The Color of Credit

The Color of Credit

Mortgage Discrimination,
Research Methodology,
and Fair-Lending
Enforcement

Stephen Ross and John
Yinger

The MIT Press
Cambridge, Massachusetts
London, England

This book was set in Palatino on 3B2 by Asco Typesetters, Hong Kong, and was printed and bound in the United States of America.

Library of Congress Cataloging-in-Publication Data

Ross, Stephen L.
 The color of credit : mortgage discrimination, research methodology, and fair-lending enforcement / Stephen Ross, John Yinger.
   p.   cm.
 Includes bibliographical references and index.
 ISBN 0-262-18228-9 (hc : alk. paper)
 1. Discrimination in mortgage loans—United States. I. Yinger, John, 1947– II. Title.
HG2040.2 .R67   2003
332.7′2′0973—dc21   2002024413

10   9   8   7   6   5   4   3   2   1

Contents

Appendixes

Acknowledgments

In the spring of 1998, Margery Turner of the Urban Institute in Washington, D.C., asked us to join a HUD-sponsored project on discrimination in mortgage lending. Our jobs were to conduct a literature review and to evaluate key issues in the debate using the best available data. Although we did not know it at the time, our decision to participate in this project put us on the road that led to this book. In fact, the chapters we wrote for that project's final report (Ross and Yinger, 1999a, 1999b, and 1999c), appear, after much revision, in chapters 5 through 8 of this book. It is safe to say that this book never would have been written if we had not had this foundation to build on.

To begin, therefore, we would like to thank Margery for inviting us to join her project and the U.S. Department of Housing and Urban Development for sponsoring it. While participating in this project, we learned and benefited from the comments of other members of the project team, and we would like to thank them: Michele DeLair, David Levine, Diane Levy, Felicity Skidmore, Robin Smith, and Kenneth Temkin.

Starting in the summer of 2000, we also received funding from the Ford Foundation. This funding allowed us to merge two data sets and to conduct the new empirical analysis in chapter 6. It also supported the new conceptual analysis that appears throughout the book. We are grateful to Melvin Oliver, Vice-President for Asset Building and Community Development, and, especially, Frank DeGiovanni, Director for Economic Development, for their support and encouragement. We would also like to thank our research assistant, Bo Zhao, who did an excellent job with the data-merger project and who drafted the data appendix.

We have been fortunate to receive very helpful comments from several colleagues, including Marsha Courchane, Edward Gramlich, John Harding, and Christopher Richardson. In addition, MIT Press found five anonymous reviewers for our original manuscript, and the final version is much better for their comments and suggestions. None of these helpful people should be held responsible for mistakes we might have made or positions we have taken.

We would probably still be working on this book were it not for the excellent support we have received from the staff at the Center for Policy Research in the Maxwell School at Syracuse University. Kitty Nasto helped with many different parts of the manuscript, especially the bibliography, figures, and tables. Mary Santy helped with the correspondence and provided word-processing advice. Denise Paul prepared the indexes.

Our most important debt is to our families, who have put up with us even during the most intense days of this project and who have given us love and support throughout. We hope that our children will someday live in an America where discrimination in mortgage lending is a thing of the past.

The Color of Credit

1 Introduction

1.1 Mortgage Discrimination and the American Dream

The last decade has witnessed a flowering of scholarly research on racial and ethnic discrimination in mortgage lending. The findings in this literature are obviously of great importance to millions of American families and also concern community groups, lenders, and public officials. This book reviews, interprets, and extends this literature. Our analysis has profound implications for fair-lending enforcement. We explain some serious flaws in the current enforcement system and show how to fix them.

The topic of discrimination in mortgage lending has, of course, great intrinsic interest. The United States is a nation of homeowners, and the homeownership rate stood at an all-time high of 67.8 percent in 2001 (U.S. Census Bureau, 2001, table 20). Homeownership is the most commonly used method for wealth accumulation,[1] and it is widely viewed as critical for access to the nicest communities and the best local public services, especially education.[2] In addition, one study (Green and White, 1997) finds evidence that homeownership provides nonfinancial benefits, such as problem-solving and management skills, that help the children of homeowners stay in school and stay out of trouble. Another recent study (DiPasquale and Glaeser, 1999) presents evidence that homeownership is associated with investments in social capital, such as membership in nonprofit organizations or helping to solve local problems.

Homeownership and mortgage lending are linked, of course, because the vast majority of home purchases are made with the help of a mortgage loan. In fact, about 8.3 million applications for home purchase mortgages were received by lenders in 2000 alone (FFIEC, 2001b, tables 4-1 and 4-2).[3] In this setting, barriers to obtaining a

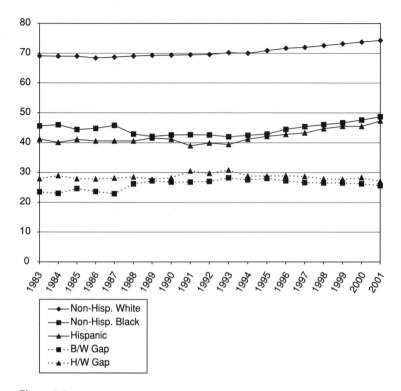

Figure 1.1
Homeownership rates, 1983–2001.
Source: HUD (2002).

mortgage must be taken seriously because they represent obstacles to attaining the American dream of owning one's own home. These barriers take on added urgency when they are related to race or ethnicity, that is, when they draw on and compound social divisions that have troubled this nation for centuries.

A hint about the potential power of mortgage discrimination is provided by the long-standing gaps in homeownership rates between black and white households and between Hispanic and white households.[4] In 2001, the homeownership rate for non-Hispanic whites, 74.3 percent, was 26.6 percentage points higher than the homeownership rate for blacks, 47.7 percent, and 27.0 points higher than the rate for Hispanics, 47.3 percent (U.S. Census Bureau, 2002, table 20). As shown in figure 1.1, these gaps have exceeded twenty-five percentage points since 1988 and are now higher than they were in the early 1980s.[5] They could be caused, of course, by many factors other than discrimination in mortgage lending, such as intergroup income differences resulting from past discrimination in labor markets or current discrimination by real estate brokers. Nevertheless, the magnitude and persistence of these gaps suggests that all the factors potentially contributing to them, including mortgage discrimination, should be carefully investigated.

1.2 Seeds of Change

Despite the intrinsic importance of discrimination in mortgage lending, few scholars addressed the topic before 1990. Although, as we will see, some important research on the topic was conducted before this time, articles and books on the topic were few and far between, and the results of this research were not widely known.

The first seed for the new burst of attention to the subject was planted in 1988 by a series of Pulitzer Prize–winning articles called "The Color of Money," which were published in the *Atlanta Journal-Constitution*.[6] These articles described practices by Atlanta's lending institutions that appeared to be discriminatory and documented a relatively small flow of mortgage funds to Atlanta's black neighborhoods. Similar articles later appeared in several other newspapers.[7]

A second seed was planted in 1989 when Congress amended the reporting requirements in the 1975 Home Mortgage Disclosure Act (HMDA). The original purpose of this act was to provide information about the geography of loan origins, so it required the vast majority of lenders to indicate the location of each property associated with a mortgage application and the ultimate disposition of the application.[8] This purpose was reendorsed when HMDA was renewed in 1980 and made permanent in 1987. In 1989, the Financial Institutions Reform, Recovery, and Enforcement Act amended HMDA by requiring lenders to provide information on the race and ethnicity of each loan applicant.[9] With these new requirements, therefore, lenders had to report their loan denial rates by racial and ethnic group, as well as by location.

When the HMDA data collected under these amendments were first released in 1991, they revealed a striking disparity in the loan denial rates for different groups. In fact, the denial rate for blacks on conventional home purchase loans was almost two-and-a-half times the rate for whites, and the Hispanic rate was 50 percent higher than the white rate (Canner and Smith, 1991). Although, as we will see, these results do not provide definitive evidence of discrimination, they are still quite troubling, and they received a great deal of publicity at the time they were released. They were, for example, the focus of front-page articles in the *New York Times* and the *Wall Street Journal* (see Quint, 1991, and Thomas, 1991, 1992a, 1992b).

The third seed was planted by the Justice Department. Thanks to the "Color of Money" series, the Justice Department initiated an investigation of Decatur Federal Savings and Loan, one of the Atlanta lenders that appeared to be discriminating, based on the information in the series. The 1990 HMDA data were released in the middle of this investigation, adding motivation—and evidence—to the Justice Department's case. Ultimately, the Justice Department was able to document extensive discrimination, and Decatur Federal signed a consent decree in the fall of 1992: the first high-profile settlement of a mortgage discrimination case.[10] Under this consent decree, Decatur Federal paid $1 million to 48 black applicants whose loans had been denied and altered its marketing practices (Ritter, 1996). This case also made a major contribution to the understanding of discrimination in mortgage lending through the development of new enforcement tools, including regression analysis of loan approval decisions.

The 1990 HMDA data also made an impression on many officials in the federal financial regulatory agencies, including the Federal Reserve Board and the U.S. Department of Housing and Urban Development (HUD). With support and advice from people in these agencies and from some academics, researchers at the Boston Federal Reserve Bank planted a fourth seed. Specifically, they decided to supplement the HMDA data with extensive information on individual loan applications so that it would be possible to isolate discriminatory behavior by lenders.[11] The resulting study, widely known as the Boston Fed Study, first appeared in 1992 (Munnell et al., 1992), and a revised version was published in 1996 (Munnell et al., 1996). The revised version of this study received a great deal of attention in part because it was published in the *American Economic Review*, which is widely regarded as the leading journal in economics.

The original version of this study concluded that "even after controlling for financial, employment, and neighborhood characteristics, black and Hispanic mortgage applicants in the Boston metropolitan area are roughly 60 percent more likely to be turned down than whites" (Munnell et al., 1992, p. 2), a result that can be interpreted as a sign of lending discrimination. After the study was revised in response to the comments of many readers, including anonymous referees for the *American Economic Review*, the final version concluded that black and Hispanic applicants were about 80 percent more likely to be turned down than were comparable whites.

1.3 Profound Change and Unanswered Questions

These seeds have produced profound change in the public and academic debate about mortgage lending discrimination. To cite a few examples: The agencies involved in fair-lending enforcement, including the Federal Reserve, have developed new enforcement procedures and filed fair-lending complaints against several major lenders. Secondary mortgage market institutions have developed programs to promote loans for low-income and minority households. HUD has sponsored research on mortgage discrimination, and dozens, if not hundreds, of articles about mortgage lending discrimination have been published.[12]

For at least two reasons, however, all this activity has failed to produce a consensus on the magnitude or consequences of mortgage lending discrimination, and debate on these subjects remains very lively. First, many commentators believe that trends in the mortgage market since 1990, when the Boston Fed Study's data were collected, have resulted in a reduction in discrimination, but no such decline is apparent in the HMDA data. Second, a huge number of publications, both academic and nonacademic, have commented on the Boston Fed Study's findings and methodology, but opinions on the study vary enormously. Some commentators praise it as a significant advance in the study of lending discrimination. Others criticize its data and methods, and some even conclude that its conclusions are incorrect or at least highly misleading. Moreover, this literature has raised a variety of important new issues, but the data are not yet available to resolve them. This section pursues these two points. We review the HMDA data for the last several years and introduce the recent literature on mortgage lending discrimination, which is the foundation of this book.

1.3.1 The HMDA Data since 1994

Despite the attention given to lending discrimination over the last decade by lenders, financial regulators, federal officials, secondary mortgage market institutions, and community groups, mortgage

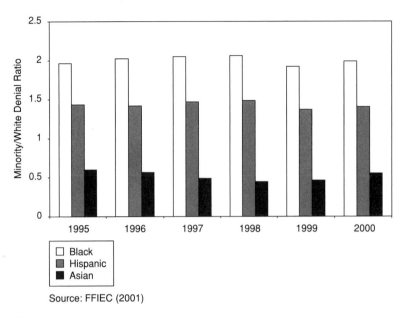

Source: FFIEC (2001)

Figure 1.2
Conventional home purchase loan denial ratios by year.
Source: FFIEC (2001b).

loan applications from black and Hispanic households are still much more likely to be denied than are applications from whites. For conventional home purchase loans in 2000, the loan denial rate for blacks divided by the loan denial rate for whites (the black/white denial ratio, for short) was 2.00, which indicates that blacks were twice as likely as whites to be turned down for a loan.[13] Similarly, the Hispanic/white denial ratio was 1.41. In contrast, the Asian/white denial ratio was only 0.55, indicating that applications from Asians were far more likely to be accepted than were applications from whites. These ratios are summarized in figure 1.2.

These numbers cannot be directly compared to the 1990 numbers, because the coverage of the HMDA data was greatly expanded in 1992.[14] Clear comparisons can be made over the last several years, however, and, as shown in figure 1.2, the black/white denial ratio has fluctuated around 2.0 since 1995, with a high of 2.07 in 1998 and a low of 1.92 in 1999. The current ratio, 2.0, is slightly higher than the 1995 ratio, 1.95. The Hispanic/white denial ratio has fluctuated around the lower value of 1.5, but it exhibits a similar pattern over time, with a relatively high value in 1998 and a relatively low value

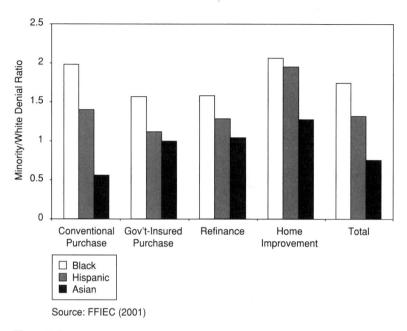

Figure 1.3
Loan denial ratios by loan type, 2000.
Source: FFIEC (2001b).

in 1999. Its current value, 1.41, is slightly below its value in 1995, 1.43. The Asian/white denial ratio has stayed fairly close to 0.5, but it follows a smoother pattern. It declined steadily from 0.61 in 1995 to 0.45 in 1998 and then increased steadily to 0.55 in 2000.

Two other persistent results in the basic HMDA data raise additional questions about mortgage lending that have intrigued scholars and policy makers (Avery, Beeson, and Sniderman, 1996a). First, blacks and Hispanics are also more likely than whites to be turned down for government-insured home purchase loans, refinance loans, and home improvement loans. For these types of loans, Asians also face a higher denial probability than do whites (see figure 1.3). These results raise, but do not answer, two important questions: Is there discrimination in the market for government-insured loans? Do black, Hispanic, and Asian households face discrimination when they apply for refinancing or a home improvement loan, even though these applicants have, by definition, demonstrated their creditworthiness by receiving a home purchase mortgage and then meeting the obligations associated with it?

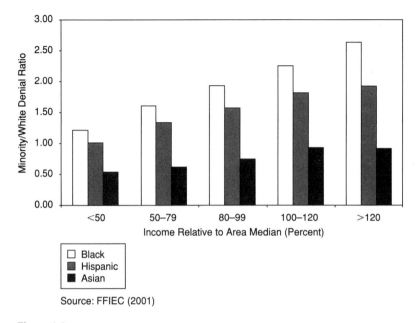

Source: FFIEC (2001)

Figure 1.4
Loan denial ratios by income class, 2000.
Source: FFIEC (2001b).

Second, loan denial rates are higher for black and Hispanic applicants than for white applicants at all income levels. Moreover, for blacks, Hispanics, and Asians, the minority/white denial ratio increases steadily with income. This increase is particularly striking for blacks; the denial ratio is only 1.19 in the lowest income category but climbs to 2.48 in the highest category (see figure 1.4). Thus, the higher denial rates for blacks and Hispanics do not appear simply to reflect the fact that these groups have lower average incomes than do whites.[15]

Of course, these higher denial rates also do not prove that blacks and Hispanics face discrimination in mortgage lending, because they do not account for possible differences in loan features or borrower creditworthiness across groups. The differences are so dramatic, however, that they focus attention on the possibility that this type of discrimination might exist. Indeed, the academic literature reviewed in this book is largely devoted to finding out the extent to which the loan approval disparities in the HMDA data and in other indicators of lender behavior reflect racial and ethnic discrimination.

1.3.2 The Literature since the Boston Fed Study

For at least three reasons, no consensus has emerged from the huge literature on mortgage lending discrimination that has appeared since the original version of the Boston Fed Study was released.

First, opinions on the Boston Fed Study vary widely, to say the least.[16] One commentator declared, in the title of his piece, that the study "deserves no credit" (Liebouitz, 1993); another argued that the study is "invalid" (Becker, 1993a). In contrast, one review and reanalysis of the Boston Fed Study's data concluded that the study "clearly demonstrated" the existence of discrimination (Carr and Megbolugbe, 1993). To some degree, this range of opinion reflects the inherent complexity of the topic. As we will see, any study of mortgage lending discrimination must grapple with a complex set of methodological issues, and scholars do not agree about which methodology is best for the issues and data involved. They also do not agree on the best way to interpret the Boston Fed Study's findings. Nevertheless, many of the issues in this debate concerning methodology and interpretation can be clarified, if not resolved, by a careful examination of the Boston Fed Study's data, which have been made available to interested scholars.

Second, disagreements about the Boston Fed Study persist because no comparable data set has yet been assembled. A great deal of research on mortgage lending discrimination, some of it very informative, has been conducted since the initial report on the Boston Fed Study was released. Nevertheless, the study has not been replicated for another place or time, let alone improved. All subsequent studies that apply to more than one lender must rely on data that are less complete than the data used for the Boston Fed Study. Given the importance of the topic and the striking nature of the Boston Fed Study's findings, this lack of replication is unfortunate and puzzling. Many institutions, including the federal financial regulatory agencies, the large secondary mortgage market institutions, and HUD clearly have the authority to collect the type of data needed for such a replication. Why haven't any of these institutions collected such data? We do not know the answer to this question, but we do know that scholars and policymakers cannot come to credible conclusions about the current importance of mortgage lending discrimination without access to data of this type.

Third, the debate about mortgage discrimination must grapple with a series of striking changes in mortgage markets over the last decade or two. These changes, which include dramatic growth in nondepository lenders and in automated underwriting, have raised new issues that the Boston Fed Study was not designed to address. Some scholars argue that these changes will lead to less discrimination; others argue that they will lead to more. The impact of these changes on mortgage discrimination has not been widely studied, however, and these arguments have hardly been addressed, let alone resolved, with empirical evidence.

1.4   The Plan of This Book

The main purposes of this book are to explain what has been learned about mortgage lending discrimination in recent years and then, building on that understanding, both to reanalyze existing data and to devise new tests for discrimination in contemporary mortgage markets. Although we do not have any new data to work with, we show that many of the contentious issues that appear in the recent literature can be addressed with the publicly available data collected for the Boston Fed Study, merged, in some cases, with other data that are also publicly available. Much of the recent debate concerns the best methodology for estimating mortgage lending discrimination. We blend the strengths of several existing methods to develop new, straightforward procedures that provide clear estimates of discrimination and avoid the statistical and interpretive problems that have plagued other approaches. These procedures rely on data that could easily be collected by governmental agencies or secondary mortgage market institutions and that could, in principle, be made available to scholars. In addition, these procedures could eliminate a major weakness in the current fair-lending enforcement system, namely, that it looks for only one, narrowly defined type of discrimination. They could also be applied not only to discrimination in loan approval, but also to discrimination in credit-scoring schemes or in loan pricing.

We begin, in chapter 2, by providing some background information on mortgage markets and on the definition of discrimination. We present some basic facts about the operation of the mortgage market and explore recent trends in this market, with a focus on trends that may affect minority households' access to mortgage loans. These trends are important in part because they are one source of the existing confusion about the importance of mortgage lending discrimination. In addition, we describe in some detail both the laws against lending discrimination and the enforcement system these laws create. The chapter concludes by presenting a preliminary framework for estimating the extent of lending discrimination, employing a definition of discrimination that is consistent with existing fair-lending legislation. This framework is then used to introduce some of the methodological issues that appear throughout the book, such as the biases that can arise when a study does not control for all relevant credit characteristics.

In chapter 3, we lay down a conceptual foundation for our work by reviewing the literature on mortgage markets in general. This review is designed to highlight the complex setting in which a loan approval decision takes place. More specifically, we build on the literature to derive a series of lessons, which we draw on in later chapters, concerning the specification of tests for discrimination in loan approval. For example, we show that a study of lending discrimination may not be able to eliminate biases without controlling not only for variables that directly influence the loan approval decision, but also for variables that influence lender actions during earlier stages of the lending process.

Chapter 4 turns to the early literature on mortgage lending discrimination, defined as the literature up to and including the Boston Fed Study (Munnell et al., 1996). We review all the early studies of which we are aware and discuss the major contributions to the literature. Not surprisingly, many, if not most, of the issues we struggle with in this book were first raised by one or more of these early studies. The chapter also describes the Boston Fed Study, but an evaluation of this study is postponed until the following chapter.

As noted above, the Boston Fed Study has been widely criticized. In chapter 5, we evaluate in detail every criticism of which we are aware, including those concerning problems arising from omitted variables, from data errors in the explanatory variables, from misclassification in the dependent variable, from incorrect specification, and from endogenous explanatory variables. We examine the claims of both the critics and the defenders of the Boston Fed Study. We then formally model the issues raised by each criticism and employ the public-use version of the Boston Fed Study's data set to determine which of these criticisms have merit. Although several other studies have explored potential flaws in the Boston Fed Study, our evaluation is the most comprehensive review yet attempted.

We find that several critics of the Boston Fed Study raise legitimate issues that are worthy of further exploration. Our analysis of these issues leads to two principal conclusions. First, the large minority-white disparity in loan approval found by the Boston Fed Study cannot be explained by data errors, misclassification, omitted variables, or the endogeneity of loan terms. Second, the interpretation of the Boston Fed Study's results depends heavily on an issue not adequately considered by the study's authors, namely, whether different lenders use different underwriting standards. More specifically, the Boston Fed Study cannot rule out the possibility that the minority-white disparity in loan approval reflects variation in underwriting standards across lenders, not discrimination.

The issue of across-lender variation in underwriting standards is so important that we give it a chapter of its own, chapter 6. This issue has been one of the central themes of the literature since the Boston Fed Study, and we begin by reviewing this literature in some detail. We then merge the public-use version of the Boston Fed Study's with the comparable HMDA data, a step that allows us to identify lenders, and provide new estimates of the impact of across-lender variation in underwriting standards on estimated minority-white disparities in loan approval. We find evidence that underwriting standards do, indeed, vary across lenders. We also find, however, using several different methods, that accounting for this variation has no impact on the estimated loan approval disparity. We conclude that the minority-white disparity in the Boston Fed Study's data does provide strong evidence of discrimination in loan approval.

Chapters 7 and 8 complete our review of recent literature. Chapter 7 concentrates on dimensions of discrimination that are related to but distinct from discrimination in loan approval. Specifically, it explores recent literature on redlining, defined as lending discrimination based on a property's location, and on discrimination in loan terms.[17] This literature is in its infancy, but several studies suggest that redlining and discrimination in the setting of mortgage interest rates appear to occur in some circumstances. In addition, this chapter reviews the literature on the causes of discrimination in loan approval. For example, we explore the hypothesis, developed in several recent articles, that discrimination arises because white lending officials often lack a "cultural affinity" with minority applicants. Clear evidence on the causes of lending discrimination does not yet exist, but our review of the conceptual literature provides background both for the subsequent chapter and for the policy issues discussed at the end of the book.

Chapter 8 addresses an alternative approach to studying discrimination in loan approval, namely, an investigation of minority-white differences in loan defaults. According to this approach, discrimination in loan approval involves holding minority applicants to a higher standard than white applicants. If discrimination exists, the argument goes, minority loans, that is, approved applications, will be of higher quality than white loans, as determined by their default rate. This "default approach" has received a great deal of attention, in part because several scholars have claimed that it refutes the Boston Fed Study's finding that discrimination exists.

The literature on the default approach performs a valuable service by bringing loan performance information into the discussion. Despite its intuitive appeal, however, this approach runs into unsurmountable methodological obstacles. Most importantly, we show that the default approach cannot detect discrimination unless some underwriting variables are excluded from the analysis but yields biased results if the variables that are excluded are correlated with minority status. No study even observes the correlation between excluded variables and minority status, let alone demonstrates that this correlation equals zero. Several recent studies have introduced creative methods for overcoming these obstacles, but we show that all of these methods meet with limited success, at best. We conclude that an analysis of loan defaults alone cannot provide credible evidence concerning the existence of discrimination in loan approval.

Chapter 9 brings together the literatures on loan approval, loan performance, and types of lending discrimination. We first show that a certain type of discrimination can easily be incorporated into a credit-scoring or other automated underwriting system, even one derived from seemingly group-neutral statistical procedures. This type of discrimination is likely to be missed by most current research and enforcement procedures, but it can serve as a substitute for other types of discrimination that these procedures are designed to uncover. Second, we devise new tests for discrimination based on a data set combining information on loan performance, as measured, say, by defaults, and on loan approval. These tests capture all types of discrimination and avoid the methodological problems that have plagued other approaches. Finally, we bring several key themes of the book together by demonstrating that our new tests can provide an accurate estimate of discrimination even if different lenders use different underwriting standards.

In our final chapter, chapter 10, we apply our results to an analysis of the current federal fair-lending enforcement system. We begin by reviewing court decisions and regulations concerning fair lending. Most of the relevant court cases and virtually all of the relevant regulations have been developed for cases involving discrimination in employment. We explore what is known about the application of these cases to discrimination in mortgage lending and develop principles to guide regulations for the enforcement of fair-lending legislation. Moreover, we also draw on our analysis in chapters 6 and 9 to develop fair-lending enforcement procedures that are consistent with existing legal standards. Specifically, we develop two new enforcement tools that capture all types of discrimination if (and only if) they exist. One of these tools is based on loan approval data, and the other combines data on loan approval and on loan performance. We also explain how tools blending approval and performance data could be adapted to consider discrimination in the scores produced by automated underwriting systems and in loan pricing.

Chapter 10 also offers an evaluation of existing fair-lending enforcement procedures. We show that these procedures are seriously inadequate in the sense that they are incapable of identifying many cases of discrimination. Indeed, as currently designed, the enforcement system picks up only extreme cases of a certain type of discrimination in loan approval among a subset of lenders! To put it another way, existing procedures completely miss certain types of discrimination in loan approval and virtually all discrimination in credit scoring and other automated underwriting practices or in loan pricing. We do not know how much discrimination actually exists in these types of behavior, but our analysis in chapter 9 demonstrates that discrimination is easy to introduce into an automated underwriting scheme, even one with apparently group-neutral procedures. It is certainly inappropriate for enforcement officials to ignore large categories of discrimination without any evidence about their incidence. The implementation of our new enforcement tools, or equivalent ones, is required to preserve access to the American dream for all Americans.

2

The Mortgage Market and the Definition of Mortgage Lending Discrimination

2.1 Introduction

Any analysis of mortgage lending discrimination must be based on an understanding of the institutions and practices in the mortgage market, of recent changes in those institutions and practices, and of the legal definition of discrimination. This chapter provides these basic ingredients. It also brings these ingredients together by developing a simple framework for thinking about the impact of discrimination on a lender's loan approval decision. This framework leads to an analytical definition of discrimination and to a basic methodology for determining whether discrimination exists. We use this framework to introduce some of the key issues in the book, such as the methodological challenges that face any study of mortgage lending discrimination.

2.2 The Mortgage Market

The mortgage market has undergone significant change over the last few decades. This section describes the current state of the mortgage market, explores several important trends that will shape the mortgage market in the future, discusses the likely impact of these trends on black and Hispanic households' access to credit, and describes the stages of a mortgage transaction.

2.2.1 Characteristics of the Market

Not too many decades ago, the mortgage market went through a period described by one scholar (Lea, 1996) as "A Wonderful Life," after the famous movie. During this period, the market could be

roughly characterized as one in which people opened savings accounts in their local savings and loan association and the association
then used the funds in these accounts to issue mortgages to others in
the community.

This description no longer bears any resemblance to reality. The
mortgage market is now far more complex, with many different
types of institutions offering home mortgage loans and with far
more than two parties participating in most mortgage transactions.
For example, many mortgages are now granted by lenders called
mortgage bankers, which have no deposits to draw on, and then sold
as income-producing assets to a secondary mortgage market institution, which in turn packages them as mortgage-backed securities
(MBSs) for sale to households or pension funds looking for a good
return on their investments.

The key to understanding these developments is the recognition
that lending institutions deliver four different types of services:
mortgage origination, mortgage servicing, default and prepayment
risk acceptance, and capital provision. Traditional savings and loans,
also called thrifts or savings banks, provided all of these services.[1]
They raised capital through deposits, originated and serviced local
mortgages, and held these mortgages in their own investment portfolios. In today's market, however, these four services are unbundled
for many mortgages.[2] Small local mortgage brokers may originate
loans and then sell these loans to larger wholesale mortgage brokers.
This sale takes place at the closing of the housing transaction, so the
proceeds of the sale, minus the broker's commission, provide the
mortgage amount to the home buyer, and the broker never has to
draw on deposits. The larger wholesale brokers, in turn, resell the
loans on the secondary market but retain the right to service them
(Lederman, 1995). Default risk is accepted by private investors,
secondary-market institutions, and mortgage insurers, and capital is
provided by investors who purchase MBSs. Traditionally, investors
accepted prepayment risk, but new types of MBSs allow the risk to
be held by the issuer of the securities.[3]

Three types of lenders now dominate the mortgage market: commercial banks, savings and loans (or thrifts), and mortgage bankers.
In 1995, approximately 99 percent of conventional and 97 percent of
government-insured one- to four-family mortgages were originated
by one of these three types of institutions. Mortgage bankers ac-

counted for over half of the conventional mortgage originations and almost 80 percent of the government-insured originations during that year (Clauretie and Sirmans, 1999, p. 210).

The federal government insures mortgages through the Federal Housing Administration (FHA) and the Veterans Administration (VA). This insurance raises the cost of a mortgage to the borrower but increases the willingness of a lender to provide the mortgage. The size of an FHA or VA mortgage is capped, so these mortgages are not available for the highest-priced houses in a metropolitan area. Of the almost five million home purchase loans that originated in 1999, about 22 percent were FHA or VA loans.

The dominance of mortgage bankers in the FHA/VA segment of the market reflects the history of the secondary market (see Lea, 1996). Specifically, the Federal National Mortgage Association (FNMA, or Fannie Mae) was established in 1938 to purchase and sell FHA- and VA-insured mortgages.[4] This created a secondary market for these loans and an opportunity for mortgage bankers. Even without deposits as a source of capital, mortgage bankers could issue mortgages, because they knew that these mortgages would be purchased by Fannie Mae. In the early 1970s, Fannie Mae's charter was changed to allow it to buy conventional mortgages, and two new secondary mortgage market institutions appeared. The Government National Mortgage Association (GNMA, or Ginnie Mae) was established to purchase FHA and VA mortgages from any source, and the Federal Home Loan Mortgage Corporation (Freddie Mac) was established to purchase conventional mortgages from savings and loans. These institutional developments, along with tremendous growth in the popularity of MBSs as an investment, have made it possible for mortgage bankers to move into the conventional market, as well.

Today, two key differences exist between depository lenders, such as banks and thrifts, and mortgage banks. First, depository lenders face an increased number of regulations, because their deposits are federally insured through the Federal Deposit Insurance Corporation (FDIC). In particular, savings and loans are regulated by the Office of Thrift Supervision, and banks are regulated by the Comptroller of the Currency, the Federal Reserve, or the FDIC.[5] These financial regulatory agencies establish capital requirements for the lenders in their purview and regularly examine the lenders they supervise for compliance with a wide range of lending legislation. Mortgage bankers are regulated by the Federal Trade Commission (FTC), which does not conduct regular examinations.

Second, banks and thrifts may still use their deposits to purchase mortgages to hold in their own portfolio, whereas mortgage bankers must raise all of their capital by reselling mortgages to other financial institutions or private investors. Several major banks, however, have established holding companies that own large mortgage banks, and these major banks may purchase the mortgages issued by their subsidiary mortgage companies.

Mortgage loans are often classified according to whether or not they conform to the underwriting standards of the major secondary mortgage market institutions. Loans may fail to conform to these standards on one or both of two dimensions: the size of the mortgage and the estimated default risk of the application. FHA/VA mortgages have a maximum amount, and both Fannie Mae and Freddie Mac face restrictions on the size of the mortgages that they can buy. In 2001, for example, Fannie Mae's limit on single-family home purchase mortgages was $275,000 (outside of Alaska and Hawaii).[6] Banks and thrifts can hold large mortgages in their own portfolios, but mortgage companies must market large mortgages to private investors or to other financial institutions. In addition, the charters of Fannie Mae and Freddie Mac limit their ability to purchase mortgages with a loan-to-value ratio above 0.95, mortgages without private mortgage insurance and a loan-to-value ratio above 0.8, or mortgages with a relatively high ratio of housing expense or debt payments to income.[7]

Some mortgage bankers specialize in relatively risky loans that do not meet the government-sponsored enterprises' (GSEs') underwriting standards (see U.S. Department of Housing and Urban Development–U.S. Treasury National Predatory Lending Task Force, 2000). These so-called subprime lenders obviously concentrate on borrowers with relatively poor credit qualifications.[8] The mortgages issued by these lenders have higher interest rates and/or costs to make up for their higher risk, and they are typically sold to private investors.[9] In recent years, subprime lenders have faced increased competitive pressures as commercial banks expand their operations into higher-cost mortgage loans (Bergsman, 1999), and the major secondary-market institutions also are beginning to operate in the higher end of the subprime market (Royer and Kriz, 1999).

HMDA data reveal some of the complexity in today's mortgage market. In 2000, 7,713 lending institutions reported mortgage loan applications (FFIEC, 2001c). These institutions include commercial banks, thrifts, and mortgage bankers, both independent and subsidiary. In 1997, depository institutions (commercial banks and thrifts) and their nondepository subsidiaries issued about 65 percent of all home purchase loans in metropolitan areas (Avery et al., 1999), and independent mortgage bankers issued the rest.

2.2.2   Important Recent Trends in the Mortgage Market

The broad trends affecting mortgage markets over the last two decades include the unbundling of mortgage services, the growth of MBSs, and growth in the number of nondepository lenders (Follain and Zorn, 1990; Van Order, 2000). These broad trends have been accompanied by several more specific trends that provide important background for this study.

To begin, the increase in nondepository lenders is associated with the rapid growth of subprime lending, which involves the issuing of mortgages with lower credit standards but higher costs. Although there is not an exact match between the growth in nondepository lenders and the growth in subprime lending, the two phenomena are highly correlated, because the vast majority of subprime loans are issued by nondepository lenders (see U.S. Department of Housing and Urban Development, 1997).[10] In 1993, only 0.7 percent of conventional mortgage loans were offered by lenders specializing in the subprime market; by 1998, this share had risen to 6.2 percent (Canner and Passmore, 1999).[11] Moreover, the number of subprime refinancing loans increased from 80,000 in 1993 to 790,000 in 1999, and the number of lenders specializing in subprime loans increased from 104,000 to 997,000 over this same period. Similarly, subprime loans made up less than 5 percent of all mortgage originations in 1994, but by 1999 this share was up to 13 percent, and outstanding subprime mortgages constituted 8 percent of single-family residential mortgage debt (U.S. Department of Housing and Urban Development–U.S. Treasury National Predatory Lending Task Force, 2000).

A disturbing feature of the growth in subprime lending is that it appears to be associated with growth in predatory lending, loosely defined as lending that relies on consumer ignorance, misleading

sales techniques, and, in some cases, outright fraud, to issue mortgages with interest costs above the full-information, competitive
level. Of course, not all subprime lending is predatory lending;
indeed, in many if not most cases, the existence of relatively high-
cost loans makes homeownership possible for people who could not
otherwise obtain credit. Moreover, there exists no widely recognized
method for determining which loans are "predatory" and which
loans are not. Some commentators believe that most subprime lending is beneficial to both borrowers and lenders and that only a few
"rogue lenders" use predatory practices, whereas others believe that
a large share of subprime lending has a predatory component.[12]

We do not, of course, know how many subprime loans are predatory. For several reasons, however, we believe the possibility of
predatory lending needs to be taken seriously. First, the anecdotal
evidence of predatory lending practices is voluminous (see U.S.
House of Representatives, 2000). In 1999, for example, the FTC settled cases against seven subprime mortgage lenders for the use of
prohibited loan terms and the failure to provide required information to borrowers. The settlement called for $572,000 in redress to
past borrowers, changes in procedures to protect future borrowers,
and, in the case of one lender, a "ban against any future involvement
with high-cost loans secured by consumers' homes." The FTC also
settled another case in 1999 involving disclosure violations by Fleet
Finance, Inc. The settlement in that case "provides for $1.3 million in
consumer redress as well as injunctive relief" (Medine, 2000, p. 8).

Second, several commentators have argued that many people who
pay the relatively high costs of subprime loans do not need to do so.
Gensler (2000) claims that "between 15 and 35 percent of those currently borrowing in the subprime market could qualify for a prime
loan." Taylor (2000) cites estimates by Fannie Mae and Freddie Mac
that set an even higher range, between 30 and 50 percent.[13] We
do not know how good these estimates are, but if they are even
approximately correct, then the increase in subprime lending involves an unwarranted increase in the cost of borrowing for many
households.

Third, the increase in subprime lending has been concentrated
in refinancing loans. Indeed, one study estimates that refinancing
loans constitute 80 percent of subprime lending (U.S. Department of
Housing and Urban Development, 2000). The growth in subprime
refinancing loans is troubling because it took place in an era of rising

interest rates when homeowners could not save money by shifting to a new, market rate mortgage. Instead, this growth appears to represent an increase in the packaging of refinancing with borrowing for home improvements, for the consolidation of credit card debt, or for some other purpose combined with an increase in the mortgage interest rate (see Mansfield, 2000). Although this type of packaging might make sense under some circumstances, its main effect in many cases appears to be an increase in both the monetary costs of borrowing and the possibility that a household will lose its house.

This leads to the fourth reason for concern about the possibility of predatory lending, namely, the startling recent increase in mortgage foreclosures in some areas. Mansfield (2000) examined all the loans sold on the secondary market by sixteen large subprime lenders in 1998. Taken together, these lenders provided almost half of the outstanding subprime home equity debt. By December 1999, 4.7 percent of these loans were foreclosed, in foreclosure proceedings, in bankruptcy proceedings, or at least ninety days in delinquency, compared to 1.5 percent for all mortgages and 2.57 percent for FHA loans. At one subprime lender, an astonishing 25 percent of the loans fell into one of these four categories. Another study of foreclosures in the Chicago area (Cincotta, 2000) found that the number of foreclosures on loans from subprime lenders increased from 131 in 1993, which was only 1 percent of all foreclosures, to 4,958 in 1999, which was 38 percent of all foreclosures. Finally, HUD-sponsored studies in Atlanta, Boston, and Chicago found dramatic increases in subprime foreclosures over the 1996–1999 period. These increases ranged from 158 percent in Boston to 4,623 percent in Chicago, even though foreclosure in the prime market was increasing modestly or even declining over the same period (Bunce et al., 2001).

Although it is not unreasonable to expect a somewhat higher default rate on subprime mortgages than on prime mortgages, this evidence is disquieting. Something is wrong when so many families are losing their homes, particularly in a time of robust economic growth.

The recent growth of nondepository lenders also is associated with a steady increase in the share of mortgages sold by the originator to another institution or to private investors.[14] One study estimates that half of the $3.2 trillion in mortgage debt outstanding in 1994 had been securitized and sold on the secondary market (Chinloy, 1995), and another estimates that 45 percent of total mortgage debt in 1999 was securitized (LaCour-Little, 2000). Neither the HMDA data nor any other currently available data allow a full accounting of the disposition of mortgage sales each year, but one study estimates that 52 percent of the debt issued in 1999 fell into the "securitized" category (LaCour-Little, 2000). Moreover, the Federal Financial Institutions Examination Council (FFIEC) (2001b, table 3) reports on the number of mortgage loans sold in 2000, by type of purchaser. It is important to note that loans sold in 2000 are not necessarily loans issued in 2000; they could have been issued in earlier years. Moreover, lenders are not required to include all loan sales in their HMDA reports. To be specific, only loan sales by the issuing institution need to be reported.[15] Even with these caveats in mind, however, the number of loans sold in 2000, over 5.9 million, is striking. This amounts to 74.8 percent of the number of loans originated in 2000. These loans were sold to Fannie Mae (22.9%), Freddie Mac (14.1%), Ginnie Mae (14.2%), commercial banks (3.2%), savings and loan associations (1.6%), affiliated institutions (10.9%), and other purchasers (33.0%) (FFIEC, 2001b, table 3).[16]

There is potential for interaction between the growing role of the GSEs and the growth in predatory lending. Because predatory lending appears to be concentrated among nondepository lenders, it depends on access to investors, something the GSEs can provide. However, the GSEs are also in a position to limit predatory lending by forbidding certain abusive practices in the loans that they purchase. Fannie Mae and Freddie Mac have recently taken steps in exactly this direction (See Brendsel, 2000).

Another important trend in mortgage markets is the increased use of automated underwriting tools, such as credit scoring.[17] These tools are designed to make the underwriting process fairer and more efficient. Credit scoring, for example, uses statistical techniques to estimate the likelihood that an applicant will repay a debt based on his or her characteristics, including performance on previous loans. This likelihood takes the form of a credit score, which lenders can purchase from a credit bureau.[18] As Avery et al. (2000, p. 523) put it, these scores "are increasingly being used as an initial and sometimes primary screen for applicants seeking credit and are also a prescreening tool for credit solicitations."

In the underwriting process, credit scores typically are combined with other factors, such as the loan-to-value ratio or the payment-to-income ratio. This may result in a formal "application score" or "origination score" (Avery et al., 2000).[19] A credit score also might be incorporated into (or generated by) an automated underwriting system, which provides a lender with a series of steps that lead to an underwriting decision. The major secondary mortgage market institutions, Fannie Mae and Freddie Mac, set underwriting guidelines for the loans that they will buy. Moreover, these two GSEs have developed automated underwriting systems based on the determinants of default for the loans in their portfolios.[20] These systems reveal whether an mortgage is clearly eligible for sale to one of these institutions or whether the lender must provide additional information to show that it meets the secondary-market guidelines (see Avery, Beeson, and Calem, 1997). They are currently being provided to selected lenders with the commitment that loans identified as eligible will be sold to the GSEs (Royer and Kriz, 1999). The FHA is developing a similar automated underwriting system for government-insured mortgages (Bunce, Reeder, and Scheessele, 1999).

The trends toward more automated underwriting and more subprime lending are related. As lenders become more confident about their ability to predict default, they also become more willing to issue credit, at a relatively high price, to higher-risk borrowers. In fact, the increased variation in credit pricing appears to be quite general; even commercial banks specializing in high-quality mortgages often provide lower-cost mortgages to customers perceived to be lower risks (Royer and Kriz, 1999). Overall, therefore, these trends, along with the increased flow of funds into the mortgage market associated with the growth in MBSs, suggest that, as time goes on, fewer people will be denied access to credit, but the range in the price of credit will continue to grow. Indeed, it is not too far-fetched to imagine a world in which anyone can obtain a mortgage if he or she is willing to pay the price that compensates the lender for the perceived riskiness of the loan. However, the 2000 denial rates in the HMDA data (22.3 percent on conventional home purchase loan applications from whites, for example) (FFIEC, 2001b) reveal that such a world is still a long way off.

A final trend worth discussing is consolidation in the lending industry. Thanks largely to changes in the laws concerning interstate banking, the number of commercial banks and savings associations dropped by over 40 percent between 1975 and 1997 (Avery et al., 1999). This trend affects not only the number of lenders but also the link between the location of a lender's office and the location of the properties for which loans are given. In the "Wonderful Life" period, borrowers went to a local office to obtain a mortgage. This is no longer true. In 1997, two-thirds of all home purchase loans in metropolitan areas were made either by a commercial bank or savings and loan association without a branch office in the neighborhood where the relevant property was located or by a mortgage bank, which has no deposit-taking offices (Avery, Beeson, and Calem, 1997). Moreover, the industry for servicing loans has become increasingly consolidated, with large wholesalers purchasing both loans and the servicing rights to them from small mortgage bankers (Follain and Zorn, 1990).

2.2.3 Implications of Recent Trends for Minority Access to Mortgage Credit

The recent trends in the mortgage market may have important implications for minority access to mortgage credit. First, minority borrowers are more likely than white borrowers to receive their loans through independent mortgage companies.[21] In 1997, 44 percent of loans to minorities were supplied by these institutions, compared to 35 percent of loans to whites. To some degree, this difference reflects the relatively heavy reliance of black and Hispanic customers on FHA loans (see Gabriel, 1996; FFIEC, 2001b), combined with the fact that many mortgage bankers specialize in the FHA market. In any case, the fact that mortgage companies have different incentives and face different regulations than depository lenders may result in differential loan access for groups who rely heavily on them for credit.

Second, minority borrowers are much more likely than white borrowers to borrow in the subprime market. According to HMDA data, lenders specializing in subprime loans make 7.6 percent of home purchase loans to minority borrowers and only 4.0 percent to whites (Joint Center for Housing Studies, 2000, table A-11). Indeed, upper-income blacks are almost twice as likely as low-income whites (25 percent compared to 13 percent) to apply for a subprime loan (U.S. Department of Housing and Urban Development–U.S. Treasury National Predatory Lending Task Force, 2000). Moreover, the share of home purchase loans from subprime specialists is 14.1 percent in predominantly minority neighborhoods, compared to only 1.6 percent in predominantly white neighborhoods. These disparities are even greater for refinancing loans.[22] The share of refinancing loans by subprime specialists is 19.2 percent for black borrowers compared to 2.0 percent for white borrowers and 42.2 percent in predominantly black neighborhoods compared to only 5.1 percent in largely white neighborhoods.

These findings are reinforced by evidence from specific urban areas. The National Community Reinvestment Coalition examined home purchase loans by the twenty largest lenders in the New York and Baltimore metropolitan areas in 1998 (Taylor, 2000). In New York, subprime lenders made 4 percent of the home purchase loans in largely white areas, but 25 percent of the home purchase loans in largely black areas. In Baltimore, subprime lenders did not supply any home purchase loans in white areas, but made 28.7 percent of the loans in largely black areas. Similar disparities exist for refinancing loans. According to a recent study (U.S. Department of Housing and Urban Development, 2000), 39 percent of households in upper-income black neighborhoods have subprime refinancing loans, compared to only 18 percent of households in low-income white neighborhoods and only 6 percent in high-income white neighborhoods.

Finally, a recent analysis by Pennington-Cross, Yezer, and Nichols (2000) finds that black and Hispanic borrowers are significantly more likely than white borrowers to obtain a subprime mortgage, even after controlling for a wide range of financial variables, including credit history. This analysis applies to almost 50,000 fixed-rate loans in 1996.[23]

The heavy use of subprime loans by minority borrowers arises primarily because they have poorer credit qualifications than whites, on average, and hence poorer access to the prime mortgage market. To some degree, however, these disparities also reflect the fact that the minority/white denial ratios are much higher for prime lending than for subprime lending (see FFIEC, 1998). For conventional loans in 1997, the black/white denial ratio was 2.28 in the prime market but only 1.27 in the subprime (plus manufactured home) market. In the case of Hispanics, the same two ratios were 1.84 and 1.11, respectively. Moreover, the black/white denial ratio in the prime market has not declined since 1993. For Hispanics it has declined from 1.97 to 1.84. In the subprime market, both groups have experienced small declines in the denial ratio for their group compared to whites over this period. Thus, even if application rates to the two markets were the same, loans to minority groups would be relatively concentrated in the subprime market.

The implications of this concentration are difficult to untangle. To some degree, the growth in subprime lending represents new opportunities for minority borrowers, many of whom cannot obtain credit in the prime mortgage market. Unfortunately, however, the concentration of subprime lending among minorities and in minority neighborhoods also may represent a new opportunity for lenders to charge higher prices to minorities than to equally qualified whites; as noted earlier, the limited available evidence suggests that many subprime borrowers are qualified for mortgages in the prime market. In addition, this concentration implies that predatory lending, to the extent that it exists, is likely to have a disproportionate impact on minority borrowers, in terms of both higher loan costs and higher foreclosure rates.

The growing role of the secondary market for mortgages also may prove to have important implications for access to credit by people in legally protected classes. As the accuracy of automated underwriting increases and variation in pricing replaces credit rationing, for example, the GSEs are likely to increase their purchasing of lower-quality prime and subprime mortgages (Zorn et al., forthcoming). The resulting increase in competition in both the primary and secondary markets may substantially reduce the cost of credit for many low-income and minority borrowers (Mahoney and Zorn, 1999). Moreover, the GSEs have implemented a variety of programs designed to promote minority homeownership (see Raines, 2000; Brendsel, 2000) and, as noted earlier, they are taking steps to minimize predatory lending practices.

In contrast, within the secondary market, different GSEs appear to play quite different roles in purchasing mortgages issued to minority households. Among all loans purchased in 1998, for example, the share going to Fannie Mae and Freddie Mac combined was 19.1 percent for blacks, 29.4 for Hispanics, and 51.0 for whites, whereas the share going to "other" purchasers was 46.0 for blacks, 35.6 for Hispanics, and 27.4 for whites. In addition, Ginnie Mae purchases government-insured loans, which have long been the major source of mortgages for blacks and Hispanics (see Gabriel, 1996). It is not surprising, therefore, that for black and Hispanic borrowers, the share of purchased loans going to Ginnie Mae is over 22 percent, whereas the comparable figure for whites is only 9.4 percent. These differences are not, of course, proof of discrimination by any of these institutions, but, like the basic HMDA disparities, they call out for further explanation.

The increasing reliance on automated underwriting is an issue of great importance to all borrowers but may prove to be particularly important for black and Hispanic borrowers. On the one hand, it appears to minimize the role for individual judgments by loan officers that may be the source of discriminatory decisions. As discussed in chapter 9, however, imperfections in automated underwriting systems may magnify other dimensions of discrimination.

Moreover, improvements in automated underwriting systems are likely to expand borrowing opportunities, perhaps at subprime rates, for borrowers with some credit flaws, who are disproportionately minority, because these improvements give lenders more confidence that they can accurately identify and price risks (Zorn et al., forthcoming).[24] Of course, these trends also might increase lending barriers for applicants with those credit problems weighted most heavily by the automated underwriting system. The current evidence on these points is inconclusive. Zorn et al. show that the "approval" threshhold for Freddie Mac's automated underwriting system, Loan Prospector, has declined over time. As a result, the "accept" rate for black and Hispanic applicants tripled between 1995 and 1999. However, Zorn et al. also point out that many applications given a "caution" rating were ultimately approved, and the loans made to them were purchased by Freddie Mac, presumably after a more traditional underwriting process. Because Zorn et al. do not examine changes in this traditional process, they cannot determine the net impact of all underwriting changes on minority applicants.

The importance for minority borrowers of consolidation in the lending industry is unclear. Consolidation might hurt minority borrowers by eliminating small lenders with expertise in the credit needs of individual neighborhoods, or it might help minority borrowers by allowing lenders to take advantage of returns to information scale in the provision of loans to minority neighborhoods.[25] Some troubling evidence from a recent study, Figlio and Genshlea (1999), indicates that the bank closings that accompany consolidation are more likely to take place in minority neighborhoods and in neighborhoods that are more integrated than in white neighborhoods.

2.2.4 The Stages of a Mortgage Transaction

Another important feature of mortgage markets is the complexity involved in each individual mortgage transaction. As shown in figure 2.1, the process leading to a mortgage transaction can be divided into three stages: advertising and outreach, preapplication inquiries, and loan approval. Loan administration can be thought of as a fourth stage. Each stage involves different types of decisions and may involve different actors.

The complexity of this process has two important implications for the study of mortgage lending in general and of lending discrimination in particular. First, one cannot gain a full appreciation of the mortgage market by looking only at the loan approval process, which is the heart of stage 3. Instead, one must also recognize that access to mortgages depends on many other types of actions by borrowers, by lenders, and by affiliated organizations. Thus, a focus on one stage should not blind us to the potential complexity of discriminatory behavior. Discriminatory barriers are cumulative, so discrimination in preapplication inquiries, for example, adds to the difficulties imposed on applicants by discrimination in loan approval. A finding of discrimination in one stage does not, however, imply that there is discrimination at every other stage. A full understanding of discrimination in lending requires research on all stages of the lending process.

Second, the behavior in the various stages is interconnected, so one cannot gain a full or accurate understanding of the behavior in any single stage without considering how that behavior is influenced by behavior at other stages. For example, lenders may, in stage 2, discourage certain types of borrowers from applying for loans. If so, then any sample of loan applications is not a random sample of the people who want mortgages, and estimations based on a sample of loan applications may yield biased results. Similarly, the second part of stage 2, namely, the setting of terms and conditions, must be considered simultaneously with the loan approval decision. As many scholars have pointed out, an analysis of loan applications may yield biased results if one does not consider the factors that influence the size of the loan request. As it turns out, accounting for these types of interactions across stages and substages is critical for accurate estimation of discrimination.[26] Consequently, these interactions are

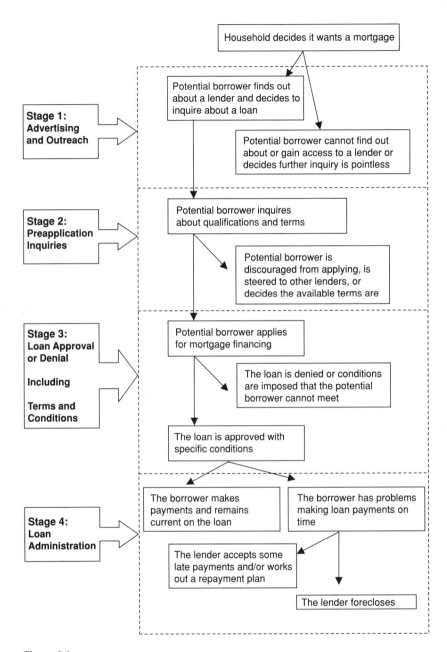

Figure 2.1
Stages in the mortgage-lending process.
Source: Adapted from Turner and Skidmore (1999, exhibit 1).

introduced into the simple conceptual framework presented later in this chapter and are a central theme of this book.

2.3 Fair-Lending Legislation

Fair-lending legislation in the United States gives a specific meaning to the concept of discrimination. This section describes the legislation that prohibits discrimination, discusses the types of discrimination covered by this legislation, and considers the related concept of redlining.

2.3.1 The Fair Housing Act and the Equal Credit Opportunity Act

Discrimination in mortgage lending is prohibited by the Fair Housing Act of 1968 (FaHA) and the Equal Credit Opportunity Act of 1974 (ECOA), both of which have been amended in important ways since passage.[27] According to ECOA, as amended,

It shall be unlawful for any creditor to discriminate against any applicant, with respect to any aspect of a credit transaction—

(1) on the basis of race, color, religion, national origin, sex or marital status, or age (provided the applicant has the capacity to contract). (U.S. Code Title 15, Chapter 41, Section 1691)

This language does not imply that a lender must lend to anyone, only that the standards used to make lending decisions must be the same for all groups. Because few cases have been brought to court on the basis of FaHA and ECOA, however, the courts have not yet provided clear guidance on the types of evidence required to prove that mortgage discrimination exists. (We return to this issue in chapter 10.)

ECOA also assigns fair-lending enforcement authority to the same federal financial institutions (namely the Office of Thrift Supervision, the Office of the Comptroller of the Currency, the Federal Reserve, and the FDIC) that oversee other aspects of lender behavior.[28] Each of these institutions regulates a different set of lenders (see FFIEC, 2001a). According to ECOA, enforcement authority for nondepository lenders is assigned to the FTC.[29]

FaHA also takes a strong stand against lending discrimination. In particular, this act, as amended, says, in part:

It shall be unlawful for any person or other entity whose business includes engaging in residential real estate–related transactions to discriminate against any person in making available such a transaction, or in the terms or conditions of such a transaction, because of race, color, religion, sex, handicap, familial status, or national origin.

As used in this section, the term "residential real estate-related transaction" means any of the following:

(1)   The making or purchasing of loans or providing other financial assistance—

(A)   for purchasing, constructing, improving, repairing, or maintaining a dwelling; or

(B)   secured by residential real estate. (U.S. Code, Title 42, Chapter 45 [Fair Housing], Subchapter 1, Section 3605)[30]

FaHA gives enforcement power to both HUD and the Department of Justice. In general, Justice is entitled to prosecute cases involving a "pattern and practice" of discrimination or an issue of national importance, whereas HUD is the main agency for dealing with discrimination complaints.[31]

These fair-lending laws are implemented through regulations written by the governmental bodies with enforcement authority, including HUD and the financial regulatory institutions. The FFIEC, which consists of all the federal financial regulatory institutions, provides a guide to the fair-lending regulations of its members. This guide says that it would constitute discrimination for a lender to take any of the following actions involving people in a protected class:

• Fail to provide information or services or provide different information or services regarding any aspect of the lending process, including credit availability, application procedures or lending standards
• Discourage or selectively encourage applicants with respect to inquiries about or applications of credit
• Refuse to extend credit or use different standards in determining whether to extend credit
• Vary the terms of credit offered, including the amount, interest rate, duration, or type of loan
• Use different standards to evaluate collateral
• Treat a borrower differently in servicing a loan or invoking default remedies
• Use different standards for pooling or packaging a loan in the secondary market (FFIEC, 1999, p. ii)

The legislative basis for fair-lending enforcement creates overlap among the responsibilities of the various enforcement agencies. As noted above, the financial regulatory agencies are supposed to refer any cases involving a "pattern and practice" of discrimination to the Justice Department, for example, even if they continue to pursue these cases themselves. Moreover, HUD is authorized to investigate practices by mortgage bankers or by depository lenders that might involve violations of FaHA.[32]

2.3.2 Types of Discrimination

ECOA and FaHA also make a key distinction between different types of discrimination. As the FFIEC guide to fair lending puts it:

The courts have recognized three methods of proof of lending discrimination under the ECOA and the FH Act:
- Overt evidence of disparate treatment
- Comparative evidence of disparate treatment
- Evidence of disparate impact

The existence of illegal disparate treatment may be established either by statements revealing that a lender explicitly considered prohibited factors (**overt** evidence) or by differences in treatment that are not fully explained by legitimate nondiscriminatory factors (**comparative** evidence)....

When a lender applies a racially or otherwise neutral policy or practice equally to all credit applicants, but the policy or practice disproportionately excludes or burdens certain persons on a prohibited basis, the policy or practice is described as having a "disparate impact."...

Although the precise contours of the law on disparate impact as it applies to lending discrimination are under development, it has been clearly established [that] the single fact that a policy or practice creates a disparity on a prohibited basis is not alone proof of a violation.

When an Agency finds that a lender's policy or practice has a disparate impact, the next step is to seek to determine whether the policy or practice is justified by "business necessity." The justification must be manifest and may not be hypothetical or speculative. Factors that may be relevant to the justification could include cost and profitability. Even if a policy or practice that has a disparate impact on a prohibited basis can be justified by business necessity, it still may be found to be in violation if an alternative policy or practice could serve the same purpose with less discriminatory effect. Finally, evidence of *discriminatory intent* is not necessary to establish that a lender's adoption or implementation of a policy or practice that has a disparate impact is in violation of the FH Act or ECOA. (FFIEC, 1999, pp. ii–iv)

Throughout this book, the behaviors identified by the first two "methods of proof," overt and comparative, will be called "disparate-treatment" discrimination, and careful attention will be paid to both disparate-treatment and disparate-impact discrimination. Although the prohibition against disparate-impact discrimination is clearly expressed in many court decisions, the legal standards for a case involving disparate-impact discrimination, such as the type of evidence required to prove that a practice meets the "business necessity" test, are complex and not always clear. Moreover, the applicability of these standards to fair lending has not been carefully worked out by the courts. As a result, we will return to these concepts and to the legal standards associated with them when we evaluate fair-lending enforcement procedures in chapter 10.

Not all types of behavior that lead to intergroup disparities in mortgage markets are covered by existing fair-lending legislation. Suppose, for example, that one set of nondepository institutions provides subprime loans in minority neighborhoods, that another set of nondepository institutions provides conventional loans in white neighborhoods, and that because of consumer ignorance, not lender fraud, many people qualified for prime loans accept subprime loans. In this case, minorities may receive loans on worse terms than do equally qualified whites even though no individual lending institution is providing loans on a differential basis to whites and minorities. Our current laws are not designed to combat this type of differential treatment.

2.3.3 Redlining and the Community Reinvestment Act

FaHA and ECOA prohibit certain actions "on the basis of" or "because of" the characteristics that define protected classes. Regulators, supported by the courts, have interpreted this language to cover *redlining*, defined as unfavorable actions by a lender toward loans involving properties in neighborhoods where members of a protected class are located. As the FFIEC puts it:

A lender may not discriminate on a prohibited basis because of the characteristics of

• An applicant, prospective applicant, or borrower
• A person associated with an applicant, prospective applicant, or borrower (for example, a co-applicant, spouse, business partner, or live-in aide)

• The present or prospective occupants of either the property to be financed or the neighborhood or other area where property to be financed is located (FFIEC, 1999, p. ii)

Another type of redlining is covered by the Community Reinvestment Act (CRA) of 1977. This act requires depository lenders to meet the credit needs of all the communities in their designated lending area but does not require them to implement loan programs that are not profitable.[33] CRA, which does not apply to mortgage bankers, is enforced by the same financial regulatory agencies that enforce ECOA.[34] As a result, compliance with CRA regulations is considered during regular examinations of all depository lenders. This arrangement gives depository lenders an incentive to implement programs designed to provide new credit opportunities in low-income and minority neighborhoods, but no consensus has emerged on CRA's effectiveness in stimulating the creation of such programs.

CRA implicitly introduces an *outcome-based* definition of redlining that differs from the *process-based* definition in ECOA and FaHA. In particular, the outcome-based definition says that redlining exists if the credit opportunities provided by a lender in a minority neighborhood in its lending area fall short of the credit opportunities provided to white neighborhoods with comparable risk characteristics. In effect, therefore, CRA not only reinforces the prohibition against process-based redlining in ECOA and FaHA, but also goes beyond those acts by requiring depository lenders to take affirmative steps to make sure all areas in their territory are well served. As a result, a depository lender might not be able to satisfy its CRA obligations simply by eliminating discrimination, both disparate-treatment and disparate-impact, in its loan approval process.[35]

2.4 A Simplified Framework for Thinking about Discrimination in Loan Approval

This section presents a simplified framework for thinking about discrimination in the approval of mortgage loan applications, which is the core of stage 3 in figure 2.1 and is the focus of this book. It offers our framework for thinking about the decision to lend, provides formal definitions of discrimination and redlining, and discusses the implications of the framework for empirical work on discrimination in loan approval.

Discrimination in the approval of mortgage loan applications has dramatic consequences for minority access to housing, it has been the focus of the academic literature, and it obviously could be part of the explanation for the minority-white loan denial disparities in the HMDA data. The conceptual framework presented here is simplified in the sense that it leaves out several aspects of a mortgage transaction. It is intended simply to introduce both the concepts of discrimination and redlining and several key methodological issues that we address in detail in later chapters. Extensions presented in the following chapters are necessary before the framework can be used to isolate discrimination in an empirical study.

2.4.1 The Decision to Lend

A mortgage is an economic transaction in which a lender provides money to a borrower in exchange for a stream of payments in the future. Mortgages must compete with other types of investments by the lender, so a lender will agree to a mortgage transaction, that is, approve a mortgage application, if and only if the profitability of the mortgage exceeds some threshold acceptable to the lender.[36] Let π indicate the profitability of a mortgage measured by the return per dollar of loan, and let π^* be the lender's required profitability threshold. Then the lender's decision rule for an application is[37]

$$\text{accept if:} \quad \pi \geq \pi^*,$$
$$\text{reject if:} \quad \pi < \pi^*. \tag{2.1}$$

Profitability can vary from one loan to the next for a variety of reasons. The terms of the loan itself obviously matter. All else equal, for example, a higher interest rate makes a loan more profitable. Moreover, profitability depends on the characteristics of the applicant. For example, an applicant with poorer credit qualifications is more likely to default, that is, to stop making payments on the loan. When a default occurs, the bank must pay various administrative costs to claim ownership of the property and then must sell the property to try to recoup its investment. The characteristics of the property and of its neighborhood may influence the outcome of this process. If the value of the house has dropped below the remaining principal on the mortgage, for example, the lender will not be able to fully recoup its investment. The profitability of a loan with given characteristics could also be influenced by factors other than default, such as prepayment by the borrower or the liquidity of the loan based on the lender's ability to sell the loan in the secondary mortgage market.

Now let L stand for the characteristics of the loan, such as its interest rate and loan-to-value ratio; A for the characteristics of the applicant, such as his or her past credit problems; and P for the characteristics of the property, such as whether it is in a declining neighborhood. Then a detailed statistical analysis of experience with previous loans can yield an accurate, although probabilistic, prediction of loan profitability based on these characteristics, or

$$\pi = \pi(L, A, P). \tag{2.2}$$

By substituting equation (2.2) into equation (2.1), we arrive at the most basic decision rule for loan approval behavior based on observable information:

accept if: $\pi(L, A, P) \geq \pi^*$,

reject if: $\pi(L, A, P) < \pi^*$. $\tag{2.3}$

The key problem with this description of decision rules for loan approval is that the relationship between loan profitability and loan, applicant, and property characteristics is difficult to establish. Of course, lenders have an incentive to figure out this relationship, but actually doing so requires detailed information on loan performance over a long period of time, along with a complex analysis of this information using advanced statistical procedures. Few lenders have the data or the expertise to conduct such an exercise.

As noted earlier, mortgage markets have recently seen increased use of automated underwriting tools, such as credit scoring. For several reasons, however, it would be inappropriate to assume that these tools provide a lender with the information needed to determine the π function. First, the main tool available to lenders, namely a credit score, is intended to indicate a borrower's "intrinsic" default probability, that is, to reflect the role of A in equation (2.2). This tool therefore does not consider the roles of loan and property characteristics, L and P. A lender can also bring information on loan and property characteristics into an underwriting decision, but this step may be based on an underwriter's judgment or on rules of thumb. Thus, even if the credit score provides the best possible prediction of a borrower's intrinsic default probability, the introduction of other elements that are not subject to the same statistical standards as the credit score implies that the lender's decision rule is unlikely to replicate the "true" π function.

Second, both standard credit scores and complete automated underwriting systems are intended to measure a borrower's default probability, not the expected profitability of a loan.[38] Thus, lenders may want to supplement automated underwriting systems with other, more ad hoc underwriting factors designed to predict the cost of default if it does occur.[39] Alternatively, lenders may base their decisions simply on the predicted probability of default, which differs from predicted profitability. Regardless of the accuracy of the automated underwriting system in predicting the borrower's default probability, therefore, the final underwriting decision may reflect factors that are not subject to careful statistical standards and may, once again, deviate from the best possible π function. Indeed, given the trend toward more diversity in loan products, the factors perceived to influence the cost of default may play an increasing role in the loan approval decision. If so, default-based automated underwriting systems could become less accurate in predicting profits even if they become more accurate in predicting defaults.

Third, no existing credit-scoring scheme, let alone a full automated underwriting system, has been subjected to the scrutiny of disinterested scholars. There is a significant literature (reviewed in Thomas, 2000) on the technical dimensions of credit scoring, that is, on the best method for devising a credit score. As Thomas points out, however, "comparisons [across methods] by academics are often limited as some of the most significant data like the credit bureau reports are too sensitive or too expensive to be passed to them by the users" (p. 160). As a result, the accuracy of credit-scoring schemes remains an open question.[40] In addition, there exists a large literature on the relationship between default and characteristics observable at the time of default, which obviously cannot be used in a credit-scoring scheme (see Quercia and Stegman, 1992; Deng, Quigley, and van Order, 2000). This literature reveals how complex the determinants of default can be and therefore implicitly questions the accuracy of credit-scoring schemes based on limited information about loan, applicant, and property characteristics. Obviously even less is known about the impact of applicant, loan, and property characteristics on loan profitability, so the accuracy of automated underwriting systems also remains in doubt.

Almost inevitably, therefore, lenders must estimate loan profitability using rules of thumb, inexact evaluations of their recent experience, or inexact additions to credit scores (which may, themselves, be inexact). Thus, a more realistic decision framework is based on an estimated profitability that not only is probabilistic, but also depends on the lender's information base and skill at evaluating it. With π^E as the lender's estimated loan profitability, we can restate the decision framework as[41]

accept if: $\pi^E \geq \pi^*$,

reject if: $\pi^E < \pi^*$,   (2.4)

where

$$\pi^E = \pi^E(L, A, P),$$ (2.5)

or

accept if: $\pi^E(L, A, P) \geq \pi^*$,

reject if: $\pi^E(L, A, P) < \pi^*$.   (2.6)

Equation (2.6) can be interpreted as a formal statement of a lender's underwriting criteria; that is, it describes the loan, applicant, and property characteristics that would lead to loan approval.

The role of lender estimation can be highlighted by adding and subtracting the "true" function for π into (2.6). The word "true" is in quotation marks to emphasize that we mean the best probabilistic relationship that can be estimated with potentially observable information and the most appropriate statistical techniques. This step yields

accept if: $\pi(L, A, P) + [\pi^E(L, A, P) - \pi(L, A, P)] \geq \pi^*$,

reject if: $\pi(L, A, P) + [\pi^E(L, A, P) - \pi(L, A, P)] < \pi^*$.   (2.7)

In this version, the lending decision depends on the "true" relationship between profitability and the characteristics in L, A, and P, as well as on the difference between the lender's estimated relationship and this true relationship.

An extension of this framework that will prove to be important in the study of discrimination is to recognize that the expressions in

(2.7) may vary from lender to lender. Lenders' expectations are likely to reflect their experience and their management policies, so variation in experience and management may lead to variation in expectations. Moreover, the true relationship between profitability and L, A, and P may be different for lenders operating in different regions or in different segments of the mortgage market. Even required profitability, π^*, may vary across lenders because the cost of capital reflects differences in regulations or because of imperfect competition in the mortgage market.[42]

2.4.2 Analytical Definitions of Discrimination and Redlining

The next step is to bring in discrimination and redlining—in ways that are consistent with fair-lending legislation. The simplest definition of *discrimination* is the use of a loan approval decision rule that is affected by an applicant's membership in a minority group or, to use the more precise legal term, in a protected class. Similarly, *redlining* is said to exist whenever the lender's decision rule is affected by the location of the relevant property in a minority neighborhood. In other words, discrimination (redlining) by this definition exists whenever the probability of loan approval goes down when the applicant belongs to a protected class (the house is in a minority neighborhood).

Now let M indicate that the applicant belongs to a protected class and N indicate that the relevant house is in a neighborhood in which a relatively high proportion of the population belongs to a protected class. Discrimination (redlining) exists if $M(N)$ affects the accept/reject decision after accounting for application characteristics L, A, and P. To express this definition in our framework, let $D(M,N)$ indicate the impact of M and N on loan acceptance, controlling for expected loan profitability.[43] Then we can write:

$$\text{accept if:} \quad \pi(L,A,P) - D(M,N) + [\pi^E(L,A,P) - \pi(L,A,P)] \geq \pi^*,$$
$$\text{reject if:} \quad \pi(L,A,P) - D(M,N) + [\pi^E(L,A,P) - \pi(L,A,P)] < \pi^*. \tag{2.8}$$

In an empirical study, therefore, one can test for discrimination or redlining by determining whether the arguments of this D function, namely, M and N, have a statistically significant impact on loan approval.

This definition of discrimination corresponds to disparate-treatment discrimination, that is, to using a different decision rule for

people in protected classes than for others. The definition of redlining corresponds to a type of disparate-treatment discrimination
based on neighborhood. This is, of course, the process-based definition of redlining, not the outcome-based definition in CRA.

Disparate-impact discrimination is buried in the difference between π^E and π in equation (2.8). Even if a lender uses the same
underwriting criteria for all customers, it is practicing disparate-
impact discrimination if one or more of these criteria are highly correlated with membership in a protected class and are not accurate
predictors of loan profitability. In legal terms, a lender cannot use
practices with a disparate impact on a protected class unless it can
establish that these practices are justified by business necessity—and
have no nondiscriminatory alternative.

In our framework, a difference between π^E and π implies that the
lender is using criteria that, to some degree, are not related to loan
profitability, but it does not necessarily imply that disparate-impact
discrimination exists. For disparate-impact discrimination to exist,
the criteria leading to this difference must be particularly unfavorable to applicants in a protected class.

Because lenders cannot be expected to know the "true" relationship between loan profitability and observable loan, applicant, and
property characteristics and because many of these characteristics are correlated with membership in various protected classes,
disparate-impact discrimination is a very real possibility in mortgage
lending. In some cases, lenders may use outmoded rules of thumb
that inadvertently have a disparate impact on people in a protected
class; in other cases, lenders may purposely design underwriting
criteria that look nondiscriminatory on the surface, because they are
applied equally to everyone, but that are, in fact, discriminatory because they have nothing to do with loan profitability and are particularly unfavorable to people in a protected class.

The rapid growth of various techniques for automated underwriting alters the terms of the debate but does not eliminate these concerns. As discussed earlier, these techniques may be able to eliminate
disparate-treatment discrimination by providing decision rules that
do not consider an applicant's membership in a protected class.
Moreover, by replacing rules of thumb with statistically based
underwriting standards, and thereby narrowing the differences
between π^E and π, these techniques might eliminate some practices
that have a disparate impact. Scholars have not yet been able, how-

ever to examine these techniques and in particular to determine whether they involve disparate-impact discrimination.[44] Moreover, we show in chapter 9 that disparate-impact discrimination can be introduced into an automated underwriting system through apparently group-neutral techniques.

In principle, one could extend the disparate-impact concept to redlining. In other words, one could ask whether some underwriting criteria that are not related to loan profitability have a disparate impact on minority neighborhoods. To the best of our knowledge, however, neither courts nor scholars have pursued this idea.[45]

One final twist on these definitions is that a lender's expectations about loan profitability could be affected by M or N. This possibility is complicated, because M and/or N might actually help predict loan profitability after controlling for L, A, and P. If so, then the use of M and N as predictors of profitability is said to involve "statistical discrimination."[46] It is important not to be confused about this link to profitability. As just explained, underwriting criteria that are applied equally to all customers do not involve discrimination if they can be justified on the basis of a link to profitability. In contrast, statistical discrimination involves the use of different underwriting criteria for people in a protected class than for others and therefore is a type of disparate-treatment discrimination, which cannot be defined away by a link to profitability. The law does not allow a lender to use different criteria for people in a protected class than for other people even if it is profitable to do so.

In more formal terms, M and N might be statistically significant in an analysis of loan profitability, even after accounting for L, A, and P. Nevertheless, on both legal and policy grounds, a legitimate "true" profitability function cannot reflect these variables. Thus, the π function defined by equation (2.2) is still appropriate, but now it must be reinterpreted as the best possible estimate of profitability based on observable borrower, loan, and property characteristics except for legally proscribed variables, namely, the applicant's membership in a protected class, M, or the location in a minority neighborhood of the property to be financed, N.

To bring statistical discrimination into our framework, let us introduce M and N into the lender's estimate of loan profitability, equation (2.5):

$$\pi^E = \pi^E(L, A, P) - D^S(M, N), \tag{2.9}$$

where D^S indicates the perceived impact of M and N on profitability, controlling for observable characteristics, L, A, and P.[47] Substituting equation (2.9) into equation (2.8) yields

accept if: $\pi(L, A, P) - [D(M, N) + D^S(M, N)]$

$\quad\quad + [\pi^E(L, A, P) - \pi(L, A, P)] \geq \pi^*,$

reject if: $\pi(L, A, P) - [D(M, N) + D^S(M, N)]$ (2.10)

$\quad\quad + [\pi^E(L, A, P) - \pi(L, A, P)] < \pi^*.$

Note that statistical discrimination appears in the new D term, not in the difference between π^E and π. This result provides a formal demonstration that statistical discrimination is just another form of disparate-treatment discrimination, not disparate-impact discrimination that might be justified by a link to loan profitability.

Some scholars argue that discrimination cannot exist if lenders are "simply" maximizing profits. For example, Becker (1993a) argues that "discrimination in the marketplace consists of voluntarily relinquishing profits, wages, or income, in order to cater to prejudice" (p. 18). This definition, however, is not consistent with the law. This society has decided that to support the principle of equal treatment, it is important to require that the same underwriting criteria be used for people in protected classes and for other people, even if this requirement imposes a cost in the form of lost profits.[48] People must be treated on the basis of their own observable characteristics, not on the basis of average characteristics of groups to which they belong. This is simply one of the costs of doing business in our society. Making an exception for "profitable" discriminatory actions would magnify hostility and conflict across racial and ethnic lines, a cost that our society deems more significant than any lost profits. Thus, it does not matter whether the perceptions in equation (2.9) are accurate or not; statistical discrimination is still discrimination whether it is accurately linked to profits or simply based on inaccurate stereotypes about the profitability of loans to certain groups.

2.5 Implications for Estimating Discrimination in Loan Approval

The formal structure of the approve/deny decision appears to be ideally suited to empirical tools for examining discrete choice, particularly logit and probit analysis. These tools are designed for examining a discrete choice (in this case, whether or not to deny a loan application) as a function of an unobservable latent variable (loan profitability), which is, in turn, a function of observable variables (loan, applicant, and property characteristics) (see equations (2.8) and (2.10)). In this setting, it seems natural to add variables indicating membership in a protected class, M, or the location of the property in a minority neighborhood, N, in order to estimate discrimination and redlining, respectively. A positive, statistically significant coefficient for M, for example, would indicate that people in a protected class are more likely than other applicants to be denied a loan, controlling for L, A, and P, and would appear to provide strong evidence of discrimination. Indeed, this is the strategy followed by several of the empirical studies discussed in this book.

Not surprisingly, however, things are not so simple. In this section we introduce two of the main challenges facing a study of discrimination in loan denial. Additional challenges are addressed in later chapters.

2.5.1 Omitted Variables

The most obvious and widely recognized problem with the simple approach described above is that some of the variables observed by the lender and included in L, A, or P, as defined earlier, may not be observed by a researcher. If so, then the researcher cannot control for all factors considered by the lender in determining whether people in protected classes are more likely to be turned down for a loan. This limitation is important because it can lead to what is called "omitted-variable bias" in the estimated coefficients, including the coefficients of M and N. Moreover, the most likely bias in the coefficients of M and N is upward, which means that an empirical analysis that omits key underwriting variables is likely to overstate discrimination and redlining. Consider, for example, a variable that indicates whether an applicant has had serious credit problems in the past. Because credit problems are more likely among disadvantaged racial and ethnic groups than among whites, a failure to control for this variable would make it look as if, on average, people in these disadvantaged groups are being denied loans unfairly, that is, being discriminated against, even when they are simply being denied loans because of past credit problems.

This methodological problem is, of course, the major reason why the HMDA data cannot be used to obtain estimates of discrimination in mortgage lending. Although these data do contain several of the variables in A and P, such as applicant income and property location, they do not include several other variables that are likely to affect loan returns and to be correlated with minority status. These missing variables include applicant wealth and credit history, the payment-to-income ratio, and the loan-to-value ratio. Moreover, one-third of mortgages immediately sold to the secondary market do not indicate the race of the applicant, and almost half of such mortgages do not indicate applicant income or urban area (Canner and Gabriel, 1992). With so much missing information, the HMDA data by itself cannot be used to obtain a formal estimate of discrimination or to test the hypothesis that discrimination exists.

The only way to eliminate this problem is, of course, to gather information on all the variables that lenders use in making the loan denial decision. This is, of course, a great challenge. As we will see in chapter 5, several critics claim that even the Boston Fed Study, with its extensive data, does not meet this challenge. Moreover, some scholars argue that this challenge is so great that it cannot be met by any study. Analysis of these issues is one of the central themes of this book. We start, in chapter 3, by exploring the literature on mortgage lending in general. This step helps identify the control variables that are necessary to identify lending discrimination. In chapters 4 through 8, we discuss the control variables used by existing studies of lending discrimination. Finally, in chapter 10 we argue that the omitted-variable problem can—and indeed must—be overcome in a fair-lending enforcement system.

2.5.2 Interactions between Loan Approval and Other Stages of the Lending Process

A lender's decision to approve or deny credit is based on a completed loan application that contains detailed applicant characteristics, including credit history; loan terms, such as the loan-to-value and debt-to-income ratios; and property characteristics, such as whether the mortgage is for a condominium or a multifamily unit. Many of these variables are determined or at least influenced by either the applicant or the lender. The applicant determines the timing of the initial inquiry and the amount, type, and location of housing, which in turn influences assessed value, sales price, and equity risk. In addition, while filling out the application, the borrower may choose from among a number of loan programs and products, which in turn may imply different down payment requirements, closing costs, interest rates, and insurance payments.

In addition, the loan officer may provide assistance, advice, or information that influences the nature of the final application. This officer may suggest certain loan products, encourage a customer to go to a different branch office, or provide advice on the best way to arrange one's financial affairs before an application is actually submitted. In its investigation of Decatur Federal Savings and Loan in Atlanta, for example, the Justice Department discovered that the Decatur loan officers helped white applicants make their applications look stronger (by paying off credit card debt, for example) and did not even tell black applicants that deficiencies in applications could be resolved (see Ritter, 1996).

The traditional method for estimating a model of loan approval is to include all borrower, loan, and property characteristics as exogenous explanatory variables. This approach may lead to biased results, because some of these characteristics are chosen or at least influenced by either the borrower or the lender. This type of bias is called endogeneity bias, which can arise whenever one or more unobserved factors influence both the dependent variable, in this case the decision to approve or deny a loan, and an explanatory variable, such as the loan-to-value ratio.

A classic example of endogeneity arises in the estimation of wage equations. Individuals choose their level of education, and unobservable characteristics, such as work ethic, influence both an individual's wages and the level of education that he chooses. In this example, the coefficient on education tends to be biased upward, because education captures part of the influence of work ethic on wages. Moreover, if race is correlated with education, the endogeneity of education can also result in a bias in estimating the relationship between race and wages (see Card, 2000).

A related problem is that the approve/deny decision is observed only for submitted mortgage applications. The sample of borrowers in a loan approval regression does not include people who did not apply for a mortgage, and it specifically excludes people who decide to rent their housing, are discouraged from submitting a mortgage application, or reside in owner-occupied housing that is not financed by a mortgage. The selection process that determines who submits a mortgage application may be related to the structure of the mortgage market. For example, an individual may choose to rent if she does not have a sufficient down payment to buy a house of the size she desires, or an individual who already owns a house may choose not to buy a new house if he believes that he will have trouble obtaining a new mortgage.

These processes may create what is called a selection bias in models of a lender's approve/deny decision. An estimation suffers from sample selection bias when one or more unobservable characteristics influence both the selection for inclusion in the sample and the dependent variable.

Again, a classic example of sample selection bias can be found in the labor market literature. Wages are observed only for individuals who are working, and wage equations must be estimated using a sample of employed individuals. As in the previous example, work ethic is likely to increase both the likelihood of being employed and the wage if the individual is employed. If one individual is employed and an observationally equivalent individual is unemployed, some difference must exist between the two individuals to explain the difference in their employment status. The employed individual must be of higher quality than the unemployed individual on unobserved characteristics. In the work ethic example, education is assumed to increase the likelihood of employment. Therefore, employed individuals with low levels of education must on average have high levels of work ethic, but employed individuals with high levels of education can have lower levels of work ethic, because education compensates for the low work ethic in determining employment status. This selection process creates a negative relationship between education and work ethic in the sample. Both work ethic and education are assumed to increase wages, and therefore the selection process biases the positive relationship between education and wages towards zero (see Card, 2000).

Both endogeneity and sample selection bias can arise only if an unobserved variable is related both to the dependent variable and to either an explanatory variable or the decision that leads to the inclusion of an individual in the sample. From this perspective, these biases are closely related to omitted-variable bias. Endogeneity bias is simply a special case of omitted-variable bias in which the relationship between the omitted variable and an explanatory variable reflects a choice by the lender or applicant. Sample selection bias is distinct from omitted-variable bias but cannot exist unless important variables are omitted from the specification. In particular, selection bias cannot exist unless one or more unobservable characteristics influence both the selection process and the dependent variable, and therefore it cannot exist if all characteristics influencing loan approval are included in the regression. As a result, the possibility of these problems simply adds weight to the need for a very detailed data set in any study of loan approval.

Omitted-variable, endogeneity, and sample selection bias are potentially tractable in a loan approval model, because the underwriting decision is based predominantly on information that is recorded in loan files and that could potentially be included in a regression analysis. If all substantive underwriting variables have been included in the analysis, the results will not generally suffer from any of these problems. Thus, our review of the literature on mortgage markets in chapter 3 also is designed to help develop specifications that avoid these types of bias.

An important exception to the conclusion that including all substantive underwriting variables in an analysis generally eliminates the potential for biased results involves the role of the lender or potential borrower in influencing either the form of the final application or whether an application is even submitted. A loan officer may have private information concerning the underwriting behavior of his or her institution. If this private information influences the interaction between the loan officer and the potential applicant, the private information may be related to the likelihood of an application's being submitted or to the content of the application, which would create a sample selection or an endogeneity bias that could not be corrected with information in the loan file. In chapter 5, we will explore methods to avoid biases of this type.

The trend toward more credit pricing and less credit rationing, which was discussed earlier in this chapter, also has important implications for future research on mortgage lending discrimination. First, with extensive variation in credit pricing, any model of loan approval must include variables to indicate the interest rate and closing costs; as the framework presented earlier makes clear, for example, an applicant paying higher costs will face a weaker underwriting standard, all else equal. Without these variables, therefore, the estimated coefficients could be subject to omitted-variable bias. In addition, these pricing variables need to be treated as endogenous. Ignoring pricing variables probably biases statistical tests away from finding discrimination. If minorities are steered to more expensive loan products or simply charged more for credit, then they are more likely to be approved, all else equal, thereby mitigating intergroup differences in loan approval. Bringing in pricing variables may prove to be quite a challenge for researchers, however, because interest rate and closing cost information would have to be collected for both accepted and denied loan applications.

Second, these developments may limit the importance of discrimination in loan approval and magnify the importance of discrimination in loan pricing. As noted earlier, the mortgage market may be moving toward a world with no credit rationing, that is, toward a situation in which everyone can have access to credit if the price is right. In this world there cannot be, by definition, any discrimination in loan approval, but there can, of course, be discrimination in loan pricing. As we discuss in chapter 7, only a few studies have addressed this type of discrimination.

2.5.3 Looking Ahead

The examples in the previous two sections are only the first of many methodological issues that we will address in this book. To expand our framework, and hence to expand the set of methodological issues with which we can deal, we next turn to a review of the literature on mortgage markets in general. Subsequent chapters then consider issues raised in existing studies of mortgage lending discrimination. Not surprisingly, mortgage lending discrimination turns out to be a difficult phenomenon to isolate, but we will ultimately show that a credible methodology for achieving this task does exist.

3

A Conceptual Framework
for Mortgage Lending

3.1 Introduction

The mortgage market is complex and has many linkages to other markets in the economy. A large and diverse literature examines this market and models the key firm and household decisions that influence it. The objective of this chapter is to organize and survey this literature. The survey presented here is not intended to be comprehensive but instead focuses on issues and studies that are relevant for the validity and structure of tests for discrimination in the lender approval/denial decision, also called underwriting. The rest of this chapter is divided into four sections. The first three sections follow the structure developed in figure 2.1. The final section draws on the literature surveyed in the first three sections to offer insights into the form and validity of statistical tests for discrimination in the lender approval/denial decision.

3.2 The Housing Market

The process leading up to the submission of a mortgage application involves many individual choices that may influence both the characteristics of individual applications and the sample of applications actually submitted to lenders. The primary choice in this process is the individual's decision whether to own or rent a home, also referred to as tenure choice. Once an individual has decided to purchase a home, or at least to begin planning to purchase a home, other important decisions follow, such as savings decisions for a down payment; whether to use a real estate agency; what type, size, and quantity of housing to purchase; and where to look for housing.

3.2.1 Tenure Choice

Economists have traditionally viewed the tenure choice as determined primarily by three factors: permanent income, costs of owning relative to renting, and household life cycle attributes. The decision to buy a home is a long-term decision and should depend on a household's long-term earnings and income-generating capacity, as well as on the household's expectations concerning the future.[1] Rosen (1985) provides a survey of the literature on tenure choice.

More recently, the research emphasis has shifted to the role of constraints in affecting the decision whether to own a home. Zorn (1989) specifies a model in which households maximize utility over three options: maintaining their current residence, moving to an owned residence, or moving to a rental residence. Lenders generally require a borrower to put a certain amount of money down, say 20 percent of the value of the house being purchased. In Zorn's model, this type of down-payment constraint may force a household to settle for less owner-occupied housing that it would choose if it faced only an income constraint; this constrained amount of owner-occupied housing may even yield less utility than the (unconstrained) rental option, so the household may choose to rent instead of own.

Duca and Rosenthal (1994) and Linneman and Wachter (1989) find empirical evidence that down-payment constraints have a substantial effect on home ownership and that credit constraints matter more than income in determining home ownership. Hendershott, LaFayette, and Haurin (1997) observe that borrowers also face an income constraint and that either type of constraint may limit housing demand.[2] In their model, constrained households are assumed to purchase the largest house possible without allowing either the ratio of assessed house value to loan amount or the ratio of monthly expenses to income to exceed specific limits.

In addition, credit constraints can explain a substantial portion of the large racial differences in homeownership in the United States. Linneman and Wachter (1989) classify households into two categories: those that are predicted to be constrained by a down-payment requirement and those that are not. After controlling for wealth differences, they find no significant racial differences in the likelihood of homeownership for unconstrained households. However,

Gyourko, Linneman, and Wachter (1999) find racial differences in homeownership for constrained households. Specifically, down-payment constraints have a larger negative effect on the likelihood of homeownership for blacks than for whites. Moreover, blacks are more likely to face a down-payment constraint than whites. Deng, Ross, and Wachter (1999) find that these two factors combine to explain over half of the observed racial differences in homeownership rates in Philadelphia.[3]

Following the logic of these models, mortgage applications can be divided, at least in principle, into three groups: applications from home buyers facing a down-payment constraint, from home buyers facing an income constraint, and from unconstrained home buyers. If a household is unconstrained, the quantity of housing it purchases, as measured by the purchase price or assessed value, is unlikely to be affected by its expectations concerning the mortgage underwriting process. If a household is constrained, however, it is likely to settle for less housing than it otherwise would in order to increase the likelihood of eventual mortgage approval. As a result, the factors that determine credit constraints, such as savings behavior, have an influence on the amount of housing a household purchases and hence on the size of its mortgage. Moreover, these factors also can influence whether a household decides to apply for a mortgage at all.

The impact of credit constraints on housing outcomes may be stronger for minorities than for whites. Minorities are more likely than whites to be credit constrained, and the effects of being credit constrained appear to be larger for minorities. The larger impact of a down-payment constraint on minorities than on whites may arise because potential minority home buyers are less willing to compromise on the quantity of housing when they are credit constrained or because being credit constrained has a larger impact on the likelihood of their eventually obtaining a mortgage.[4] In any case, several factors could explain the fact that minority households are more likely to be credit constrained, including less stable income streams for minority households, racial or ethnic disparities in the wealth of extended families, mortgage lending discrimination, or higher equity risk in minority neighborhoods (see Gyourko, Linneman, and Wachter, 1999). However, Deng, Ross, and Wachter (1999) find that racial differences in the effect of being credit constrained persist even after neighborhood equity risk is controlled for.

3.2.2 Savings Behavior

The traditional model of savings determination involves an intertemporal consumption choice; to be specific, households can save in order to finance future consumption above future income levels. In these models, households often expect an age-earnings profile in which earnings first increase with age but then decrease with age later in life. Thus, households tend to borrow early in life and save during the middle portion of their life in order to smooth their consumption path. Another important consumption-smoothing activity arises from earnings uncertainty, which leads households to save as a precaution against negative earnings shocks (see Sandmo, 1985).

The decision to save may also be influenced by the need for a down payment on a home. Engelhardt (1994) develops a model for the decision to save for a down payment (see also Artle and Varaiya, 1978; Brueckner, 1986; and Haurin, Hendershott, and Wachter, 1996). The key features of Engelhardt's model are as follows:

1. The household maximizes the discounted stream of utility over a fixed lifetime with perfect foresight.

2. Utility depends on nonhousing consumption and housing.

3. Housing consumption is fixed over time and can be altered only once, when the household makes the transition from renting to owning.

4. The household faces an intertemporal budget constraint that varies by tenure status.

5. Actual monetary assets at the time of home purchase must equal or exceed the required down payment, which is based on the household's housing demand.

Although this model imposes a number of strong assumptions, it is able to capture many of the important trade-offs faced by a household in deciding when and whether to become a homeowner. Households can enter the state of homeownership earlier by reducing housing consumption or by foregoing current consumption and saving in order to accumulate a down payment. On the other hand, income increases over time, and households may desire to buy a larger house than they can afford based on current income and assets. As a result, households may delay the transition to ownership, which increases the time available for saving and allows the household to buy a larger house.

Engelhardt (1994) finds evidence that households consider all options described by this model. The model's strongest assumption is that housing consumption is fixed after the transition into owner-occupancy, but this assumption captures the high moving costs associated with changing housing consumption as an owner-occupant. With high moving costs, households may indeed delay the transition into owner-occupancy in order to buy more housing. Although Engelhardt's model may overstate this delay effect somewhat, the effect is quite real among homeowners.

Engelhardt's analysis also identifies a substantial "discouragement effect," in which households foresee their inability to purchase a home in the future and respond by decreasing their saving rate. Engelhardt (1994) finds evidence of this effect using data from Canada. He documents a negative relationship between the price level of housing and the savings of renters. Sheiner (1995) also investigates this discouragement effect as evidenced by housing price changes. Using data for the United States, she finds that the discouragement effect is smaller than the direct effect of a change in price levels, which requires an increase in savings from renters who plan to buy. The net result is that renters' savings increase with the housing price level.[5]

Gifts to households also play an important role in providing funds for down payments. Mayer and Engelhardt (1996) find that the share of the down payment from gifts increased from 8.5 percent in 1976–1978 to 13.1 percent in 1991–1993. These results suggest that first-time home buyers face an increasingly difficult job in saving for a down payment, even among households that have sufficient income to support the associated mortgage payments. Mayer and Engelhardt also find that households facing a credit constraint are more likely to receive a gift. Additional evidence concerning gifts comes from a recent study by Charles and Hurst (forthcoming). Among white renter households that became owners between 1991 and 1995, 15 percent received the funds for their down payment entirely from their extended family, and 27 percent received some family funds.

Engelhardt and Mayer (1998) also find a link between savings and the availability of gifts from relatives for down payments. On average, a $1 gift reduces savings by $0.40 and increases the down payment by $0.60. This increase in the down payment goes toward both a higher down payment percentage ($0.42) and a higher housing price ($0.18).

The savings behavior of potential home buyers can affect the terms of any mortgage application they submit by influencing both the price they can afford to pay for a house and the resources available for a down payment. Moreover, the large discouragement effect identified by Engelhardt implies that the sample of mortgage applicants may be selected based on their ability to accumulate wealth. The availability of gifts from relatives, however, may limit the importance of this discouragement effect and, as a result, affect this selection process.

Race and ethnicity may be important factors in determining the size of the effect attributable to selection based on ability to accumulate weath. On average, minorities have less wealth than whites, even controlling for income, and therefore are less likely to have saved enough money for a down payment (see Hurst, Luoh, and Stafford, 1998, and Oliver and Shapiro, 1995). Moreover, these wealth disparities reach across generations, as minorities are less likely than whites to receive gifts that contribute to a down payment. In fact, Charles and Hurst (forthcoming) find that almost nine out of ten black home buyers came up with the entire down payment for their home purchases themselves and that only 6 percent received the entire down payment from their families.

3.2.3 Real Estate Brokers and Housing Search

The housing market is characterized by a search process in which buyers and sellers search for the best available options, subject to various search costs. Sellers search for the buyer who will offer them the highest price, and buyers search for the house that best matches their needs, conditional on the price that they expect to pay for the house. Buyers and sellers face uncertainty concerning both their ability to find a match and the quality of that match. In addition, the return to search for any seller or buyer may depend on the search efforts of other sellers and buyers, which implies that externalities exist. Finally, a housing market with these characteristics may not have a single equilibrium. Instead, the equilibrium may depend on the expectations of individual sellers and buyers concerning the search effort of other actors, and many different expected levels of effort

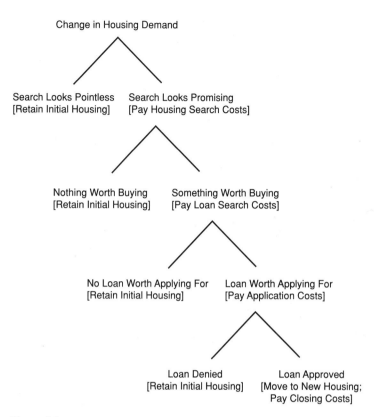

Change in Housing Demand

Search Looks Pointless   Search Looks Promising
[Retain Initial Housing]   [Pay Housing Search Costs]

Nothing Worth Buying   Something Worth Buying
[Retain Initial Housing]   [Pay Loan Search Costs]

No Loan Worth Applying For   Loan Worth Applying For
[Retain Initial Housing]   [Pay Application Costs]

Loan Denied   Loan Approved
[Retain Initial Housing]   [Move to New Housing;
                                       Pay Closing Costs]

Figure 3.1
Steps in the housing search process.
Source: Adapted from Yinger (1997, figure 2).

may result in an equilibrium (Diamond, 1982; Yavas, 1995). In this setting, there is a potential role for intermediaries, such as real estate agents and multiple-listing services, which can reduce uncertainty, internalize externalities, and potentially eliminate some equilibria that result in low levels of welfare.[6] (See Yavas, 1994, for a survey of the literature on this topic.)

Courant (1978) provides a basic model of the search problem facing a household. This model was extended by Yinger (1997) to consider multiple-listing services and lenders. One of the key insights of a housing search model is that households must make decisions in stages, with different information at each stage. In the Yinger model, which is described in figure 3.1, the search process begins when a household experiences some change in its underlying housing demand so that it might gain from moving to a different housing unit.[7] The first decision it must then make is whether to begin a formal housing search. The household must make this decision on the basis of information available to it at the time, which is likely to be informal information about the availability of housing and about the terms and conditions of mortgages. This information could come from its own previous experiences, from advertising, or from the experiences of its friends and neighbors.

If the household decides to search for housing, then the next decision it must make is whether any of the available units appear to be worth buying, that is, whether, given their prices, they appear to make the household better off. This decision will be based on the information gathered during a housing search, which, of course, is heavily influenced by the actions of real estate agents. In the 1989 Housing Discrimination Study (HDS), for example, white customers were shown or told about an average of 2.84 available houses when they visited a single real estate agent to inquire about a particular advertised unit and similar houses (Yinger, 1995, table 6.1).[8]

Moreover, Ondrich, Ross, and Yinger (2001) find evidence that real estate agents interpret a customer's initial housing request as an indication of her preferences and then concentrate on showing units consistent with those preferences, presumably to maximize the chance of a sale. Agents also deviate from this pattern, however, in some circumstances. For example, they practice redlining against integrated neighborhoods in the suburbs in the sense that they are less likely to show white customers available houses in those neighborhoods than in other neighborhoods. This effect shows up even for customers who request housing in such neighborhoods. This behavior could reflect agents' perception that lenders practice redlining against such neighborhoods, although Ondrich, Ross, and Yinger have no way to test this proposition.

Once a household decides that there is a house worth buying, it must search for a mortgage and determine if the loan terms it is offered are acceptable. As discussed in the next section, this search process may involve lenders, but it also may involve real estate agents. HDS found, for example, that lenders often offered to help customers find financing, and they also often volunteered information about the types of loans available (Yinger, 1995, chap. 5). A more recent development is that real estate agents screen many potential buyers for the mortgage market by "prequalifying" them for a mortgage. This prequalification step is designed to tell the broker what type of house a potential buyer can afford, but it obviously also sends a signal to the potential buyer about what will happen to her in the mortgage market. As a result, real estate agents may influence the lender to which the borrower eventually applies or the terms of the eventual loan application.

There are obviously many opportunities for race or ethnicity to play a role in this search process. People in different racial or ethnic groups tend to have different social networks and therefore may obtain different information about available housing or about mortgage possibilities. In addition, Yinger (1997) points out that racial or ethnic discrimination by real estate agents can influence housing searches in several ways. The most fundamental effect, of course, is that discrimination restricts the housing information available to minorities. In HDS, for example, blacks learned about only 2.26 houses on average, compared to the 2.84 figure for whites (Yinger, 1995, table 6.1). Hence, minorities are less likely than whites to find a house that is worth buying. In addition, discrimination can make the search process less pleasant and more costly for minorities than for whites. In HDS, for example, blacks were significantly less likely than whites to receive a follow-up call from the broker or to be given positive comments about an available house (Yinger, 1995, table 3.3). These impacts of discrimination on housing searches imply that, compared to similar whites, black and Hispanic households will gain less from housing searches and will be more likely to decide not to search at all.

In some cases, discrimination may be associated with real estate agents' preconceptions about where blacks can buy housing. Agents try to focus their marketing efforts on housing matches that are relatively likely to be consummated and therefore avoid showing houses when a match seems unlikely. This is an example of statistical discrimination, which was defined in chapter 2. For example, Ondrich, Ross, and Yinger (2001) find that the probability that a particular unit will be shown increases with its asking price for white customers, but not for black customers. Thus, agents act as if the higher the price of a house, the less likely it is that a black customer will be able to buy it, even if she asks about it. This behavior could reflect a belief that black customers, unlike white customers, are unlikely to be qualified for expensive houses, even if they inquire about them, or a belief that lending discrimination against blacks is more likely for more expensive houses. Ondrich, Ross, and Yinger also find that available houses that are less expensive than the one a customer inquires about are more likely to be shown if the customer is black but not if she is white. In other words, real estate agents act as if blacks, but not whites, request more expensive units than they can afford. This is another form of statistical discrimination.

No existing research sheds light on the origins of these types of agent perceptions, but they might be linked with agents' past experiences, including their past interactions with lenders. Agents might have observed lenders practicing discrimination, for example, or they might have observed that, at any given house value, blacks tend to receive loans with higher loan-to-value ratios than do whites. The latter observation is consistent with evidence in Munnell et al. (1996). Thus experience and perceptions about lender behavior can feed back to influence actions by real estate agents.

Courant (1978) explains that discrimination, actual or anticipated, also can influence the set of neighborhoods in which minority households search for housing.[9] The influence of discrimination on search could be based on perceptions by minority households, on advertising practices by real estate firms, or on actions by real estate agents that steer minority households to certain neighborhoods. Evidence of discrimination in advertising practices is found by Galster, Freiberg, and Houk (1987), Newburger (1995), and Turner (1992). Evidence of steering, based on the HDS, is found by Turner and Mickelsons (1992). This steering might involve lenders. Either potential minority home buyers or real estate agents (or both) might perceive that lenders are willing to lend to minority households only for housing purchases in certain neighborhoods.

The real estate agent's role in financing also could have an intergroup dimension. For example, prequalification is typically completed without full information on a customer's financial situation. This leaves room for agents' preconceptions. If the agents believe that minorities have inferior financial characteristics compared to whites, for example, or if agents place less trust in the information provided by minority home buyers, then agents may send minorities to mortgage lenders with lower underwriting standards, but higher prices, or may steer minorities to less expensive housing.

HDS provides some evidence of behavior like this (Yinger, 1995). First, brokers were more willing to help white than minority customers with making arrangements to finance their housing purchase.

In fact, only 13.3 percent of the black auditors were offered assistance finding a loan, compared to 24.4 of their white teammates. Similarly, only 18.1 percent of the Hispanic auditors were offered this type of assistance, compared to 22.1 percent of their white teammates. Moreover, white auditors were far more likely to be told about both conventional fixed-rate and conventional variable-rate mortgages, whereas minority auditors were steered toward FHA loans. To be specific, the probability that an auditor was told about a conventional fixed-rate mortgage was 21.5 percentage points lower for black auditors than for their white teammates and 14.7 percentage points lower for Hispanic auditors than for their black teammates. In the case of conventional adjustable-rate mortgages, the comparable gaps were 15.1 and 10.9 percentage points, respectively. In contrast, blacks were 6.7 percentage points more likely than whites (and Hispanics 3.4 percentage points more likely than whites) to be told about FHA loans.[10]

3.3 The Preapplication and Application Stages of Lending

As discussed in chapter 2, a potential home buyer must go through several steps to obtain a mortgage. She must approach one or more lenders to gather information concerning both her qualifications and the application process, choose a mortgage lender, select the type of loan and the loan terms, and submit a loan application. This process is difficult to analyze because it is intrinsically difficult to separate the borrower's choices from the lender's decisions and recommendations. The lender may influence the pool of applicants through marketing and preapplication screening, and the loan officer usually provides some advice to the borrower concerning loan products and terms, as well as some assistance in filling out the application.[11]

3.3.1 Matching Borrowers and Lenders

At the preapplication stage, the prospective borrower collects information to determine whether she can afford to purchase a home, how expensive a home she can afford, and what types of loan products are available and best fit her needs. The lender can affect this process in several ways. First, lender marketing and past originating decisions may, through word of mouth, have a substantial affect on the pool of inquiries. Second, a potential applicant who approaches a specific lender meets a loan originator (also referred to simply as a loan officer) who provides information concerning underwriting standards, loan types, loan terms, and application procedures. Moreover, this loan officer may provide an informal assessment of the applicant's creditworthiness or conduct a formal mortgage prequalification that the borrower can use during the housing search. Little has been written on these processes, however, so our strategy in this subsection is to examine briefly a few of the key interactions they involve.

Borrowers gather information on prospective lenders and then decide where to submit an application. The search process is dictated by the cost of examining the public information provided by lenders. This public information may include information disseminated by the lender's marketing as well as information gathered by the borrower during phone calls and visits to lenders' offices. Once such information has been gathered, the borrower must then select a lender to which to submit an application. All else equal, a borrower obviously will prefer a lender that offers a lower price (in terms of interest rates, closing costs, etc.). Borrowers also care, however, about the amount of credit supplied, as well as the likelihood of having the mortgage application approved. Although a borrower whose application is denied may apply to other lenders, a denial may create costly delays that interfere with the borrower's housing search. In addition, the credit check associated with the failed mortgage application can be observed by the lenders receiving any subsequent mortgage application, and its existence, along with the associated denial, may increase the likelihood of rejection by a second lender, even one who has higher prices and lower standards. As a result, a borrower may not apply to a lender with low prices and high standards, even if she is qualified for a low-cost loan.

The lender's behavior can be divided into two parts: the marketing decisions of the lending institution and the behavior of the individual loan officer during preapplication visits by potential home buyers. If lenders specialize in specific market segments, they will naturally choose marketing strategies that tend to attract individuals who are likely to submit applications that meet their standards. Lenders obviously have no objection to making loans to people who exceed their standards, but they also do not want to spend marketing resources on people who will reject their loans. In a competitive environment, at least, a lender is therefore unlikely to devote resources to attracting individuals who have the ability to qualify for credit at a price that is lower than the price the lender is willing to offer.

Individual loan officers also may have a substantial influence on the pool of applicants and on the nature of the eventual application, if it is submitted. The loan originator may serve a matching role by comparing the basic characteristics of the applicant to the lender's niche and to the associated underwriting criteria. Suppose loan officers are evaluated and compensated based on the number and value of loans they originate. In such a case, they may want to help marginal applicants make their applications as strong as possible. Loan officers might, for example, encourage their applicants to pay off credit card debt or obtain extra documentation for secondary income sources.

Moreover, borrowers who appear to be a poor fit and unlikely to receive an approval may be discouraged from submitting an application and possibly referred to an alternative lender. This type of referral could be in the interest of the borrower. If the borrower is unlikely to receive an approval from the lender that makes the referral, such steering may save the borrower valuable time in obtaining credit and may save her from having a loan denial on her record. At the same time, however, such steering probably takes place with incomplete information, and some borrowers who are steered away might have been approved if an application had been submitted.

The available evidence indicates that preapplication procedures and processing of applications for housing loans are not the same for whites and minorities. First, several pilot audit studies of preapplication behavior by lenders found numerous examples of discrimination against blacks and Hispanics. An audit that was conducted in eight major urban areas in the mid-1990s found evidence of discrimination (Smith and Cloud, 1996).[12] This study found, for example, that lenders sometimes quoted more restrictive standards and loan ratios to black and Hispanic customers than to white customers, sometimes required higher escrow or reserve account payments at closing for blacks and Hispanics, and sometimes offered constructive advice to white but not to black or Hispanic customers. A reexamination of the audit data in this study found statistically significant discrimination in several lender actions. Whites were more likely than blacks to receive an estimate of mortgage payments and of closing costs, and in some cities, whites were also quoted lower interest rates and were less likely to be steered toward FHA loans (Smith and DeLair, 1999).

Second, a careful analysis of the procedures by one large lender revealed that, compared to similarly qualified minority applicants, "whites were viewed as cases for whom the underwriters searched for compensating factors to justify acceptance" (Siskin and Cupingood, 1996, p. 454). At the time of the underwriting decision, therefore, white applicants looked better on paper than did minority applicants who were identical to them at the time an application was first filed.

Finally, mortgage lenders often provide mortgage prequalification services to potential home buyers prior to or during a housing search. In such prequalification, the borrower provides financial information to the lender, and the lender provides a written statement that the borrower qualifies for a mortgage loan of a specific size or smaller. The borrower can use this written statement to establish credibility with real estate agents or specific home sellers. Such prequalification does not imply a formal commitment on the part of either the borrower or the lender. The borrower is still free to obtain a mortgage from an alternative source, and the lender has not done a credit check or actually agreed to provide a loan. Once a borrower has obtained a prequalification, however, she is likely to remain with the lender that provided it, and, unless key information was omitted or provided and proved incorrect, the lender is likely to approve the final application.

The provision of prequalifications to those looking to purchase housing appears to be increasing in frequency. This trend is most likely moving the choice of lender to earlier in the process. In many cases, the mortgage lender may be selected well before a house is identified. Moreover, the prequalification process may limit uncertainties in the underwriting process by establishing some level of commitment by the lender up front, as well as by linking the eventual demand for credit (i.e., the loan needed to purchase the selected house) with the borrower's qualifications. We know of no data, however, on the role of prequalification or on the differential use of prequalification for minority and white customers.

3.3.2 Loan Programs, Terms, and Applications

Once an individual decides to submit a mortgage application for a specific house, a host of decisions must be made concerning the loan: type of mortgage (conventional or FHA), mortgage instrument (fixed- or variable-rate mortgage), size of down payment, whether to apply for private mortgage insurance (PMI), and whether to pay points in order to lower the interest rate charged and thus the monthly payments. In one sense, the borrower makes these decisions, because the borrower fills out and submits the application. The borrower may also face many constraints over these choices, however, or may accept offers made informally by the lender. For example, lenders often require a borrower to obtain PMI if the borrower does not have a 10- or possibly even a 20-percent down payment. Households also might be constrained because their ratio of housing payment to income is too high. If so, households might lower their initial monthly payments by paying points, choosing an ARM with a low initial interest rate, or increasing their down payment. (See Follain, 1990, for a broad survey of the literature on this topic.)

The first of these choices that we will consider is the size of the down payment. At the time an application is submitted, a house has most likely been identified, and a sales price has been negotiated. The down payment determines the size of the mortgage and the ratio of the loan amount to the appraised value of the property (the loan-to-value ratio, or LTV). If the household is not credit constrained, this down payment choice represents a portfolio allocation problem. Ranney (1981) examines this problem with a model of housing demand under certainty, and Jones (1993) extends this model to allow for uncertainty. In Ranney's model, the mortgage interest rate exceeds the return to savings. As a result, the opportunity cost of financing housing expenditures out of savings is lower than the cost of a mortgage, and savings are used whenever possible. A household incurs the higher cost of mortgage debt only after savings have been exhausted. Jones (1993) finds that when earnings or housing sales prices are uncertain, households will have a demand for liquid assets and will incur greater mortgage debt to avoid exhausting their savings.

In practice, many home buyers face some constraints in obtaining credit. If a borrower has limited resources for a down payment, for example, she may be forced to put most or all of her liquid assets into the home purchase to obtain credit. Even after depleting most of her savings, such a borrower may submit an application with a high LTV. As discussed in detail in section 3.4.2, the LTV is a key factor in any lender's underwriting model. A high LTV increases the probability of a mortgage default, because it lowers the borrower's equity in the house, and it increases the exposure of the lender to loss in the case of a default, because it raises the probability that the value of the collateral (i.e., the house) will not cover the loan. A high LTV therefore decreases the likelihood that a loan application will be approved by the lender, other things equal.[13] This leads to a more general version of the point made in section 3.2.1 that credit constraints may affect housing consumption. The household does not simply pick house size with a fixed down payment requirement, but instead must trade off the size of the house purchased against the LTV of the resulting mortgage application, which affects the likelihood of loan approval.

Moreover, for reasons discussed in section 3.4.2, a high LTV may influence other aspects of the application. When the LTV is above 0.80, the loan officer may encourage or even require the borrower to purchase PMI; if the LTV is above 0.95, the borrower may be excluded from conventional loan programs and thus compelled to apply for an FHA mortgage if she wishes to obtain financing. As a result, the price of debt increases at specific LTV thresholds. These factors can be observed in actual borrowing patterns, in which mortgage applications tend to cluster at key LTV values, such as 0.80, 0.90, and 0.95. Follain (1990) notes that even some unconstrained borrowers may cluster at such LTV values because at slightly higher values the cost of debt may jump above the return to equity.

As discussed in section 3.2.1, Hendershott, LaFayette, and Haurin (1997) observe that borrowers often face an income constraint. Lenders require that both the housing payment and total household debt payments be less than specific fractions of the household's income.[14] Hendershot, LaFayette, and Haurin focus on the requirements placed on the housing expense–to–income ratio. They show that households may sometimes select an LTV below the level they would otherwise desire in order to decrease their housing payment–to–income ratio and thereby satisfy the income constraint. They model the FHA/conventional loan choice as a function of the difference in insurance costs for FHA and PMI and two constraint variables. The first of these constraint variables measures the difference between optimal housing demand and the maximum housing demand allowed by the income ratio and LTV constraints for conventional loans, and the second measures the difference between optimal demand and the demand allowed by the FHA limit. If there were no differences in debt cost among types of mortgages, the household would simply choose the mortgage type that allowed it to minimize the gap between the desired quantity of housing and the constrained quantity.

Another rationale behind the choice to use an FHA mortgage involves the traditional "paternalistic" policies associated with FHA mortgages. In the past, FHA mortgages required home inspections, often required that any identified problems be repaired by the seller, set a limit on the interest rate paid by the borrower, and forbade the paying of discount points by the buyer.[15] If the housing market was not perfectly competitive, such policies could provide first-time home buyers with an advantage during negotiations with home sellers after an offer had been accepted. This negotiation advantage might have been especially valuable to minority home buyers, who faced discrimination in the housing market and were likely to be at a substantial disadvantage in any negotiation. Indeed, this incentive might help to explain the high rates of FHA usage among minorities historically.

Two other important choices facing conventional mortgage borrowers involve the choice between a fixed-rate mortage (FRM) and an adjustable-rate mortgage (ARM) and the choice concerning whether to pay points to lower the interest rate charged. The FRM/ARM choice may be driven by concerns about interest rate variation. Households that expect to hold the mortgage for a short time may prefer an ARM to avoid paying a premium to lock in interest rates for a long period or possibly to take advantage of ARM teaser rates (see Rosenthal and Zorn, 1993, and Harding, 1997). The mortgage holding period appears to play a role in the decision on whether to pay points. Mobile households are unwilling to pay points to lower the interest rate because they will only receive the benefit of the lower rates over a few years (Dunn and Spatt, 1988). In fact, Stanton and Wallace (1998) suggest that mortgage contracts involving points serve to separate borrowers by expected mobility. Alternatively, Dunn and McConnell (1981) suggest that points serve as a mechanism for pricing the prepayment option embedded in a fixed-rate mortgage. Both ARMs and points can be used to alter monthly housing payments and potentially minimize the effect of being income constrained.[16]

Finally, the loan officer can play a major role in influencing the application terms chosen by borrowers. The loan officer is supposed to guide the borrower through the application process. Moreover, the loan officer brings additional knowledge concerning the underwriting standard of the particular bank for which she works, and this knowledge may influence her recommendations concerning the type and terms of the final loan application. In addition, the loan officer may request explanations for specific problems with the individual's credit history and be responsible for interpreting these explanations for other bank officials in the underwriting process. This process may create a link between the eventual terms of a loan offered in response to a particular application and features of a lender's underwriting process that researchers cannot observe.

3.4 Lender Underwriting

This section examines the underwriting process and the factors potentially considered by lenders in establishing and following a system of loan underwriting. The first subsection examines models that attempt to explain why some borrowers are denied credit rather than simply being offered credit at a higher price (credit rationing), the second examines the literature on prepayment and default (both of which have a direct impact on loan profitability), and the third briefly explores the role of the secondary market. The powerful recent trends in mortgage markets, which were discussed in chapter 2, provide background for this review.

3.4.1 Adverse Selection, Moral Hazard, and Credit Rationing

Stiglitz and Weiss (1981) examine the impacts on credit markets of adverse selection and moral hazard. Adverse selection arises when the price chosen by a firm or economic agent influences the composition of the agents that are willing to trade with this firm in terms of important factors that the firm cannot observe. In the case of credit markets, a borrower's expected cost depends on both the interest rate and the likelihood that the borrower will have to make all the resulting payments. Therefore, borrowers who have a high likelihood of default, referred to as high-risk borrowers, will accept a higher interest rate than borrowers with a low likelihood of default (low-risk borrowers). In addition, as the interest rate increases, the creditworthiness of the applicant pool based on unobservable characteristics will decline.

Moral hazard arises in credit markets when a borrower has the ability to influence a lender's return in a way that the lender cannot monitor or control. Stiglitz and Weiss show that the effect of an interest rate increase on a borrower's expected return decreases with project risk, because the interest rate does not affect total borrower payments in the case of a bankruptcy. As the market interest rate increases, therefore, borrowers will choose riskier projects. Overall, both moral hazard and adverse selection cause lenders' returns to rise at a decreasing rate or even to decline with increases in interest rates.

Stiglitz and Weiss show that a nonmonotonic relationship between interest rates and lender return can lead to credit rationing. They define credit rationing as a situation in which either (1) some borrowers receive credit and others who are observationally equivalent do not or (2) some identifiable group of borrowers cannot obtain credit at any interest rate given the current supply of credit, even though they could obtain credit at a higher supply. Type-1 credit rationing arises if the quantity of credit borrowers demand (L_d) exceeds the quantity lenders supply (L_s) at the interest rate (r^*) that maximizes lender return (p^*). This situation is illustrated in figure 3.2, which shows what can happen when both gross returns and the average default probability increase with the interest rate. Beyond some interest rate, illustrated by r^*, the impact of a higher interest rate on default outweighs its impact on gross returns, and lenders' net returns start to fall. Some borrowers are willing to pay interest rates above r^*, but an offer to pay the higher interest rate would reveal a borrower's type as high risk and would result in a denied application. As a result, r^* is the equilibrium interest rate, quantity demanded exceeds quantity supplied, and some borrowers do not receive credit, whereas other identical borrowers do.[17]

Stiglitz and Weiss also examine the case in which borrowers fall into distinct groups that drop out together. In this case, the lender return curve will have multiple peaks. In figure 3.3, an equilibrium can arise in which the lower interest rate, r_1^*, is associated with the first peak in the lender return curve. Type-1 credit rationing occurs at this lower interest rate. At the higher rate, r_2^*, no credit rationing occurs, but only high-risk borrowers demand credit. Moreover, because lenders cannot distinguish between high- and low-risk borrowers, only high-risk borrowers who experience rationing at the lower interest rate enter the high-risk segment. In this equilibrium, some of the high-risk borrowers are separated from the low-risk borrowers. Note that type-1 credit rationing implies that identical applicants to the same lender may experience different outcomes.

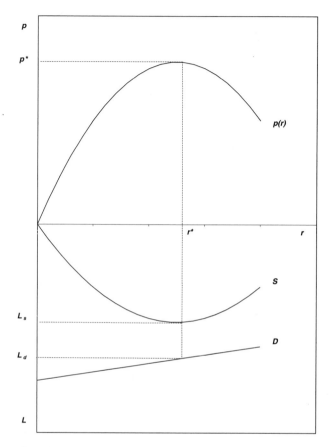

Figure 3.2
Stiglitz-Weiss credit rationing.

Type-2 credit rationing, unlike type-1, focuses on the denial of credit based on observable characteristics. In this case, the relationship between expected lender return and the interest rate depends on observable characteristics. In figure 3.4, for example, borrowers can be divided into two groups based on observable characteristics. The return for group 1, $p_1(r)$, reaches a maximum at a higher interest rate than the return for group 2, $p_2(r)$, and the maximum return is lower for group 1. In equilibrium, all capital must earn the same expected return, so if loans are made to group 1, then group 2 cannot be credit rationed (Stiglitz and Weiss, 1981). If p^* is lenders' equilibrium cost of capital, group 1 will simply face type-1 credit rationing.

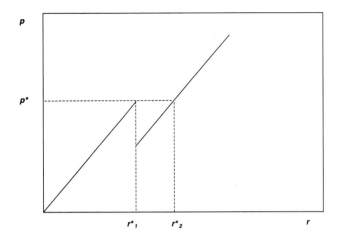

Figure 3.3
Credit rationing when borrowers vary on unobserved traits.

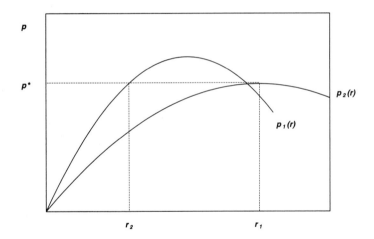

Figure 3.4
Credit rationing when borrowers vary on observed traits.

Moreover, group 1 will experience type-2 credit rationing if the cost of capital is above p^*. In this case, no member of group 1 will receive credit at any interest rate, but if the supply of capital is increased, lenders' cost of capital will fall and at least some members of this group will obtain credit.

The development of the subprime mortgage market might be explained, in part, by this model.[18] Group 1 represents borrowers who are poor credit risks based on observable characteristics. Because of the default risk, loans to this group are relatively unprofitable even at high interest rates, but the return on good-credit-risk loans peaks at a relatively low interest rate, possibly because these borrowers are more sophisticated and exercise prepayment and default options more aggressively. The development of the secondary mortgage market lowered lenders' cost of capital over time and made the provision of high-interest rate loans to less creditworthy borrowers profitable, which in turn led to the development of the subprime market. This aspect of Stiglitz and Weiss's model may help explain why lenders are observed to ration credit based on observable characteristics.[19] For example, banks may have a higher cost of capital than mortgage bankers, because they face more federal and state regulations, and as a result banks tend to provide credit to the most creditworthy applicants based on observable characteristics, whereas some mortgage bankers extend credit to the subprime market.

Calomiris, Kahn, and Longhofer (1994) argue that the adverse-selection story inherent in some of these models is not appropriate to mortgage markets. They argue that in mortgage markets lenders may have better information concerning default risk than borrowers and that the only important private information that borrowers have concerning default involves their own idiosyncratic attachment to their house. Borrowers with greater attachment are less likely to default. They also argue that borrowers with a greater attachment to their house are less likely to drop out of the mortgage market when interest rates increase. This behavior creates a selection process in which the low-risk borrowers apply for a mortgage but the high-risk borrowers do not. With such a process, adverse selection and credit rationing will not occur.[20]

However, the Calomiris, Kahn, and Longhofer model requires an implausible assumption about the formation of a household's idiosyncratic attachment to its house. In particular, the model assumes that this attachment already exists when the household decides whether to apply for a mortgage and hence whether to drop out of the mortgage market as interest rates rise. In fact, however, a household's idiosyncratic attachment to its house is more likely to develop *after* it has already bought the house and decorated or arranged it in a pleasing way. It seems unlikely that this attachment develops before a decision about whether to remain in the mortgage market as interest rates rise, so it is unlikely that this attachment can affect this decision. Instead, this decision is based on tenure choice, which is influenced by many other factors (see section 3.2.1).

Besanko and Thakor (1987) and Calem and Stutzer (1995) offer alternative credit-rationing models in which lenders choose the type of lending contracts they offer strategically to separate high- and low-risk borrowers. In both models, borrowers are observationally equivalent. Calem and Stutzer's borrowers are assumed to face a cost of loan denial that increases with the risk of default, possibly because the higher risk of default implies a riskier project with greater expected gains. Therefore, lenders offer two types of contracts: one with a low interest rate, but a high probability of denial, and the other with a high interest rate and a low probability of denial. All high-risk borrowers choose the high interest rate contract. In Besanko and Thaker, lenders also offer two types of contracts, but a down-payment requirement is used to separate low- and high-risk borrowers. Low-risk borrowers are willing to make a sizable down-payment to obtain a lower interest rate contract, and high-risk borrowers are not. If borrowers have insufficient assets to meet the down-payment requirements, however, lenders will be unable to specify contracts that will perfectly separate borrowers. A separating equilibrium will be obtained, however, if lenders ration the credit available with the low interest rate contract to make that option relatively less attractive to high-risk borrowers. In both models, credit rationing occurs among low-risk borrowers in equilibrium. Alternatively, Ben-Shahar and Feldman (2001) show that high- and low-risk borrowers can be separated without credit rationing by offering two contracts that vary over the loan term and the interest rate. In equilibrium, low-risk borrowers choose the shorter term and the lower risk premium.

The possibility that low-risk borrowers would face credit rationing may appear counterintuitive, but remember that in these models, lenders cannot tell the difference between high- and low-risk borrowers. Credit rationing arises only for borrowers who are low risk on unobservable characteristics. Again, the predicted outcomes are reasonably consistent with market outcomes. The market can be roughly divided into prime and subprime lenders. Prime-market lenders offer loan products with lower interest rates but may be more likely to reject a given loan application than subprime lenders, after controlling for all observable underwriting characteristics.

A key question that is not addressed in the papers discussed above is the implication of the models they present when borrowers differ on observable characteristics. For Calem and Stutzer (1995), the cost of loan denial increases with the risk of default, as determined by observable and unobservable borrower attributes. So borrowers with observable characteristics that imply high risk will tend to choose lenders with higher interest rates and lower underwriting standards, and borrowers with observable characteristics that imply low risk are more likely to face credit rationing in the market. Ben-Shahar and Feldman (2001) also consider the possibility that borrowers can signal their creditworthiness at a cost by working to achieve a clean credit history. In this case, borrowers separate first on the basis of their creditworthiness signal and then, for any observable creditworthiness, on the basis of the loan terms and interest rate they choose.

This logic might also be extended to explain why individual lenders may not price observable credit risk, but rather establish a fixed price and deny mortgage applications that do not meet a specific quality threshold. Specifically, assume that a lender's portfolio resale and management costs increase with the risk diversity of its portfolio. As a result, individual lenders specialize in a specific risk class of mortgages, and each lender will offer a specific interest rate and accept some subset of applications at that price. High-quality applicants on observable characteristics will tend to choose lenders with low interest rates and high standards, and low-quality applicants will choose lenders with high interest rates and low standards.

Individual lenders may use credit rationing to limit the diversity of applicants on unobserved characteristics, as well. The borrower's trade-off between facing rationed credit and receiving a lower interest rate depends on his actual credit risk, including both observable and unobservable attributes. Therefore, a contract that specifies a given interest rate, a rate of credit rationing, and potentially a specific downpayment requirement will attract all borrowers with a specific level of actual credit risk, regardless of the observed level of credit risk. This reasoning implies that all applicants to a given lender have the same actual creditworthiness, face the same level of credit rationing, and pay the same interest rate regardless of the observed credit risk they present.

We find quite compelling the argument that credit rationing is being used to separate borrowers by credit risk, but the resulting implication that borrowers whose observable characteristics make them low-risk experience credit rationing appears to be inconsistent with the stylized facts about mortgage markets. Ferguson and Peters (1997) suggest an alternative model of credit rationing that appears to be more consistent with actual outcomes in mortgage markets. In Ferguson and Peters' model, no adverse-selection problem exists in the market. Rather, the profitability of an individual loan depends on the size of the lender's portfolio. Credit rationing can occur when the marginal cost of managing a loan increases with the size of the portfolio and the market exhibits imperfect competition. Ferguson and Peters show that under these circumstances a lender will prefer a pooling equilibrium, in which the lender offers all borrowers the same interest rate, relative to the equilibrium that arises when credit is priced based on observable characteristics. As the size of the lender's portfolio grows, loans to borrowers with low credit risk become unprofitable, and the lender stops extending credit, thereby leaving some applicants without credit. Since all borrowers pay the same rate, only the least creditworthy applicants face credit rationing.

3.4.2 Default, Prepayment, and Foreclosure

A borrower's rights to default on a mortgage or prepay the mortgage balance are often modeled as options that the borrower purchases along with the mortgage. The option to default on the mortgage is considered a put option, with which the borrower has the ability to force the lender to purchase her home for the remaining value of the mortgage. Prepayment is considered a call option, because the borrower has the option of buying the mortgage based on paying the remaining balance to the lender. Kau and Keenan (1995) provide a detailed review of the literature involving the options view of mortgages. This literature views default and prepayment as choices that the borrower exercises "ruthlessly" based entirely on the value of the option. Vandell (1995) provides a review of the debate over whether the exercise of default and prepayment options are typically "ruthless."

Foster and Van Order (1984) investigate the nature of the default option. They describe the value of the option as the value of the mortgage to the borrower (that is, the present value of remaining mortgage payments) minus the sum of the house value and the costs involved in exercising the option (transaction costs). These costs may include moving costs, legal fees, and the stigma associated with a default. Since most mortgages require a down payment, the value of this option typically can become positive (or in the money) only if the house declines in value. Other factors can also affect the value of the option. Changes in interest rates can affect the value of a fixed-rate mortgage. If interest rates rise, the present value of remaining payments falls, and so does the value of the option. The mortgage also may include mortgage insurance. A decrease in house value decreases equity and would increases the amount of mortgage insurance that would be required to purchase the same home with the current level of equity. This increases the value of the current mortgage insurance policy and therefore increases the cost of exercising the default option. Finally, Foster and Van Order consider the role of a second type of transaction costs, the costs involved in selling the house. If a household is required to move, the value that the borrower places on the house declines by the amount of the sales costs. This decline could put the option in the money.

Chinloy (1989) and Van Order and Zorn (2001) investigate the option to prepay a mortgage.[21] The value of exercising the prepayment option is the value of the mortgage minus the sum of the mortgage balance and the costs associated with prepayment. Interest rates are the primary determinant of prepayment. If interest rates decrease, the value of the mortgage increases, and the option becomes more valuable. Chinloy observes that the option to prepay is actually a sequence of callable options. At any point in time, the decision to prepay requires the borrower to forgo all future options to prepay. As a result, prepayment depends upon expectations concerning future interest rates. The exercise of an option may yield a positive return, and yet the borrower may not exercise the option because the value of all future options exceeds the value of exercising the option in the current period. Chinloy also observes that the prepayment option is sometimes exercised even though it has a negative value. This action is referred to as autonomous prepayment and occurs because the household has experienced a shock to housing demand, such as a job relocation, a sudden wealth windfall, or a change in family structure.

Kau, Keenan, and Kim (1993) and Kau et al. (1995) both propose a model in which default and prepayment form a joint termination option. The two options are substitutes for each other. If the borrower exercises either option, the value of the second option becomes zero. Furthermore, the decision to terminate the mortgage involves the loss of all future termination options. Therefore, a decision to prepay requires the borrower to forgo the total value of future prepayment and default options. As in Chinloy, the existence of these future options may prevent borrowers for terminating a mortgage in the current period even if the terminate option appears to be in the money. Deng, Quigley, and Van Order (2000) estimate a joint model of prepayment and default for conventional mortgages that strongly supports the jointness of these two options. Deng and Gabriel (2002) estimate a similar model for FHA mortgages, with similar results.

Transaction costs in foreclosure create an incentive for renegotiation, often referred to as loss mitigation, that might delay or prevent a default by the borrower (see Kau, Kennan, and Kim, 1993, 1994). Riddiough and Wyatt (1994a) examine this problem using game theory and in particular develop a two-person game played between a lender and a borrower in which the mortgage contract can be extended past any given borrower default by negotiation. Kahn and Yavas (1994) show that the presence of such negotiation increases the borrower's incentive to threaten default (that is, withhold payment), lowers the lender's effective return on mortgages, and leads to higher market interest rates in equilibrium. Riddiough and Wyatt (1994b) show that lenders may foreclose more aggressively in a repeated-game framework than in a one-shot game to signal that they have low foreclosure costs and thereby lower the borrower's incentive to threaten default. Moreover, if the game is repeated for the same borrower (multiple delinquencies and defaults), the borrower may act strategically during initial negotiations to force the lender to reveal its foreclosure costs. Under many circumstances, this possibility increases the likelihood of foreclosure by the lender.

Alternatively, Ambrose, Buttimer, and Capone (1997) model foreclosure behavior by examining the impact of a delay between default and foreclosure. They find that an increase in the length of the delay decreases the value of the mortgage and as a result increases the value of the default option. Essentially, a borrower can default and still maintain the use of his home for some period of time, which makes default more appealing. Ambrose and Capone (1996a) observe that defaulters can be divided into two types: ruthless and trigger-event defaulters. Trigger-event defaulters are associated with default options that are not in the money, that is, not profitable in their own right. Instead, these borrowers fail to make the mortgage payments required to maintain current consumption after unexpected changes in income, wealth, or needs. Ambrose and Capone argue that lenders' loss mitigation programs must be targeted toward trigger-event defaulters, because ruthless defaulters will increase defaults in response to such programs. In another article, Ambrose and Capone (1996b) also find no difference in lender's propensity to foreclose on black and white borrowers, at least not with FHA mortgages.

In principle, a lender's underwriting model is designed to identify and approve only profitable mortgages. The termination option available to borrowers and the foreclosure policies established by lenders have a substantial effect on the value of a mortgage, whether it is held in portfolio or resold on the secondary market, and on the value of the servicing rights associated with the mortgage. Therefore, a lender's willingness to underwrite a loan at a given interest rate should be directly influenced by these factors.

Many features of mortgage contracts are designed to manage and price the value of these options. As discussed previously, if a borrower pays points on the mortgage to decrease the interest rate, the value of the prepayment option decreases. Therefore, the lender can lower interest rates more quickly as points are paid than would be possible if mortgages did not include a prepayment option. Similarly, the value of the default option falls as the down payment increases. Therefore, the LTV associated with a particular mortgage application has a large influence on the likelihood of that application's being approved. Moreover, the price of credit for a particular loan depends on the LTV with respect to the property whose purchase it finances. If the LTV is above .80, the borrower is likely to be required to purchase PMI, and the premiums for this insurance increase with the LTV. Finally, if the LTV is above 0.95, the borrower may be restricted to FHA loans with government-provided insurance, which can be more expensive than PMI.

If a borrower is severely credit constrained, however, her ability to select the values of the prepayment and default options may be limited. The most common way for a lender to lower the value of the default options of a mortgage is to increase the mortgage's up-front costs, such as the payment of points to obtain a lower interest rate. But this route conflicts with the typical situation in which many households struggle to raise a 5- or 10-percent downpayment, even without paying points up front.

Chinloy and Megbolugbe (1994) argue that the inclusion of a prepayment option in mortgages places many minority and low-income borrowers at a substantial disadvantage in obtaining credit. These groups of borrowers are thought to be substantially less mobile than upper-income borrowers and therefore to subsidize the prepayment option for high-income borrowers. They conclude that many minority and low-income borrowers would have increased access to credit if they had the choice to forgo the prepayment option.

3.4.3 Role of the Secondary Market

As discussed earlier, the secondary market has developed over time to unbundle the many mortgage services originally provided by depository lenders. This unbundling exploits economies of scale and advantages of diversification in servicing, taking on credit risk, and raising capital. Van Order (1996, 2000) argues that this unbundling has increased the flow of funds into the mortgage market and that as a result, mortgage interest rates have fallen in all segments of the market. To illustrate this outcome, Van Order develops a two-segment market in which the secondary market purchases mortgages only in one segment of the market. Nonetheless, the increased flow of funds in one segment will lower rates in that segment, which in turn should lead to a flow of funds between that market and the second market. Therefore, interest rates should fall in both markets.

Passmore and Sparks (1996) present an alternative view in which primary lenders have more information than agents in the secondary market. Specifically, primary lenders know the cost of screening mortgage applicants, and by incurring these costs, lenders can determine whether a particular applicant is creditworthy. Secondary-market

agents cannot observe either the cost of screening or the characteristics by which the creditworthiness of the borrower is determined.
This creates an adverse-selection problem in which primary lenders
will screen mortgages with low screening costs and hold those
mortgages that are found to be creditworthy in their portfolio. Noncreditworthy screened mortgages are either not underwritten or
underwritten and sold on the secondary market, which reduces the
quality of the sample of secondary-market mortgagees. The institutions in the secondary-market, however, can affect a lender's decision to screen. An increase in the rate paid by secondary-market
institutions to primary lenders decreases the net benefits that arise
from screening. The resulting decrease in the frequency of screening will improve the pool of secondary-market mortgages but
will also increase number of noncreditworthy mortgages that are
underwritten.[22]

Passmore and Sparks do not consider the role of differences in
creditworthiness that *are* observable to agents in the secondary
market. When borrowers also differ on characteristics observable to
secondary-market agents (as well as on those that are, not), these
characteristics may also affect primary lenders' decision to screen, as
well as the compensation rate offered by the secondary market. As a
borrower's observable creditworthiness declines, the likelihood of
her actually being creditworthy declines, and other things being
equal, the primary lender is more likely to screen. In a market that
was not characterized by adverse selection, the secondary-market
institutions would decrease the compensation offered for a mortgage
as observable creditworthiness declined. With adverse selection,
however, the secondary-market institution might not decrease compensation for loans to borrowers with low observable creditworthiness, because the likelihood of screening would be higher for these
borrowers. Since declines in observable creditworthiness cannot be
effectively priced, the secondary market may refuse to purchase
mortgages when the observable creditworthiness of the borrowers
falls below some threshold. This refusal will increase the cost of
credit for these high-risk borrowers or even preclude their access to
credit.

This failure of the market to provide access to credit for certain
borrowers may create a role for government-sponsored mortgage
lending and an associated secondary market. The provision of a
government guarantee may decrease the cost of credit and increase

the secondary market's ability to handle some level of adverse selection. Therefore, the government may be able to make loans that should be made but could not be made by the private sector because of the market failure.[23] The creation of the secondary market has probably decreased the cost of credit in the mortgage market and as a result has probably increased the flow of funds to marginal borrowers, including many low-income and minority households. On the other hand, the adverse-selection problem faced by secondary-market institutions may decrease access to credit for the marginal borrower, and the resulting increased standards in the secondary market may have a disproportionate impact on minorities and low-income borrowers.

Cutts, Van Order, and Zorn (2001) consider just such an adverse-selection problem. In their model, a secondary-market institution and competitive banks compete to provide capital to the mortgage market. Banks have private information concerning the creditworthiness of borrowers, to which secondary-market institutions do not have access, but the secondary-market institutions have a lower cost of capital than the banks. Cutts, Van Order, and Zorn find that two equilibriums exist: one in which the secondary market captures the entire market, and a second in which the secondary market charges a very high price and captures only a small, high-risk share of the market. Small changes in the environment might move the market between these two extreme equilibriums. Cutts, Van Order, and Zorn suggest that this unstable situation can be avoided by the imposition, by secondary-market institutions, of a licensing requirement for primary lenders. Such a requirement segments the markets into two markets: a prime market in which all lenders meet the licensing requirements and loans flow through the secondary-market institutions, and a subprime market in which individual lenders practice risk-based pricing.

3.5   Lessons for Estimating Underwriting Models

Chapter 2 outlined several key challenges facing statistical analyses of lenders' decisions to approve or deny mortgage appliccations. First, a statistical analysis may be biased because the researcher does not have access to all information that the lender uses in the approval decision (omitted-variable bias). Second, earlier stages of the mortgage process may influence what potential borrowers put on their applications, which results in endogeneity bias. Third, these earlier stages also may influence which households elect to submit an application (as opposed to abandoning the housing search), which results in sample selection bias. The literature reviewed in this chapter provides insight into the nature of these three challenges and leads to several additional lessons about estimating discrimination in loan approval. These lessons concern variation in underwriting standards across lenders, the price of credit, and the interpretation of a loan approval regression.

3.5.1   Bias Attributable to Omitted Variables, Endogenous Variables, and Sample Selection

In the standard case of omitted-variable bias, an important determinant of a borrower's creditworthiness, such as her credit history, is omitted from a loan approval regression. If, as is likely, this variable is correlated with race, then its omission will lead to a correlation between the error term, that is, the unobserved factors, and included variables, including the race coefficient. This type of correlation implies that the estimated race coefficient will be biased. Because blacks and Hispanics typically have poorer credit qualifications, on average, than whites, the race coefficient will pick up some of the effect of these poorer qualifications and will therefore overstate the amount of discrimination. This type of bias can be avoided through the use of a data set that includes all credit variables considered by lenders.

A second source of correlation between the error term and included variables, and hence of potential bias, in a loan approval regression is that some omitted determinants of a borrower's creditworthiness may influence, and hence be correlated with, the loan terms that appear on the application. Because there is a behavioral connection between the omitted variable and the included variable, the resulting bias is called endogeneity bias. In this case, both the dependent variable (loan approval) and the explanatory variable (loan terms) are influenced by some omitted (and hence, for the purposes of the regression, unobserved) factor. In standard omitted-variable bias, the problematic correlation between the error term and an explanatory variable arises through factors external to the lending process, such as the historical discrimination that has contributed to racial disparities in income and wealth. In this case (endogeneity bias), this correlation arises because the omitted variable influences the included variable as part of the lending process. But in either case, omitting the variable may result in biased coefficients.

The most direct effect of the problematic correlation in cases of endogeneity bias is that the estimated coefficients of the loan terms are biased. In addition, however, this problem can spill over into the estimated coefficient of the race variable. If the coefficients of loan terms are biased and the loan terms are correlated with race, then the race variable may pick up some of the loan term effects that are misstated by the biases in their coefficients. This type of bias may work in either direction (that is, to overstate or understate the amount of discrimination). In many cases, endogeneity bias, like standard omitted-variable bias, can be avoided through the use of an extensive set of credit variables.

In some cases, however, actors in the housing or mortgage market, including real estate brokers, potential home buyers, and loan officers, may have private information about the credit standards of various lenders. This knowledge may influence the advice they give (in the case of brokers or loan officers) or the decisions they make (in the case of potential buyers) about the ways to prepare for and fill out a loan application. In this way, unobserved credit standards influence both the approval decision and the loan terms—and hence create endogeneity bias. The difference between this case and the one described above is that the omitted variable, namely a lender's credit standard, is unlikely to be observed by a researcher. As a result, the only way to solve this problem is likely to be the use of a simultaneous-equations procedure, which, in effect, predicts loan terms on the basis of exogenous variables and then includes predicted loan terms, not actual loan terms, in the loan approval equation. In chapter 5, we discuss this type of procedure and the rules for the selection of appropriate exogenous variables, often called "instruments."[24]

The third possible source of correlation between the error term and included variables in a loan approval regression is that some omitted credit variable influences potential borrowers' decisions as to whether to apply for a mortgage at all. People who have not saved enough for a down payment, for example, may not apply, so the omission of a savings variable in a loan approval regression may result in sample selection bias. As in the case of endogeneity bias, this bias may affect the coefficients of many variables in a loan approval regression, including the race coefficient, and it can often be eliminated, or at least minimized, by including an extensive set of credit variables in the regression. Moreover, this bias, like endogeneity bias, may sometimes arise because of private information that is unlikely to be observed by researchers. A potential borrower may be less likely to apply for a mortgage, for example, if she is first matched with a lender who has a particularly strict underwriting standard, controlling for price. This case has been carefully modeled by Bloom, Preiss, and Trussell (1983), who summarize it as follows:

In general, prescreening biases the usual estimates of discrimination when potential applicants are screened (either by loan officers or by themselves) on the basis of factors 1) that are unobservable to the economist, 2) that affect the creditworthiness score (either positively or negatively), *and* 3) that are correlated with membership in some protected group. (p. 99)

Bloom, Preiss, and Trussell also show that in some cases such sample selection bias can be eliminated even without any information on the people who do not apply for loans.

Three principal lessons can be drawn from this discussion:

• *Lesson 1.* Biases from omitted variables arise not only because, for historical reasons, the values of these variables are correlated with race, but also because these variables may have behavioral connections with included variables, including race, through earlier stages in the mortgage process.

• *Lesson 2.* To eliminate biases associated with omitted variables, a researcher must control for a wide range of factors, including variables that are not standard determinants of an applicant's (or an application's) creditworthiness but are expected to influence loan terms and hence underwriting.[25]

• *Lesson 3.* Some omitted variables, namely, those involving private information shared by the borrower and the lender, are virtually impossible for a researcher to observe, so the biases associated with them cannot be eliminated without a simultaneous-equations procedure or a sample selection correction, as appropriate.

Examples of these three lessons appear throughout this chapter. Consider first the housing market. Any underwriting variables related to the purchase price of a house may be correlated with an applicant's overall creditworthiness, because borrowers who expect to have trouble qualifying for a mortgage are likely to choose smaller, less expensive houses, other things equal. Omitting applicant characteristics that are observed by the lender from the loan approval regression could therefore make the home purchase price and all related underwriting variables endogenous.

Household savings behavior raises similar issues. If a potential home buyer expects to have trouble qualifying for a mortgage, she may save more aggressively to increase her down payment and reduce the likelihood of having her loan application rejected. As a result, mortgage applicants may be selected based on their ability to accumulate wealth, and this ability is likely to be correlated with unobserved credit variables.

Real estate agents also may influence the composition of the pool of mortgage applicants as well as the final characteristics of the resulting applications. A real estate agent shows specific units to a potential buyer, provides advice about making an offer, and may guide prospective home buyers toward certain units or neighborhoods or lenders. Moreover, real estate agents may send minority customers to mortgage lenders with relatively low underwriting standards, but relatively high prices. These actions create more potential for endogeneity or sample selection bias.

Many of the potential biases arising from these aspects of the housing market can be prevented through the use of an extensive set of control variables. For example, even if real estate agents steer people with poor credit histories to lenders with low standards, no bias will arise in a loan approval regression that controls for applicants' credit history. The set of control variables used must, however, extend beyond traditional underwriting variables. For example, people in different ethnic groups may tend to go to different lenders and thus may, on average, go to lenders with different credit standards. In this case, a loan approval regression that does not control for differences across lenders can have a biased minority status coefficient.[26]

In the mortgage market, a potential home buyer must decide to apply for a mortgage, select a lender, and choose the terms of the application. These choices create the potential for sample selection and endogeneity bias in models of lender underwriting behavior, because characteristics of the home buyer influence these choices and influence the underwriting process. These biases are unlikely to appear, however, if many credit characteristics of the home buyer are included in the loan approval regression.

Lender actions in both the preapplication and application stages of a mortgage transaction also may influence a borrower's decision to apply to a specific lender, the terms of the final loan request, and even the credit characteristics expressed on the application. This lender influence is likely to be related to unobservable features of the lender's underwriting process, which may create a correlation between the error term in the loan approval model and unobservable factors that influence lender choice and loan terms.[27] Such actions by lenders and loan officers imply that statistical analyses of mortgage lending discrimination should include lender dummy variables in the specification.

3.5.2   Variation in Underwriting Standards

The literature points to three major factors that might lead to systematic differences in underwriting standards across lenders:

1. Adverse selection or moral hazard in the credit market may give lenders an incentive to ration credit to segment the market based on observable credit risk.

2. Lender differences in liquidity, risk tolerance, or cost of capital may influence underwriting criteria.

3. Lenders may differ in default experience because their loans draw on different pools of potential borrowers.

If borrowers have private information concerning their creditworthiness, lenders may face adverse selection and/or moral hazard. Under these circumstances, lenders may be able to affect the unobservable characteristics of their applicant pool by rationing credit. Moreover, a lender's optimal level of rationing may vary based on observable factors that influence default risk. Different lenders may specialize in different segments of the mortgage market and, based on that specialization, some lenders may impose a level of credit rationing and associated underwriting standards that differ from those of other lenders.

Even in a market with perfect information, lenders may differ in liquidity, risk tolerance, or cost of capital. They may rationally make different trade-offs among nominal return, default risk, loss exposure, and other factors and, as a result, may make different decisions about loan terms, such as interest rates, debt-to-income ratios, and loan-to-value ratios. These differences in choices may be the result of portfolio differences that affect a lender's liquidity or exposure to risk.

The roles of liquidity, risk tolerance, and cost of capital in loan decisions are minimal when all lenders use underwriting models that are based entirely on default risk. A common measure of loan performance among lenders does not rule out differences in underwriting standards across lenders, however, even across lenders that provide the same loan product in the same metropolitan or regional market. Each lender could fit into a unique market niche based on its history or marketing strategy, and borrowers are unlikely to be randomly distributed across lenders based on the unobservable determinants of their creditworthiness. Instead, the pool of applicants to a given lender may differ from other lenders' pools in terms of unobservable characteristics that are correlated with both the underwriting variables the lenders use and the future likelihood of default.[28] As a result, each lender may experience a different relationship between observable credit characteristics and default and therefore may develop unique underwriting standards.

The first two sources of variation in underwriting standards may also interact with across-lender differences in default experience. Credit rationing arises when a lender rejects some qualified applications to influence the sample of applicants. If lenders differ in the extent of rationing they engage in, borrowers will sort across lenders based on their (the borrowers') unobservable attributes. Similarly, if borrowers are uncertain concerning which of their financial characteristics will be observed by the lender, they will sort across lenders based on a broader set of attributes than are actually considered in the underwriting equation. Finally, differences across lenders in liquidity, risk tolerance, and the cost of capital may also influence foreclosure behavior. Borrowers who observe the past foreclosure behavior of lenders are likely to consider both their own risk of default and lender foreclosure behavior when choosing a lender.

This leads us to a fourth lesson:

• *Lesson 4.* Loan approval regressions need to consider the possibility that underwriting standards vary across lenders.

This lesson implies that the inclusion of lender dummy variables, as suggested in the previous section, may not be sufficient to insulate a loan approval regression from sample selection or endogeneity bias. Lenders may differ in terms of the weights placed on various loan

and borrower characteristics, and these differences may be related
to unobserved borrower characteristics, thanks to borrower self-
selection, coaching by loan officers, or the characteristics of a lender's
market niche. The biases arising from these differences may remain
unless separate underwriting models are estimated for each lender in
a sample of loan applications. Unfortunately, researchers and enforcement agencies may not observe enough applications to estimate
a separate loan approval model for many lenders.[29]

This is not the end of the story, however, because some important
countervailing forces tend to produce homogenous standards across
lenders:

1. The secondary market allows lenders to pass equity risk on either
to government-sponsored enterprises or to private investors.

2. Technological changes allow lenders and the secondary market
to assess default risk systematically, a development that has led
to the increased use of automated underwriting systems as well as to
the pricing of credit risk in mortgage contracts.

3. Increased consolidation of the industry has led to the creation of
large financial holding companies that compete in all regions of the
country and many segments of the mortgage market.

4. Increased borrower information and competition among lenders
through advertising and marketing makes it difficult for lenders to
sustain different underwriting standards in many circumstances.

The growth in the secondary mortgage market, the increasing use of
automated underwriting systems, and industry consolidation may
limit variation in underwriting models across lenders. When lenders
sell mortgages to the secondary market, they pass either part or all of
the default risk on to the purchasing institution. In this regime,
lenders need not worry about unobservable applicant characteristics.
Primary lenders are judged in the secondary market based solely
on the application of their underwriting standards to observable
underwriting characteristics.[30] In addition, many lenders now have
access to automated underwriting systems, such as those developed
by Freddie Mac and Fannie Mae, that are based on the performance
of large pools of loans. The increasing availability and use of such
systems is likely to limit the influence of a lender's idiosyncratic
performance experience on its underwriting standards. Also, many
smaller lenders with idiosyncratic applicant pools have been pur-

chased by larger lenders with portfolios that are more nationally representative.

Finally, increased borrower information and competition may eliminate some differences in underwriting standards. If an applicant had perfect information about the lenders available to her, she would obviously submit her application to the lender that both offered the lowest cost of credit and was most likely to approve her application. As a result, many across-lender differences in the evaluation of applications could not be sustained, because any given type of applicant would never be observed at two lenders using different loan performance models. Under these circumstances, borrowers who understood which lenders were likely to approve their application and which were not would sort based only on their observable credit characteristics.

This argument is illustrated in figure 3.5, which presents hypothetical loan performance models for two different types of lenders. Each loan performance model is described by the estimated relationship between loan performance, on the vertical axis, and credit characteristics, represented here by the debt-to-income ratio, on the horizontal axis.[31] The higher this ratio, the lower the estimated performance. This estimated relationship is used to calculate a loan performance score. For any given debt-to-income ratio, the score under either loan performance model is indicated by the height of the estimated line at that ratio.

In figure 3.5, lender A specializes in loans with a high debt-to-income ratio, so in its performance model, the impact of the applicant's debt-to-income ratio, measured by the steepness of the loan performance curve, is relatively low. Lender B specializes in loans with a low debt-to-income ratio, so its loan-performance curve is relatively steep. Now consider an applicant with a debt-to-income ratio of D_2. This applicant will receive a score of S_2 from lender A but a score of only S_1 from lender B. With full information, this person would obviously not apply to lender B. An applicant with a debt-to-income ratio of D_1 will receive a higher score from lender B (S_4) than from lender A (S_3) and would not apply to lender A. In other words, all applicants with a debt-to-income ratio below D^* would apply to lender B, and all those with a ratio above D^* would apply to lender A. Regardless of whether it is estimated using a pooled sample of loans or using separate samples for the two lenders, the true loan performance model therefore consists of the curve for lender B below

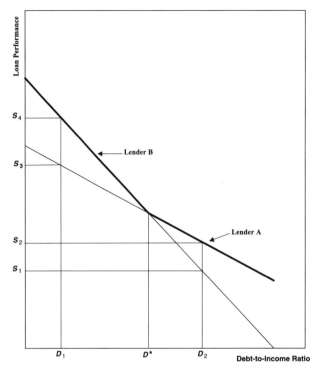

Figure 3.5
Loan performance scores with two lenders.

D^* and the curve for lender A above D^*. It follows that if different lenders have different performance models, then borrowers must be acting with imperfect information, and the mortgage market cannot be characterized as a perfectly competitive market.[32]

This leads us to another lesson:

• *Lesson 5.* Current trends and market forces are likely to reduce differences in underwriting standards across lenders who draw on the same applicant pools, but such differences can persist over time when borrowers and lenders have asymmetric information.

3.5.3 *Variation in the Price of Credit*

The shift toward credit pricing and away from explicit denial of credit could dramatically change the debate over discrimination in mortgage lending. Most data on lender underwriting contain no information on the price of credit of the loans underwritten, and yet a lender may be more likely to approve a mortgage application that offers a higher interest rate and therefore higher profits. This implies that researchers need to examine a simultaneous model of underwriting and the price of credit in which discrimination may occur on either dimension or both. The prospects for dealing with this issue are unclear, however, largely because price variables are difficult if not impossible to observe for denied mortgage applications.

One might argue that ignoring pricing probably biases statistical analyses of loan approval away from finding discrimination. If minorities are steered to more expensive lenders and loan products or simply charged more for credit than whites, this should increase the likelihood that minority applications are approved and mitigate racial differences in underwriting. Given the complexity of the mortgage process, however, this simple result may not hold in practice.

Finally, when pricing is considered, the up-front costs of obtaining credit may also represent an important treatment variable. As discussed earlier, a household can lower its cost of credit by paying points and thereby reducing the value of the prepayment option, but households may be prevented from reducing the value of this option if they are credit constrained. Similarly, holding the cost of credit constant, lenders are more likely to approve a mortgage when part of the cost of credit is paid up front, because this reduces the value of the termination options that the lender is providing to the borrower. If minorities have fewer assets available for closing, on average, than whites, they may be unable to pay points and therefore face a higher cost of credit, which might bias underwriting models toward finding discrimination.

In short, borrower treatment in the underwriting process may be characterized according to three separate outcomes: approval or denial, the cost of credit, and up-front costs. At the very least, the literature on underwriting models needs to explore the linkages between loan approval and both credit pricing and up-front costs. This discussion can be summarized as another lesson:

• *Lesson 6.* In a world with relatively little credit rationing, studies of mortgage discrimination should investigate not only rates of loan approval but also the price of credit, that is, the interest rate, and the up-front costs of borrowing, such as points and closing costs; if possible, these studies should also account for the relationships among these three outcomes.

3.5.4   Interpreting the Results of a Loan Approval Regression

The analysis in this chapter also reveals that a loan approval regression is more difficult to interpret than commonly believed. The problems of interpretation lead to three more lessons about these regressions.

Our seventh lesson addresses the first of these interpretation problems:

• *Lesson 7.* Whenever private information influences the matching of borrowers and lenders, not only may it lead to endogeneity bias or sample selection bias in the estimated coefficients in a loan approval regression, but it also may change the interpretation of the minority status coefficient.

In particular, the issue of interpretation of the minority status coefficient arises whenever blacks and Hispanics select or are steered to lenders in part on the basis of lenders' propensity to discriminate. Suppose, for example, that real estate brokers know that half of all lenders discriminate and steer all black and Hispanic customers to the other half of lenders, which do not. In this case, no discrimination will be observed in the loan approval process, even though half of lenders would discriminate if given the chance. This process could, of course, work in the opposite direction if real estate brokers steered black and Hispanic customers toward discriminating lenders. In this case, discrimination would be observed for every loan, even though half of lenders would never discriminate.

Real estate brokers are not the only actors who can play this type of role. Black and Hispanic customers may have private information about which lenders will discriminate and therefore avoid these lenders. Even loan officers can get into the act by discouraging (or encouraging) black and Hispanic customers who inquire about loans before they ever fill out an application.

In short, the minority status coefficient may reveal the level of discrimination in loan approval encountered by a typical black or Hispanic applicant, but it does not reveal the level of discrimination in loan approval practiced by the typical lender.[33] The difference between these two estimates is that the first, but not the second, is affected by the process linking borrowers to lenders. This process may involve not only the behavior of loan underwriters, but also the behavior of real estate brokers, potential borrowers, and loan officials who have nothing to do with the underwriting decision.

This difference is important, because discrimination in loan approval can impose costs on a minority households even if that particular household does not literally experience it. If minority households select or are steered to certain lenders because of private information about discrimination by other lenders, then they may have to pay extra search costs, and they may not receive mortgages on the same terms as comparable whites or deal with offices in the most convenient locations. Indeed, minority households may even submit to less favorable terms than comparable whites in an attempt to overcome anticipated discrimination in loan approval. Moreover, as noted earlier, anticipated discrimination in loan approval may convince some minority households not to apply for a mortgage at all. In this case, discrimination clearly lowers the well-being of minorities relative to comparable whites. The effect of such discrimination can be quite large. Using the search model described in section 3.2.3, Yinger (1997) estimates that 21 percent of potential moves by minority households are discouraged by discrimination in housing and mortgage markets. Most of this effect is due to mortgage discrimination.

Overall, therefore, a loan approval regression cannot reveal the level of discrimination in loan approval by the average lender without a sampling or weighting scheme that removes the effects of lender selection and steering. No study has taken this step.[34] If properly specified, a loan approval regression might be able to determine the extent to which minority households directly experience discrimination in loan approval. Even in this case, however, the regression may not capture the full impact of this discrimination, because minority households may take steps, and pay costs, to avoid it.

A second interpretation problem is encompassed by our eighth lesson:

• *Lesson 8.* A loan approval regression may reflect discrimination that occurs before the loan approval decision.

As explained earlier, discriminatory offers and advice from lenders (and perhaps real estate agents) can result in differences in the applications of minority and white households that appear identical when they first inquire about a loan. Thus, discrimination may be built into the explanatory variables in a loan approval regression. For example, whites may be told to pay off their credit card debts before filling out their applications, whereas minorities may not be given any such advice (e.g., see Siskin and Cupingood, 1996). A credit card debt variable would reflect such discriminatory advice.

This lesson has two key implications. First, even in a correctly specified loan approval regression, the minority status coefficient may not indicate the full impact of lender discrimination on loan approval. In particular, lender discrimination in offers and advice may alter the application characteristics of minorities relative to whites in ways that increase minorities' relative chance of rejection.

Second, the presence of other forms of lender discrimination might result in biased estimates of discrimination in the loan approval decision. Suppose, for example, that some lenders have a high propensity to discriminate in both advice and loan approval and that other lenders rarely discriminate. Then there is an unobserved variable, propensity to discriminate, that is correlated with the applicant characteristics, such as credit card debt, that are influenced by discrimination in lender advice. The coefficients of these characteristics may therefore pick up some of the effect of discrimination in loan approval, even if a minority status variable is included in the regression.

Unfortunately, neither the magnitude of this potential bias nor the circumstances under which it is likely to arise have been documented in the literature. Moreover, the data needed to generate such documentations, namely, applicant characteristics uninfluenced by lender discrimination, are not likely to be available.[35] This type of bias therefore remains merely a theoretical possibility that has not been investigated.

The chapter's final lesson is related to variation in underwriting standards across lenders:

• *Lesson 9.* Interpretation of a loan approval regression, and in particular of the minority status coefficient, depends on whether different lenders have different underwriting standards.

As explained in section 3.5.2, lenders may base their underwriting criteria on different experiences or different sources of information or even different objectives. As a result, underwriting criteria may not be the same for all lenders. This possibility greatly complicates the interpretation of the minority status coefficient in a loan approval regression. Because it is particularly relevant for our review of the Boston Fed Study and the related literature, we postpone our discussion of this issue until chapter 5 and, especially, chapter 6.

3.6 Conclusions

At first glance, a test for discrimination in loan approval appears to be straightforward. All one has to do, it seems, is estimate the extent to which minority applicants are more likely to be turned down than are equally qualified whites. As it turns out, however, the loan approval decision is only part of a complex process, and the complexity of this process has important implications for the estimation of discrimination in loan approval.

The behavior of households, real estate agents, and loan officers other than underwriters can create correlations between explanatory variables that are included in a loan approval regression and others that are omitted. The result may be endogeneity bias or sample selection bias. In many cases, biases of this type can be eliminated through the use of an extensive set of control variables. To eliminate bias, however, this set may have to be broader than the set of variables in lenders' loan files, and some types of omitted variables, particularly those reflecting private information, are intrinsically difficult for a researcher to observe. Thus, statistical methods to correct for these biases may be necessary.

The nature of the loan approval decision implies that lenders may not all use the same underwriting standards. This possibility complicates the specification of a loan approval regression and could, under some circumstances, result in biased coefficients even in a regression with extensive control variables. The extent of variation in underwriting standards, however, is not known, and the widespread use of automated underwriting systems and of loan sales on the secondary market suggest that it may be limited. In addition, the trend toward credit pricing and away from credit rationing implies that loan approval regressions may need to account for elements of the price of credit.

The complexity of the process leading up to loan approval also complicates the interpretation of a loan approval regression, even one that is completely and correctly specified. Actions by households, real estate agents, and loan officers may result in the matching of minority households with lenders that tend not to discriminate, for example, so that the minority status coefficient is much lower than it would be for a random sample of lenders, even a random sample weighted by loan volume. Focusing on discrimination by the lenders actually visited by minority households ignores the potential costs that these households face because their selection of a lender is influenced by anticipated lender discrimination. Moreover, the minority status coefficient in a loan approval regression does not necessarily reveal the full impact of lender discrimination on loan approval. Lenders may also diminish the likelihood that minority applicants will be approved by discriminating in the provision of offers and advice at earlier stages of the lending process. Finally, loan approval regressions are usually interpreted under the implicit assumption that all lenders have the same underwriting standard. If, as seems likely, this assumption is violated, then the most straight-forward interpretation of these regressions may no longer hold. We will return to this issue, and indeed to all of these issues, in chapter 5.

4

The Literature on
Mortgage Lending
Discrimination up to and
Including the Boston Fed
Study

4.1 Introduction

Although discrimination in mortgage lending received little attention from policymakers before the "Color of Money" series was
published in 1988 and the first HMDA data with denial rates by race
were released in 1991, several scholars had made serious efforts to
address this issue before then. This chapter reviews this early literature on discrimination in loan approval.[1] The review presented in
the chapter provides valuable perspective on the Boston Fed Study
(Munnell et al., 1996), which is discussed at the end of the chapter,
and serves as an introduction to many of the key issues in studying
mortgage discrimination that are still under debate. The chapter
also examines the efforts by a few of these early studies to estimate
process-based redlining by mortgage lenders.

4.2 Early Studies of Discrimination in Loan Approval

The principal early studies of discrimination in mortgage loan approval include Black, Schweitzer, and Mandell (1978), King (1980),
Peterson (1981), Schafer and Ladd (1981), and Maddala and Trost
(1982). In this section we review all of these studies except for Peterson, which focuses on sex-based discrimination in consumer loans.[2]

4.2.1 Black, Schweitzer, and Mandell (1978)

The first major study of discrimination in loan approval was conducted by Black, Schweitzer, and Mandell (1978). This study is based
on a survey mailed to a sample of 300 lenders in 1976 by the Comptroller of the Currency and the FDIC. Perhaps the most significant
limitation of the study is that this survey was voluntary, and only

Table 4.1
Control variables used by Black, Schweitzer, and Mandell (1978)

Demographic information	Loan characteristics
Age	Loan amount
Male	Down payment
Single	Loan origination fees
Black	Years to maturity
Female	Annual interest rate
	Monthly loan payment
	Loan insurance status
Financial information	
Years employed	
Self-employed	
Income	
Net worth	
Price of property	
Age of property	
Assessed value of property	

Source: Black, Schweitzer, and Mandell (1978, pp. 188–189).

176 of the 300 lenders decided to participate. Moreover, even though the survey resulted in some information on almost 14,000 loan applications, missing data on many of those applications reduced the final sample size to 3,456.[3] One sign that the resulting sample is not representative is that the loan rejection rate is only 2.7 percent, which is far below the 12.5-percent rejection rate for non-subprime mortgage applications in the 1993 HMDA data (FFIEC, 1998, table 4).[4]

The resulting data set provided extensive information on loan terms and basic financial characteristics of the applicant and the property but did not include any information on the applicant's credit history or on the neighborhood characteristics of the property associated with the loan (see table 4.1). The dependent variable was set equal to one for a rejected application and zero for an accepted application. The study defined only two racial categories, namely, black and nonblack; Hispanics were included in the nonblack category. Black et al. estimated their loan approval model using probit analysis, which is appropriate for this type of model. They found that applications from blacks were more likely to be rejected than those from nonblacks, although this result was significant only at the 10-percent level (one-tailed test).

The Black, Schweitzer, and Mandell study is notable for including the loan terms, including the amount requested, as exogenous explanatory variables. This step anticipates a key focus of later research. Black, Schweitzer, and Mandell do not, however, consider the possibility that loan terms are endogenous, an issue raised by Madalla and Trost (1982) and addressed by many later studies.[5] In addition, the lack of information on either credit history or neighborhood characteristics is undoubtedly a source of omitted-variable bias.

4.2.2   King (1980)

King (1980) is an important milestone both because it is based on extensive data and because it raises many of the important issues with which the literature on mortgage discrimination continues to struggle. In terms of framework, King points out that discrimination can occur at many stages of the lending process, including prescreening, property appraisal, loan approval, and setting loan terms. In addition, King points out that loan approval decisions may be affected by factors that do not directly involve race or sex, but that are nevertheless not "proper" business considerations in the sense that they do not predict loan default or loss. Although King never mentions disparate-impact discrimination, his discussion of business considerations provides a preview of work on this important issue. Finally, King points out that in his regressions, which pool data across lenders, "[a]pparent discrimination in the pooled results does not imply that all lenders discriminate, nor does failure to detect discrimination in the pooled sample exclude discriminatory behavior by an individual institution" (p. 3). As we will see in chapter 10, this is an important, but still unresolved, issue for fair-lending enforcement.

The data for this study come from applications to savings and loans associations for home purchase, refinancing, and construction loans in 1978 for owner-occupied properties in three metropolitan areas: Miami, San Antonio, and Toledo. The final sample sizes for these three areas were 2,733, 555, and 1,020, respectively. As shown in table 4.2, King was able to collect extensive information on applicant, property, and loan characteristics. Some key variables, including lender dummies, are in the data set, but full information on credit history is limited. In fact, King's variable for the applicant's

Table 4.2
Control variables used by King (1980)

Applicant characteristics	House characteristics
Age	Age
Single	Neighborhood dummies
Black	Census tract characteristics (1970)
Spanish-American	Percentage black
Female	Percentage Hispanic
Proportion of gross income from co-applicant	Percentage owner-occupied
Payment-to-income ratio	Percentage old housing
Debt-to-income ratio	Poverty rate
Unacceptable credit history	
Loan characteristics	*Other*
Loan-to-assessed-value ratio	Lender dummies
Involves FHA or VA insurance	
Involves private mortgage insurance	

Source: King (1980, table 5.1).

credit history is available only for those cases in which an applicant has been rejected for the cause of "unacceptable credit information." This information about credit history is similar to what is available in the HMDA data, and including it in a loan approval regression is, as we will see in chapter 5, quite problematic. As a result, we focus on regressions that omit it, recognizing, as does King, that this could result in (unavoidable) omitted-variable bias.[6]

King's regressions examine a lender's decision to reject a loan application as a function of the control variables in table 4.2. An offer by the lender to lend on terms different from the terms requested by the borrower is treated as an acceptance.[7] King estimates his regressions using ordinary least squares (OLS).[8] He includes two loan terms, namely, LTV (loan to assessed value ratio) and the payment-to-income ratio, which are treated as exogenous variables. Like Black, Schweitzer, and Mandell (1978), therefore, King does not consider the possibility that loan terms are endogenous.[9]

King finds a significantly higher probability of rejection for black than for white applicants in Miami and Toledo and a higher probability of rejection for Hispanic than for white applicants in Miami and San Antonio. In these cases, the denial rate is between 30 and 100 percent higher for minorities than for whites. All but one of these results hold up even when the suspect credit history variable is included.

King also provides the first estimates of process-based redlining in loan denial. His regressions include the racial and ethnic composition of the census tract in which the relevant property is located. In the case of Toledo, they also include dummy variables for neighborhoods defined by the Toledo Department of Community Development. King finds that the probability of denial is higher in black than in white neighborhoods in San Antonio. The racial and ethnic composition variables are not significant in the other cities; neither are the neighborhood dummies in Toledo.

Finally, King initiates research on discrimination in mortgage terms by estimating regressions to explain the interest rate, LTV, and the loan amount for approved loans. The explanatory variables in these regressions include those in table 4.2, along with the maturity and LTV requested by the borrower. King recognizes that the different terms are determined simultaneously, and he estimates these regressions with a simultaneous equations procedure. These regressions provide little evidence of discrimination or redlining in the setting of mortgage terms.

4.2.3 Schafer and Ladd (1981)

Schafer and Ladd (1981) assembled the largest data set of all the early studies, with information for each application similar to that in King (1980). They took advantage of the fact that, even before HMDA, California and New York required state-regulated lenders to keep records on mortgage applications. Because of this requirement, Schafer and Ladd were able to obtain detailed data on mortgage loan applications for state-regulated savings and loans in California in 1977 and 1978 and for commercial banks, mutual savings banks, and savings and loans in New York in 1976–1978. Their data set covered sixteen metropolitan areas in California and six in New York. It included extensive information on applicant, property, and loan characteristics but did not include information on applicant credit history (see table 4.3).

Schafer and Ladd's study makes an important contribution by recognizing the complexity of the loan denial decision. In fact, the authors do not define one choice, namely approve or deny, but instead analyze a four-way choice using multinomial logit analysis. For California, the four choices are "approved as applied for, approved after increasing the requested loan amount, approved after

Table 4.3
Control variables used by Schafer and Ladd (1981)

California sample	New York sample
Applicant characteristics	
Income	Income
Income relative to requested loan	Income relative to requested loan
Age	Age
Female	Female
Black	Black
Hispanic	Hispanic
Income of secondary earner	Net wealth
	Years at present occupation
Loan characteristics	
Ratio of requested loan amount to income	Ratio of requested loan amount to income
Ratio of requested loan amount to appraised value of property	Ratio of requested loan amount to appraised value of property
Property characteristics	
Neighborhood income	Neighborhood income
Change in neighborhood income	Change in neighborhood income
Change in neighborhood population	Change in neighborhood population
Neighborhood average sales price[a]	Neighborhood average sales price
Change in neighborhood average sales price[a]	Neighborhood mortgage delinquency rate
Neighborhood vacancy rate[a]	Neighborhood mortgage foreclosure rate
Fraction of units built before 1940	

Source: Schafer and Ladd (1981, pp. 85–88, 187–188).
[a] In selected areas only.

decreasing the requested loan amount, and denied" (p. 132). A somewhat different set is used for New York, namely "approved as applied for, approved with modifications, denied, and withdrawn" (p. 187).[10] The study also conducts a separate examination of discrimination in loan terms, but it does not treat loan terms as endogenous in the loan approval regressions.[11]

Schafer and Ladd (1981, tables 5.19 and 5.20) find evidence of widespread, but not universal, discrimination against blacks and Hispanics in loan approval decisions. In California in 1977, the black/white denial ratio was significantly greater than one in nine of the sixteen metropolitan areas.[12] Moreover, this ratio was usually greater than 2.0 and exceeded 7.0 in two areas. In 1978, blacks faced a significantly higher denial probability than did whites in ten of the sixteen areas, with black/white denial ratios ranging from 1.59 to 4.15. Differences between Hispanics and whites also appeared, but they were not as large or as common. In particular, Hispanics faced a significantly higher denial probability in five of the metropolitan areas in both 1977 and 1978, with Hispanic/white denial ratios ranging from 1.16 to 2.52.[13]

The New York sample covered six metropolitan areas and up to three different types of lenders (commercial banks, mutual savings banks, or savings and loan associations) in each area. The denial ratio was higher for blacks than for whites in four of the six metropolitan areas and six of the ten area/lender type combinations. In these cases, the black/white denial ratios ranged from 1.58 to 3.61. These results provide additional evidence of substantial, widespread discrimination against blacks in the lending process. In contrast, the Hispanic/white denial ratio was significantly greater than one in only one case and significantly less than one in another.

Finally, Schafer and Ladd also test for process-based redlining in loan approval by determining whether denial rates are higher either in neighborhoods with large concentrations of blacks or Hispanics or in neighborhoods where redlining has been alleged. They find (Schafer and Ladd, 1981, tables 5.33 and 5.34) that in California in both 1977 and 1978, loan applications in largely black neighborhoods had a significantly higher probability of loan denial (compared to largely white neighborhoods) in up to five metropolitan areas, but they also had a significantly lower probability of denial in a somewhat smaller set of areas. The results for Hispanic neighborhoods in California are similar. These results indicate that process-based redlining is not a widespread phenomenon. Moreover, if these regressions do capture redlining, then reverse redlining appears to exist in a few metropolitan areas. In New York, only one of the ten area/lender type combinations exhibited a significantly higher loan denial probability in largely nonwhite neighborhoods than in other neighborhoods (table 7.18).

The results for allegedly redlined neighborhoods are also quite mixed (Schafer and Ladd, 1981, tables 5.23–5.25 and 7.2–7.17). In California, only two of the twelve allegedly redlined neighborhoods in Los Angeles had a denial probability greater than that of other neighborhoods (and only in one of the two years), and several other neighborhoods had lower than average denial probabilities.

Moreover, the single allegedly redlined neighborhoods identified in Oakland/San Francisco and in Sacramento had denial probabilities below those of other neighborhoods. For mutual savings banks in New York, one allegedly redlined area in Albany and one in Troy had denial probabilities far above those of other neighborhoods; in fact, these denial probabilities were over 10 times the probabilities elsewhere, a difference that is highly significant statistically. There was no evidence, however, of redlining for six other allegedly red-lined neighborhoods in this metropolitan area. Moreover, evidence of redlining appeared in only three of the seven allegedly redlined neighborhoods in the New York City area, one of the two such neighborhoods in Rochester, and none of the six such neighborhoods in Buffalo or Syracuse.

Overall, therefore, these results indicate that redlining may some-times occur, but that it is hardly a widespread phenomenon.

4.2.4   Maddala and Trost (1982)

Maddala and Trost (1982) make another important contribution by providing a simultaneous model of the demand and supply of mortgage funds. If a loan is approved, they argue, the loan amount represents the minimum of two unobserved quantities, namely, the loan amount demanded by the applicant and the loan amount the lender is willing to supply. If a loan is denied, then the loan amount in the application is assumed to equal the loan demand by the ap-plicant, and loan supply is assumed to be less than this amount.

Maddala and Trost develop two formal econometric models of this situation. In the first model, the interest rate is treated as endoge-nous. This model applies when interest terms are negotiated be-tween borrower and lender. In the second model, all parties treat the interest rate as fixed. This model applies when a lender makes a separate decision about the interest rate and applies it to all loans. The second model leads to an important lesson, namely, that an analysis of loan approval may yield biased estimates of discrimina-tion unless it includes the amount of loan demanded as an explana-tory variable. As we will see, however, this lesson is difficult to implement because, as the Maddala and Trost models demonstrate, the amount of loan demanded cannot be directly observed.

Finally, Maddala and Trost estimate their models using data for 750 mortgage loan applications made to seven lenders in the

Columbia, South Carolina, metropolitan area in 1976 and 1977. Unfortunately, these data include only two variables describing an applicant's creditworthiness, namely, applicant income and debt. The data also include indicators of race, sex, and marital status; the age of the house; and three neighborhood variables. When applied to these data, both of their models yield the same conclusion: The loan amount supplied to blacks was smaller than the loan amount supplied to whites, but the *t*-statistic is about 1.5, which does not reach statistical significance at conventional levels.

Overall, therefore, this article's main contribution is methodological, not empirical. It demonstrates the limitations of a simple analysis of the loan denial decision, but its data are not sufficient to provide compelling results for the alternative models it develops.

4.3   The Boston Fed Study

The studies discussed above all lead up to the so-called Boston Fed Study (Munnell et al., 1996), which originally appeared as a working paper by the same authors (1992). This study estimates a loan denial equation using a sample of about 3,000 loan applications for conventional mortgages in the Boston area in 1990. The sample includes all applications in the area by blacks and Hispanics in that year (about 1,200), along with a random sample of white applications. As discussed in chapter 1, the main purpose of this study was to shed light on the patterns observed in the HMDA data by collecting and, ultimately, controlling for a comprehensive set of applicant, loan, and property characteristics. Implicitly, therefore, its purpose was also to improve on previous studies by adding information on applicants' credit histories. An important secondary purpose was to enhance the generality of a study of lending discrimination by covering all types of lenders, instead of the restricted sets in all previous studies.

In more technical terms, this study focused on minimizing omitted-variable bias by supplementing the HMDA data with thirty-eight additional variables. "These variables were selected based both on expectations of what should be important and on numerous conversations with lenders, underwriters, and others familiar with the lending process about what they believe is important" (p. 28). The final data set includes virtually all of the variables in any of the previous studies, plus extensive information on each applicant's credit

Table 4.4
Control variables used by Munnell et al. (1996)

Risk of default	*Loan characteristics*
Housing expense/income	Two- to four-family house
Total debt payments/income	Lender ID
Net wealth	
Consumer credit history	
Mortgage credit history	
Public record history	
Probability of unemployment	
Self-employed	
Loan/appraised value is low	
Loan/appraised value is medium	
Loan/appraised value is high	
Costs of default	*Personal characteristics*
Denied private mortgage insurance	Black or Hispanic
Census tract dummies	

Source: Munnell et al. (1996, table 2).

history. As Munnell et al. (1996) put it (p. 43), their data set "includes every variable mentioned as important in numerous conversations with lenders, underwriters, and examiners, and it contains all of the information on the application form and almost all of the information in the loan file." The set of control variables in this study's main regressions, organized by categories the authors define, is presented in table 4.4.[14]

The control variables employed in Munnell et al.'s studies go far beyond those used in previous studies. The "consumer credit history" and "mortgage credit history" variables measure the seriousness of applicants' previous credit problems, ranging from no "slow pay" accounts or late payments to serious delinquencies or extensive late payments. The "public record history" variable indicates whether the applicant has any record of past credit problems, and the "probability of unemployment" variable is the previous year's unemployment rate in the applicant's industry. These variables provide extensive information about an applicant's credit history.

Munnell et al. estimate a loan denial equation using logit analysis, which is appropriate for analyzing discrete choices, such as the decision to grant or deny a mortgage in response to an application. The dependent variable is whether the lender either denies the application or makes a counteroffer that is rejected by the applicant.[15] In their preferred specification, Munnell et al. find that the probability of loan denial is 8.2 percentage points higher for blacks and Hispanics than for whites, controlling for all the varibles in table 4.4. This result is highly significant statistically. The rejection rate for white applicants is 10 percent, so this result implies that the rejection rate is 82 percent higher for minorities than for whites with comparable loan, property, and personal characteristics.

To determine whether this result is robust, Munnell et al. also estimate a variety of alternative specifications. They replace the census tract dummies with census tract characteristics, such as the rate of housing appreciation; they add additional loan characteristics, such as whether a grant contributed to the down payment; they add the age, gender, and family status of the applicant; they develop a more elaborate method for predicting the probability of unemployment; they drop the "denied private mortgage insurance" variable and exclude cases in which this insurance was denied; they treat application withdrawals as a third discrete outcome; they run separate regressions for single-family houses, condominiums, and multifamily units; they examine various interaction terms; they run separate regressions for lenders that specialize in loans to minorities; and they run separate regressions for minority and white applicants. These alternative specifications have remarkably little impact on their estimate of the disadvantage faced by black and Hispanic applicants; indeed, this effect is strong and statistically significant in every one of these alternative specifications.

In a separate manuscript, Tootell (1996a), one of the authors of the Boston Fed Study, uses the Boston Fed Study's data set to examine process-based redlining.[16] The Boston Fed study itself does not focus on whether particular neighborhood characteristics influence the loan approval decision. Instead, its main loan approval regressions include census tract dummy variables to capture the impact of all characteristics of the neighborhood in which a house is located. Tootell replaces these dummy variables with a set of census tract characteristics, including the vacancy rate, the poverty rate, and the perceived risk to owners of home equity in a neighborhood. The last of these variables is measured by the ratio of apartment rents to property values. It is likely to have a high value in neighborhoods where rental housing is an attractive option relative to owner-occupied housing, that is, where the risk to home equity is relatively high. To test for redlining, Tootell also includes the percentage of the census tract population belonging to a minority group. This variable is not statistically significant, and Tootell concludes that there is no evidence of redlining in Boston.[17]

4.4   Conclusion

In our view, Munnell et al. (1996) represents a significant improvement over previous research, both because of its careful data collection efforts and because of its extensive examination of alternative specifications. As it turns out, however, the publication of this study was just the opening salvo in an intense debate. Dozens of scholars have commented on this study, and as noted in chapter 1, the comments run the gamut from praise to condemnation. Much of this commentary has focused on the study's methodology, and several scholars have raised methodological issues that are worthy of further investigation. Moreover, legitimate questions have been raised about the interpretation of this study, and in particular, about whether the results provide evidence of discrimination in mortgage lending. We now turn to this debate and to these questions.

5   Evaluating Criticisms of
the Boston Fed Study

5.1   Introduction

The Boston Fed Study and its findings have been the focal point of the literature on mortgage lending discrimination over the last ten years.[1] It is nearly impossible to find a publication on the topic that does not at least cite the Boston Fed Study as motivation for further research, and many of these publications have been dedicated to a reexamination or critique of this study's findings. The study plays the important role that it does in the debate on the existence and nature of mortgage lending discrimination because, as discussed in chapter 4, no other study comes close to using as many potential underwriting variables or investigating as many specifications with a data set that is representative of mortgage transactions in a major U.S. metropolitan area.

Because of its centrality, the Boston Fed Study and criticisms of it are the subject of this chapter. We identify the major criticisms of this study and explore their validity using the public-use version of the data set the study itself employed. We also examine the responses of the Boston Fed Study's authors to their critics.[2] This analysis builds on the analytical framework developed in the preceding chapters.

Critics of the Boston Fed Study have identified many potential flaws in it. All the potential flaws of which we are aware are reviewed in this chapter.[3] To be specific, we investigate the claims that the Boston Fed Study overstates discrimination because of

- omitted variables
- data errors in the explanatory variables
- misclassification in the dependent variable

- incorrect specification
- endogenous explanatory variables

5.2   Omitted Variables

As explained in chapter 4, Munnell et al. (1996) supplement the 1990 HMDA data for Boston with a survey of lenders that provides extensive information on an individual applicant's credit history, among other things. The resulting data set allows the authors to estimate a model of loan denial that depends on an extensive list of variables associated with the probability and cost of default, including variables to measure an individual's credit history and dummy variables for the census tract in which the house whose purchase is being financed is located and for the lender to which the application is submitted. This model indicates that the probability of loan denial is significantly higher for a black or Hispanic applicant than for a white applicant with the same applicant, loan, and property characteristics.

Chapter 4 also points out that Munnell et al. estimate a number of alternative models that add additional control variables. These models yield the same result. Furthermore, the Boston Fed Study's data set includes additional individual characteristics, such as years of job experience, education, and tenure in current job. The estimated minority status coefficient is unaffected by the inclusion of these variables, as well (Ross and Tootell, 1998).

5.2.1   The Critics' Claims

Although the Boston Fed Study has more control variables than any previous study, many critics of this study, including Zandi (1993), Liebowitz (1993), Horne (1994), Zycher and Wolfe (1994) and Day and Liebowitz (1996), argue that it still omits key explanatory variables. As discussed in earlier chapters, this type of omission can be very troubling. According to a well-known econometric theorem, the coefficient of one variable (in this case, minority status) will be biased if the estimating equation omits variables that are correlated with that variable and that help explain the dependent variable (loan denial). Moreover, if these omitted variables have a positive impact on loan denial (i.e., if higher values make loan denial more likely) and are positively correlated with minority status, then their omission will bias upward the coefficient of the minority status variable, or, to put it another way, will lead to an overstatement of discrimination. Because, on average, blacks and Hispanics have poorer credit qualifications, certain critics have concluded that the Boston Fed Study probably exaggerates discrimination because of these omitted variables. Examples of the omitted variables these authors discuss are "presence of cosigner," "loan amount," "dollar amount of gifts," "home equity," "lender toughness," "whether data could not be verified" (henceforth called "unable to verify") and "whether the applicant's credit history meets loan policy guidelines for approval" (henceforth called "meets guidelines").[4]

The available evidence reveals that most of these variables are not a source of bias in the Boston Fed Study's equations. As noted by Browne and Tootell (1995), "cosigner" and "loan amount" are present in the Boston Fed Study's data set, and their inclusion in a loan denial model has no effect on the estimated minority status coefficient. The study's data set also includes variables indicating "whether a gift was used for the downpayment" and "whether the applicant is a first-time homebuyer." In addition, the "net worth" variable included in the Boston Fed Study's equation includes "home equity." The "net worth" variable is included in the Munnell et al. equations and is insignificant, and the inclusion of the "gift" or "first-time homebuyer" variables has no effect on the estimated minority status coefficient (see Browne and Tootell, 1995, or Tootell, 1996b). It seems unlikely that including the (unavailable) "actual amount of the gift" or "home equity" variables separately would have much influence on the minority status coefficient, given that these related variables have no effect. In addition, Glennon and Stengel (1994a) investigate many alternative sets of explanatory variables using the Boston Fed Study's data. They find that the estimated minority status coefficient is "remarkably" unaffected by the changes they made in the explanatory variables tested.

The inclusion of the "unable to verify" and "meets guidelines" variables has a larger effect. With the Boston Fed Study's data, the coefficients of the "unable to verify" and the "meets guidelines" dummy variables are statistically significant in a denial model. Moreover, according to Day and Liebowitz, the inclusion of "unable to verify" lowers the minority status coefficient by 27 percent, and the inclusion of both "unable to verify" and "meets guidelines" lowers the minority status coefficient by 62 percent. Thus, including both variables substantially reduces the magnitude and significance of the minority status coefficient; in fact, in some of Day and Liebowitz's specifications, the minority status coefficient is no longer statistically significant when these variables are included.

Carr and Megbolugbe (1993) also examine the effects of these variables on the minority status coefficient. They find that including "unable to verify" lowers the minority status coefficient by 15 percent and that including both variables lowers the minority status coefficient by 40 percent. The minority status coefficient is still statistically significant at the 1-percent level of confidence in Carr and Megbolugbe's regressions, however, even after including both variables. The findings of Glennon and Stengel (1994a), Browne and Tootell (1995), and Tootell (1996b) are similar to those of Carr and Megbolugbe.

Carr and Megbolugbe (1993) and Browne and Tootell (1995) argue that these variables, especially "meets guidelines," should not be included in the denial equation, because these two variables were not recorded in the original loan files. Rather, they involve the after-the-fact judgment of the individual completing the HMDA data forms. The "unable to verify" variable could reflect the fact that lenders make extra efforts to verify the information of white applicants, and the "meets guidelines" variable could simply reflect the lender's loan denial decision. In particular, Browne and Tootell contend that the "meets guidelines" question, which was answered roughly one year after the loan approval decision, was interpreted by the respondents as whether "the sum total of applicant characteristics meet the institution's guidelines for approval" (p. 61). They note that some unsuccessful applications were coded as not meeting credit history guidelines even though those applicants had no credit problems. Browne and Tootell test their claim by estimating a model of the "meets guidelines" variable. As predicted by their claim, they find that loan terms, such as housing expense–to–income ratio, debt-to-income ratio, and LTV, help explain the "meets guidelines" variable—a result that does not make sense if the "meets guidelines" variable concerns only the quality of an applicant's credit history.

Horne (1994) and Day and Liebowitz (1996) counter that the "meets guidelines" variable is a suitable proxy for details of an individual's credit history that were not collected for the Boston Fed Study. For example, Day and Liebowitz suggest that the "age of the credit problem" and the "size of the credit problem" should have been included in the analysis. They also suggest that standards may vary across lenders and claim that this is another justification for including the "meets guidelines" variable. Because credit history information often is provided by an outside agency, lenders also might determine whether an applicant meets their guidelines simply by comparing an external credit score to their internal standard; if so, then the "meets guidelines" variable can be considered exogenous and hence a legitimate explanatory variable.

Finally, Day and Liebowitz (1996) also develop a "lender toughness" variable by matching the Boston Fed Study's data to HMDA data. They add both the "lender toughness" and the "unable to verify" variables to the denial equation. Including both variables lowers the minority status coefficient by 27 percent, which is the same as the effect of including only "unable to verify." Therefore, "lender toughness" alone probably has little effect on the minority status coefficient. Moreover, the basic equation in Munnell et al. (1996) already includes a set of lender dummy variables, which capture, of course, lender toughness and other fixed lender characteristics that affect loan denial. These variables lower the minority status coefficient by about 20 percent, an effect that is already included in Munnell et al.'s basic estimate.[5]

5.2.2 Evaluation

The Boston Fed Study's data contains an extensive set of underwriting variables, including variables on credit history, as well as controls for the lender and the location of the housing unit. Moreover, the magnitude and statistical significance of the minority status coefficient in a loan denial equation are largely unaffected by the inclusion of a large array of risk, loan, borrower, unit, and neighborhood variables that are not included in the Boston Fed Study's main equations. In our view, the Boston Fed Study's equations contain a remarkably complete set of explanatory variables, and most claims concerning omitted-variable bias are implausible or have been shown to be incorrect. As we discussed at length in chapter 3, we agree that an underwriting model cannot yield credible results without controlling for a wide range of factors (see lessons 1 and 2). Unlike the critics, however, we conclude that the Boston Fed Study has a more complete list of control variables—and hence more credible results—than any previous study.

Nevertheless, two variables omitted from the Boston Fed Study, namely "unable to verify" and "meets guidelines," have been shown to have a substantial effect on the estimated minority status coefficient. Browne and Tootell (1995) find that the minority status coefficient is still large and statistically significant after including the variables. More importantly, they also argue that "meets guidelines" should not be included in the regression because it represents a subjective, after-the-fact opinion that could be influenced by a lender's discriminatory behavior.

In our view, this argument illustrates a more general concern that the "unable to verify" and "meets guidelines" variables may be endogenous and that their inclusion as exogenous variables in the underwriting model may lead to biased results. To be specific, the individual who determines the final value of these variables clearly has private information concerning the lender's underwriting criteria, which as discussed in chapter 3 (lesson 3) creates the potential for endogeneity bias. Nevertheless, no consensus has yet emerged on the magnitude of the impact that these variables have on the minority status coefficient or on the appropriate way to treat these two variables in a loan denial equation.

5.2.3   Reanalysis

The first question we examine here is the magnitude of the drop in the minority status coefficient when "meets guidelines" and "unable to verify" are included in a denial equation. The Browne and Tootell (1995) and Tootell (1996b) conclusions on this point are not convincing, because they are based on a specification that is more parsimonious than many of the specifications investigated by Munnell et al. (1996) and others.

We reexamine this issue with a more complete specification that includes additional loan, borrower, and neighborhood characteristics. The dependent variable in our analysis is loan approval, not loan denial, as in most other studies. This shift is designed to focus attention on the *provision* of credit; it changes the sign of all the estimated coefficients, but it obviously has no substantive impact on the results. We start with a base specification that does not include any credit history variables but does include an extensive list of control variables, namely, housing expense–to–income ratio; debt-to-income ratio; net worth; a proxy for the likelihood of unemployment; term;

dummy variables for LTV between 0.6 and 0.8, LTV between 0.8 and 0.95, and LTV above 0.95; fixed-rate mortgage; down payment includes gift; special program application; cosigner; age over 35; gender; marital status; self-employed; percentage minority in tract above 30; median income in tract over $39,111; multifamily unit; owner-occupied unit; PMI application denied; and, of course, minority status (which means, as in Munnell et al., black or Hispanic).[6] The definitions, means, and standard errors of these variables are presented in table 5.1.

As shown in the first column of table 5.2, a probit regression to explain loan approval using these explanatory variables performs quite well. Most of the estimated coefficients have the expected sign, and well over half of them are statistically significant at the 5-percent level (two-tailed test) or above. The minority status coefficient is negative and highly significant, which means that minority applications are significantly less likely to be approved than are comparable white applications.

We then successively add to the regression the Boston Fed Study's credit history variables, the "unable to verify" variable, and the "meets guidelines" variable. The results for these three variations on the baseline regression are presented in table 5.2 as well. The pseudo-R^2 or goodness-of-fit values for the baseline model and these three variants are 0.454, 0.511, 0.568, and 0.611, respectively.[7] Thus, each additional variable or set of variables has a substantial impact on the fit of the model. The minority status coefficients (with absolute values of t-statistics in parentheses)[8] for the four models are −0.537 (6.39), −0.356 (3.97), −0.327 (3.43), and −0.218 (2.047). When all these variables are added, therefore, minority status is still significant, but only at the 5-percent level (two-tailed test) instead of the 1-percent level. Moreover, the effect of minority status on loan approval falls dramatically as these variables or sets of variables are included. Based on the characteristics of the minority applicants, the average effect of minority status on the probability of approval is −12.3, −7.7, −6.2, and −3.3 percentage points for the four models.[9]

We conclude that the two variables in question, "unable to verify" and "meets guidelines," do, indeed, have a dramatic impact on the minority status coefficient. As a result, the key question is whether it is appropriate to include these variables in the equation, include them as endogenous variables, or exclude them altogether. To answer this question, we first reestimate the model using a

Table 5.1
Variable definitions and values

Name	Definition	Mean	Standard deviation	Minimum	Maximum
EXPENSE-TO-INCOME	Housing expense–to–income ratio	25.4282	9.8228	0.0000	300.0000
DEBT-TO-INCOME	Total debt expense–to–income ratio	0.3323	0.1134	0.0000	3.0000
NET WORTH	Net worth in thousands	0.3911	2.1040	−43.3340	53.4480
PREDICTED UNEMPLOYMENT	Predicted probability of unemployment	3.7050	2.2101	0.2000	10.6000
SELF EMPLOYED	Self-employed	0.1174	0.3219	0.0000	1.0000
LTV60_80	Loan-to-value ratio between 0.60 and 0.80	0.4255	0.4945	0.0000	1.0000
LTV80_95	Loan-to-value ratio between 0.80 and 0.95	0.3640	0.4812	0.0000	1.0000
LTV95	Loan-to-value ratio above 0.95	0.0822	0.2748	0.0000	1.0000
DENIED PMI	Applied for and denied PMI	0.0263	0.1600	0.0000	1.0000
MULTI-FAMILY	Multifamily unit = 1	0.1344	0.3412	0.0000	1.0000
FIXED RATE	Fixed-rate mortgage = 1	0.6605	0.4736	0.0000	1.0000
SPECIAL	Whether application made for a special loan program	0.1894	0.3919	0.0000	1.0000
TERM	Term in years	28.7076	5.0766	0.5000	40.0000
GOT GIFT	Whether received gift for down payment	0.1764	0.3812	0.0000	1.0000
COSIGNER	Whether a cosigner on application	0.0372	0.1893	0.0000	1.0000
MINORITY	Minority applicant (black or Hispanic)	0.2337	0.4233	0.0000	1.0000
AGE	Age greater than 50	0.4654	0.4989	0.0000	1.0000
MALE	Male applicant	0.7823	0.4127	0.0000	1.0000
MARRIED	Applicant married	0.5984	0.4903	0.0000	1.0000
OWNER-OCCUPIED	Owner-occupied residence	0.9638	0.1867	0.0000	1.0000

POOR TRACT	Tract income below area median	0.7864	0.4099	0.0000	1.0000
MINORITY TRACT	Percentage African American in tract above 30%	0.1177	0.3223	0.0000	1.0000
BANKRUPTCY	Public-record bankruptcy = 1, otherwise = 0	0.0795	0.2706	0.0000	1.0000
MORTGAGE CREDIT	Boston Fed study's ordinal mortgage credit history variable	1.7434	0.5339	1.0000	4.0000
CONSUMER CREDIT	Boston Fed study's ordinal consumer credit history variable	2.1720	1.6996	1.0000	6.0000
UNABLE TO VERIFY	Unverified information in application	0.0566	0.2312	0.0000	1.0000
MEETS GUIDELINES	Whether application met lender's credit guidelines	0.8983	0.3023	0.0000	1.0000
APPROVE	Loan approved = 1, denied = 0	0.8543	0.3528	0.0000	1.0000

Source: Authors' calculations based on public-use version of Boston Fed Study's data set.

Table 5.2
Results for basic loan approval regressions

Variable	Model 1	Model 2	Model 3	Model 4
EXPENSE-TO-INCOME	0.0081	0.0054	0.0077	0.0096
	(1.560)	(0.994)	(1.341)	(1.553)
DEBT-TO-INCOME	−3.364	−3.119	−3.293	−3.066
	(−7.850)	(−7.003)	(−6.931)	(−6.130)
NET WORTH	0.0060	0.0032	0.0058	−0.0020
	(0.363)	(0.180)	(0.314)	(−0.106)
PREDICTED UNEMPLOYMENT	−0.0282	−0.0296	−0.0230	−0.0186
	(−2.005)	(−2.007)	(−1.457)	(−1.088)
SELF EMPLOYED	−0.2182	−0.2282	−0.2281	−0.2634
	(−2.256)	(−2.242)	(−2.112)	(−2.279)
LTV60_80	−0.2699	−0.2655	−0.2399	−0.1322
	(−2.116)	(−1.951)	(−1.666)	(−0.877)
LTV80_95	−0.4288	−0.3875	−0.3903	−0.2397
	(−3.271)	(−2.766)	(−2.631)	(−1.532)
LTV95	−0.6440	−0.6764	−0.7155	−0.6555
	(−4.189)	(−4.150)	(−4.176)	(−3.663)
DENIED PMI	−2.548	−2.668	−2.582	−2.447
	(−10.52)	(−10.40)	(−9.890)	(−9.085)
MULTI-FAMILY	−0.2207	−0.2170	−0.2242	−0.3128
	(−2.425)	(−2.245)	(−2.185)	(−2.813)
FIXED RATE	−0.0178	−0.0665	−0.1059	−0.1901
	(−0.259)	(−0.900)	(−1.348)	(−2.207)
SPECIAL	0.2045	2.076	0.2834	0.3035
	(2.247)	(2.166)	(2.749)	(2.682)
TERM	0.0044	0.0043	0.0029	−0.0084
	(0.687)	(0.636)	(0.407)	(−1.048)
GOT GIFT	0.0052	0.1012	0.1153	0.0333
	(0.061)	(1.115)	(1.197)	(0.320)
COSIGNER	0.2037	0.2148	0.2158	0.2256
	(1.117)	(1.101)	(1.048)	(0.977)
MINORITY	−0.5366	−0.3554	−0.3266	−0.2184
	(−6.398)	(−3.975)	(−3.430)	(−2.047)
AGE	−0.1403	−0.1653	−0.1834	−0.2006
	(−2.099)	(−2.333)	(−2.440)	(−2.448)
MALE	−0.1026	−0.1046	−0.1574	−0.1272
	(−1.198)	(−1.160)	(−1.638)	(−1.223)
MARRIED	0.1798	0.1837	0.2371	0.2736
	(2.541)	(2.450)	(2.982)	(3.167)
OWNER-OCCUPIED	0.3748	0.5212	0.3668	0.1699
	(2.297)	(3.004)	(1.936)	(0.863)
POOR TRACT	0.0767	0.0225	0.0112	0.0522
	(0.790)	(0.219)	(0.106)	(0.437)

Table 5.2
(continued)

Variable	Model 1	Model 2	Model 3	Model 4
MINORITY TRACT	−0.0398	−0.1165	−0.1324	−0.1289
	(−0.334)	(−0.926)	(−0.993)	(−0.871)
BANKRUPTCY		−0.7284	−0.7952	−0.2718
		(−6.987)	(−7.311)	(−2.046)
MORTGAGE CREDIT		−0.2079	−0.1761	−0.0537
		(−3.224)	(−2.578)	(−0.718)
CONSUMER CREDIT		−0.1701	−0.1656	0.0001
		(−9.042)	(−8.337)	(0.005)
UNABLE TO VERIFY			−1.747	−1.508
			(−13.58)	(−10.77)
MEETS GUIDELINES				1.943
				(14.84)
Intercept	2.246	3.007	3.296	1.224
	(7.070)	(8.492)	(8.654)	(2.817)

Note: *t*-statistics are given in parentheses. All models are estimated using probit analysis. APPROVE is the dependent variable.

simultaneous-equations technique that is appropriate for detecting a simple form of endogeneity when the dependent variable is binary (i.e., accept or reject).[10] This simple form of endogeneity arises when the unobservable factors in the equation to explain loan approval are correlated with the unobservable factors in an equation to explain one of the explanatory variables in the approval equation, that is, when some unobserved factors simultaneously influence both variables. The procedure we use allows us to calculate the correlation between unobservable factors across equations; a high value for this correlation indicates that endogeneity may be a serious problem.[11]

We consider first the case of "unable to verify," which may be endogenous because the probability of approval influences data verification efforts. We find that the across-equation correlation in unobserved factors is quite large (−0.574, with a *t*-statistic of 0.94). This correlation could arise either because some underwriting variables are omitted from the specification or because "unable to verify" is influenced by the probability of denial. In either case, a loan approval equation that treats "unable to verify" as exogenous will yield biased results, but the simultaneous-equations model we estimate will not. In this model, the estimated coefficient of "unable to verify" in the loan approval equation is −0.410 (*t*-statistic: 0.27), which is small and statistically insignificant. The coefficient of "unable to verify" without the endogeneity correction, -1.747 (t-statistic: 13.58), is obviously biased. Moreover, the estimated minority status coefficient is basically unaffected by the inclusion of "unable to verify" when this variable is treated as endogenous; to be specific, it changes only from -0.356 (t-statistic: 3.97) to -0.364 (3.68).[12] The probability of loan approval is 7.4 percentage points lower for minorities than for whites with "unable to verify" treated as endogenous, which is close to the 7.7-percentage-point effect we obtained based on a single-equation specification without the "unable to verify" variable.[13] We conclude that, when properly treated as endogenous, the "unable to verify" variable has little or no impact on the minority status coefficient, and we drop it from all further analysis.[14]

Now let us consider the "meets guidelines" variable, which may be endogenous because the actual underwriting outcome may influence a conclusion about whether an application meets a particular lender's guidelines. As a point of reference, the minority status coefficient in an equation that includes the "meets guidelines" variable but not the "unable to verify" variable is -0.245 (t-statistic: 2.43), and the effect of minority status on the probability of approval is -4.1 percentage points. Our simple simultaneous-equations procedure estimates that the correlation between the unobservable factors in the loan approval and "meets guidelines" equations is 0.214 (t-statistic: 0.81). The estimated minority status coefficient from a model in which "meets guidelines" is allowed both to be endogenous and to influence approval is -0.270 (t-statistic: 2.44), and the influence of minority status on the probability of approval is -6.5 percentage points. This "corrected" estimate of the impact of minority status on loan approval (-6.5 percentage points) is bracketed by the single-equation estimate with the "meets guidelines" variable included (-4.1 points) and the single-equation estimate with this variable excluded (-7.7 points), but it obviously is closer to the latter. Thus, treating "meets guidelines" as endogenous eliminates most of its impact on the minority status coefficient; correcting for the endogeneity of this variable makes a big difference.

This result may arise because this simultaneous-equations model is too simple. As noted earlier, Browne and Tootell (1995) contend that the "meets guidelines" variable represents an after-the-fact judgment concerning the entire loan file made when someone filled out the Boston Fed Study's survey. If this contention is correct, the issue is not simply whether unobservable factors are correlated across equations, but whether the loan approval decision itself influences the "meets guidelines" variable. Thus, we must ask whether denied applications are more likely than accepted applications to be coded as "does not meet guidelines," all else equal. If so, then one would have to reject the Day and Liebowitz (1996) claim that "meets guidelines" is determined entirely by additional credit history details.

A full examination of these issues requires a complex model in which both loan approval and the "meets guidelines" indicator depend on a loan officer's unobserved opinion concerning whether the applicant meets the lender's credit history standards and in which the "meets guidelines" statement by another bank employee could be influenced by the loan denial decision. With this formulation, the observed "meets guidelines" variable depends on both the approval decision and the variables describing the applicant's creditworthiness and the loan terms. Except for the influence of the loan approval decision, the process that determines the "meets guidelines" variable is assumed to be the same for the loan officer who makes the loan approval decision and the bank official who later fills out the survey form. The "meets guidelines" variable itself cannot influence the loan approval decision because it is set at a later point in time; instead, the loan approval model depends on the likelihood that the applicant would meet the lender's guidelines based on the estimated coefficients from the "meets guidelines" equation. We estimate such a model, and the results are presented in the first two columns of table 5.3.[15]

The estimation results reveal that loan approval has a large influence on the "meets guidelines" variable; the coefficient is 2.040 (t-statistic: 2.48).[16] This finding leads us to reject the view that lenders fill in the "meets guidelines" variable simply by comparing an applicant's external credit score with some standard. Moreover, the fact that an application is coded as meeting the lender's standards has a large influence on the likelihood of the loan's being approved; the coefficient is 0.437 (t-statistic: 8.33). The estimated minority status coefficient in the approval equation after controlling for the likelihood that the original loan officer felt that the application met the lender's standards is -0.248 (t-statistic: 2.60), and the effect of minority status on the probability of approval is -5.3 percentage points. Thus, the effect of minority status on the loan approval probability is still bracketed by the results from the two

Table 5.3
Results for simultaneous-equations estimation

Variable	Model 1: APPROVE	Model 1: MEETS GUIDELINES	Model 2: APPROVE
EXPENSE-TO-INCOME	0.0076	−0.0050	0.0076
	(1.390)	(−0.594)	(1.257)
DEBT-TO-INCOME	−3.029	−0.2148	−3.025
	(−7.183)	(−0.216)	(−7.134)
NET WORTH	−0.0099	0.0299	−0.0099
	(−0.435)	(0.504)	(−0.389)
PREDICTED	−0.0187	−0.0250	−0.0187
UNEMPLOYMENT	(−1.285)	(−0.950)	(−1.193)
SELF EMPLOYED	−0.2890	0.1380	−0.2884
	(−2.784)	(0.727)	(−2.476)
LTV60_80	−0.0439	−0.5074	−0.0441
	(−0.314)	(−1.703)	(−0.285)
LTV80_95	−0.1332	−0.5828	−0.1332
	(−0.911)	(−1.923)	(−0.765)
LTV95	−0.5227	−0.3525	−0.5225
	(−3.165)	(−0.979)	(−2.778)
DENIED PMI	−2.548	−0.2754	−2.548
	(−9.395)	(−0.424)	(−9.507)
MULTI-FAMILY	−0.3561	0.3201	−0.3567
	(−3.486)	(1.750)	(−3.165)
FIXED RATE	−0.1985	0.3014	−0.1980
	(−2.499)	(2.398)	(−2.278)
SPECIAL	0.3059	−0.2247	0.3057
	(3.253)	(−1.342)	(2.906)
TERM	−0.0096	0.0318	−0.0096
	(−1.463)	(2.794)	(−1.165)
GOT GIFT	−0.0064	0.2469	−0.0065
	(−0.072)	(1.597)	(−0.059)
COSIGNER	0.2757	−0.1396	0.2757
	(1.224)	(−0.400)	(1.338)
MINORITY	−0.2477	−0.2466	−0.2477
	(−2.599)	(−1.455)	(−2.755)
AGE	−0.1715	0.0145	−0.1716
	(−2.271)	(0.122)	(−2.426)
MALE	−0.0480	−0.1299	−0.0479
	(−0.517)	(−0.840)	(−0.480)
MARRIED	0.2188	−0.0799	0.2186
	(2.832)	(−0.627)	(2.582)
OWNER-OCCUPIED	0.3654	0.3609	0.3637
	(2.085)	(1.569)	(2.001)

Table 5.3
(continued)

Variable	Model 1: APPROVE	Model 1: MEETS GUIDELINES	Model 2: APPROVE
POOR TRACT	−0.0032	0.0573	−0.0025
	(−0.029)	(0.346)	(−0.023)
MINORITY TRACT	−0.1059	−0.0247	−0.1057
	(−0.803)	(−0.117)	(−0.781)
BANKRUPTCY	−0.3107	−0.9565	−0.3109
	(−2.340)	(−4.134)	(−2.179)
MORTGAGE CREDIT	−0.0881	−0.2746	−0.0880
	(−1.249)	(−2.483)	(−1.235)
MEETS GUIDELINES	0.4366		0.4364
	(8.327)		(8.587)
CONSUMER CREDIT		−0.3897	
		(−7.377)	
APPROVE		2.040	
		(2.478)	
Intercept	1.547	3.347	1.547
	(4.136)	(4.553)	(3.459)

Note: t-statistics are given in parentheses. All models are estimated using probit analysis.

single-equation specifications, one excluding and the other including the "meets guidelines" variable. In other words, "meets guidelines" is clearly influenced by the approval decision but still has some impact on the minority status coefficient even when this influence is taken into account.

Because we are ultimately interested in only the loan approval equation, not the "meets guidelines" equation, we also explore a simpler estimating procedure that could be used in our subsequent analysis. To be specific, we use the results of our complex estimating procedure to construct a variable, based solely on exogenous information, to measure the likelihood that an applicant meets a lender's credit standards, as seen by the original loan officer. In other words, we "cleanse" the usual "meets guidelines" variable of any influence that flows from the loan approval decision. As shown in the third column of table 5.3, the introduction of this cleansed variable into a single-equation estimate of loan denial yields coefficient estimates that are very similar to those obtained with our more complicated simultaneous-equations procedure. Moreover, the effect of minority status on loan approval in the simplified procedure is still highly significant, and its magnitude, -5.6 percentage points, is almost the same as the effect with the full model, -5.3 percentage points. In subsequent models we estimate, therefore, we make use of the simpler procedure.

5.2.4 Interpreting the "Meets Guidelines" Results

This is not quite the end of the story, however, because the impact of the "meets guidelines" variable on the minority status coefficient in the approval equation could have two different causes. The first possible cause is omitted variables. As noted earlier, Horne (1994) and Day and Liebowitz (1996) propose that the Boston Fed Study's loan denial equation omits crucial credit history variables that are captured by the "meets guidelines" variable. Under this interpretation, the inclusion of "meets guidelines" eliminates an omitted-variable bias that would otherwise exist in the loan denial (or loan approval) equation. Similarly, the "meets guidelines" variable might capture differences across lenders in the stringency of their underwriting guidelines, that is, in "lender toughness."[17]

If either of these causes is at work, then there should be a strong negative correlation between the unobservable factors in the loan approval equation and in the "meets guidelines" equation; after all, the argument is that unobserved lender or borrower characteristics that show up in the "meets guidelines" rating are omitted from (and therefore obviously unobserved in) the loan approval equation. This prediction is not supported by the evidence. In our simultaneous-equations procedure, the correlation between the unobserved factors in these two equations is only -0.032 (t-statistic: 0.070). Thus, we conclude that the issue here is not a simple omitted-variable problem.

The second possible cause of this impact is that the "meets guidelines" equation varies with minority status. This type of variation could have two different sources: bias in the evaluation of applications or variation in underwriting guidelines across lenders. The first source is new, but the second source was discussed in chapter 3. To be specific, chapter 3 pointed out that many factors might cause lenders to chose different underwriting guidelines: differences in market power, differences in market niches due to an adverse-selection problem, or differences in portfolio mix (lesson 4). It also pointed out that variation in underwriting guidelines results in difficult interpretation problems for a loan denial regression (lessons 5 and 9).

Consider the first of these sources, namely, the possibility that intergroup differences in "meets guidelines" arise because of discrimination in determining whether an applicant meets a lender's underwriting standards. This discrimination could exist at two different points in the process. First, the loan officer who processes an application might use tougher standards for minorities, so that the bank official who later answers the "meets guidelines" question on the survey form, and who reads the comments entered by the loan officer, systematically gives lower ratings to minority applicants. Second, the bank official who fills out the survey form may simply be less likely to say that a minority applicant meets the lender's standards than does a white applicant, even when the two applications are otherwise identical. The first type of behavior is obviously more troubling, but both types of behavior have the same impact on the "meets guidelines" variable. In particular, these types of behavior lead to a negative correlation between minority status and "meets guidelines," so the inclusion of the "meets guidelines" variable in an underwriting model may mask discrimination in the underwriting process. Moreover, the two types of behavior might interact. If the bank official filling out the survey form observes a case in which a minority applicant who actually meets the lender's guidelines is denied a loan by a discriminatory underwriter, then that official might indicate that the applicant failed to meet the guidelines as a rationale for the underwriter's earlier decision.[18]

Now consider the second possible source of intergroup differences in the "meets guidelines" variable, namely, that some lenders use underwriting guidelines that are particularly hard on applicants with characteristics that are relatively common among their minority applicants. Up to this point, our discussion has focused on disparate-treatment discrimination, which involves lenders' treating minority applicants differently than equally qualified white applicants. Underwriting differences across lenders then create the possibility that the system of mortgage underwriting within a metropolitan area has a disparate impact on minority borrowers. As explained in chapter 2, the key issue in this case is whether these differences have an economic rationale, or, to use the legal terminology, whether they can be justified on the basis of "business necessity." Underwriting guidelines that fail this test are said to involve disparate-impact discrimination.

Disparate-impact discrimination by some lenders clearly could result in a negative correlation between minority status and the probability than an application meets the lender's guidelines—and thus a significant coefficient for the (endogenous) "meets guidelines" variable in a loan approval regression. In this case, including the (endogenous) "meets guidelines" variable must be interpreted as a way to isolate disparate-treatment discrimination, not as a way to prevent the minority status coefficient from overstating discrimination. To put it another way, the coefficient of the "meets guidelines" variable may simply show how much of the minority status coefficient can be attributed to this type of disparate-impact discrimination.

This is still not the end of the story, of course, because differences in underwriting guidelines across lenders may be fully justified on the basis of business necessity, so that despite these differences, there is no disparate-impact discrimination. Even in this case, the "meets guidelines" equation could vary with minority status if blacks and Hispanics are not as successful as whites in selecting a lender that meets their credit needs. This "mismatch" would be picked up by the "meets guidelines" variable, so that including this variable in the loan approval equation might simply correct for the fact that different groups go to different lenders. The issue here is not that minorities simply go to "tougher" lenders or, indeed, to lenders with any particular characteristics; as just shown, the "meets guidelines" variable does not capture omitted variables in the loan approval equation. Instead, it reflects the possibility that black and Hispanic customers have poorer information than do white customers about the underwriting standards used by different lenders and therefore, on average, find a poorer match between their qualifications and the standards used by lenders to which they apply. In this case, white customers might be more likely than minority customers to be seen as meeting the lender's standards, even though no individual lender used different standards for minorities than for whites. As a result, adding the "meets guidelines" variable, treated endogenously, can be interpreted as a way to extract the portion of the minority status coefficient that reflects legitimate differences in underwriting guidelines, or, to put it another way, that is justified on the basis of business necessity.

A "mismatch" between the credit needs of minority borrowers and the lenders to which they apply does not involve any discrimination in loan approval, but it might involve discrimination in other lender behavior, such as preapplication counseling or loan marketing. After all, the key to this interpretation is that minorities have poorer information than whites about lenders' underwriting guidelines.[19] Such an information disparity could arise without any discrimination as defined by our civil rights laws. To use an example presented in chapter 2, one set of nondepository lenders offering one set of loan products might operate in minority neighborhoods, whereas another set of nondepository lenders offering another set of loan products might operate in white neighborhoods. On the other hand, such an information disparity might really reflect discrimination. As discussed in chapter 3, for example, some studies find that lenders provide more information to customers who inquire about loans when those customers are whites than when they are black or Hispanic. Moreover, several lenders have been found to have discriminated against minority neighborhoods in decisions about the opening or closing of branch offices (see Ritter, 1996; Lee, 2001).

This discussion leaves a bewildering set of possible interpretations for the results of a loan approval regression that includes the "meets guidelines" variable, treated as endogenous. These possibilities are summarized in table 5.4. Several of these possibilities involve discrimination by lenders, although only one of them, case II.B.1, involves discrimination, specifically, disparate-impact discrimination, in the loan approval decision.

5.2.5 Conclusions

The dilemma we face at this point is that we do not know which interpretation in table 5.4 is correct. We can rule out cases I.A and I.B because, as noted earlier, the unobserved factors in the loan approval and "meets guidelines" equations are not correlated, as these cases require. Moreover, as explained earlier, case I.B is definitively ruled out by the use of lender dummy variables in Munnell et al. and by the fact that, even without these dummies, a "lender toughness" variable has no impact on the minority status coefficient.

Table 5.4
Interpreting the MEETS GUIDELINES variable

I. MEETS GUIDELINES captures omitted dimensions of underwriting

    A. MEETS GUIDELINES captures omitted credit history variables.
[No discrimination]

    B. MEETS GUIDELINES reflects variation in lender "toughness."
[No discrimination]

II. Determinants of MEETS GUIDELINES vary with minority status

    A. Lender evaluations of applications involve bias

        1. Loan officers who process applications may use a tougher standard for minorities. [Discrimination in processing applications]

        2. Bank officials who filled out the Boston Fed Study's survey form may be less likely to say that a minority applicant meets the lender's guidelines than that a white applicant does, even when the two applications are otherwise identical. [Discrimination in evaluating loan files]

        3. Bank officials who filled out the Boston Fed Study's survey form may rationalize the loan officer's decision to deny a loan to a qualified minority applicant by saying that the applicant failed to meet the lender's guidelines. [Discrimination in processing applications and in evaluating loan files]

    B. Underwriting guidelines vary across lenders

        1. Differences in underwriting guidelines *are not* based on "business necessity." [Disparate-impact discrimination in loan approval]

        2. Differences in underwriting guidelines *are* based on "business necessity" and minorities have a poorer match than do whites between their lender and their credit qualifications.

            a. The minority mismatch with lenders is caused by illegal lender behavior. [Discrimination in preapplication procedures and loan marketing]

            b. The minority mismatch with lenders is caused by legal disparities in lender marketing. [No discrimination by lenders]

            c. The minority mismatch with lenders reflects discrimination by the people other than lenders who participate in mortgage markets, such as real estate brokers, and discrimination stemming from intergroup disparities, such as those in education, that reflect past discrimination. [No current discrimination by lenders]

This moves us into the second set of cases, in which the "meets guidelines" equation varies with minority status. We do not know, however, which of these cases applies. Two of these cases, namely, II.B.2.b and II.B.2.c, do not involve any current discrimination by lenders. If either of these cases applies, then "meets guidelines" should be introduced as an endogenous variable in the loan approval regression. Moreover, the impact of this step on the minority status coefficient can then be interpreted as the overstatement of discrimination, caused by omitting the "meets guidelines" variable.

In this case, therefore, the procedure near the end of section 5.2.2 implies that the Boston Fed Study overstates lender discrimination by 45.3 percent $[(7.7 - 5.3)/5.3]$.[20]

Of the other cases, one, namely, II.B.1, involves discrimination in loan approval; all of the others involve discrimination in some other type of lender behavior. Case II.B.2.a involves discrimination in preapplication procedures and loan marketing. This case calls for the same estimating method as cases II.B.2.b and II.B.2.c, although the results obviously have a different interpretation. In particular, the impact of the (endogenous) "meets guidelines" variable on the minority status coefficient can, if case II.B.2.a holds, be interpreted as an indication of the extent to which intergroup disparities in loan approval reflect lender discrimination in the earlier stages of the mortgage process. Under this interpretation, for example, the above result implies that 45.3 percent of the discrimination uncovered by the Boston Fed Study is really discrimination in preapplication procedures and loan marketing, not discrimination in loan approval.

Case II.B.1 and the three cases under II.A require a procedure that does not build discrimination, either disparate-impact discrimination (case II.B.1) or discrimination in deciding who meets the lender's guidelines (all cases under II.A), into the "meets guidelines" variable. Thus, the correct procedure in all these other cases involves the introduction into the loan approval equation of a minority status–neutral "meets guidelines" variable indicating the likelihood that a candidate meets the lender's guidelines. In other words, this variable must not be influenced by observed differences in this likelihood based on minority status, after controlling for other observable factors. Such a procedure can reveal whether omitting the non-discriminatory component of "meets guidelines" results in an overstatement of discrimination.

Under this alternative procedure, the "meets guidelines" variable no longer has a substantial impact on the minority status coefficient. To be specific, the minority status coefficient in an equation with a cleansed and minority status–neutral variable for "meets guidelines" is -0.355 (t-statistic: 3.81), and the impact of minority status on the probability of approval is -7.3 percentage points. This estimated impact is, of course, close to the estimated impact for a single-equation specification that omits the meets guidelines variable altogether, namely, -7.7 points.

As this stage in our analysis, we do not have any evidence to determine which of these possibilities reflects the actual reality of the situation. Moreover, no study has yet identified the type of behavior that leads to the cases under II.B.2, so it is difficult to determine whether any of these cases might apply. The most direct explanation for these cases is that something in the market limits the ability of minority borrowers to uncover lender underwriting standards and to identify the lender that best fits their specific characteristics and credit needs. This explanation can be valid only if lenders differ in the underwriting weights they place on various applicant, property, and loan characteristics. The resulting type of mismatch between minority applicants and lenders might arise, for example, if minority households tend to apply to lenders that specialize in lending to minorities and these lenders, ironically, have underwriting guidelines that are relatively unfavorable to minority households. The available evidence, however, does not support a key implication of this explanation, namely, that the minority-white difference in loan approval should be larger among lenders that specialize in lending to minorities.[21] Alternatively, minority borrowers might simply have less information about lenders and therefore choose a lender who is a relatively poor fit for their characteristics and needs, regardless of whether they apply to a lender that specializes in serving minority households. Evidence on this possibility is not yet available.[22]

In short, we cannot yet determine whether it is appropriate to include the "meets guidelines" variable in a loan approval regression, even when it is treated as endogenous. One possibility is that the decline in the absolute value of the minority status coefficient caused by including an (endogenous) "meets guidelines" variable reflects a correlation between discrimination in loan approval and other types of discrimination, which are identified in part II.A of table 5.4. Thus, this decline may not imply that the Boston Fed Study overstates lender discrimination, but may instead reflect biases caused by introducing an inappropriate variable. It is also possible, however, that there exists some kind of minority mismatch with lenders so that it is appropriate to include an endogenous "meets guidelines" variable. In this case, the impact on the minority-status coefficient of including such a variable has two possible interpretations, with no way to determine which one applies.[23] The first interpretation, which follows case II.B.2.b or II.B.2.c, is that the Boston Fed Study overstates discrimination. The second, which follows case II.B.2.a, is that it accurately states overall discrimination but fails to recognize that this discrimination occurs in preapplication procedures and loan marketing, as well as in loan approval.

To account for the range of possibilities concerning the "meets guidelines" variable, we explore all other potential flaws in Munnell et al. (1996) using three models of the loan approval equation. Model 1 includes the "meets guidelines" variable in a single-equation estimation, Model 2 replaces the original "meets guidelines" variable with a cleansed (but not minority status–neutral) version of the variable, and Model 3 excludes the "meets guidelines" variable from a single-equation estimation. Model 1 provides an unrealistically low measure of discrimination, because it ignores the possibility (supported by evidence presented here) that the "meets guidelines" variable is endogenous, so that including it as an exogenous variable leads to an underestimate of discrimination. Model 2 accounts for this possible endogeneity and provides the most accurate estimate of discrimination in loan approval if the observed across-group differences in the "meets guidelines" equation have nothing to do with discrimination. This model also covers case II.B.2.a, in which the "meets guidelines" variable extracts discrimination in preapplication behavior and loan marketing from the minority status coefficient. Model 3 provides the most accurate estimate of discrimination if there exists either disparate-impact discrimination (case II.B.1) or discrimination in determining who meets a lender's guidelines (the three cases under II.A).

The first row of table 5.5 reviews our estimates of discrimination in loan approval for the baseline version of these three models. In particular, this table indicates that the estimated impacts of minority status on loan approval in these three models are −4.1, −5.6, and −7.7 percent, respectively. All of these estimates are highly significant statistically (significant at the 5-percent level or above using a two-tailed test). We believe that models 2 and 3 impose bounds on the estimated minority status effect for reasonable alternative assumptions about the "meets guidelines" variable. The assumptions behind Model 1 are not so reasonable, but results from this model are still instructive. They reveal that even if, despite the evidence to the contrary, the strongest claims of the critics about "meets guidelines" are correct, then blacks and Hispanics still face a significantly lower probability of loan approval than do equally qualified whites.

Table 5.5
Impact of minority status on loan approval for various models (in Percentage Points)

	Model 1	Model 2	Model 3
1. Basic model	−4.1	−5.6	−7.7
2. No applications that were reconsidered by the lender	−7.1	−10.0	−12.0
3. No condos or multifamily houses	−5.1	−7.0	−9.0
4. No applications with PMI denied or special program	−6.4	−6.4	−9.0
5. Use actual LTV, not LTV categories	−4.3	−6.0	−8.1
6. Use actual LTV and treat it as endogenous	−4.2	−5.3	−7.7
7. Treat LTV and housing expense–to–income ratio as endogenous	−4.4	−5.1	−8.6
8. No applications for special programs	−5.7	−7.2	−9.5
9. Estimation conditional on choice of a special program	−6.6	−8.0	−11.1

Note: Model 1 includes the MEETS GUIDELINES variable, with no correction for endogeneity; model 2 includes the MEETS GUIDELINES variable, with a correction for endogeneity; model 3 excludes the MEETS GUIDELINES variable. All entries in this table are based on regression coefficients that are statistically significant at the 5-percent level (two-tailed test) or above.

5.3   Data Errors in the Explanatory Variables

Loan files contain a great deal of information, some of which may be inconsistent or recorded with error. Thus, any study of loan approval faces a major challenge in obtaining data that are relatively free of errors, particularly errors that might influence analysis results, such as the estimated minority status coefficient.

5.3.1   The Critics' Claims

Liebowitz (1993), Horne (1994, 1997), Zycher and Wolfe (1994) and Day and Liebowitz (1996) present evidence of errors in loan terms and in other application characteristics in the Boston Fed Study's data. They claim that these errors lead to biased results and, in particular, to an overstatement of discrimination.

Horne focuses on a subsample of the Boston Fed Study's data. This subsample begins with a set of applications provided to the FDIC to help it explore the underwriting policies of the lenders it oversees. This set was made up of all rejected loan applications in which the predicted denial probability based on a statistical model was below

50 percent: the so-called exceptions list. The subsample examined by Horne consisted of applications on the exceptions list that were filed with lenders that had at least one minority rejection on the exceptions list. Horne (1994) claims that he identified many coding errors in the Boston Fed Study's data in this subsample. Munnell et al. (1996) and Browne and Tootell (1995) obtained Horne's corrected data, reestimated the original Boston Fed Study equations using these data (along with the observations that Horne did not correct), and found no substantial effect on the minority status coefficient.[24]

Leibowitz and Day and Leibowitz analyze the public-use version of the Boston Fed Study's data set, which is the same data set we use, and identify many observations that appear to have unreasonable values, such as a large negative net worth, an LTV above 0.8 without an application for PMI, a low or negative imputed interest rate, an annual income that does not match monthly incomes, or obligation ratios that are inconsistent with other variables. They conclude that these problems cast doubt on the integrity of the Boston Fed Study's data—and hence on the credibility of the results based on it.

In addition, Day and Leibowitz reexamine the Boston Fed Study's data after removing observations with questionable interest rates.[25] The impact of minority status on loan denial drops from 0.0325 (t-statistic: 2.45) to 0.0293 (t-statistic: 2.12) when observations with interest rates above 14 percent or below 5 percent are deleted. This coefficient drops to 0.0249 (t-statistic: 1.69) when observations with interest rates above 12 or below 7 percent are deleted.[26]

Munnell et al. (1996), Browne and Tootell (1995), and Tootell (1996b) argue that many of these problems are not errors at all. Some applicants actually have negative net worth, and the Boston Fed Study used the monthly incomes in the actual loan files, not the more problematical annual income in the HMDA data. Moreover, even though secondary-market institutions generally require PMI when LTV is above 0.8, a lending institution may not impose this requirement if it does not intend to sell the loan on the secondary market. The Boston Fed Study's authors also explain that they contacted lenders to verify the accuracy of the information in many applications with unusual values and corrected many extreme values before conducting their regressions.

The Boston Fed Study's authors also note that interest rates must be imputed from housing expense, loan term, and loan amount. This procedure does not work well for multifamily units, they say, and most of the applications with very low imputed interest rates are for loans on multifamily units. It also does not work well for applications with very low LTVs, which are the applications that tend to have very high interest rates. In addition, they point out that the obligation ratios used in the Boston Fed Study were taken directly from each lender's worksheets in the loan files. Browne and Tootell and Tootell also estimate several alternative models that omit observations with unusual values, with little or no impact on the minority status coefficient.

Browne and Tootell (1995) also argue that the critics of the Boston Fed Study cannot eliminate the statistical significance of the minority status coefficient without combining a large set of questionable steps. In fact, this coefficient becomes insignificant only if one eliminates a large number of observations because of potential data errors, includes both "unable to verify" and "meets guidelines," and takes a strong position concerning possible misclassification in the dependent variable. For example, Liebowitz (1993) claims that the minority status coefficient is not significant in a sample of single-family homes with LTVs below 0.8 if six influential outliers are eliminated. However, Browne and Tootell show that this subsample contains only fourteen minority denials to begin with (out of the original 200 in the Boston Fed Study's data), and yet Liebowitz must still eliminate almost half of those observations to eliminate the impact of minority status.

These claims are supported by Carr and Megbolugbe (1993), who clean the Boston Fed Study's data by removing observations with very high LTVs or inconsistencies between housing expenses and debt payments and by performing various other consistency checks. They also delete all observations with imputed interest rates either above 20 percent or below 3 percent. In all, Carr and Megbolugbe delete 1,045 observations out of 2,816. The results of the analysis of data obtained under this procedure do not support the claim that data errors lead to an overstatement of discrimination; in fact, the estimated effect of minority status actually increases when these observations are deleted.

In addition, Carr and Megbolugbe acknowledge that many of their so-called inconsistencies may not be data errors at all. About 800 of their deletions are for one of three reasons: the HMDA and Boston Fed Study's income variables are not consistent, the housing expense–to–income ratio is not consistent with house expense and income considered separately, and the house price is greater than the loan amount plus liquid assets plus other money available. As noted earlier, differences between these income sources probably reflect problems in the HMDA data, not in the Boston Fed Study's data. Moreover, the housing expense–to–income ratio often includes adjustments to account for the temporary nature of some income or the uncertain nature of rental income in multifamily houses. Finally, the house price may exceed apparent resources because the applicant plans to make a down payment with equity from a house that he has not yet sold.

5.3.2 Evaluation

Overall, the key finding of the Boston Fed Study appears to be remarkably unaffected by corrections in the explanatory variables, both corrections that take the form of cleaning individual variables and those that take the form of dropping observations with extreme values on some variables. As shown particularly by Carr and Megbolugbe (1993), this conclusion holds for a wide range of variables and alternative cleansing procedures.

The only possible exception appears in Day and Leibowitz (1996), which finds that the estimated minority status coefficient declines by 24 percent when one drops observations with an imputed interest rate above 12 or below 7 percent. On the surface, at least, this data correction exercise appears to be independent of minority status, so it warrants further explanation. Moreover, the explanation provided by Browne and Tootell (1995) concerning problems with the imputation process for multifamily properties and for applications with low LTVs is not very satisfying. The estimated minority status coefficient is not affected by the elimination of applications for multifamily properties and with low LTVs.[27] If these applications are the ones with unreasonable interest rates, why does filtering out unreasonable interest rates affect the minority status coefficient?

5.3.3 Reanalysis

To check the Day and Leibowitz (1996) claim that the minority status coefficient is no longer significant when observations with extreme interest rates are dropped, we devised our own procedure for imputing interest rates. The formula for a mortgage is well known; it expresses the mortgage amount as a function of the monthly payment, the interest rate, and the term of the mortgage.[28] Interest rates are not included in the Boston Fed Study's data set, but this formula can be used to calculate the interest rate on a particular loan using data on the mortgage amount, monthly payment, and term. The Boston Fed Study's data set includes the mortgage amount and term. It also includes monthly housing expense, but this variable includes property taxes and homeowner's insurance in addition to the monthly mortgage payment. This variable also includes condominium fees, and, in the case of multifamily housing, it is reduced by the expected rent from other units. One cannot estimate the interest rate, therefore, without making assumptions about these other components of the monthly housing expense variable.

Our procedure begins by dropping condominiums and multifamily units from the sample, as well as units with missing information on term, monthly housing expense, or loan amount. The resulting sample has 1,780 applications; with this sample the effects of minority status on the probability of approval in our three models are −5.1, −7.0, and −9.0 percentage points (See the third row of table 5.5). To cover a range of possibilities, we explore cases in which the sum of annual taxes and insurance expenses equals −2.0, −2.5, and −3.0 percent of the house price (equivalent to 20, 25, and 30 mills, respectively). Finally, we examine different possible interest rate cutoffs, in each case discarding observations with interest rates that are above one threshold or below another.

The results of these estimations reveal no clear pattern. When we use Day and Leibowitz's criteria of imputed interest rates between 7 and 12 percent, we delete between 20 and 40 percent of the sample, depending on the assumption we make about housing expense. Under the 20-mill assumption, the minority status effects with our three models are −3.9, −6.7, and −8.7 percentage points, and the minority status coefficient in the first model is significant only at the 10-percent level. Under the 25-mill assumption, the minority status effects are −1.9, −4.6, and −6.8 percentage points, and the minority status coefficients in the first two models are both insignificant. Under the 30-mill assumption, however, the minority status effects are −6.7, −8.0, and −10.2 points, and the minority status coefficients are highly significant in all three models. To make matters more confusing, when we use Day and Leibowitz's criteria of imputed interest rates between 5 and 14 percent, the largest minority status effects (−4.5, −6.7, and −8.6 points) occur under the 25-mill assumption, which was the mill rate that made the minority status coefficient go away with the alternative interest rate cutoffs, and the minority status coefficients are statistically significant in all three models.

5.3.4 Conclusions

The Boston Fed Study's data set is large and complicated and may contain some errors in the explanatory variables. The study's authors made extensive efforts, however, to check the data and to investigate the possible impacts of errors on their results. Several other scholars have also performed various tests for the possible impacts of data errors on the results. All reasonable tests support the Boston Fed Study's conclusion. Thus, there is no reason to think that errors in the explanatory variables lead the Boston Fed Study to overstate the extent of discrimination.

Day and Liebowitz (1996) make the reasonable suggestion that one way to check the accuracy of the data in a mortgage lending study is to determine whether, using the standard mortgage formula, the payment, term, and mortgage amount imply a reasonable mortgage interest rate. This suggestion cannot be implemented in a compelling way, however, with a data set, such as the one used for the Boston Fed Study, that does not include information on the mortgage payment. Because it is impossible to impute interest rates accurately without observing actual mortgage payments, any imputation procedure introduces measurement error, perhaps substantial error, into the interest rate variable. Any check based on such an imputation will identify many observations as having a data error when, in fact, there is nothing more than an error in the imputation procedure. Thus, we do not find it surprising that the application of this procedure leads to such confusing results.

More importantly, this type of procedure opens the door to another potentially serious source of bias in estimating the impact of minority status on loan approval. If minorities tend to live in areas with relatively high property taxes and insurance rates, for example, then assuming a low mill rate for tax and insurance costs may disproportionately—and inappropriately—filter out minority applications. Moreover, property taxes and insurance rates are undoubtedly negatively correlated with loan approval, so this filtering process is correlated with the dependent variable. As is well established (see Greene, 2000), any sample selection process that is correlated with the dependent variable creates a sample selection bias in the estimated coefficients. Thus, an interest rate filter seems far more likely to create a sample selection bias than to eliminate measurement error.

5.4   Misclassification in the Dependent Variable

A lender's decision concerning a particular loan application cannot be adequately characterized with a dichotomous approve-or-deny variable. In some cases, rather than simply accept or deny an application, the lender makes a counteroffer to the borrower with a loan amount that is somewhat smaller than the borrower's request. Moreover, this counteroffer can be accepted by the buyer, or the buyer can apply again at yet another loan amount, or the buyer can withdraw. Decisions about the way to handle this type of complexity might influence the results of a loan approval study.

5.4.1   The Critics' Claims

Several authors have argued that the results in the Boston Fed Study are biased because the study's data misclassify the outcome of many applications (See Horne, 1994, 1997; Day and Liebowitz, 1996). The Boston Fed Study's authors were themselves concerned about this issue and address several aspects of it (Munnell et al., 1996). Their basic model excludes applications that were withdrawn before the lender made a decision about them; they support this approach by showing that the factors determining withdrawals are very different from those determining loan denials. Moreover, they checked their final data set data carefully to remove "[r]efinancings, home improvement loans, and some business loans that institutions had mistakenly coded as mortgage originations in their original filings" (p. 31).

Based on the FDIC review conducted to assess underwriting policies, Horne (1994, 1997) argues that many apparently rejected loan applications on the exceptions list should not be considered "denied" applications. The FDIC reviewed files on 62 minority and 33 white loan applications that had been rejected (see section 5.3.1).

Out of these Horne (1994) identifies five applications (three minority and two white) that were actually approved; eight applications (six minority and two white) that were withdrawn prior to an accept/reject decision; six minority loan applications to which the bank made a counteroffer that was turned down by the applicant; five minority loans applications in which the applicant applied for a special-program loan and was overqualified; one minority application that was rejected because the VA would not approve the loan; and one minority application that was rejected because PMI was denied.

Day and Liebowitz (1996) find that the removal of these 26 applications (plus two others that they identify as being in a bank-specific special program) from the Boston Fed Study's sample reduces the impact of minority status on loan denial by 39 percent from 0.0531 (t-statistic: 3.96) to 0.0325 (t-statistic: 2.45). Even after this step, however, the estimated coefficient is still significant at the 1-percent level. Day and Liebowitz nevertheless observe that the FDIC reviewed only a small number of applications from the Boston Fed Study sample and argue that reviews of additional files in that sample would certainly yield additional errors and that these errors, taken together, might account for the significance of the minority status variable in the Boston Fed Study.

Horne (1997) also examines the effect of observations with a potentially misclassified dependent variable using just the FDIC subsample of the Boston Fed Study's data. First, Horne drops 111 observations because the application had one of the following characteristics: it was withdrawn, it involved a unit under construction, it involved refinancing, it was an investor application, it involved an applicant who was overqualified for a special program, or it had an LTV below 0.30. He also recoded four applications in the subsample as approvals, arguing that they had been incorrectly coded as denials. The impact of minority status on loan denial for the entire FDIC subsample is 1.12 and is highly significant statistically. After observations are deleted and recoded as discussed above, the minority status coefficient falls to 0.67 but is still significant at the 1-percent level. Next, Horne drops 61 applications in which he believes that the outcome is ambiguous. (For example, counteroffers were made by some lenders and turned down by applicants, or applicants were denied PMI. The FDIC file reviews also uncovered other instances in which the lender appeared to be willing to provide credit, but the transaction was precluded by outside factors, such as title problems or housing code violations.) The exclusion of these applications and some modifications to the model specification result in a minority status coefficient of 0.35 that is no longer statistically significant at even the 10-percent level.

The Boston Fed Study's authors follow the HMDA reporting requirements and consider counteroffers that are accepted to be approvals and counteroffers that are denied to be rejections. They argue that an accepted counteroffer implies that the borrower received credit based on his application package and his preferences. A rejected counteroffer implies that the lender was not willing to provide a loan at terms that were acceptable to the borrower. Not all counteroffers may be equal. Some counteroffers may involve small changes to the terms of the loan, whereas others may involve dramatic changes. The data contain no information concerning the magnitude of the change proposed by lenders in their counteroffers, so, according to Munnell et al., the fact that a counteroffer was accepted is the best available indicator that the change involved in that counteroffer was minimal.

Horne (1994, 1997) proposes that all counteroffers should be considered acceptances, because a counteroffer indicates that the lender is willing to provide credit. He goes on to claim that the effect of minority status would probably decline considerably if counteroffers were treated in this manner. As he puts it (1994, p. 7), "to the extent that some counteroffers are reasonable, an approach that classifies all rejected counteroffers as lender denials is likely to exaggerate the race effect to the extent that minorities receive a disproportionate number of counteroffers." One could also argue, however, that all counteroffers should be considered rejections, because the lender was not willing to provide credit based on the terms in the application package, which are in fact the terms that are included in the Boston Fed Study's data set.

A study of an alternative sample yields some insight into the issues raised by Horne. Stengel and Glennon (1999) examine applications from three different lenders. They find, on average, a significant impact of minority status on loan denial.[29] They identified all applications in which the applicant rejected the bank's counteroffer and all files in which the applicants were determined to be overqualified for special loan programs to which they had applied. The deletion of all of these applications did not affect their findings.

Moreover, they review all denied files at one lender. They detected forty-one withdrawals that had been previously missed. The deletion of these withdrawals did not affect the estimated minority status coefficient for that bank.

An alternative approach is to see if the Boston Fed Study's results are driven by a few "influential" observations. If so, a few data errors or misclassifications might drive the results. Rodda and Wallace (1996) rank applications in the Boston Fed Study sample according to their influence on the minority status coefficient. Most of the highly influential applications are minority denials, and the elimination of the twenty-three most influential minority denials causes the minority status coefficient to become insignificant. Rodda and Wallace conduct this analysis to determine which applications should be subject to file review, not to determine whether estimates of discrimination are flawed. Moreover, they point out that this finding is driven predominantly by sample size: There are nearly four times as many white applications as minority applications, and most applications are approved. A related approach that focuses on outliers in a broader sense is provided by Carr and Megbolugbe (1993), who calculate the influence of every observation on the minority status coefficient and on all other coefficients. They exclude twenty-seven applications that are highly influential on either measure and find that the minority status coefficient does not change.

5.4.2 Evaluation

In the Boston Fed Study's data, as in any large, complex data set, it is reasonable to explore the accuracy and interpretation of the information, as Horne and Day and Liebowitz have done. Many of the cases that they identify as "errors", however, are in fact cases that raise issues of interpretation about which reasonable people may disagree.

Consider first the issue of counteroffers. We find the interpretation of counteroffers by Munnell et al. to be entirely reasonable, although not the only interpretation possible. Moreover, it is important to remember that the loan officer may play an important role in encouraging or discouraging the borrower to apply or reapply, matching the borrower to a loan product, or guiding the borrower through the application process. One cannot ignore the possibility that a loan officer's reaction to a borrower's minority status influences the likelihood that a borrower receives a counteroffer and the nature of that counteroffer (lesson 8 in chapter 3). As a result, we are not ready to accept Horne's claim that all "reasonable" counteroffers should be treated as acceptances.

As noted earlier, Horne also argues that excluding rejected counteroffers leads to an overstatement of the minority status effect whenever minorities receive more counteroffers than whites. A key question, therefore, is whether counteroffers are tilted toward minorities. Schafer and Ladd (1981) provide some evidence on this point. As discussed in chapter 4, they have somewhat different information for New York and California. In California, they observe when a loan is approved at a lower amount than requested and when it is approved at a higher amount than requested. Although Schafer and Ladd cannot identify withdrawn applications in this data set, the counteroffers that are rejected by the borrowers are not likely to be the ones involving an amount higher than the borrower's request; after all, a borrower need not borrow the entire amount. In the California data, therefore, the question is whether minorities are more likely than whites to receive an approval at an amount lower than requested. Schafer and Ladd find that they are not; the probability of downward modification is the same for whites and minorities in virtually all of the sixteen metropolitan areas they studied.[30]

For most metropolitan areas in Schafer and Ladd's New York data, all modifications are lumped together, so it is not possible to focus on the counteroffers that are treated as denials in the Boston Fed Study.[31] In the case of New York City, however, Schafer and Ladd are able to identify applications withdrawn after a counteroffer. They find that the probability of modification followed by withdrawal is not significantly different for blacks and whites, but is significantly higher for Hispanics than for whites (table 7.9). With the exception of this last result for Hispanics in New York City, therefore, the results in Schafer and Ladd indicate that counteroffers unacceptable to the buyer are not more common for minorities than for whites. Even if one agrees with Horn's view that these counteroffers should be treated as acceptances, therefore, it seems unlikely that this step would alter the Boston Fed Study's main result.

There is obviously room for more research on this topic.[32] The evidence in Schafer and Ladd refers to an earlier decade and different metropolitan areas than the data in the Boston Fed Study. Moreover, the circumstances that lead to counteroffers, the range of provisions contained in counteroffers, and the factors determining these provisions remain largely unexplored. Research on these issues would undoubtedly shed light on the role of counteroffers in estimating discrimination in loan approval.

A second issue concerns the insights to be gained by examining the applications on the FDIC's exceptions list. In our view, the selection process the FDIC used to identify files within the Boston Fed Study's sample for review makes this list inappropriate for assessing the validity of the Boston Fed Study. This selection process was designed to help bank examiners, not to shed light on a loan approval equation. For example, the FDIC did not review files at lenders that did not reject any minority applications. As a result, two-thirds of the files reviewed are minority rejections, despite that fact that over half of the rejections in the Boston Fed sample are applications from whites. This feature of the FDIC exceptions list makes it inappropriate for use in a loan approval equation. The FDIC's exclusive focus on rejected applications also is problematic for estimation purposes; after all, some, even many, denied or withdrawn applications could have been miscoded as approvals. Similarly, the Boston Fed Study's data set may include underqualified minority applicants who were approved because they applied for a special program. Overall, Day and Liebowitz's and Horne's filtering of the data and the resulting conclusions must be rejected because they are not based on a random sample of the applications in the Boston Fed Study's data. Indeed, alternative approaches to possible misclassification due to counteroffers and withdrawals that are neutral with respect to minority status, such as the one in Stengel and Glennon (1999), find that misclassification has little or no impact on the relationship between minority status and loan denial.

Finally, studies such as Rodda and Wallace (1996) that identify and drop "influential" observations also do not shed much light on data errors or misclassification, although they might be useful for other purposes. In particular, it is not surprising that minority denials have the most influence on the minority status coefficient in the Boston Fed Study; after all, this coefficient is supposed to determine whether applications with this outcome are treated differently than comparable white applications. Moreover, it is not surprising that the list of influential observations did not include any white approvals, the effects of which are "watered down" by the presence of so many similar observations. As a result, this type of analysis sheds no light whatsoever on the credibility of the Boston Fed Study's result. The study by Carr and Megbolugbe (1993) is more to the point, because it defines "influential" in a way that is relatively neutral with respect to minority status, but it also does not provide a compelling conceptual or methodological argument for dropping influential observations. We conclude that any procedure for identifying and dropping "influential" observations in a loan approval study, particularly one that defines "influence" by the impact on the minority status coefficient, is not appropriate for evaluating the role of errors or of misclassification in a study of mortgage lending discrimination.

5.4.3   Reanalysis

The public-use data from the Boston Fed Study contain some information to help shed light on the issues raised by Horne and by the FDIC file reviews. First, these data contain variables to indicate "whether an application for PMI was denied" and "whether a mortgage application was made for a special program." We find that dropping all applications coded affirmative for "PMI denied" or "application for special program" actually increases the negative impact of minority status on loan approval. For our three models and the full sample, the effects of minority status are −4.1, −5.6, and −7.7 percentage points. When these applications are dropped, the remaining sample contains 2,336 applications, the effects of minority status are −6.4, −6.4, and −9.0 percentage points, respectively, for the three models, and the estimated minority-status coefficient is highly significant in all three models (see row 4 of table 5.5).

Although the public-use version of the Boston Fed data does not contain information on withdrawals and rejected counteroffers, which were deleted from the sample, the study does contain information on the number of times a particular application was reconsidered by the lender. A reconsideration is likely to have been precipitated by modifications or clarifications made to the original application, perhaps in response either to a counteroffer made by the lender during this process or to suggestions made by the loan officer. Thus, one could think of reconsidered applications as examples of successful negotiations between the borrower and the lender, compared to counteroffers that resulted in withdrawn applications, which represent failed negotiations. Horne and Day and Liebowitz argue that the Boston Fed Study's findings are likely to be biased because minority applicants are overrepresented among the failed negotiations, which are treated as rejections, whereas white applicants are overrepresented among the successful negotiations, which are treated as acceptances. One way to test this argument is to drop all the applications that appear to involve negotiations, whether failed or successful. According to the Horne/Day-Liebowitz (henceforth HDL) hypothesis, this step should eliminate the upward bias in the minority status coefficient.

It should be noted that this test makes sense only if lenders bear no responsibility for the relatively high failure rate of negotiations with minority applicants. If some lenders simply refuse to negotiate with minority applicants, for example, then minority-white differences in the ultimate acceptance of counteroffers should affect the estimated minority status coefficient, and the procedure followed by the Boston Fed Study is entirely appropriate. In contrast, if some minority households simply refuse to negotiate with lenders, despite lenders' willingness to negotiate with them, then treating failed negotiations as rejections could bias the minority status effect upward. In other words, finding that the minority status effect decreases when applications involving negotiation are excluded is necessary but not sufficient for the HDL hypothesis to hold.

To test the HDL hypothesis, we first drop from the sample all applications that were considered four or more times (i.e, *recon*sidered three or more times), a sign of extensive negotiation, and reestimate the baseline models. This step, which results in a sample size of 2,717, changes the impact of minority status in our three loan approval models to -4.1, -6.7, and -8.4 percentage points. For the second two models, these effects are larger than our baseline estimates, which contradicts the HDL hypothesis, although the differences from the baseline estimates are not very large. As a further test, we drop all applications that were considered three or more times (i.e., *re*considered two or more times), resulting in a sample size of 2,301. According to the HDL hypothesis, this step should lower the bias still further and hence lower the estimated impact of minority status compared to the first step. In fact, however, the impacts of minority status on loan denial are -3.9, -5.7, and -8.7, which contradicts the HDL hypothesis for the first two models. Finally, we drop all applications considered two or more times (i.e., all applications with evidence of any negotiation). This step, which reduces the sample size to 1,454, provides a further rejection of the HDL hypothesis; specifically, the minority status impacts increase for all three models to -7.1, -10.0, and -12.0 percent, respectively. Indeed, these estimates, which are entered in the second row of table 5.5, are all substantially larger (in absolute value) than the baseline estimates, which are given in the table's first row.

Overall, therefore, we find no evidence that the minority status effect is overstated because only a subset of applications involving counteroffers, namely, those that resulted in successful negotiations, are treated as acceptances. Indeed, the evidence presented here suggests, but does not prove, that bias from this source may actually work in the opposite direction.

5.4.4 Conclusion

Although the available data do not permit a definitive conclusion concerning the impact of misclassification on the Boston Fed Study's results, we find that these results are not affected by many of the misclassification problems discussed by Horne and by Day and Liebowitz. Moreover, the strongest claims that have been made about bias due to misclassification are not compelling, because they are based on a nonrandom sample of applications. There currently exists no evidence indicating that the elimination from the data set of misclassified observations that are identified on a minority status–neutral basis has any substantial influence on the estimated minority status coefficient.

5.5 Incorrect Specification

Anyone studying loan approvals must decide how to "specify" the equation used to study them, that is, determine what algebraic form to use for estimating purposes. Different specifications may lead to different results. Munnell et al. (1996) were, of course, aware of this issue and investigated several different forms. For example, they conducted a test to determine whether the same model applied to applications for single-family houses, multifamily houses, and condominiums. On the basis of the affirmative test results, they pooled all these types of applications. They also investigated several "interaction" terms, which determine whether the impact of one explanatory variable depends on the value of another one, and could not find any such terms that affected the impact of minority status on loan denial.

5.5.1 The Critics' Claims

Liebowitz (1993) and Day and Liebowitz (1996) suggest that the underwriting process may vary across the sample used in the Boston Fed Study. For example, Liebowitz suggests that the sample should be split by type of unit or by LTV, with a separate analysis of each subsample. As noted above, however, Munnell et al. reject the hypothesis that the model differs by type of unit. Moreover, Browne and Tootell (1995) report that when separate equations are estimated for each type of unit, the minority status coefficient actually increases in the single-family housing regression. The minority status coefficient is insignificant only in the two- to four-family housing regression, which contains only 393 loan applications. Browne and Tootell also find that the minority status coefficient is still significant in what Liebowitz characterizes as the "core" sample, namely, single-family houses that do not involve an application for PMI, even though this subsample contains only fourteen minority denials.

Buist, Linneman, and Megbolugbe (1999) separate the sample into applications that meet all standard underwriting criteria, based on LTV, housing expense–to–income ratio, and so on, and applications that fail to meet at least one of these criteria. They find that the minority status coefficient is highly significant in the second subsample but is not significantly different from zero in the first. This result suggests that discrimination may arise in underwriters' decisions concerning the interpretation of or compensation for an applicant's failure to meet one or more underwriting criteria.

Although Buist, Linneman, and Megbolugbe's specification differs from that used by Munnell et al., their conclusion is actually quite consistent with that of the Boston Fed Study. To be more specific, Munnell et al. find that a minority applicant whose characteristics equal the average for the white sample has a loan denial probability that is 5.5 percentage points above that of a comparable white applicant. This differential is considerably smaller than the eight-percentage-point differential facing a minority applicant with characteristics equal to the average for the minority sample. These results reflect the nonlinearity of a logit model used by Munnell et al. In fact, their results imply that the higher the quality of the application, the smaller the minority-white differential in the probability of loan denial.

Glennon and Stengel (1994a) suggest that the loan denial model should vary by minority status. They estimate separate models by minority status and use the Blinder-Oaxaca decomposition approach (a common approach in the literature on wage differentials) to estimate the effect of minority status on the likelihood of denial. They find that the average impact of minority status on loan approval is the same with this alternative specification as with a single loan denial model. Munnell et al. (1996) perform a similar test in which they allow all the coefficients except those of the census tract and lender dummy variables to vary with minority status. They obtain the same result.

A related point is made by Bostic (1996) and Hunter and Walker (1996), who suggest that individual elements of the underwriting model may vary with minority status.[33] They interact minority-status with credit history, education, and obligation ratio. Only the obligation ratio interaction is statistically significant. They find that at low obligation ratios the minority status coefficient is relatively small and significant only at the 10-percent level, but at high obligation ratios the minority status coefficient is large and highly significant. A similar result is found by Bostic and by Munnell et al. (1996).[34] These results have no impact whatsoever on the average impact of minority status on loan denial, however, which is the focus of the Boston Fed Study and most of the other literature.

LaCour-Little (1996b) estimates a model of loan demand and supply using the Boston Fed Study's data and the model developed by Maddala and Trost (1982), which was described in chapter 4. LaCour-Little finds that minorities have a higher demand for credit than whites, but that lenders supply less credit to minorities. In fact, the significance of the minority status coefficient in LaCour-Little's supply equation is comparable to the significance of the minority status coefficient in Munnell et al. (1996) This finding is consistent with Maddala and Trost's results and confirms the view that lenders treat minority applicants less favorably than comparable whites.

LaCour-Little (1996a) also applies the so-called reverse-regression approach to the Boston Fed Study's data. In a reverse regression, a model of the variable of interest, in this case loan denial, is estimated and is used to generate a quality index for each individual observation. The quality index is used as the dependent variable in a second-stage regression that controls for the original variable of interest and the minority status and/or gender of the individual. This approach has been used in the wage discrimination literature (see Goldberger, 1984). It is especially appropriate when the actual explanatory variables deviate from the ones that are called for theoretically, but it also may be useful when the explanatory variables suffer from measurement error. Typically, reverse regression is employed when the variable of interest is continuous, as in the case of earnings, but LaCour-Little argues that the approach is also reasonable for a discrete dependent variable, such as loan denial. He predicts the probability of denial for all observations and uses this probability as the dependent variable in the second stage. Based on this analysis, LaCour-Little reverses the findings of the Boston Fed Study and concludes that minority applications are favored, on average, in the Boston Fed Study's sample.

Finally, Glennon and Stengel (1994a) and Stengel and Glennon (1999) argue that changes are needed in the specification of a loan approval regression to account for the fact that different lenders may use different underwriting guidelines.[35] This is a critical issue, because the interpretation of a loan approval regression depends upon whether underwriting guidelines vary across lenders. Using the disparate-treatment standard, for example, discrimination exists if common underwriting guidelines used by all lenders are not the same for white and minority applications, but does not exist if minorities and whites with the same qualifications receive different treatment because they visit different sets of lenders with different guidelines. After a brief treatment of this issue here, we return to it in chapter 6.

Stengel and Glennon argue that the best way to isolate disparate-treatment discrimination is to estimate a separate loan denial regression for each lender. They cannot implement this approach with the public-use version of the Boston Fed Study's data, which does not identify lenders, but they can implement it using an entirely different data set for three large lenders. As discussed more fully in chapter 6, they find that the minority status coefficient is not always significant in the results of regressions for individual lenders. They conclude that the Boston Fed Study's results may therefore reflect a specification error rather than market-wide discrimination.

The issue of variation in underwriting criteria across lenders is also raised by Horne (1997), who argues that the minority status coefficient in the loan denial equation estimated by the Boston Fed Study reflects the behavior of lending institutions, perhaps even minority-owned ones, that specialize in lending to minorities.[36] According to this argument, lenders that attract many minority applications have unusually high rates of minority denials either because those applications have a high incidence of credit problems that are not observed in the Boston Fed Study's data or because those lenders have unusual underwriting standards. For example, Horne finds that if two large minority-owned lenders are excluded from his subsample of the Boston Fed Study's data, the minority status coefficient is no longer significant. Munnell et al. (1996) include lender dummies in their basic equation, however, which rules out fixed lender effects for minority-owned or any other lenders, and they show that the minority status coefficient is virtually the same in a regression for lenders that have a high volume of loans to minorities as in a regression for lenders that do not.[37] Moreover, Browne and Tootell (1995) drop minority-owned lenders from the sample, and Tootell (1996b) drops the lenders identified by Horne. These changes also do not affect the minority status coefficient in the resulting regressions.

5.5.2   Evaluation: Introduction

Most of the specification changes discussed in the literature have little or no impact on the Boston Fed Study's main result. These include allowing the underwriting model to vary by type of unit, by application or property characteristics, by minority status of the applicant, or by minority status of the lender. In other words, this result appears to be remarkably unaffected by changes in specification. There are, however, two possible exceptions to this conclusion: reverse regression and the use of different regressions for each lender. These two possibilities are examined in the next two sections.

5.5.3   Evaluation and Reanalysis: Reverse Regression

One specification change that has a substantial effect on the Boston Fed Study's main result is the reverse-regression approach in LaCour-Little (1996a). We reject the reverse-regression approach, however, for an equation with a discrete dependent variable. In the wage discrimination literature, the reverse regression asks the following question: Among workers that earn the same amount, do minority (or female) workers have higher average quality than white workers? This question is appropriate for examining wage differentials. If female workers make the same amount and yet are higher-quality workers, they must be facing discrimination. A similar question arises for the loan denial decision. Among applicants with the same outcome (either denial or approval), are minority applications more creditworthy, on average? This question is not appropriate, however, for a discrete outcome like approval/denial. Even if a greater number of marginal white applications are approved, the average quality of approved loans might be higher for white applications because the high-quality applications are predominantly from whites. Thus, the LaCour-Little conclusion that minorities are favored in loan decisions, on average, is unwarranted.

To shed further light on this issue, we first obtain a measure of "loan quality" by estimating a loan approval model using only the applications from whites and then using the coefficients to predict the probability of acceptance for every application, regardless of minority status. A distribution of the resulting loan quality measure illustrates the problem with the reverse-regression approach (see table 5.6). This table reveals that most of the very-high-quality applications are from whites and that many of the very-low-quality applications are from minorities. There probably exist some applications that are of such high quality that they will be approved (or of such low quality that they will be rejected) regardless of minority status. The existence of such applications should not influence a test for discrimination. As explained earlier, however, these applications undermine reverse regression, because the very-high-quality approved loans and the very-low-quality denied loans enter the calculation of average loan quality. In other words, LaCour-Little incorrectly uses data on the average difference between minority and white borrowers to test a hypothesis about the difference between the marginal (i.e. lowest quality) minority and white borrowers.[38]

5.5.3 Evaluation: Lender-Specific Underwriting Guidelines

Stengel and Glennon (1999) argue that an analysis based on a pooled sample of lenders may not be able to isolate disparate-treatment discrimination. We agree with this conclusion. This puts us at odds with Munnell et al. (1996), who claim to isolate disparate-treatment

Table 5.6
Distribution of application quality for minority and white applications

Application quality (1 = highest)	Number of white applications	Number of minority applications	Minority share of applications (%)
1	11	0	0.0
2	80	3	3.6
3	459	48	9.5
4	758	167	18.1
5	470	161	25.5
6	210	101	32.5
7	96	68	41.0
8	56	36	39.1
9	32	30	48.4
10	29	15	34.1
11	13	11	45.8
12	15	12	44.4
13	2	3	60.0
14	6	8	57.1
15	7	6	53.3
16	1	6	85.7
17	0	4	100.0
18	0	4	100.0
19	1	0	0.0
25	1	0	0.0

Note: The application quality index is the propensity to be denied as predicted by an econometric model of loan denial, based on the public-use version of the Boston Fed Study's data and scaled so that it falls between 1 (*highest quality*) and 25 (*lowest quality*).

discrimination with their pooled approach. If lenders do, in fact, use different underwriting guidelines, then a pooled regression cannot separate cases in which individual lenders apply different guidelines to minority and white applicants from cases in which minority and white customers apply to lenders with different guidelines. This is an application of lesson 9 in chapter 3.

Scholars should be concerned however, about discrimination based on disparate impact, as well as discrimination based on disparate treatment. A separate loan approval regression for each lender might be able to isolate disparate-treatment discrimination, because it could indicate whether a lender applies the same underwriting standards to minority and white applicants, but it cannot observe disparate-impact discrimination. As explained in chapter 2, disparate-impact discrimination is based on a difference between actual underwriting standards and the "true" relationship between expected loan profitability and applicant, loan, and property characteristics. When focusing on a single lender, data on loan profitability or some other measure of loan performance are needed to estimate this true relationship. Discrimination would exist by the disparate-impact standard if the weight given to loan or applicant characteristics in a lender's actual underwriting standards differed from the impact of those variables on expected loan profitability—and this difference was particularly hard on minority applicants.

Although no published study has yet estimated the relationship between loan and applicant characteristics and loan profitability with a data set that includes applicant credit history, one could argue that lenders have an incentive to figure out this relationship and to incorporate it into their actual underwriting standards. After all, lenders can make more money if they can accurately forecast the profitability of each loan application. Because the data do not exist to make this type of forecast with much precision, individual lenders will forecast with error, but lenders may get the relationship about right, on average. If so, then deviations from average standards could indicate "errors" (perhaps intentional) by individual lenders that may impose a disparate impact on minority applicants—and may therefore be discrimination under the disparate-impact standard. In this case, a pooled regression, which controls for average actual underwriting standards (using applicant, loan, and property characteristics), might capture both disparate-treatment discrimination and disparate-impact discrimination. Switching to separate regressions for individual lenders might provide a better estimate of disparate-treatment discrimination (assuming that sample sizes are large enough), but only at the cost of ignoring disparate-impact discrimination.

Even if lenders' underwriting standards accurately predict loan performance on average, however, one cannot be confident that simply controlling for applicant, loan, and property characteristics accurately captures the effects of disparate-impact discrimination. The problem arises because the relationship between loan profitability and these characteristics may vary across lenders. In that case, deviations from the average relationship might be legitimate, that is, they might not involve disparate-impact discrimination. At best, therefore, the standard pooled regression approach provides a rough approximation for the sum of disparate-impact and disparate-treatment discrimination.

A more accurate approach requires additional controls for legitimate variation in underwriting standards across lenders. If, for example, the lenders to which minority and white customers apply have different underwriting standards, but each set of lenders gets the underwriting model right, on average, the appropriate procedure is to estimate a separate model for minority and white applicants. As noted earlier, however, one cannot reject the hypothesis that the coefficients of the explanatory variables are the same for the minority and white applicants (Munnell et al., 1996), and splitting the sample in this way does not alter the estimated impact of minority status on loan denial (Stengel and Glennon, 1999). Moreover, Horne's (1997) claim that the Boston Fed Study's results are driven by two minority-owned lenders is not compelling, because it is based on a non-random subsample of the Boston Fed Study's data. Results from the whole sample indicate that these results do not depend on the behavior of a few lenders, minority-owned or otherwise. These findings provide further support for the use of a pooled model as a useful, if approximate, way to estimate the combined impact of disparate-impact and disparate-treatment discrimination.

5.5.5 Conclusions

The conclusion that applications from minority households are less likely to be approved than are applications from equally qualified white households follows from virtually all specifications of the underwriting equations that have appeared in the literature. One apparent exception is the reverse-regression specification, but our investigation of this approach indicates that it is not appropriate for analyzing discrete dependent variables. Thus, reverse regression does not provide a legitimate alternative to a loan approval regression, and one cannot legitimately reject the Boston Fed Study's findings on the basis of reverse-regression results.

Finally, with a large number of applications from each individual lender, a loan approval study might provide a clearer picture of disparate-treatment discrimination by conducting separate regressions for each lender. The cost of this approach, however, is that it hides disparate-impact discrimination. Pooling all lenders, as in the Boston

Fed Study, provides the best approach currently available for measuring discrimination under both the disparate-treatment and the disparate-impact standards.

This approach, however, depends on several untested assumptions, and further research is needed on these important issues. One key question is whether different lenders use different underwriting standards. Another is whether existing underwriting standards can be justified by a link to loan profitability. Data to answer these questions fully are not publicly available at this time, but several recent studies have addressed the questions, and we consider them at length in the following chapters. We also provide a more complete analysis of disparate-impact discrimination in chapter 9.

5.6   Endogenous Explanatory Variables

Another challenge facing a study of loan approval is to account for the interactions between the loan approval decision and other aspects of lender behavior. These interactions are important because some of the explanatory variables in a loan approval model might be endogenous, and statistical procedures that do not account for this possibility might lead to biased results.

5.6.1   The Critics' Claims

Rachlis and Yezer (1993) argue that single-equation models of loan denial are biased because many loan terms are actually the result of borrower choices. They highlight the endogeneity of LTV. In particular, Rachlis and Yezer argue that LTV is endogenous because negotiation with a lender will induce marginal loan applicants to increase their proposed down payment.[39] They show that this type of response will bias the coefficient of LTV downward and the coefficient of minority status upward. Yezer, Phillips, and Trost (1994) explore this issue further by constructing a model in which the lender rejection decision depends on LTV and on an index of default likelihood, LTV depends on indices of approval and default likelihood, and default likelihood depends upon LTV. Using simulations, they demonstrate that if this structure is correct, a single-equation model of loan denial will overstate the minority status coefficient. As evidence for the plausibility of their approach, they cite evidence from Schafer and Ladd (1981) that the effect of minority status on loan denial varies with the number of times an application is reconsidered by the lender. During any reconsideration, they argue, loan terms may be altered and more negotiation may take place.

Browne and Tootell (1995) argue that Yezer, Phillips, and Trost have not established that negotiation is widespread. In addition, Tootell (1996b) argues that negotiation does not imply simultaneity. Endogeneity bias will not arise, he says, so long as any adjustments to loan terms have been finalized prior to the denial decision. To examine this issue, Brown and Tootell estimate a model in which LTV is treated as endogenous. As in most such procedures, they make use of new exogenous variables, called "instruments," to "identify" the model, that is, to separate the true effect of the endogenous variable (LTV) on the dependent variable (loan denial) from the factors that affect both of these variables. The variables they use as instruments are (1) the applicant's age minus years of education and (2) the applicant's income. They find that the minority status coefficient in the loan denial equation is actually larger using this procedure than when LTV is treated as exogenous. Tootell (1996b) estimates a similar model with a somewhat different set of instruments and obtains a similar result. Yinger (1996) provides a conceptual basis for these findings. He points out that if white applicants receive additional aid in preparing their loan application (as found by Siskin and Cupingood, 1996) or loan officers are more willing to negotiate with white applicants, then treating LTV as exogenous leads to an understatement—not an overstatement—of the minority status coefficient in a loan denial equation.

Another explanatory variable that may be endogenous is whether the application involves a special loan program. Phillips and Yezer (1996) investigate this possibility. Previous studies either control for whether an application is for a special program or drop all applications involving a special program. Phillips and Yezer observe that neither of these approaches yields consistent estimates if applying for a special program loan is, in fact, endogenous. They estimate a model in which the applicant first decides whether to apply for a special program and then, if she does not, the lender decides whether to accept her application for a regular loan. In technical terms, this model corrects for the "selection" of applications into a special loan program.[40] Phillips and Yezer observe that the applicant must decide whether to apply for a special program before the property is assessed, so the assessed value cannot influence the special-program decision. This observation identifies the exogenous variables they need for their simultaneous-equations procedure; in particular, they include the ratio of the loan amount to the house price in the special-program equation and the ratio of the loan to the assessed value in the loan denial equation. Using the Boston Fed Study's public-use sample, they find that the minority status coefficient in this model is not statistically significant and is almost 30 percent lower than the minority status coefficient in a model that simply omits the applications that involve a special loan program.

For two reasons, however, one should be cautious in interpreting this result. First, Phillips and Yezer's model also includes both the "unverified information" and "meets guidelines" variables, and the minority status coefficient in the model that simply drops special-program applications was significant only at the 10-percent level. Second, the estimated correlation between the error terms in the two equations was only -0.155 (t-statistic: 0.53), which provides only weak support for the claim that special-program choice is endogenous.[41]

In a study of redlining, Ross and Tootell (1998) treat yet another variable as endogenous, namely, whether the applicant obtained PMI.[42] The first stage of their model explores the factors that determine the receipt of PMI, and the second stage involves a loan denial equation in which one of the explanatory variables indicates whether the applicant obtained PMI. In estimating this model, Ross and Tootell drop all seventy-seven cases in which an applicant applied for and was denied PMI. Dropping these observations greatly simplifies the model, because it avoids the necessity of estimating the PMI denial decision, and Munnell et al. (1996) show that this step has no impact on the minority status coefficient in the loan denial equation. Ross and Tootell find little evidence to indicate that PMI is endogenous. The correlation between the unobservable factors in the PMI and denial equations is only -0.135 (t-statistic: 0.49), and the minority status coefficient in their loan denial equation is not affected by allowing PMI to be endogenous.

5.6.2 Evaluation

The findings of Yezer, Phillips, and Trost (1994) are thought-provoking because they indicate that the Boston Fed Study's results may be biased even if the data are not flawed and no important underwriting variable is omitted from the equation. Such bias, if it exists, arises because information about a lender's treatment of an application affects the borrower's behavior, which is lesson 3 in chapter 3. In particular, LTV may decrease with the likelihood of loan rejection, even after controlling for all borrower characteristics that enter the underwriting problem, so LTV may be correlated with the unobservable factors in the loan denial equation. This type of correlation leads to biased coefficients, and the sign of any such bias in the minority status coefficient depends on the correlation between minority status and LTV. Empirically, minorities submit loan applications with higher LTVs than do otherwise equivalent whites, which supports Yezer, Phillips, and Trost's argument that single-equation loan denial models are biased toward finding discrimination. This does not prove, of course, that other biases are not also at work. For example, the possibility that whites receive more coaching or are treated better during negotiations, as suggested by Yinger, would lead to a bias in the other direction. The net impact of these and perhaps other biases on the estimated minority status coefficient is, of course, an empirical matter.

Furthermore, we are not convinced by Tootell's argument that the influence of the lender on LTV precedes the denial decision and so is not endogenous. An individual loan officer knows about his bank's underwriting procedures and can probably give applicants a good indication about whether their applications will be approved in any given form. This unobservable information about an application's probability of denial may influence both LTV and the eventual denial decision. Thus, a single-equation model of loan denial could suffer from endogeneity bias even if LTV is fixed at the time of the final loan denial decision. It may indeed be the negotiation that matters, not the timing.

Although it makes a valuable contribution, the model provided by Yezer, Phillips, and Trost understates the complexity of the problem. In fact, LTV is influenced by three sets of unobservable factors. First, in addition to the unobservable factors in the loan denial equation, there are unobservable factors in the LTV equation itself. Second, because LTV depends on the likelihood of default as well as the likelihood of rejection, LTV is influenced by the unobservable determinants of default. Third, the likelihood of default may influence loan denial, in which case the unobservable factors in the default equation are imbedded in the unobservable factors in the loan denial equation. Yezer, Phillips, and Trost investigate only one of these relationships (and potential biases). They allow the unobservable factors in the default and loan denial equations to be correlated, a step that leads to a decrease in the minority status coefficient in the loan denial equation. Accounting for the other relationships among unobservable factors, however, is likely to have the opposite impact on this minority status coefficient and could even reverse the findings of Yezer, Phillips, and Trost. We conclude that their findings are far from definitive.

Although these studies do not convince us that endogeneity results in an overstatement of the minority status coefficient, we also are not convinced that existing studies adequately deal with the endogeneity problem. A simultaneous-equations procedure generally requires the use of variables (instruments) that are highly correlated with the endogenous explanatory variable, in this case LTV, but not with the dependent variable, in this case loan denial, when the endogenous variable is also included in the regression. To put it more formally, good instruments must meet three criteria. First, they must make conceptual sense. Second, they should be significant in a regression to explain the endogenous explanatory variable, in this case LTV. Third, they should not have explanatory power in the regression of interest, in this case a regression to explain loan denial, when the potentially endogenous variable is also included.[43] In our view, the last criterion requires a stronger standard than the usual significance test; if a variable is even marginally significant in the regression of interest, then it should not be used as an instrument.

Now consider the analysis by Browne and Tootell (1995). To account for the possible endogeneity of LTV, they use an applicant's income and age minus education as instruments. We do not find this approach to be compelling.[44] First, income is often significant in the loan denial equation, which violates the third of the above criteria. Age minus years of education is not available in the public-release data set, but the education variable in that data set is not statistically significant in the LTV model, which violates the second criterion. We conclude that Browne and Tootell have not eliminated the bias from an endogenous LTV. The instruments proposed by Tootell (1996b) are no more compelling. He uses liquid assets, marital status, gender, and years in current line of work, but also includes years on the job (which is close to age minus education) and education. The new variables on this list all have explanatory power in some of the loan denial regressions in Munnell et al., which implies that they violate the third criterion for a good instrument.

5.6.3 Reanalysis

The review in the previous section reveals that LTV may indeed be endogenous in a loan denial equation and that estimates of the effect of minority status on loan denial may be biased if this endogeneity is not taken into account. On conceptual grounds, this bias could work in either direction, however, so the nature of the bias is ultimately an empirical question that is not adequately answered by existing analysis.

The bias identified by Yezer, Phillips, and Trost (1994) arises from negotiation, so one might also ask whether the minority status coefficient is different when more negotiation takes place. Yezer, Phillips, and Trost suggest that there is more opportunity for negotiation when an application is considered more than once; if so, the bias in the minority status effect should be larger for applications that are considered more often. A reasonable test of this negotiation hypothesis involves the elimination from the sample of applications that were considered more than some preset number of times, a sign of extensive negotiation, and reestimation of the model with LTV treated as exogenous. This procedure, which was presented in section 5.4.3, does not find a clear relationship between minority-white differences in loan approval and the number of times an application is reviewed. If anything, more negotiation appears to be associated with a smaller minority status effect, which is the opposite of the Yezer-Phillips-Trost prediction (see the second row of table 5.5). We conclude that either negotiation is not the source of endogeneity in loan amount or else the number of times an application is reviewed is a poor measure of the extent to which negotiation takes place.

To further investigate this issue, we estimate a simultaneous-equations model to explain loan approval with LTV treated as endogenous. This model uses a new set of instruments, namely, house price plus the pairwise interactions between income, house price, and liquid assets. These instruments meet the first criterion stated above, that is, they make sense conceptually. The interaction between liquid assets and house price may indicate the ability of the household to make a down payment. Moreover, the interaction between income and liquid assets or income and house price may explain a household's desire to make a larger down payment and reduce monthly housing expenses. Finally, none of these interactions is likely to influence the loan denial decision, because the link between the underlying variables and default is already captured in LTV and in the housing expense–to–income ratio.

These hypotheses are confirmed by the data in the sense that all of these variables are statistically significant in an equation to explain LTV. Thus, these variables appear to meet the second criterion for an appropriate instrument. In addition, each of these four variables has a small, insignificant coefficient in a loan denial equation that includes LTV, even at the 50-percent confidence level, which indicates that they meet the third criterion as well.[45]

Having identified appropriate instruments, we then estimate the loan approval equation accounting for the endogeneity of LTV.[46] As a point of comparison, we first estimate the loan approval equation with the continuous version of LTV instead of the categories in our base case. The coefficients (t-statistics) of the minority status variable for our three models are −0.260 (2.57), −0.272 (3.06), and −0.375 (4.19), and the impacts of minority status on loan denial are −4.3, −6.0, and −8.1 percentage points (see row 5 of table 5.5). When LTV is treated as endogenous, the estimated minority status coefficients are −0.253 (2.50), −0.233 (2.35), and −0.354 (3.62), and the minority status effects are −4.2, −5.3, and −7.7 (see row 6 of table 5.5).[47] Accounting for the endogeneity of LTV lowers the minority status effect in every case, but the largest decline, in model 2, is only 0.7 percentage points, or less than 12 percent. These results support the view that single-equation estimates of the impact of minority status on loan approval can be biased upward but also indicate that this bias is likely to be small in magnitude.[48]

LTV is endogenous because borrower or lender behavior may affect its numerator, the size of the loan. If loan size is endogenous, however, then so is the size of the mortgage payment, which is a key component of the housing expense–to–income ratio.[49] For each additional explanatory variable it wishes to treat as endogenous, an analysis generally must have at least one additional instrument. In this case, we know that the Boston Fed Study data for housing expense include insurance and property taxes, as well as mortgage payments, and that the relationship between the loan amount and the monthly mortgage payment depends on the term of the mortgage.[50] Because insurance and taxes may vary by location, we include as instruments both a dummy variable for the central county in the Boston area and this dummy variable interacted with several factors that might influence insurance or assessments, namely, whether the unit is to be owner-occupied, whether the unit is a multifamily unit, and three census tract characteristics: racial composition, tract income, and whether the percentage of units that are boarded up exceeds the metropolitan median value. It also seems reasonable to suppose that these instruments will affect loan denial only indirectly through the housing expense–to–income ratio. Finally, the term of the mortgage is interacted with the age of the applicant on the assumption that older households may want a shorter mortgage. All of these instruments fulfill the second and third criteria listed earlier; that is, they are statistically significant in an equation to explain the housing expense–to–income ratio but have no explanatory power in the loan approval equation when the housing expense–to–income ratio is also included.

With both LTV and the housing expense–to–income ratio treated as endogenous, the minority-status coefficients (t-statistics) in our three loan denial models are -0.265 (2.49), -0.218 (2.16), and -0.398 (4.38).[51] The corresponding impacts of minority status on loan denial are -4.4, -5.1, and -8.6 percentage points (see row 7 of table 5.5). Hence, treating this additional variable as endogenous actually increases the impact of minority status on loan approval in the first and third models and lowers it only slightly, from -5.3 to -5.1 percentage points, in the second.

These results complicate our conclusions about the role of the endogeneity of the loan amount. If model 1 or model 3 is correct, then single-equation estimates actually understate the impact of minority status on loan denial to a small degree, but if model 2 is correct, then single-equation estimates overstate this impact by about 15 percent (row 7 relative to row 5 in table 5.5). Even in model 2, however, the impact of minority status on loan approval remains large and statistically significant when we account for this endogeneity. It is, of course, possible that a different set of instruments would lead to different results, but we believe that the instruments we have used clearly meet all the criteria for good instruments and that minority status has a large, significant impact on loan approval using any reasonable set of instruments from the Boston Fed Study's public-use data set.[52]

Following Phillips and Yezer's (1996) lead, we also estimate a simultaneous-equations model in which an individual decides whether to apply to a special program. We use the same three specifications that we have used all along, except that we change one of the explanatory variables. Our previous models of loan approval include the ratio of loan amount to the minimum of assessed value and house price. Like Phillips and Yezer, we now include the ratio of loan amount to assessed value in the approval model and the ratio of loan amount to house price in our model of the special-program application decision. As a point of comparison, we first estimate our three loan approval models after deleting all applications that involve a special program. The minority status coefficients (t-statistics) from these models are −0.329 (2.93), −0.291 (2.90), and −0.418 (4.24), and the impacts of minority status on the probability of denial are −5.1, −6.5, and −8.7 percentage points. With a correction for the selection of some applications into special programs, the minority status coefficients in the three denial equations, which in this case apply just to loans that do not involve special programs, are −0.375 (3.70), −0.312 (3.64), and −0.439 (5.20), and the minority status effects increase substantially to −10.0, −9.7, and −13.7 points. These results differ from Phillips and Yezer's and indicate that, if anything, the failure to treat special programs as endogenous biases downward the impact of minority status on loan approval.

One possible explanation for the difference between our results and Phillips and Yezer's is that they use a much more parsimonious specification and, in particular, omit a number of variables that are statistically significant in the approval model. For our three models, the estimated correlation between the unobservable factors in the special-program choice equation and the unobservable factors in the loan approval equation is close to one.[53] This result implies that the model is not well identified; that is, it cannot accurately account for the endogeneity of special-program choice because we cannot distinguish between the unobserved factors in the two equations.[54] Phillips and Yezer do not run into this problem because they drop several variables from the denial equation, thereby lowering the correlation between the unobservable factors in the two equations— and thereby introducing omitted-variable bias into their results. In other words, they solve the identification problem but cause another, more serious one. Given the difficult trade-off facing researchers in this case, we think future research should investigate other ways to identify the model.

As in the case of an endogenous LTV, variables for house price, liquid assets, and applicant income, along with their interactions, appear worth investigating as possible determinants of the choice to apply for a special program. In fact, all six variables are statistically significant in a single-equation model for explaining the choice to apply for a special program, which indicates that these variables meet the second criterion listed above for a good instrument. These variables also are insignificant in a denial specification that controls for whether the applicant applied for a special program, which indicates that they also meet the third criterion.

On the basis of these results, we estimate three simultaneous-equations models of loan approval and special-program choice, with these additional variables included only in the special-program choice equation. In addition, these models include the traditional LTV variable in the loan approval equation and exclude the "meets guidelines" variable (or its instrument) from the special-program choice equation, because the borrower does not gain insight into whether he meets the lender's underwriting standards until after he has submitted his application. This approach appears to do a better job of identifying the model. In particular, the estimated correlations between unobserved factors in the two equations are now all close to 0.5, instead of the almost-perfect correlation in the previous approach.[55] Again for comparison, we find that the impacts of minority status on the probability of loan denial when special program loans are dropped are −5.7, −7.2, and −9.5 percentage points. With special program choice treated as endogenous, these impacts become −6.6, −8.9, and −11.1 points. See rows 8 and 9 of table 5.5. These results also support the conclusion that a failure to treat special-program choice as endogenous biases the minority status coefficient toward zero, but the bias is smaller in this case than in the previous one.

5.6.4   Conclusion

In conclusion, the key finding of the Boston Fed Study is unaffected when the model includes a complete accounting for the endogeneity of LTV—or of any other variable that can plausibly be called endogenous. In all the models examined here that take account of the endogeneity of various variables, the impact of minority status on loan approval is statistically significant and close to the value in the Boston Fed Study's equations. Moreover, we find that accounting for the endogeneity of special-program choice actually boosts the impact of minority status on loan approval.

5.7 Conclusions Concerning the Boston Fed Study

Munnell et al. (1996), otherwise known as the Boston Fed Study, has been subjected to a phenomenal and, in our experience, unprecedented volume of criticism. Critics have argued that the study's main finding, that minority applicants are over 80 percent more likely to be turned down for a loan than are equivalent white applicants, which is an indication of discrimination in mortgage lending, is biased upward because the study omitted variables, used data with errors in the explanatory variables, used a dependent variable that misclassifies loan outcomes, used the wrong algebraic form (also known as misspecification), and failed to account for endogeneity in several different explanatory variables.

We have examined all of these arguments and, where possible, explored them with the public-use version of the Boston Fed Study's data. In some cases, we find that the critics are simply wrong: the problem they identify does not exist, or the bias involved is empirically insignificant. In several cases, however, we agree with the critics that a limitation in the Boston Fed Study could potentially lead to a serious overstatement of discrimination, and we have explored these cases in detail. Moreover, we find that the literature has raised several important issues concerning the interpretation of the Boston Fed Study's results. This analysis leads us to five main conclusions.

1. The large differences in loan approval between minority and white applicants that are identified by Munnell et al. cannot be explained by data errors, omitted variables, or the endogeneity of loan terms. No study has identified a reasonable procedure for dealing with any of these potential problems that eliminates the large negative impact of minority status on loan approval. One cannot, of course, prove that no bias exists in any particular equation, but one can examine all the potential sources of bias identified by scholars for that case. Scholars have been unusually creative in identifying potential biases in the Boston Fed Study, but our analysis, based on the best data currently available, reveals that none of these potential biases can explain why the estimated minority status coefficient in the study's loan approval equation is so far from zero.

For example, some scholars have claimed that the "meets guidelines" variable should be included to correct for elements of applicants' credit histories that are omitted from the explanatory variables in the Boston Fed Study. If this variable does indeed capture such omitted elements, however, then the unobserved factors influencing "meets guidelines" would be correlated with the unobserved factors influencing loan approval. We show that this is not the case. In addition, we find that accounting for the endogeneity of various loan terms never results in a substantial reduction in the estimated minority status coefficient, and in some plausible cases, this step actually makes that coefficient larger.

2. No study has demonstrated either the presence or the absence of disparate-treatment discrimination in loan approval, at least not in a large sample of lenders.[56] This conclusion puts us at odds both with the authors of the Boston Fed Study, who claim that they measure disparate-treatment discrimination, and with several of their critics, who claim that there is no discrimination at all.

In our view, the Boston Fed Study's results measure disparate-treatment discrimination only under the assumption that all lenders use the same underwriting guidelines. With this assumption, any group-based difference in treatment after controlling for underwriting variables implies that the guidelines are applied differentially across groups, which is, by definition, disparate-treatment discrimination. As discussed in chapter 3, virtually all lenders sell some of their loans in the secondary mortgage market, so they have some incentive to use the underwriting guidelines that institutions in that market, such as FannieMae, have established. Many loans are not sold in the secondary market, however, and the lending process often involves many individuals in the same lending institution who may not all have the same incentives. Even on conceptual grounds, therefore, the same-guidelines assumption is a strong one, and no existing empirical study can confirm (or deny) it.

3. No study has demonstrated either the presence or the absence of disparate-impact discrimination in loan approval. The Boston Fed Study's results measure disparate-impact discrimination only under the assumptions that (1) different lenders use different underwriting guidelines, (2) existing guidelines are accurately linked to loan profitability, on average, and (3) existing deviations from average guidelines cannot be justified on the basis of business necessity. These assumptions could be justified, for example, if underwriting guidelines vary across lenders solely for idiosyncratic reasons or if some lenders purposefully develop guidelines that have a disparate impact on minority applicants. No existing study, however, sheds light on whether these assumptions are met.

4. *The Boston Fed Study provides strong, but not irrefutable, evidence that in 1990 lenders in Boston engaged in either disparate-treatment discrimination, or disparate-impact discrimination, or both.* The study shows that the probability of loan denial is higher for minority than for white applicants, controlling for a wide range of applicant, loan, and property characteristics. The higher denial rate for minorities could reflect disparate-treatment discrimination, that is, the use of harsher underwriting standards for minority than for white applicants. To the extent that underwriting standards vary across lenders, that this variation is particularly hard on minority applicants, and that this variation is not justified on the grounds of business necessity, this higher denial rate for minorities also could reflect disparate-impact discrimination.

The Boston Fed Study's main result could be refuted with evidence that the observed minority-white differences in loan approval can be entirely explained by nondiscriminatory differences in underwriting standards across lenders that are justified on business grounds. Legitimate differences in underwriting guidelines must be associated with real differences in lenders' experiences and therefore are most likely to arise among lenders that specialize in groups of borrowers with different average creditworthiness. If the minority-white difference in loan approval simply reflects legitimate across-lender variation in underwriting standards, therefore, this difference should disappear when underwriting standards are allowed to vary across lenders that serve different segments of the mortgage market.

Several studies present evidence that this is not the case. Munnell et al. (1996) can reject the hypothesis that the underwriting model is different for single-family houses, multifamily houses, or condominiums. Moreover, both Munnell et al. and Hunter and Walker (1996) find little evidence that individual underwriting variables receive different weights for minority and white applicants. In addition,

Munnell et al. show that the minority status coefficient is virtually the same when separate regressions (and hence separate underwriting standards) are estimated for lenders that specialize in lending to minorities and for other lenders. Finally, Browne and Tootell (1995) show that the minority status coefficient is literally unaffected if one excludes two minority lenders that together account for half of the minority applications in the Boston Fed Study's sample.

As explained earlier, the "meets guidelines" variable might be related to the issue of business necessity. Under the assumptions that minority households do a poorer job than white households in selecting lenders that meet their credit needs and that this mismatch is not influenced by lender actions, such as discrimination in pre-application procedures or in loan marketing, including the "meets guidelines" variable (and treating it as endogenous) can be interpreted as a way to account for legitimate differences in underwriting guidelines across the lenders visited by minorities and whites. In this case, we find that roughly 37.5 percent [$(7.7 - 5.6)/5.6$ from the first row of table 5.5] of the minority-white difference in loan denial is due to business necessity, not discrimination. This assumption is not consistent, however, with the results in the previous paragraph. If minority households simply do a poorer job of finding just the right lender, then, contrary to this evidence, the minority-white difference in loan approval should be larger for lenders that specialize in lending to minorities. Moreover, even if this "meets guidelines" result does reflect differences in underwriting guidelines across the lenders visited by minorities and whites, these differences could be the result of lender discrimination in preapplication procedures and loan marketing, not of benign differences in the way minorities and whites select lenders.

5. *The role of across-lender variation in underwriting standards has not been adequately studied, and more definitive conclusions about the extent of discrimination in loan approval must await further controls for this variation in a loan approval study or a study that combines loan performance and loan approval information.* Although the evidence presented above is suggestive, it does not, in our view, adequately explore the possibility that underwriting standards vary across lenders. As discussed in chapter 3 (lesson 4), underwriting standards may vary for many legitimate reasons, that is, for many reasons that would pass the business necessity test. Although the existing literature explores

a few possible sources of across-lender variation in these standards, it does not, in our view, consider the full range of possible legitimate sources for this variation. Of course, some across-lender variation in underwriting standards may not be legitimate in this sense (chapter 3, lesson 5). As a result, more compelling tests for discrimination must be careful not to remove minority-white differences in loan approval associated with lender-specific underwriting standards that cannot be justified on the grounds of business necessity. We develop such tests the next chapter and in chapter 9.

By collecting, analyzing, and releasing their data, the authors of the Boston Fed Study have made an enormous contribution to the literature on lending discrimination, but their study is certainly not the last word on the subject. A number of important questions concerning the Boston Fed Study's findings have been identified in this chapter. Do lenders engage in disparate-treatment discrimination, or disparate-impact discrimination, or both? To what extent can observed minority-white differences in loan denial, controlling for applicants' credit histories, be explained by legitimate differences in underwriting guidelines across lenders instead of by discrimination? Although these questions cannot be definitively answered with publicly available data, they will be further explored throughout the rest of this book.

6

Accounting for Variation in Underwriting Standards across Lenders

6.1 Introduction

Numerous articles on mortgage lending discrimination have been published since the Boston Fed Study first appeared. A key theme of this literature is variation in underwriting standards across lenders. More specifically, many of these articles struggle with one of the key limitations of the Boston Fed Study identified in chapter 5: It cannot distinguish between disparate-treatment discrimination, disparate-impact discrimination, and intergroup differences in loan denial that arise because different lenders have different underwriting standards and applicant groups differ in the way they are matched with lenders. In this chapter we review recent studies that explore variation in underwriting standards across lenders, and we add to this literature with some analysis of our own.

The studies reviewed in section 6.2 demonstrate that lenders may have complex, even idiosyncratic underwriting standards and that these standards differ from one lender to another. Several studies also find significant minority-white disparities in loan approval by some lenders, even after controlling for an extensive set of underwriting variables that are designed specifically for a particular lender. This is, of course, powerful evidence that these lenders practice disparate-treatment discrimination. A few studies also show, however, that accounting for all the idiosyncratic variation in underwriting behavior across lenders tends to lower the estimated minority-white disparity in loan approval, sometimes substantially. These findings indicate that the main result in the Boston Fed Study might not be a sign of disparate-treatment discrimination but might instead reflect either disparate-impact discrimination or legitimate variation in underwriting standards across lenders that is, because of the way borrowers are matched with lenders, correlated with minority status.

In section 6.3 we investigate the possibility that the minority-white disparity in loan approval in the Boston Fed Study reflects legitimate differences in underwriting standards across lenders. This empirical analysis is based on the public-use version of the Boston Fed Study's data supplemented with HMDA data that identify lenders. Because these data do not include performance information, we cannot directly determine whether variation in underwriting standards across lenders is based on variation in the relationship between underwriting variables and loan profitability. To use the legal terminology, we cannot directly determine whether this variation is justified on the grounds of business necessity. We can determine, however, whether the minority-white disparity in loan approval disappears when we allow for systematic variation in underwriting weights across lenders.

We investigate variation in underwriting weights using two different methods. First, we estimate several models in which a lender's underwriting weights depend on its portfolio, as one would expect if variation in weights reflects variation in lenders' applicant pools and loan performance experience. We find substantial evidence to support the view that the underwriting weights a given lender employs depend on its portfolio. We also find no evidence, however, that this variation in underwriting weights is the source of the minority-white disparity in loan approval. Second, we allow the weights for standard underwriting variables to vary across a subsample of large lenders. Again, we find no evidence that this idiosyncratic variation in underwriting weights can explain minority-white disparities in loan approval.

Because they focus on variation in underwriting weights for standard underwriting variables, these results cannot rule out the possibility that minority-white disparities in loan approval arise because of idiosyncratic variation in the set of underwriting variables across lenders. They do, however, provide new insight into the studies that provide evidence to support this possibility. As these studies recognize, the impact of idiosyncratic variation in underwriting variables on the minority-white disparity in loan approval must reflect either legitimate differences in loan experience across lenders or else disparate-impact discrimination. Our analysis examines a wide range of underwriting and portfolio variables. Any variation in underwriting standards across lenders that we do not account for must be associated, therefore, with underwriting variables that are essentially unique to each lender. It is difficult to imagine loan performance information that would justify the use of a particular variable by one lender but not by others. In other words, any remaining variation in underwriting standards is unlikely to be justified on the grounds of business necessity. Our findings therefore lend credence to the possibility that lenders practice disparate-impact discrimination.

6.2   The Literature on Variation in Underwriting Standards

The first step in untangling the possible interpretations of a loan approval regression is to drop the assumption that all lenders use the same underwriting standards.[1] Two approaches to this step have appeared in the literature. The first approach is to estimate underwriting models for individual lenders. This approach makes it possible to interpret intergroup differences in loan approval, controlling for loan, property, and applicant characteristics, as measures of disparate-treatment discrimination.

The second approach is to pool the data across lenders and to allow the underwriting model to depend on some variables in the data, such as lender characteristics. This approach has the potential to provide insight into the extent to which different lenders use different underwriting standards, but it cannot distinguish between discrimination and intergroup differences in loan approval that arise from idiosyncratic differences in underwriting systems across lenders. Nevertheless, this approach may shed light on the extent to which these differences are associated with loan practices that are most likely to be justified on the grounds of business necessity and therefore least likely to involve disparate-impact discrimination.

6.2.1   Studies of Underwriting Standards for Individual Lenders

In several instances, detailed information on applicant, loan, and property characteristics for loans submitted to one or a few lenders has been assembled as part of a fair-lending investigation. This section reviews studies based on this type of data. These studies shed light both on the complexity of a single lender's underwriting standards and also on the variation in these standards across lenders. In addition, we consider one study that uses the data from the Boston

Fed Study to conduct a detailed investigation of variation in under-writing standards across lenders.

6.2.1.1   Studies Based on Data for a Single Lender

Two detailed explorations of loan approval decisions by a single lender have appeared in the literature, one (Siskin and Cupingood, 1996) based on data collected for an investigation by the U.S. Justice Department, and the other (Calem and Longhofer, 2000) based on data collected for an investigation by the Federal Reserve Board.

The study by Siskin and Cupingood (1996) grew out of the Justice Department's antidiscrimination case against Decatur Federal Savings and Loan, a large lender in Atlanta.[2] In particular, the study examines 1,479 conventional, fixed-rate mortgage applications and 1,431 variable-rate mortgage applications processed by Decatur Federal in 1988 and 1989. The data are based on detailed file reviews, which make it possible to estimate loan denial equations with explanatory variables covering a wide range of loan, borrower, and credit history characteristics. These equations reveal that blacks are far more likely than equivalent whites to be turned down for both fixed- and variable-rate loans.

Because this study is based on detailed information about applicants and loans, it provides compelling evidence that Decatur Federal practiced disparate-treatment discrimination.[3] The main issue with the results is that they cannot be generalized to other lenders.[4] Thus, this study provides a powerful illustration of the lengths to which some lenders will go to avoid lending to black households but does not reveal how common these practices are.

Calem and Longhofer (2000) present the results of a regression-based investigation by the Federal Reserve Board.[5] Their sample consists of 340 conventional home purchase loan applications submitted to one large lender. Their loan approval model is based on extensive information on credit characteristics collected by Federal Reserve examiners and extensive evidence on the lender's underwriting policies. They find that minority status has a negative and significant impact on loan approval. More specifically, they find that the probability of loan approval is 4.56 percentage points lower for minority than for white applicants. Given that the denial rate for whites is only 2.62 percent, this is a large effect.

Further inspection of the loan files, however, led the investigators in this case to the conclusion that no discrimination had taken place. As Calem and Longhofer put it:

Ultimately, however, this finding was attributed to a possible omitted variable (unpaid collections) and to factors that are not amenable to statistical modeling. The latter included incomplete or unverifiable information in the file and idiosyncratic factors specific to individual applications, such as property deficiencies. (p. 20)

The relationship between regression results and loan file reviews is a key issue for fair-lending policy. We discuss this issue in detail in chapter 10.

6.2.1.2 Studies Based on Data for Several Lenders

Several studies examine loan approval decisions using data for a few lenders collected as part of the fair-lending enforcement activities of the Office of the Comptroller of the Currency (OCC).[6] Stengel and Glennon (1999) evaluate three nationally chartered banks based on data collected by the OCC. Random samples of applications for one- to four-family, conventional, nonpurchased (by secondary mortgage market institutions), home purchase mortgage loan applications were drawn from the 1993 HMDA data for each of the three banks. The data contain applications from various minority groups, including Native Americans, Asians, blacks, and Hispanics, but, to preserve confidentially, Stengel and Glennon sort the applications into minority groups I, II, and III, without revealing the identity of any group.

The first step Stengel and Glennon take is to estimate a loan denial equation for each lender using a common set of explanatory variables, including variables to indicate the three minority groups. Because there are so few applications from some minority groups at some lenders, they are able to estimate coefficients for only one of the minority groups for the first bank and for only two of the minority groups for the third. Based on a general specification, they find statistically significant minority status coefficients (significance levels) of 0.59 (0.0062) and 0.72 (0.0029) for minority group I at banks A and B, respectively. The minority status coefficient for group I at bank C is 0.31 (0.2970) and is not statistically significant. The only other significant minority status coefficient is for group III at bank B; this coefficient is 0.71 (0.008).[7]

Stengel and Glennon's next step is to allow for the possibility that different lenders have different underwriting criteria by varying the estimating equation across lenders. For example, they replace LTV with the difference between LTV and a lender-specific threshold value based on the loan size, type, or program; this variable is set to zero if LTV is below the threshold or PMI is obtained. They also modify the debt-to-income ratio variable based on lender-specific criteria and include a variable to indicate whether the applicant had sufficient available liquid assets to cover closing costs. Based on these and other changes, the minority status coefficient for group I at bank A is 0.47 (significance level: 0.0791) and is not statistically significant. At bank B, the minority status coefficient for group I is 0.66 (significance level: 0.0108) and the coefficient for group III is 0.94 (significance level: 0.0001), both of which are significant.[8] Finally, Stengel and Glennon find that their lender-specific model has more explanatory power than their basic model and therefore reject the hypothesis that the underwriting guidelines are the same at all three lenders.[9] They conclude that the use of a common set of control variables across all lenders in a regression is inappropriate and, in the case of bank A and minority group I, leads to a false finding of discrimination.

As a follow-up to this analysis, OCC conducted detailed file reviews and comparisons at bank B and failed to corroborate the existence of disparate-treatment discrimination against any minority group. Stengel and Glennon argue that this apparent contradiction can be explained by two factors: first, several applications had unusual characteristics that were subject to special underwriting guidelines, and second, several data errors were found in the variables measuring credit history, debt ratios, and special-program status. They suggest that bank B's underwriting model contained dozens of detailed limits and guidelines, some of which are only rarely applicable, and conclude that a statistical model cannot possibly capture every provision. They conclude that even their bank-specific model is insufficient and may itself have led to a false finding of discrimination.

Courchane, Nebhut, and Nickerson (2000) provide statistical analyses of the underwriting models of ten additional lenders using a different data set collected by OCC. Based on the pilot program described in Stengel and Glennon (1999), OCC adopted statistical modeling as part of its fair-lending procedures. Under this program, OCC considers conducting statistical analysis only if the number of denied minority applications at a particular lender exceeds fifty. In these cases, OCC draws a sample of loans from the lender's files that is stratified by race and by key underwriting criteria.[10]

Following Stengel and Glennon (1999), Courchane, Nebhut, and Nickerson use a specification that is tailored to each individual lender. Some examples of variables included in the models are credit scores based on lender-specific guidelines, LTV, public-record default, debt-to-income ratio and whether this ratio exceeds lender guidelines, housing expense–to–income ratio and whether this ratio exceeds lender guidelines, job stability as defined by the lender, and low LTV as a compensating factor if it is below a lender-specific threshold.

Statistical evidence of adverse treatment was identified in two of the ten banks included in this study.[11] The authors point out, however, that these ten lenders were included in the paper to illustrate the findings of OCC investigations over the previous five years and that no other statistical examinations during this time period uncovered evidence of adverse treatment of minority borrowers.

Blackburn and Vermilyea (2001) examine the same sample of applications from ten large lenders as Courchane, Nebhut, and Nickerson. They estimate the minority-white difference in loan approval (1) after controlling for the lender-specific models developed by Courchane, Nebhut, and Nickerson and (2) in a pooled regression in which all lenders are assumed to use the same underwriting factors and impose the same underwriting weights. They find substantially higher minority-white disparities with the pooled model. In this sample, in other words, variation in underwriting standards across lenders explains a substantial portion of the intergroup loan approval disparities. This result supports our conclusion in chapter 5 that a pooled regression cannot be used to test for disparate-treatment discrimination. It also suggests, however, that lender-specific regressions may miss important intergroup differences in loan approval, which might constitute disparate-impact discrimination.

Blackburn and Vermilyea also investigate another model of loan approval in which all lenders use the same underwriting variables, but the weights placed on these variables are allowed to vary across lenders. This model yields a minority-white difference in loan approval that is similar to that of their simpler pooled model. This result indicates that minority-white disparities in loan approval arise because different lenders use different underwriting variables, not because they use different underwriting weights for the same variables. The Blackburn and Vermilyea study cannot determine, however, whether differences in the set of underwriting variables can be justified on the grounds of business necessity.

6.2.1.3   Lender-Specific Guidelines in the Boston Fed Study's Data

Buist, Linneman, and Megbolugbe (1999) use the Boston Fed Study's data to pursue the possibility that different lenders have different underwriting standards. Because they cannot directly observe each lender's underwriting standards, their approach is to infer each lender's standards on the basis of its loan approval decisions. In particular, they search for a unique set of implicit underwriting criteria for each lender that best differentiates between accepted and rejected applications.[12] In other words, they identify the criteria that, if violated, always lead to a rejection. This procedure leads to an implicit "meets guidelines" variable, which is set equal to one for all applications that meet the implicit underwriting standards of the lender to which they are submitted. The implicit standards vary widely across lenders. Although the Boston Fed Study's data do not contain all the specialized variables in the studies discussed above, they do contain a large number of variables (see chapter 4), and the procedure developed by Buist, Linneman, and Megbolugbe clearly allows each lender to have idiosyncratic underwriting standards.

The final step taken by Buist, Linneman, and Megbolugbe is to include this new implicit "meets guidelines" variable in a loan denial regression similar to the one estimated by Munnell et al. (1996). This step cuts the minority status coefficient by almost one-third and eliminates its statistical significance.

On the surface, this result appears to indicate that minority applicants do not face discrimination after one accounts for the unique underwriting standards of each lender. For two fundamental reasons, however, such an interpretation is not correct. First, as Buist, Linneman, and Megbolugbe are careful to explain, this finding simply shows that there exists a set of lender-specific, minority status–neutral underwriting criteria that can explain a large portion of observed intergroup differences in loan denial. Information on loan performance was not used to derive these criteria. Thus, even if these criteria accurately describe how lenders actually behave, the Buist, Linneman, and Megbolugbe procedure cannot distinguish between two possibilities: that variation in underwriting standards across lenders has a legitimate, performance-based business justification, or that this variation has a disproportionate impact on minority applicants without any business justification and therefore constitutes discrimination under the disparate-impact standard.

Second, Buist, Linneman, and Megbolugbe's finding that the minority status coefficient is no longer significant once the implicit "meets guidelines" variable is included does not prove that the same underwriting standards are used for both minority and white applicants. Because the underwriting criteria in Buist, Linneman, and Megbolugbe's procedure are inferred, not observed, they could simply reflect a correlation between minority status and various applicant or loan characteristics that arises precisely because minority and white applicants face different criteria. If that is the case, Buist, Linneman, and Megbolugbe's procedure serves only to disguise disparate-treatment discrimination.

Such a disguise also might be facilitated by the econometric properties of their procedure. Specifically, the implicit "meets guidelines" variable is endogenous by definition because it reflects information in the dependent variable.[13] Consequently, the coefficient of this variable, and indeed of all other variables in the regression, might be severely biased.

In short, Buist, Linneman, and Megbolugbe's result reinforces the lesson that a standard loan denial regression alone cannot distinguish among disparate-treatment discrimination, disparate-impact discrimination, and the possibility that minority and white applicants visit lenders with legitimate differences in underwriting standards. Moreover, their result suggests that virtually the entire minority status coefficient could be explained by any one of these three possibilities. The Buist, Linneman, and Megbolugbe procedure cannot reveal, however, which possibility—or which combination of the three possibilities—is the source of the large minority status coefficient in the Boston Fed Study.

6.2.1.4 Discussion

The studies reviewed in this section show that underwriting standards can vary widely across lenders and that lender-specific regressions can be effective in identifying disparate-treatment discrimination in loan underwriting. Indeed, some of the studies reviewed here provide powerful evidence of discrimination against minority applicants.

This approach has several serious limitations, however. First, the data requirements of the approach imply that it can be applied only to a few large lenders. Because it must control for so many underwriting variables, a study of this type cannot be conducted unless a lender makes a large number of loans. Problems of interpretation can arise when the sample size is too small. In the Stengel and Glennon study, for example, the fact that the statistical significance of the group I coefficient at bank A becomes insignificant when the model allows for the possibility that different lenders have different underwriting criteria could reflect the study's small sample size, not a problem with the common model. In fact, the magnitude of the coefficient for this group is not much smaller in the lender-specific regression than in the common one, and we doubt if one could reject the hypothesis that these two coefficients are the same.

Because it must explain the difference between minority and white denials, a study of this type also cannot be conducted unless a large number of minority denials are observed. As illustrated by the Decatur Federal case, however, discriminatory lenders may take extreme steps to limit the number of minority applicants. This behavior obviously limits the power of statistical analysis to determine the circumstances under which minority applications are denied and may even make it impossible to analyze with any level of statistical confidence the behavior of the most discriminatory lenders.

Second, and most important, this method cannot determine whether differences in underwriting guidelines across lenders are legitimate, in the sense that they can be justified on the grounds of business necessity. In Stengel and Glennon (1999), for example, there is such a large number of detailed limits and guidelines at bank B, many of which are only rarely applicable, that it appears highly unlikely this lender has empirical evidence to support the use of these limits and guidelines. This suggests that these guidelines are not legitimate indicators of default risk. Moreover, these policies appear to have a disparate impact on minority applicants. Under such circumstances, switching to a lender-specific model may sharpen the focus on disparate-treatment discrimination at the expense of hiding disparate-impact discrimination.

Indeed, both Buist, Linneman, and Megbolugbe (1999) and Blackburn and Vermilyea (2001) show that it is possible to make minority-white differences in loan approval virtually disappear by allowing different lenders to use different sets of underwriting variables. This type of variation in underwriting systems might have a legitimate business justification (although it is difficult to see why so many credit characteristics would affect default or some other measure of loan profitability for some lenders and not others offering similar loan products). If this type of variation does not have a legitimate business justification, however, then the results in these studies demonstrate that lenders can transform disparate-treatment discrimination, which is easily observed as a significant coefficient for the minority status variable, into disparate-treatment discrimination, which is buried in the coefficients of the idiosyncratic underwriting variables. This possibility makes it imperative that scholars and regulators find better methods for understanding the legitimacy of existing underwriting systems.

6.2.2 Studies of Systematic Variation in Underwriting Standards across Lenders

The alternative to specifying a lender-specific model is to examine underwriting in a pooled sample, but to allow the model to vary across lenders in some systematic manner. The studies discussed in this section estimate underwriting models that fall into one of three categories: (1) models that control for observed lender characteristics, (2) models that allow underwriting standards to vary across loan applications based on lender information, and (3) models that divide lenders into groups (white- and minority-owned banks) and allow a separate underwriting model for each group.[14] All of the studies discussed are based on HMDA data, which do not contain information on borrower credit history or on loan terms, such as the LTV and debt-to-income ratios. As a result, the findings of these studies must be interpreted with caution.

6.2.2.1 Controlling for Lender Characteristics

Black, Collins, and Cyree (1997) incorporate detailed lender financial characteristics as control variables in separate analyses of white- and minority-owned lenders using the 1992–1993 HMDA data. These characteristics include "loan-loss reserves divided by total assets, total mortgages divided by assets, net charge-offs of the bank scaled by assets, core deposits divided by assets, bank equity divided by assets, and the return on assets" (p. 192). They compare loan approval specifications based on just loan application characteristics to extended specifications that include both census tract and lender characteristics. For white-owned lenders, they find that the minority status coefficient is large and statistically significant in the initial specification, but not statistically significant in the expanded specification.[15]

Harrison (2001) examines HMDA data from Pinellas County (St. Petersburg), Florida, in 1993–1995.[16] He estimates four loan approval models: a basic one, one with extensive neighborhood characteristics, one with neighborhood characteristics and lender fixed effects, and one with neighborhood characteristics and, instead of lender fixed effects, lender characteristics. He finds no significant difference between Hispanic and non-Hispanic white applicants in any model, but all four models indicate that blacks are significantly less likely to be approved than are equivalent whites. Moreover, the introduction of either lender fixed effects or lender characteristics increases the magnitude of this race effect substantially, which is the opposite of the direction found for this effect in other studies. To be specific, the race coefficients (absolute values of t-statistics) in the four models are -0.281 (3.47), -0.293 (3.59), -0.365 (4.41), and -0.343 (4.11), respectively. Because Harrison uses a fairly extensive list of lender characteristics, the results for the race coefficient do not depend on whether the model includes these characteristics or uses the preferred method, namely, to include lender fixed effects.[17] This preferred approach was used, of course, by the Boston Fed Study (Munnell et al., 1996).

Because the Harrison study is based on HMDA data, it does not include information on applicant credit history and therefore is undoubtedly subject to omitted-variable bias. Nevertheless, it provides some additional support for the view that it is important to control for differences in underwriting standards across lenders. Moreover, it provides the helpful reminder that accounting for across-lender variation in underwriting standards might either decrease or increase the magnitude of the minority status coefficient. For example, disparate-treatment discrimination against minority applicants could to some degree be hidden if minority applicants tend to visit lenders with less stringent underwriting standards.

6.2.2.2 Controlling for Lender Information

Lang and Nakamura (1993) argue that different lenders have different information about equity risk. The Lang-Nakamura hypothesis begins with the observation that lenders are uncertain about future developments in any particular neighborhood. Because they are risk averse, a greater degree of uncertainty about the condition of the housing market in a particular neighborhood is associated, all else equal, with a higher probability of denying applications for loans to buy houses there.

Lang and Nakumura hypothesize that lenders gain information by observing house sales, so, controlling for other factors, the probability of loan denial in a neighborhood should decline as the number of house sales in that neighborhood goes up.[18] Calem (1996), Ling and Wachter (1998), and Harrison (2001) test this hypothesis using HMDA loan approval data.[19] All three studies confirm the basic hypothesis that loan approval is positively related to the volume of housing transactions in a given neighborhood and conclude that information plays a role in lender underwriting decisions.

Calem also finds, however, that this relationship does not hold in minority neighborhoods; specifically, he finds lower denial rates in minority tracts with poor information than in white tracts with poor information. Moreover, the results of these three studies should be interpreted with care, because the number of housing transactions in a particular neighborhood may be correlated with many unobserved neighborhood characteristics that are relevant for loan profitability. In addition, these studies might suffer from endogeneity bias: A small number of recent transactions in a neighborhood could be the result of a high rate of loan rejections in that location.

Two existing studies address these methodological problems by considering the possibility that the information available about a given neighborhood differs across lenders. Avery, Beeson, and Sniderman (1999) measure the quality of a lender's information in a specific census tract using the number of applications submitted to that lender in that tract, instead of the total number of houses sold there. They show that a substantial portion of the denial rate differences between high- and low-income tracts or between high- and low-percentage minority tracts can be explained by differences in quality of information.

Lin (2001) argues that the number of applications received by a lender from a particular census tract is likely to be influenced by the lender's previous actions in that area. If so, the number of applications received may be endogenous, and its estimated impact on loan denials may be biased. To address this problem, Lin uses, as a measure of lender information, the distance between the tract in which a given housing unit is located and the tract that contains the lender's main office, a variable that appears to be exogenous. In other words, the greater the distance between a neighborhood and a particular lender's office, the less that lender is likely to know about the housing market in that neighborhood, and the more likely it is, all else equal, to reject an application for a loan to buy a house in that neighborhood. Using HMDA data for Connecticut, Lin finds that distance (and hence information) is more important for applications from women and minorities than for applications from white men. She concludes that women and minorities have a particularly difficult time obtaining credit in "thin" housing markets.

The models of Avery, Beeson, and Sniderman and Lin are designed to test a specific hypothesis concerning the role of information in lender underwriting, but they also provide important evidence that underwriting behavior does indeed differ across lenders. Moreover, both Avery, Beeson, and Sniderman and Lin find that these differences have an adverse impact on minority households in the mortgage market. These results should be carefully qualified, because they are based on HMDA data without credit history controls. Even taken at face value, however, these results are difficult to interpret. If application volume or proximity actually provides lenders with better information about the loan risks in a particular neighborhood, then the intergroup differences in loan approval associated with these variables might be justified by business necessity. As illustrated by the Decatur Federal case (Ritter, 1996), however, lenders may consider a location's group composition when deciding whether to open a branch office or even to solicit applications there. As a result, intergroup differences in application volume or proximity to lenders could themselves reflect previous discriminatory actions by lenders. If so, the business necessity defense obviously fails, and these studies reveal that disparate-impact discrimination in loan approval can arise from a lender's past discrimination in marketing decisions.

6.2.2.3 Separate Underwriting Models by Type of Lender

Black, Collins, and Cyree (1997) argue that if discrimination arises because of intergroup prejudice, then discrimination, and hence intergroup differences in loan approval, will appear in white-owned lending institutions but are unlikely to appear in a lending institution that is owned by blacks (or by people in some other minority group). A similar argument has been applied to discrimination by housing agents (Yinger, 1986, 1995) and by car salesmen (Ayres and Siegelman, 1995). Some scholars have called this the "cultural-affinity" hypothesis. Further implications of this hypothesis are explored in chapter 7.

To test this hypothesis, Black, Collins, and Cyree identify black-owned lending institutions in major metropolitan areas and matched or comparable white-owned lending institutions in the same locations. Then they obtain the 1992–1993 HMDA data for all applications to these lenders. The resulting data set contains 2,393 white applications and 925 black applications from eighty-one lenders, thirty-two of which were owned by blacks.

The first step in the analysis conducted by Black, Collins, and Cyree is to estimate, for both black- and white-owned lending institutions, the relationship between loan denial and the applicant and loan characteristics in the HMDA data. This estimation indicates large intergroup differences in loan denial for both black-owned and white-owned lending institutions, but the size and significance of the minority status coefficient is substantially larger for institutions owned by blacks. The second step is to estimate an enhanced equation that includes neighborhood characteristics and detailed financial characteristics of the individual lending institutions as explanatory variables. With this enhanced equation the minority status coefficient is not significant for white lenders, but it is still highly significant for black lenders.

These results appear to contradict the cultural-affinity hypothesis, but it is not clear what they mean. One possibility is that they reflect lenders' trade-off between the potential economic gains from discrimination, a topic to which we return in chapter 7, and the potential costs of being caught by federal regulators. If black-owned banks assume that their lending practices with regard to applicant minority status will receive little scrutiny, those banks may be more inclined to practice discrimination. Another possibility is that the results simply reflect limitations in the study's data, which, after all, do not indicate applicants' credit history. As we have seen throughout this book, omitted-variable bias is likely in this situation.

Another possibility is investigated by Bostic and Canner (1997), who argue that the Black, Collins, and Cyree results could arise because the applicants at black-owned banks are different from the applicants at white-owned banks on characteristics that are not recorded in the HMDA data. More specifically, they argue that "cultural affinity" applies to applicants, as well as to lenders:

Minority applicants may feel more comfortable applying for mortgages at minority-owned banks, which could result in a relatively large volume of marginally qualified applicants at minority-owned banks. In such a case, minority-owned banks could have higher rejection rates than white-owned banks, even if only minority lenders exhibit cultural affinity or if lenders of both races applied the same underwriting standards. (p. 1)

To test this view, Bostic and Canner identify minority-owned banks and comparable white-owned banks, following procedures similar to those in Black, Collins, and Cyree. They then use the 1994 and 1995 HMDA data to determine the share of applications at each bank that come from whites, blacks, and Asians. Their sample consists of twenty-nine minority-owned and fifty-two white-owned banks in 1994 along with thirty-two minority-owned and sixty-two white-owned banks in 1995.

These data make it possible to explain the share of a lender's applications from a minority group (or from low-income neighborhoods) as a function of the financial characteristics of the bank and whether it is minority-owned. Bostic and Canner find that the share of applications from blacks at black-owned banks was five times the share at white-owned banks, on average, in 1994 and eight times the share in 1995.[20] Black-owned banks also had a much higher share of their applications from low-income neighborhoods.

Bostic and Canner then estimate a loan denial equation and reproduce the Black, Collins, and Cyree result. To account for the possibility that the applicants to black-owned lenders are less creditworthy than those to white-owned lenders, they then reestimate this equation using a subsample that consists of applications at black-owned banks along with applications at white-owned banks that are comparable in terms of observable characteristics. In this matched subsample, there is no evidence that the black/white denial ratio is any higher at black-owned banks than at white-owned banks.

These results generally support the Bostic-Canner hypothesis. They indicate, in other words, that black-owned banks attract black applicants and applicants with relatively low credit qualifications, on average, and that a failure to account for this effect leads to the false impression that black-owned banks are the only ones to discriminate against blacks. Bostic and Canner's results do not show, however, that blacks or applicants with low creditworthiness are attracted to black-owned banks because of "cultural affinity." These applicants could, as Bostic and Canner say in their fourth footnote, end up at black-owned lenders because the marketing practices of those lenders differ from those of white-owned lenders. They point out, for example, that black-owned banks might be more likely than white-owned banks to work with black real estate brokers, who might, in turn, be more likely than other brokers to have black customers. Moreover, the results do not support the standard prediction from the cultural-affinity hypothesis, namely, that the black/white denial ratio will be higher at white-owned than at black-owned banks.

Thus, the results in Bostic and Canner's study support the notion that applicants sort themselves by group in selecting lenders but do not explain why this sorting occurs, and they find no evidence that cultural affinity affects lenders' loan denial decisions. However, the sorting indicated by this study confirms one of the key concerns raised in chapter 5 concerning the effect of lender differences in underwriting standards. Minority borrowers appear to be responding to information about lenders in an attempt to increase their likelihood of receiving mortgage credit. Intergroup differences in information about individual lenders may have a direct impact on minority loan denial rates in a sample of pooled mortgages.

6.3   New Estimates of Variation in Underwriting Standards

As the preceding literature review makes clear, the key challenge facing scholars as they try to understand discrimination in loan approval is that different lenders may use different underwriting standards. An analysis that does not recognize this possibility could lead to incorrect or invalid conclusions. Results generated by disparate-impact discrimination might mistakenly be interpreted as evidence of disparate-treatment discrimination. Moreover, results generated by legitimate, that is, nondiscriminatory, differences in underwriting standards across lenders might mistakenly be interpreted as evidence of discrimination. In this section we explore these possibilities through further investigation of the Boston Fed Study's data.

To be specific, we conduct an empirical investigation of the possibility that the minority-white disparity in loan approval in the Boston Fed Study reflects differences in underwriting standards across lenders. Because the data collected for this study do not include performance information, we cannot directly determine whether variation in underwriting standards across lenders reflects variation in the relationship between underwriting variables and loan profit-ability, or, to use the legal terminology, whether this variation is justified on the basis of business necessity. We can take a significant step in this direction, however, by accounting for systematic varia-tion in underwriting standards across lenders.

The relationship between underwriting variables and loan profit-ability is most likely to vary across lenders when lenders specialize in different loan products or draw applications from different pools of potential borrowers. As a result, lender-specific underwriting standards that reflect a lender-specific relationship between under-writing variables and loan profitability, which are the lender-specific standards most likely to be justified on the grounds of business necessity, are inevitably correlated with the types of loans a lender issues. To put it another way, these lender-specific standards are correlated with a lender's loan portfolio. Allowing underwriting standards to vary with key measures of a lender's portfolio is there-fore equivalent to controlling for the type of variation in underwrit-ing standards across lenders that is most likely to meet the business necessity test.

Any minority-white disparities that remain after such variation is allowed must be the result of either disparate-treatment discrimina-tion or idiosyncratic variation in underwriting standards across lenders that is correlated with minority status. In principle, this type of idiosyncratic variation in underwriting standards could have a business justification; after all, we cannot directly observe the per-formance-based justification for any underwriting practice.[21] Be-cause a lender's loan performance experience is related to the pool of applications it attracts, however, this possibility is unlikely. As a re-sult, minority-white differences in loan approval that persist after variation in underwriting standards according to lender's portfolios is allowed provide strong, if not unambiguous, evidence that lenders either practice disparate-treatment discrimination or have idiosyn-cratic variations in underwriting practices that constitute disparate-impact discrimination.

Our analysis proceeds in three steps. First, we merge the Boston Fed Study's data with HMDA data to identify individual lenders. Second, we account for variation in underwriting standards based on loan terms. Third, we account for variation in underwriting stan-dards across lenders and explain the implications of our results for an interpretation of minority-white disparities in loan approval.

6.3.1   Identifying Lenders in the Boston Fed Study's Sample

We begin our analysis of across-lender variation in underwriting standards by matching the Boston Fed Study's data to HMDA data using a procedure developed by Day and Liebowitz (1996).[22] This procedure allows us to identify the lenders associated with most of the loans in the Boston Fed Study's data and then to incorporate into these data the characteristics of each lender's portfolio, based on all its HMDA loans or on just the loans in the Boston Fed Study's sample. In this section we describe this procedure and the data set that results from it.

6.3.1.1   The HMDA Matched Sample

The Day and Liebowitz (1996) matching procedure involves the identification of unique observations based on a set of comparison variables that exist in both the Boston Fed Study's data and the comparable HMDA data. These two data sets can be unambiguously matched by finding two observations, one in each data set, that have the same values for all the comparison variables. Once a match has been found, the lender identification in the HMDA data can be attached to an observation in the Boston Fed Study's data. The comparison variables are loan action, race and sex of applicant, race and sex of coapplicant, income and loan amount in thousands of dollars, if and by whom the loan was purchased, and whether the applicant intended to occupy the home.

This process successfully matched, and hence identified the lender for, 2,343 loans in our cleaned, public-use version of the Boston Fed Study's sample, which contains 2,896 loans. One might think that it would be impossible to match many loans in the Boston Fed Study's data because they have the same values on the comparison variables as several different loans in the HMDA data or because one loan in the HMDA data has the same values on these variables as several loans in the Boston Fed Study's data. As it turns out, however, such cases are rare. Instead, the main reason for a failure to find a match for a particular loan in the Boston Fed Study's data is that there does not exist a loan in the 1990 HMDA data for the Boston metropolitan area with the same values for the comparison variables.[23] Overall, the matching process works well, but over 500 loans in the Boston Fed Study's data remain unmatched, thereby reducing our sample size for analysis that includes lender characteristics.

6.3.1.2   Basic Analysis with the Matched Sample

To provide perspective for our later analysis, we begin our investigation of the matched sample by returning to the basic specification of a loan approval model, as developed in chapter 5. Our objectives are to determine whether this specification yields similar results with the full sample and the matched sample and, if not, to investigate the reasons for the differences.

We begin by making a few minor modifications to the specification in chapter 5. First, we treat LTV as a continuous variable instead of a series of discrete categories to facilitate the use of interactions in later specifications. Second, we drop loans with missing information on LTV or with LTV values above 1.5 to make certain that our analysis is not unduly influenced by outliers. Third, we use a logit specification instead of a probit, because a logit provides a particularly straightforward way to account for individual lender effects, usually called "fixed effects" (Chamberlain, 1980). This is not a major change; logit and probit results tend to be quite similar. Fourth, we exclude both the "meets guidelines" variable and the instrument for this variable. As shown in chapter 5, once a loan approval equation controls for legitimate differences in underwriting standards across lenders, the minority status coefficient will understate discrimination if the "meets guidelines" variable is included in the regression.[24] Fifth, we do not treat any loan terms as endogenous. The results in chapter 4 reveal that allowing for this type of endogeneity has little impact on the results. Moreover, our analysis eventually includes both lender fixed effects and variables to describe a lender's portfolio; these additions greatly weaken the case for an endogeneity correction, which depends on the presence of unobserved lender characteristics.

The results for this basic loan approval specification are presented in table 6.1. The first column shows the results for the Boston Fed Study's sample, with the minor modifications indicated above. The next two columns show the results for the matched sample with and without lender fixed effects. The variables in these regressions are defined in table 5.1. All three regressions work quite well, with similar coefficients for most variables. In all three cases, the coefficient of the minority status variable is large and statistically significant.

When evaluated at the average characteristics for the minority sample, the results in the first column imply that the probability of loan approval is 7.9 percentage points lower for minorities than for whites. The comparable differences for the matched sample are 4.8

Table 6.1
Results for baseline loan approval regressions with matched sample

Variable	Boston Fed Study's sample	Matched sample	Matched sample with lender fixed effects
EXPENSE-TO-INCOME	0.860	0.004	−0.133
	(0.857)	(0.400)	(−0.107)
DEBT-TO-INCOME	−5.837	−5.194	−6.190
	(−6.701)	(−5.508)	(−5.483)
NET WORTH	−0.002	0.017	−0.024
	(−0.063)	(0.425)	(−0.407)
PREDICTED UNEMPLOYMENT	−0.061	−0.063	−0.059
	(−2.179)	(−2.100)	(−1.788)
SELF EMPLOYED	−0.462	−0.502	−0.706
	(−2.419)	(−2.510)	(−3.152)
LTV	−1.846	−2.301	−2.879
	(−3.886)	(−4.317)	(−4.666)
DENIED PMI	−4.843	−4.612	−5.009
	(−8.854)	(−7.263)	(−6.834)
MULTI-FAMILY	−0.436	−0.459	−0.509
	(−2.477)	(−2.441)	(−2.390)
FIXED RATE	−0.208	−0.176	−0.237
	(−1.455)	(−1.158)	(−1.068)
SPECIAL	0.310	0.946	1.410
	(1.211)	(2.695)	(3.447)
TERM	0.090	0.000	0.004
	(6.923)	(0.000)	(0.222)
GOT GIFT	0.264	0.159	0.163
	(1.517)	(0.864)	(0.799)
COSIGNER	0.350	0.470	0.568
	(0.972)	(1.146)	(1.246)
MINORITY	−0.647	−0.392	−0.409
	(−3.994)	(−2.292)	(−2.108)
AGE	−0.248	−0.307	−0.325
	(−1.865)	(−2.147)	(−2.044)
MALE	−0.155	−0.205	−0.207
	(−0.912)	(5.435)	(−1.005)
MARRIED	0.283	0.257	0.283
	(1.993)	(1.669)	(1.655)
OWNER-OCCUPIED	0.981	0.992	0.973
	(2.982)	(2.918)	(2.527)
POOR TRACT	0.007	−0.026	−0.054
	(0.038)	(−0.131)	(−0.240)
MINORITY TRACT	−0.205	−0.313	−0.259
	(−0.911)	(−1.272)	(−0.925)

Table 6.1
(continued)

Variable	Boston Fed Study's sample	Matched sample	Matched sample with lender fixed effects
BANKRUPTCY	−1.255	−1.279	−1.502
	(−7.011)	(−6.661)	(−6.559)
MORTGAGE CREDIT	−0.356	−0.405	−0.401
	(−2.967)	(−3.115)	(−2.747)
CONSUMER CREDIT	−0.311	−0.322	−0.391
	(−9.147)	(−8.944)	(−9.093)
Intercept	6.438	6.988	7.568
	(8.493)	(8.319)	(6.168)

Note: All models are estimated using logit analysis. APPROVE is the dependent variable; *t*-statistics are in parentheses. Results for lender fixed effects in the third regression are not presented.

and 4.5 percentage points for the specifications that exclude and include lender fixed effects, respectively. Thus, intergroup differences in loan approval are considerably lower for the merged sample than for the set of loans that could not be matched to the HMDA data. In fact, estimating these equations for the 553 observations in the full sample that could not be matched, we find that the probability of loan approval is 24.6 percentage points lower for minorities than for whites.[25] The experiences of minority applicants appear to be quite different in the matched and unmatched samples of loans!

We can think of several potential explanations for this difference:

• The lender fixed effects explain a substantial portion of observed intergroup differences in loan approval.

By definition, lender fixed effects cannot be estimated for the unmatched sample, and the estimated impact of minority status might drop considerably if they were included. The evidence from the matched sample does not, however, support this explanation. In fact, the estimated effect of minority status is almost the same for the specifications that exclude and include lender fixed effects. Although the inclusion of lender fixed effects might have a much larger impact in the unmatched sample, this possibility appears to be inconsistent with the evidence in Munnell et al. (1996). Specifically, as pointed out in chapter 4, Munnell et al., who have access to lender identities for the entire sample, include lender fixed effects in their basic model and still find a large, statistically significant minority status coefficient.

• The loans in the matched and unmatched samples are significantly different.

Another possibility is that the loans that are successfully matched differ significantly from other loans. This explanation has some intuitive appeal. Munnell et al. (1996) establish that intergroup differences in underwriting increase with the debt-to-income ratio. If the unmatched sample of loans has a higher debt-to-income ratio, on average, than the matched sample, then it also will have a larger estimated intergroup difference in underwriting.

As it turns out, however, this explanation is not supported by the evidence. In the matched sample, the mean obligation ratios are 32.5 and 34.7 for white and minority applicants, respectively. In the unmatched sample, the corresponding means are 33.6 and 34.8. Thus, the mean obligation ratio for minorities is almost identical across the two samples, and the mean obligation ratio for whites is higher in the unmatched sample. The explanation also is not supported by a comparison of estimated intergroup differences in loan approval in the full and matched samples that accounts for the possible role of obligation ratio. To make this comparison, we introduce a new variable, namely, the interaction between minority status and debt-to-income ratio, into our basic specification. When this interaction variable is included in a regression for the matched sample, the predicted average minority-white difference in loan approval is 5.0 percentage points. Applying the estimated coefficients from the matched sample to the entire sample yields an average minority-white difference of 4.9 percentage points.[26] As before, therefore, accounting for differences in the characteristics of loans in the matched and unmatched samples has little impact on the estimated minority status coefficient.

• The actual level of discrimination varies with the likelihood of finding an HMDA match.

Another possibility is that loans we are unable to match with the HMDA data have unobserved characteristics that are associated with a higher probability of discrimination. To examine this possibility, we must consider why HMDA matches do not exist for some of the Boston Fed Study's loans. Day and Liebowitz (1996) suggest that the Boston Fed researchers either worked with an early, error-prone sample or made errors in constructing their sample. This explanation does not seem very likely, however, because the Boston Fed researchers did not rely on the information in the HMDA data, whether or not it was an early, error-prone release. The information used in the Boston Fed Study comes directly from the loan files. As discussed earlier, the Boston Fed researchers also did extensive checking of their data. In addition, the sample of unmatched loans appears to be significantly different from other loans. Random data entry and transcription errors in the creation of the Boston Fed Study's data could not have created this type of systematic difference.

Instead, we believe that the failure to obtain matches for some loans arises from flaws in the HMDA data. As is well-known, the HMDA data are often missing information on race/ethnicity, income, and other applicant characteristics (see Avery, Beeson, and Sniderman, 1996a, and Huck, 2001). In addition, by comparing the HMDA data with data on FreddieMac loan purchases, Van Order and Zorn (1995) show that the HMDA data do not contain information on all the mortgage applications they are intended to cover. Thus, the unmatched sample of loans is likely to consist largely of loans that are missing, incomplete, or incorrect in the HMDA sample. Using HMDA data for 1993 to 1999, Dietrich (2001, p. 1) provides compelling evidence for this type of data problem. He finds that "applications that contain race data have higher origination rates than applications without race data, and applications from Blacks and Hispanics may be more likely to be without race data than whites."

Errors in HMDA reporting might arise because some lenders place a low priority on providing information on fair lending to government agencies, because some lenders are careless with loan files and in documenting mortgage applications in general, or because many lenders are occasionally careless in the handling of individual loan files and mortgage applications. Any of these factors might lead to higher intergroup differences in loan denial for the unmatched sample. Lenders that place a low priority on fair lending may not monitor their employees carefully for compliance with antidiscrimination guidelines and may even be willing to engage in statistical discrimination to increase the quality their loan pool. Alternatively, carelessness in the handling of mortgage applications and loan files may insert noise into the underwriting process, thereby creating an opportunity for prejudiced employees to discriminate or for racial stereotypes to influence underwriting decisions.

One way to test this carelessness hypothesis is to determine whether discrimination depends on the number of times an application is considered. The reconsideration of an application presumably results in less noise, as bank officials correct errors or applicants supply additional information. As a result, the lender's written underwriting standards become more decisive, and there is less room for personal judgments or interpretations, including those based on prejudice or stereotypes. Thus, we explore this hypothesis further using a variable, introduced in chapter 5, indicating the number of times an application was considered.

To conduct our test of the carelessness hypothesis, we introduce into our basic loan approval model both the number of times an application was considered ("considerations" for short) and an interaction between considerations and minority status. We estimate this model for both the matched and unmatched samples. In the matched sample, the number of considerations does not appear to vary by race; 69.8 percent of white applications and 68.3 of minority applications were reconsidered only one, two, or three times. In this sample, the coefficients (t-statistics) on considerations and the interaction variable are 0.145 (1.86) and 0.127 (0.93), respectively. The first coefficient is significant at the 10-percent level, but the interaction is not statistically significant. In the unmatched sample, however, minority applications are less likely than white applications to be reconsidered. To be specific, 81.7 percent of minority applications, compared to 61.4 percent of white applications, were considered only one, two, or three times. In this sample, the coefficients (t-statistics) on considerations and its interaction with minority status are 0.167 (0.49) and 0.899 (1.69). The latter coefficient, which is statistically significant at the 10-percent level (two-tailed test), implies that additional considerations increase the likelihood that a minority application will be approved. This result supports our hypothesis that noisy underwriting criteria create additional opportunities for discrimination against minority applicants.

In short, the HMDA data make it possible to identify the lender for the vast majority of the observations in the Boston Fed Study's data. The minority-white differences in loan approval are significantly larger, however, for the unmatched observations than for the matched ones. The most likely explanation for this difference appears to be that the unmatched observations are more likely to involve incomplete information in the loan files and are thereby more likely to provide an opportunity for loan officers to exercise their prejudices, stereotypes, or discriminatory inclinations.

6.3.2   Estimating Variation in Underwriting Based on Loan Terms

Before examining the possibility that different lenders have different underwriting standards, it is important to determine whether the weights lenders place on various loan and borrower characteristics depend upon the nature of the loan. If this type of interaction exists but is omitted from the analysis, a researcher might incorrectly conclude that underwriting standards vary across lenders. This possibility arises because these interactions might create a correlation between the underwriting weights placed on various loan terms and the characteristics of a lender's loan portfolio. Consider, for example, a lender that specializes in high-LTV loans and a common underwriting process in which the weight placed on the debt-to-income ratio is higher for loans with a high LTV. Under these circumstances, this lender will appear to place a higher weight on the debt-to-income ratio than do other lenders, even though this is not the case.

Our strategy for determing whether lenders' weights on various criteria vary according to the type of loan is to estimate a series of models in which all the variables in our baseline specification with lender fixed effects are interacted with one of the following application characteristics: debt-to-income ratio, housing expense–to–income ratio, LTV, public-record default, mortgage credit history, consumer credit history, multifamily unit, fixed-rate mortgage, term of mortgage, gift included in down payment, and unit in high–poverty-rate census tract. We then test whether each set of interaction variables is statistically significant.

We find that several sets of interaction variables are statistically significant, namely, the sets associated with the following variables: debt-to-income ratio (significant at the 0.001 level), housing expense–to–income ratio (0.01 level), consumer credit history (0.01 level), public-record default (0.05 level), and LTV (just misses significance at the 0.05 level). These results imply that any attempt to determine whether underwriting standards vary across lenders must proceed with great caution. Interactions among loan characteristics, combined with differences in lenders' portfolios, could easily be mistaken for differences in underwriting standards.

As an aside, it is worth noting that the estimated intergroup differences in loan approval are essentially unaffected by the introduction of these interaction variables. Specifically, the estimated minority-white differences in loan approval for models that include these interaction variables fall between 4.3 and 4.7 percentage points, compared with the 4.5 percentage points for the baseline specification in table 6.1. These results reinforce the evidence on specification presented in chapter 5: The large minority-white differences in loan approval cannot be attributed to a misspecification of the loan approval equation.

Table 6.2 presents our results for the interactions with the debt-to-income ratio and with consumer credit history.[27] Columns 1 and 2 presents the results for the model that includes interactions with the debt-to-income ratio. The first column reveals, for example, that holding the debt-to-income ratio fixed, an increase in the housing expense–to–income ratio, which implies a decrease in nonhousing debt, leads to a significant increase in the likelihood of loan approval. The second column indicates that the positive effect on loan approval of a decrease in nonhousing debt is smaller at a high debt-to-income ratio than at a low debt-to-income ratio. Similarly, the positive effect on loan approval of a high net worth or of good credit history is smaller when the debt-to-income ratio is high than when it is low. These results indicate that lenders are less willing to consider other compensating factors as the share of income consumed by debt increases.

Finally, intergroup differences in underwriting are much larger at high debt-to-income ratios than at low debt-to-income ratios. One possible explanation for this result is that, on average, lenders expect minorities to have less-stable income streams than whites. With this expectation, loans at a given debt-to-income ratio will be seen as riskier if the customer is minority than if the customer is white. This is, of course, an example of statistical discrimination; lenders are using minority status as a predictor of income variation and hence of credit risk. In other words, this result supports the view, discussed at length in chapter 7, that mortgage lending discrimination persists because lenders believe it will increase their profits.

Columns 3 and 4 of table 6.2 present the results for the model that includes interactions with consumer credit history.[28] The two significant interactions in the fourth column involve the housing expense–to–income ratio and the debt-to-income ratio. The underwriting

Table 6.2
Results for regressions with interactions between loan terms, matched sample

Variable	Model 1		Model 2	
	Coefficient	Coefficient of interaction with DEBT-TO-INCOME	Coefficient	Coefficient of interaction with CONSUMER CREDIT
EXPENSE-TO-INCOME	8.148 (2.651)	−21.449 (−3.085)	3.392 (1.575)	−1.348 (−1.934)
DEBT-TO-INCOME	14.618 (1.622)		−11.047 (−5.793)	1.725 (3.273)
NET WORTH	0.765 (2.211)	−2.181 (−2.320)	−0.087 (−0.926)	0.038 (0.760)
PREDICTED UNEMPLOYMENT	−0.206 (−0.002)	0.441 (1.205)	−0.113 (−1.982)	0.016 (0.941)
SELF EMPLOYED	−0.569 (−0.741)	−0.163 (−0.077)	−0.611 (−1.501)	−0.044 (−0.328)
LTV	0.163 (0.069)	−9.036 (−1.403)	−3.168 (−2.931)	0.003 (0.009)
DENIED PMI	−8.845 (−2.060)	9.678 (0.831)	−6.021 (−5.142)	0.481 (1.419)
MULTI-FAMILY	0.416 (0.459)	−2.197 (−0.875)	−0.126 (−0.330)	−0.148 (−1.358)
FIXED RATE	0.978 (1.306)	−3.530 (−1.725)	−0.642 (−1.845)	0.145 (1.576)
SPECIAL	2.263 (0.975)	−2.330 (−0.361)	0.566 (0.840)	0.242 (1.337)
TERM	0.008 (0.145)	0.003 (0.020)	0.038 (1.357)	−0.011 (−1.375)
GOT GIFT	−1.826 (−1.920)	5.628 (2.139)	0.141 (0.365)	−0.006 (−0.059)
COSIGNER	1.353 (0.546)	−1.994 (−0.303)	1.614 (1.590)	−0.318 (−1.320)
MINORITY	2.044 (2.172)	−7.005 (−2.688)	−0.375 (−1.856)	
AGE	−0.002 (−0.003)	−1.082 (−0.530)	−0.563 (−1.889)	0.062 (0.747)
MALE	−0.745 (−0.831)	1.431 (0.583)	−0.375 (−0.974)	0.055 (0.514)
MARRIED	0.199 (0.252)	0.060 (0.027)	0.740 (2.357)	−0.156 (−1.733)
OWNER-OCCUPIED	2.669 (2.576)	−6.609 (−2.076)	0.364 (0.538)	0.248 (1.000)
POOR TRACT	1.574 (1.676)	−4.810 (−1.810)	0.414 (1.010)	0.155 (1.384)

Table 6.2
(continued)

	Model 1		Model 2	
Variable	Coefficient	Coefficient of interaction with DEBT-TO-INCOME	Coefficient	Coefficient of interaction with CONSUMER CREDIT
MINORITY TRACT	1.329	−4.626	−0.131	−0.131
	(0.921)	(−1.146)	(−0.257)	(−0.230)
BANKRUPTCY	−3.985	7.135	−0.668	−0.220
	(−3.985)	(2.580)	(−1.277)	(−1.833)
MORTGAGE CREDIT	−0.225	−0.758	−0.020	−0.119
	(−0.395)	(−0.474)	(−0.070)	(−1.587)
CONSUMER CREDIT	−0.769	1.025	−0.323	
	(−3.944)	(1.881)	(−0.626)	
Intercept	1.061		7.709	
	(0.324)		(4.136)	

Note: All models are estimated with logit analysis. APPROVE is the dependent variable; *t*-statistics are in parentheses.

weights placed on the debt-to-income and housing expense–to–income ratios are closer to zero if an applicant has a poor credit history (i.e., a large value for the credit history variable) than if he has a good credit history. This is, of course, exactly the same result obtained from the previous specification; a high debt-to-income ratio has a large negative impact on the approval probability of an application that is otherwise attractive, as indicated, in this case by a good credit history.

We do not present detailed results for any of the other interaction specifications mentioned earlier. Although these other specifications are statistically significant compared to a specification with no interactions, they are not significant compared to the specification with the debt-to-income interactions, which is the first one presented in table 6.2.[29]

6.3.3 Accounting for Across-Lender Variation in Underwriting Standards

We now turn to our central questions: Do underwriting standards vary systematically across lenders? If so, does accounting for this systematic variation affect the minority-white disparity in loan approval? We address these question in three different ways. The first two ways determine whether the underwriting model used by a lender depends on the lender's portfolio, that is, on the characteristics of the loans the lender has approved. The first way determines the characteristics of a lender's portfolio based on that lender's loans in the Boston Fed Study's data, and the second determines these characteristics based on all the loans by that lender in the HMDA data.

As indicated earlier, this approach is designed to shed some light on the possibility that observed minority-white differences in loan approval reflect legitimate differences in underwriting standards across lenders. In this context, "legitimate" means that these differences accurately reflect differences in expected profitability and therefore are, in the legal sense, justified on the grounds of business necessity. Any underwriting differences that are legitimate in this sense must reflect either differences in the applications lenders receive or differences in lenders' past experiences. As a result, a finding that minority-white differences in loan approval disappear after accounting for the link between a lender's underwriting standards and its portfolio satisfies a necessary condition for the business necessity defense. In other words, such a finding would not prove that minority-white differences in loan approval are justified on the basis of business necessity, but it would tell us that this possibility cannot be ruled out. A finding that minority-white differences in loan approval remain after these new controls indicates that these differences result from disparate-treatment discrimination, from disparate-impact discrimination built into idiosyncratic variation underwriting standards across lenders, or from idiosyncratic variation in underwriting standards across lenders that is justified on the grounds of business necessity (but somehow is uncorrelated with variation in lenders' portfolios).

The third way we address the question of variation in underwriting standards across lenders is to estimate separate underwriting models for all the lenders with a relatively large number of loans in the Boston Fed Study's sample. This approach picks up any differences in underwriting standards across lenders associated with key underwriting variables, regardless of whether these differences are correlated with lenders' portfolios, and provides another type of test about the source of the minority-white difference in loan approval.[30] The test is whether the estimated minority-white difference in loan approval disappears in a model that allows for differences across lenders in the weights placed on key underwriting variables. If it does, then we can conclude that the higher likelihood of loan denial for minorities is caused by differences in underwriting standards across lenders that reflect either legitimate business considerations or else disparate-impact discrimination. If it does not, however, then we can conclude that the higher likelihood of loan denial for minorities is a product of disparate-treatment discrimination, of disparate-impact discrimination that appears in the idiosyncratic variation in the list of underwriting variables across lenders, or of idiosyncratic variation in the list of underwriting variables that is justified on the grounds of business necessity.

6.3.3.1 Underwriting Standards and Lender Portfolios Based on the Boston Fed Study's Sample

We start by asking whether underwriting models vary systematically with the characteristics of a lender's portfolio, where the portfolio is described by the average characteristics of the lender's applications in the Boston Fed Study's data. In addressing this question, we recognize the key lesson from the previous section, namely, that the underwriting weights attached to various applicant, loan, or property characteristics depend upon the value of the debt-to-income ratio and various other variables. As explained earlier, a failure to recognize this dependence could lead a researcher to draw an incorrect or invalid conclusion about variation in underwriting standards across lenders. Thus, all the models in this section include the types of interactions described in table 6.2.

To investigate differences in underwriting standards across lenders, the models in this section introduce new sets of interaction variables that interact applicant, loan, and property characteristics with the average value of some characteristic for the loans in a lender's portfolio. In other words, we determine whether the underwriting weights placed on various application characteristics vary with the type of applications a lender receives. Our strategy is to examine portfolio characteristics one at a time. For example, one model introduces a set of interactions between individual application characteristics and the average debt–to–income ratio in a lender's portfolio, and another introduces a set of interactions between the same individual application characteristics and the average housing expense-to-income ratio.

To facilitate interpretation, we also coordinate the two sets of interaction variables in each model, namely, the applicant-level interactions based on section 6.3.2 and the portfolio-level interactions introduced in this section. To be specific, we make certain that the same variable (debt-to-income ratio, housing expense–to–income ratio, and so on) is used to define the applicant-level interactions and the portfolio-level applications.[31] For example, the model to determine whether underwriting weights vary with the average debt-to-income ratio in a lender's portfolio also includes the set of interactions in the second column of table 6.2, which are defined by the debt-to-income ratio in each application. This strategy ensures that the coefficients of the portfolio-level interactions will not inadvertently measure the role of applicant-level interactions.

We examine separate sets of portfolio-level interactions for five variables: debt-to-income ratio, housing expense–to–income ratio, LTV, public-record default, and consumer credit history. Each set is statistically significant at the 0.05 level or above, except for the set based on public-record default.[32] Table 6.3 presents the estimation results for the portfolio-level interactions involving the debt-to-income ratio, LTV, and consumer credit history. (The comparable results for the housing expense–to–income ratio are not shown in the table because they are very similar to the results for the debt-to-income ratio.)[33]

Our first key result from these regressions is that different lenders do, indeed, use different underwriting standards. Consider, for example, the role of a lender's mean debt-to-income ratio. We find that the negative influence of the applicant-level debt-to-income ratio is smaller when portfolio-level debt-to-income ratio is high (significant at 0.10 level).

Our second key result is that the minority-white difference in loan approval depends on the nature of a particular lender's portfolio, or, to put it another way, on the market niche that the lender fills. We find, for example, that the minority-white disparity in loan approval increases with the applicant-level debt-to-income level (significant at 0.01 level) but decreases with the portfolio-level debt-to-income ratio (0.05 level). In other words, minority applicants appear to face more discrimination if they have a high debt-to-income ratio but less discrimination if they visit a lender with a high average debt-to-income ratio among the loans in its portfolio.

Table 6.3
Results for regressions with interactions between lender portfolio and applications characteristics, matched sample

Variable	Model 1: Interaction with lender's mean DEBT- TO-INCOME	Model 2: Interaction with lender's mean LTV	Model 3: Interaction with lender's mean CONSUMER CREDIT
EXPENSE-TO-INCOME	−70.944	66.57	2.766
	(−1.094)	(1.815)	(0.995)
DEBT-TO-INCOME	109.738	17.393	0.940
	(1.808)	(0.533)	(0.398)
NET WORTH	−3.816	0.874	0.085
	(−1.312)	(0.591)	(0.675)
PREDICTED	−01.968	−2.284	0.031
UNEMPLOYMENT	(−0.569)	(−2.250)	(0.425)
SELF EMPLOYED	3.807	5.733	−0.141
	(0.319)	(0.907)	(0.276)
LTV	10.182	16.178	1.209
	(0.364)	(0.904)	(0.829)
DENIED PMI	17.914	15.963	−2.485
	(0.576)	(0.426)	(−0.699)
MULTI-FAMILY	−7.136	−8.030	−0.203
	(−0.660)	(−1.216)	(−0.395)
FIXED RATE	−11.837	−18.779	−0.491
	(−1.137)	(−2.756)	(−0.968)
SPECIAL	−56.622	33.330	−1.962
	(−1.631)	(1.226)	(−1.023)
TERM	0.606	−0.898	−0.057
	(0.827)	(−2.123)	(−1.462)
GOT GIFT	6.479	−7.772	−1.318
	(0.646)	(−1.225)	(−2.865)
COSIGNER	34.829	−2.391	−1.722
	(1.781)	(−0.247)	(−1.854)
MINORITY	27.022	1.177	0.922
	(2.492)	(0.251)	(1.962)
AGE	4.010	2.674	−0.093
	(0.527)	(0.466)	(−0.256)
MALE	−9.360	−2.693	0.558
	(−0.853)	(0.557)	(1.232)
MARRIED	−15.885	9.520	−0.328
	(−1.953)	(0.646)	(−0.822)
OWNER-OCCUPIED	−6.588	−12.028	−1.344
	(−0.376)	(−1.588)	(−1.183)

Table 6.3
(continued)

Variable	Model 1: Interaction with lender's mean DEBT-TO-INCOME	Model 2: Interaction with lender's mean LTV	Model 3: Interaction with lender's mean CONSUMER CREDIT
POOR TRACT	−13.445	−2.357	−0.196
	(−1.257)	(−0.229)	(−0.380)
MINORITY TRACT	9.409	−0.919	−0.018
	(0.497)	(−0.149)	(−0.028)
BANKRUPTCY	−2.859	5.138	0.175
	(−0.240)	(0.711)	(0.357)
MORTGAGE CREDIT	−3.073	2.667	0.364
	(−0.534)	(0.799)	(3.434)
CONSUMER CREDIT	−1.772	1.991	0.013
	(−0.747)	(1.399)	(0.038)

Note: All models are estimated with logit analysis. APPROVE is the dependent variable; t-statistics are in parentheses. All models also include application characteristics not interacted with anything and interactions between loan terms; these results are not presented. Lender mean values are based on the Boston Fed Study's data for each lender.

One possible interpretation of these results is that lenders specialize in loans with different debt-to-income ratios or have compensating factors that explicitly or implicitly allow for "compensating factors" at high debt-to-income ratios. In this case, a lender's concern about minority applicants with a high debt-to-income ratio might be mitigated if the lender specializes in similar loans. To test this hypothesis, we estimate an alternative model in which we control for the difference between the applicant's debt-to-income ratio and the mean debt-to-income ratio for the lender, instead of simply controlling for the mean ratio.[34] We find that, for all applicants, the likelihood of approval falls as the debt-to-income ratio increases above the average for the lender (significant at 0.01 level), but we also find that this effect is stronger for minority applicants (0.05 level). This finding is consistent with specifications used by Stengel and Glennon (1999), in which they include the debt-to-income ratio above a lender-specific threshold as a control variable.

As pointed out in section 6.3.2, a link between the applicant-level debt-to-income level and minority status supports the hypothesis that lenders practice statistical discrimination. The results obtained when we control for the difference between the applicant's debt-to-income ratio and the lender's mean debt-to-income ratio indicate that this statistical discrimination is not as severe for lenders that specialize in loans with high debt-to-income ratios. Unobserved intergroup differences in credit qualifications, which are the source of statistical discrimination, may not be as severe (or may not be perceived by lenders to be as severe) in the pool of applications attracted by lenders with high average debt-to-income ratios as in the pool of applications attracted by other lenders.

Another example of the link between a lender's portfolio and the minority-white approval gap arises in the case of average credit history (see the third column of table 6.3). We find that an increase in portfolio-level consumer credit history reduces the impact of an applicant's credit problems on the likelihood of loan approval (significant at 0.001 level). Moreover, an increase in the portfolio-level consumer credit variable (i.e., a decrease in application quality) lowers the gap between minority and white approval rates.

These results provide further evidence that statistical discrimination exists but varies with the circumstances.[35] Loan officers with extensive experience in evaluating applications with poor credit histories appear to be more likely to approve low-quality loans in general and less likely to rely on the belief that minority applicants have poorer qualifications than whites with the same observable credit characteristics.

Our third key result, which addresses the central issue in this chapter, is that accounting for underwriting differences across lenders has no impact on the average minority-white difference in loan approval. For the regressions in table 6.3, this average difference ranges from 4.2 to 4.6 percent, which is virtually identical to the difference in the baseline regressions that assume all lenders use the same underwriting standards. The same result holds for the alternative specification based on the difference between an applicant's debt-to-income ratio and the mean debt-to-income ratio of the lender. In this case, minority applicants are 4.4 percentage points less likely to be approved than are equally qualified whites.

These results contradict the view that the minority-white differences in loan approval found by Boston Fed Study reflect legitimate differences in underwriting standards across lenders, not differences in the treatment of minority and white applicants. As explained earlier, legitimate across-lender differences in underwriting standards are likely to be associated with differences in the characteristics of applicant pools and hence of loan portfolios. We find that minority-white differences in loan approval remain after allowing for differences in underwriting standards based on a variety of loan portfolio characteristics.

6.3.3.2 Underwriting Standards and Lender Portfolios Based on HMDA Data

The second way we examine lender differences in underwriting is the same as the first, except that we measure the characteristics of a lender's portfolio using all the information in the HMDA data, not just the information in the Boston Fed Study's sample. Given the consistent importance of debt-to-income ratio in our earlier analysis, we define a baseline model that is a modification of the specification in section 6.3.2. This baseline starts with a specification in which the applicant-level debt-to-income ratio is interacted with all application characteristics. Then we add the difference between the applicant-level and the portfolio-level debt-to-income ratios is interacted with the applicant-level debt-to-income ratio and, separately, with minority status. This specification builds on the possibility, supported by earlier results, that each lender specializes in underwriting loans with a debt-to-income ratio that falls into a certain range and penalizes applicants with ratios that fall far from this range. More specifically, this specification allows for the possibility that a large difference between the applicant-level and portfolio-level debt-to-income ratios raises the weight placed on the applicant-level debt-to-income ratio and leads to a greater penalty for minority applications.[36]

Finally, we add interactions between all application characteristics and selected average characteristics of all the applications received by each lender that are present in the HMDA data. We consider the following portfolio-level characteristics: percentage minority, average loan amount, average ratio of loan amount to applicant income, loan volume, percentage of loans rejected, and percentage of loans sold on the secondary market. The baseline specification is rejected (at the 0.01 confidence level) in favor of the specifications including interactions with percentage minority and with the ratio of loan amount to income. It is also rejected (at the 0.05 level) in favor of the specification containing interactions with the number of loans a lender issued. The portfolio-level interaction terms from these three specifications are presented in table 6.4.

Table 6.4
Results for regressions with interactions between lender portfolio and applications characteristics, matched sample plus HMDA data

Variable	Model 1: Interaction with lender's percentage of applications from minorities	Model 2: Interaction with lender's average housing price–to–income ratio	Model 3: Interaction with lender's loan volume
EXPENSE-TO-INCOME	0.120	−0.014	0.010
	(1.091)	(−0.286)	(0.625)
DEBT-TO-INCOME	−23.370	2.746	−2.273
	(−2.512)	(0.640)	(−1.380)
NET WORTH	−0.254	−0.004	−0.613
	(−1.050)	(−0.029)	(−1.670)
PREDICTED UNEMPLOYMENT	−0.467	−0.093	0.013
	(−1.717)	(−0.838)	(0.277)
SELF EMPLOYED	−3.612	1.474	−0.129
	(−1.902)	(1.677)	(−0.424)
LTV	−0.109	−0.411	−1.305
	(−0.019)	(−0.216)	(−1.292)
DENIED PMI	−2.068	0.103	−12.788
	(−0.315)	(0.044)	(−1.487)
MULTI-FAMILY	2.421	0.106	0.451
	(1.304)	(0.148)	(1.611)
FIXED RATE	−2.477	0.476	−0.153
	(−1.368)	(0.591)	(−0.528)
SPECIAL	13.113	−3.579	0.822
	(1.933)	(−2.037)	(1.720)
TERM	−0.384	0.070	−0.071
	(−1.662)	(1.228)	(−1.543)
GOT GIFT	−2.983	−2.123	−0.178
	(−1.823)	(2.754)	(−0.695)
COSIGNER	−2.667	−0.045	0.122
	(−0.518)	(−0.047)	(0.109)
MINORITY	2.011	0.217	−0.568
	(1.151)	(0.344)	(−2.119)
AGE	2.564	−0.235	0.368
	(1.854)	(−0.447)	(1.680)
MALE	−1.911	1.080	−0.057
	(−1.037)	(1.574)	(−0.206)
MARRIED	0.141	0.500	−0.364
	(0.100)	(0.879)	(−1.576)
OWNER-OCCUPIED	−5.956	2.251	0.481
	(−1.317)	(1.278)	(1.071)

Table 6.4
(continued)

Variable	Model 1: Interaction with lender's percentage of applications from minorities	Model 2: Interaction with lender's average housing price–to–income ratio	Model 3: Interaction with lender's loan volume
POOR TRACT	7.162	−0.049	0.264
	(3.599)	(−0.070)	(0.953)
MINORITY TRACT	3.070	−0.211	0.105
	(1.252)	(−0.219)	(0.308)
BANKRUPTCY	1.516	1.133	−0.034
	(0.842)	(1.200)	(−0.109)
MORTGAGE CREDIT	−0.011	−0.584	0.090
	(−0.010)	(−1.295)	(0.425)
CONSUMER CREDIT	−0.259	0.075	−0.002
	(−0.649)	(0.472)	(−0.033)

Note: All models are estimated with logit analysis. APPROVE is the dependent variable; *t*-statistics are in parentheses. All models also include application characteristics not interacted with anything and interactions between loan terms; results for these variables are not presented. Lender characteristics are based on the HMDA data for each lender.

Although several of the interaction terms in table 6.4 are statistically significant, we find that these regressions, like those in table 6.3, imply that the average minority-white difference in loan approval is unaffected by allowing underwriting standards to vary with lender characteristics. Again, these regressions provide no evidence to support the view that the large minority status coefficient in the Boston Fed Study simply reflects legitimate differences in underwriting standards across lenders.

The model in which a lender's loan volume is interacted with loan characteristics deserves special discussion. The only interaction coefficient that is statistically significant at the 5-percent level is the interaction between minority status and loan volume. The estimated coefficient is negative, implying that discrimination is greater at large lenders. To gain further insight into this result, we first tried splitting the sample between the ten largest lenders and all other lenders. This resulted in a sample of 901 applications to large lenders, of which 289 applications were from minority customers. The sample for small lenders contained 1,442 applications, 272 of which were from minorities. Among the large lenders, the probability of loan approval was 6.8 percentage points higher for whites than for minorities. We found no minority-white difference in loan approval, however, for the sample of small lenders.

These results do not imply that small lenders never practice discrimination. In fact, even though minorities and whites have the same average chance of loan approval in the small-lender sample, we find signs that minorities are treated unfavorably under the same circumstances in both the large-lender and the small-lender samples. Specifically, we find that in both samples, group differences in underwriting vary by loan volume and by the difference between the applicant-level and portfolio-level debt-to-income ratios (results not shown in table). Furthermore, these two relationships are quite similar in magnitude in the two samples. One cannot simply conclude, therefore, that discrimination is present only among the large lenders. Systematic intergroup differences in underwriting appear to exist for the population of lenders in Boston at the time of the Boston Fed Study. These differences are not associated with across-lender variation in loan portfolios and therefore are unlikely to be justified on the grounds of business necessity.

6.3.3.3 Lender-Specific Underwriting Differences for Large Lenders

Finally, we search for systematic differences in underwriting models across lenders that cannot be explained by differences in lenders' portfolios. To conduct this search, we restrict our attention to applications received by lenders that rejected at least ten applications.[37] This restriction results in a sample of 929 applications submitted to eight lenders. These lenders include all but one of the nine lenders with the highest number of applications in the Boston Fed Study's sample. The exception is a lender with seventy-two applications and only one denial. The number of applications received by the eight included lenders ranged from 63 to 318.

We start by estimating a baseline model that adds lender dummy variables to the model with the same variables as the regressions in table 6.1. The estimated coefficients from this baseline model imply that the average minority-white difference in loan approval is 9.8 percentage points, compared to 4.5 percentage points for the complete matched sample. This increase in intergroup underwriting differences is consistent with the earlier finding that these differences increase with a lender's loan volume.

We then allow each lender to place a different weight on three key application characteristics: debt-to-income ratio, LTV, and consumer credit history.[38] Table 6.5 shows the core results. The first column shows the estimated weight for these three underwriting variables for one of the eight lenders. The next seven columns apply to the other seven lenders. Each column shows the difference between the estimated weight for the first lender and the estimated weight for one of these other lenders. The most significant differences across lenders arise for the underwriting weight placed on LTV.[39] This analysis therefore provides clear evidence that accounting for underwriting differences across lenders may boost the explanatory power of a loan approval model.

These results also demonstrate, however, that accounting for underwriting differences across lenders, at least the underwriting differences examined here, has no impact on the estimated minority-white difference in loan approval. Specifically, the minority-white difference based on the coefficients of the regression in table 6.5 is still 9.8 percentage points, just as it is with common underwriting variables. This result is consistent with the analogous finding in Blackburn and Vermilyea (2001). As explained earlier, this evidence supports the conclusion that the minority-white difference in loan approval identified by the Boston Fed Study cannot be explained by legitimate business considerations but may reflect disparate-impact discrimination.

6.4 Conclusions

The literature reviewed in this chapter provides clear evidence that underwriting standards vary across lenders and that borrowers may respond to these differences. Some evidence suggests that differences in underwriting standards arise because lenders have different financial characteristics, have different information about the equity risk associated with houses in different neighborhoods, or specialize in loans with different levels of equity risk. Other studies find that variation in lender underwriting standards may explain the minority-white differences in loan approval models observed in loan samples that are pooled across lenders. This result raises questions about the existence of widespread disparate-treatment discrimination in the mortgage market. The literature does not determine, however, whether across-lender variation in underwriting standards

Table 6.5
Results for regressions with lender-specific underwriting coefficients, matched sample, for lenders with sufficient denials

| | Coefficient for | | | | | | | |
Variable	Lender 1	Difference between lenders 1 and 2	Difference between lenders 1 and 3	Difference between lenders 1 and 4	Difference between lenders 1 and 5	Difference between lenders 1 and 6	Difference between lenders 1 and 7	Difference between lenders 1 and 8
DEBT-TO-INCOME	−23.796	21.050	11.803	16.099	14.729	21.688	0.265	−46.806
	(11.806)	(12.947)	(12.046)	(12.375)	(12.700)	(12.210)	(15.565)	(38.774)
CONSUMER CREDIT	−0.373	0.106	−0.079	0.165	0.112	−0.236	−0.359	−2.572
	(0.219)	(0.274)	(0.248)	(0.252)	(0.264)	(0.299)	(0.419)	(1.586)
LTV	6.225	−7.106	−12.532	−13.273	−10.106	−17.263	−8.622	−35.250
	(2.974)	(3.377)	(3.580)	(4.553)	(4.458)	(5.035)	(4.684)	(21.400)

Note: All results are obtained with logit analysis. APPROVE is the dependent variable; *t*-statistics are in parentheses. All models also include other application characteristics; results for these variables are not included. Only lenders with ten or more observed denials are included.

has a disparate impact on minority applicants or, instead, is justified on business necessity grounds. As a result, existing studies do not reveal the magnitude of disparate-impact discrimination.

This chapter provides further evidence on across-lender variation in underwriting standards using the public-use version of the Boston Fed Study's data combined with HMDA data. We then explore three different ways to account for variation in underwriting standards across lenders. The first way is to determine whether these weights depend on the average level of characteristics observed for each lender's applications in the Boston Fed Study's sample. The second way is similar, except that it broadens the set of information used to determine lender averages by considering the characteristics of all the applications submitted to each lender and recorded in the HMDA data. The third way is to estimate separate underwriting weights for each lender for several key credit variables and to determine whether these weights are significantly different across lenders.

All three methods yield the same two main results. First, underwriting standards differ significantly across lenders. Second, accounting for systematic variation in underwriting standards across lenders has no significant impact on the estimated minority-white disparity in loan approval. Similar results are provided by Blackburn and Vermilyea (2001) using a sample of ten large lenders.

These results cast serious doubt on the view that the minority-white disparities in loan approval in the Boston Fed Study (or in other studies based on the same data, including ours in chapter 5) arise because of differences in underwriting standards across lenders that are legitimate (in the sense that they can be justified on the grounds of business necessity). Any business necessity defense requires a link to loan performance and therefore must be linked to factors that differentiate one lender's loan performance experience from others'. Such factors must appear in the nature of the lender's applicant pool and will be reflected in its loan portfolio. Allowing lenders' underwriting standards to vary with their loan portfolios is therefore roughly equivalent to controlling for the factors associated with business necessity. Our results therefore support the claim that the authors of the Boston Fed Study did not exaggerate discrimination by ignoring across-lender differences in underwriting standards.[40]

Our approach cannot reveal whether our estimated minority-white disparity in loan approval reflects idiosyncratic variation in the set of underwriting variables across lenders.[41] Studies that can observe this type of variation, namely, Glennon and Stengel (1999), Courchane, Nebhut, and Nickerson (2000), Blackburn and Vermilyea (2001), and Buist, Linneman, and Megbolugbe (1999), all indicate that, to a large degree, it probably does; in all of these studies, the minority-white disparity is much smaller, or even nonexistent, when this variation is accounted for. These studies indicate that it is possible to exaggerate disparate-treatment discrimination by failing to account for each lender's unique underwriting variables, but they do not demonstrate that discrimination does not exist. Indeed, one of their most striking implications is that lenders may be able to transform disparate-treatment discrimination into disparate-impact discrimination through the use of unique underwriting standards that are correlated with minority status but not with business necessity.

Neither these studies nor our study has access to loan performance information, so we cannot determine whether idiosyncratic variation in underwriting standards across lenders is associated with across-lender variation in the relationship between underwriting variables and loan performance. This type of association would indicate that this variation can be justified on the basis of business necessity and therefore does not constitute disparate-impact discrimination. Although we cannot provide a direct test of this type, our approach provides an indirect test. By allowing underwriting weights for a wide range of variables to vary based on a lender's portfolio, we control for the variation in underwriting standards that is most likely to have a business justification. This step has virtually no impact on the minority-white loan approval disparity. In our analysis, idiosyncratic variation in underwriting standards is defined to be variation not associated with a lender's portfolio and is likely to reflect lender-specific rules of thumb that are not based on current performance information. Even if this variation fully explains the minority-white disparity in loan approval, therefore, this effect is far more likely to be a sign of disparate-impact discrimination than of legitimate business considerations.

Overall, our results make a case for a strong presumption that the estimated minority status coefficient reflects either disparate-treatment or disparate-impact discrimination that is built into idiosyncratic variation in underwriting standards across lenders. They do not, however, prove that discrimination exists. The minority status coefficient might be explained by idiosyncratic variation in underwriting weights across lenders that is not correlated with variation in lenders' portfolios, at least not as measured by our portfolio variables, or it might be explained by idiosyncratic variation in underwriting variables that we cannot observe. The impact of idiosyncratic variation in underwriting standards on the minority-white loan disparity is more likely to be explained, however, by disparate-impact discrimination than by business necessity.

7

Other Dimensions of Discrimination: Pricing, Redlining, and Cultural Affinity

7.1 Introduction

The voluminous recent literature on mortgage lending discrimination is not just concerned with variation in underwriting standards across lenders.[1] Several other important issues, including the causes of discrimination, the extent of discrimination in mortgage pricing, and the extent of redlining, are also addressed in this literature. In this chapter we review the recent research on these three topics.

7.2 The Causes of Discrimination

Many studies of mortgage lending discrimination recognize that different lenders may use different underwriting standards and attempt to account for this possibility in their estimating equations. Another possibility is that loan approval decisions differ across lenders because discrimination is the result of economic or other incentives that vary across lenders. This possibility is, of course, the central focus of the studies that focus on the "cultural affinity" between blacks and whites, which were mentioned in chapter 6. In particular, these studies investigate the possibility that white-owned lenders behave differently from black-owned lenders. This section addresses the more general questions: What are the causes of lending discrimination? To what extent should loan approval regressions account for the possibility that different lenders may face different incentives to discriminate? Although these questions have been raised in the literature, they have not been given a great deal of attention, so this section focuses more on conceptual models than on empirical results.

7.2.1 Statistical Discrimination

As discussed in chapter 2, statistical discrimination is said to exist if lenders use minority status as a signal concerning unobserved credit characteristics. It seems possible, given their relatively disadvantaged socioeconomic outcomes, that black and Hispanic applicants are more likely than white applicants to be rated unfavorably on these unobserved characteristics—or at least that lenders perceive this to be the case. In either event, lenders will believe that minority applicants are more likely to default than are white applicants with the same observed credit characteristics; this belief gives lenders an economic incentive to discriminate against minority applicants. This behavior is illegal—under the pertinent laws, a lender must base his or her decision on the *observed credit characteristics* of an applicant—but some lenders may respond to the economic incentive instead of to the requirements of the law.

The concept of statistical discrimination was developed by Phelps (1972) and Arrow (1973), with applications to the labor market.[2] For example, an employer can readily determine a job applicant's years of education but may not be able to determine the quality of that education. If the employer assumes that black applicants received lower-quality educations, on average, than white applicants, then he may hire white applicants instead of black applicants who have the same number of years of education and are equally qualified on other observable characteristics.

Statistical discrimination also has been studied by Ondrich, Ross, and Yinger (2001), in their case as it applies to real estate brokers. Using HDS data, these authors find that brokers interpret a customer's initial housing request as an indication of the customer's housing and neighborhood preferences, but that brokers are willing to override an initial request from a black customer when it contrasts with their beliefs about what blacks really want or can afford. "Marketing effort" is defined as an agent's willingness to show a particular unit in his files. These authors find that

agents' marketing efforts increase with sales price for whites but not for blacks. This difference is smaller, but still exists, for the advertised unit. We interpret these results as an indication that agents practice statistical discrimination based on a preconception about the ability of black customers to purchase expensive homes. Agents appear to believe that the higher the price range, the less likely it is that a black customer will be able to complete a transaction; to avoid wasting time on unlikely transactions, therefore, agents are reluctant to show high-priced units to blacks.

This preconception could take the form of a belief that black customers, unlike white customers, are unlikely to be qualified for expensive houses, even if they explicitly ask to see them, or a belief that the more expensive the housing, the more likely it is that blacks will encounter discrimination from lenders. Moreover, this preconception might accurately reflect an agent's past experience with black customers, or it might draw on general societal stereotypes and have no predictive power at all. In either case, acting on the basis of this preconception, as agents appear to do, constitutes statistical discrimination because it involves using a perceived average trait for a group to predict an outcome for an individual member of that group. This preconception also appears to be so strong that it is not offset by the information in a customer's initial housing request.

Ondrich, Ross, and Yinger also point out (in footnote 30) that this belief could be based on brokers' knowledge about the mortgage market. Specifically, they point out that Munnell et al. (1996) find that, "on average, black mortgage applications have higher loan-to-value and debt-to-income ratios than do white applications."[3]

In another paper, Ondrich, Ross, and Yinger (2001) find that, in some urban areas, discrimination by real estate brokers is related to general conditions in the mortgage market, as indicated by HMDA data. In the Atlanta area, for example, discrimination by brokers increases with the percentage of loan applications denied in census tracts far from black areas, but it decreases with the percentage of loans denied in tracts near black areas. One possible interpretation of these results is that a high denial rate near black areas is seen by brokers as a sign that many blacks are applying, so that other blacks are likely to be considered by lenders. A high denial rate far from black areas, however, is seen as a sign that lenders use underwriting standards that blacks will be unable to meet, either because those standards involve discrimination or because blacks are thought to have poorer credit characteristics (even if they inquire about the same house).

Munnell et al. (1996) do not provide a formal analysis of the causes of mortgage discrimination, but they do discuss statistical discrimination. In particular, Munnell et al. (and, in a follow-up piece, Tootell, 1996b) argue that statistical discrimination is unlikely to be at work in mortgage markets because there is no compelling evidence that blacks actually have higher default rates, controlling for observable characteristics. However, they do not directly test this hypothesis, or any other hypothesis about the causes of discrimination. In fact, even though statistical discrimination in lending has been widely discussed in the literature (see, for example, Swire, 1995), no clear evidence concerning its existence has yet appeared.

7.2.2 The Cultural-Affinity Hypothesis

Another hypothesis about the cause of lending discrimination is one mentioned earlier, namely, the cultural-affinity hypothesis. This hypothesis, which is formally developed by Calomiris, Kahn, and Longhofer (1994), begins with the argument that the limited affinity of white loan officers for the culture of certain minority groups implies that these officers make less effort to determine the creditworthiness of minority than of white applicants. The resulting information disparity implies, in turn, that minority clients are more likely to be rejected.

Hunter and Walker (1996) interpret the cultural-affinity hypothesis as a form of statistical discrimination. Loan officers must decide how much effort to make in finding additional information about an applicant and use group membership as a signal about the difficulty of obtaining this information. In the standard version of statistical discrimination, group membership is used as a signal for elements of creditworthiness that are unobservable or at least expensive to observe and that, in the loan officer's estimation, differ across groups. For example, if blacks are believed to be less creditworthy than whites by these unobserved indicators, on average, then the loan officer has an economic incentive to use race as an indicator of creditworthiness. Hunter and Walker suggest, however, that statistical discrimination could arise even if the two groups do not differ in their underlying creditworthiness. Specifically, they suggest that statistical discrimination could arise if the cost of collecting extra information is higher for minority applicants, presumably because the white loan officer is uncomfortable collecting this information.

The existence of higher information costs for minorities than for whites does not imply that minority applicants will encounter discrimination. After all, lenders might assume that the characteristics that are not observed for minority applicants have the same values, on average, for both groups. Thus, the key question is why the extra information collected for white applicants results in a more favorable outcome for whites, on average.

We see three possible answers to this question.[4] The first is that standard statistical discrimination is at work, after all. In other words, lenders presume that if the extra information were available for minorities, then it would indicate that minorities are less qualified than whites with the same observable characteristics. This presumption might be based on lenders' past experience or simply on untested stereotypes. In either case, lenders' behavior constitutes standard statistical discrimination, and the concept of "cultural affinity" adds nothing to the discussion.

The second possible answer, due to Longhofer (1996a), begins with the assumption that the credit characteristics lenders cannot observe have a larger variance for minority than for white applications, precisely because a lack of "cultural affinity" with minority applicants makes it more difficult for lenders to find extra information or corroborating information. If lenders are risk averse, this assumption implies that lenders will be more likely to turn down a minority than a white application even if the two applicants have the same observed creditworthiness. In other words, lenders seek compensation for the added uncertainty in minority applications by holding those applications to a higher standard. This possibility is another form of statistical discrimination, equivalent to the one discussed in Lundberg (1991) for the case of labor markets, but one based on the perceived variance, instead of the mean, in unobserved credit characteristics.[5]

The third possible answer is that white loan officers are not trying to learn more about white applicants' creditworthiness but are instead trying to build the best possible case for each white applicant, often by collecting additional supporting information. One could say that white loan officers do not provide this service to black or Hispanic applicants because they do not feel a "cultural affinity" with them, but this view is indistinguishable from the more traditional explanation that white loan officers are simply prejudiced against minority applicants.[6] In this context, the term "cultural affinity" is nothing more than euphemism for "a lack of prejudice." Thus, no one should think that a loan officer's behavior is either legal or in keeping with widely held values just because it is driven by a lack of "cultural affinity" for a particular group. In short, this version of the "cultural-affinity" hypothesis boils down to this: Loan officers are prejudiced against people in some groups, and this prejudice induces them to withhold some services from applicants in those groups, that is, to discriminate against them.

The existing empirical evidence does not provide clear support for any of these possibilities. Consider first the studies discussed in chapter 6. Black, Collins, and Cyree (1997) and Bostic and Canner (1997) argue that if lender prejudice is at work (the third possibility), black-owned lenders should be less likely than white-owned lenders to discriminate against black applicants. Black, Collins, and Cyree find that the opposite is true, that is, that black-owned lenders are more likely than white-owned lenders to discriminate against blacks, and Bostic and Canner find that this difference disappears once one accounts for differences in the quality of the applicants to black-owned and white-owned lenders. Thus, neither study supports the prediction that lenders with white owners are more likely to discriminate against blacks.

Kim and Squires (1998), argues that "cultural affinity" depends upon the group composition of the lender's workforce, not the group composition of its ownership. After all, it is the employees, not the owners, who actually have contact with customers.[7] To test this view, Kim and Squires match 1993 HMDA data in five urban areas with Equal Employment Opportunity Commission records on the group composition of lenders' workforces and with census data. They find that in most areas, for most types of lender (commercial bank, savings and loan, or mortgage banker), the probability that a black customer's application will be approved increases significantly, all else equal, with the share of the lender's professional employees who are black.[8] The probability of approval for a Hispanic applicant increased in several cases with the share of employees who were Hispanic.[9] This study suggests that the prejudice version of the cultural-affinity hypothesis does play a role in the interactions between loan applicants and the employees at lending institutions.

Hunter and Walker (1996) investigate their version of the cultural-affinity hypothesis (the first possibility above) by determining whether underwriting standards differ for minority and white applicants. They begin with the Boston Fed Study's data set, then delete observations associated with a special program and observations identified as having a data error according to the procedure developed by Carr and Megbolugbe (1993). The resulting data set contains 1,516 white applications and 475 black or Hispanic applications. Hunter and Walker use this data set to test "whether loan officers' decisions on white applicants depend less on formal information, such as credit history, financial obligations, and the like, than they do for minorities" (p. 60). This informal information is what the loan officer collects, because of her "cultural affinity" with white clients, to help make the best possible case for white clients. By relying on this extra, informal, largely positive information, the hypothesis goes, loan officers inevitably place less weight on formal information.

The main form of Hunter and Walker's test is to determine if two key variables, the obligation ratio and their credit history indicator, have a larger impact on loan denial for blacks and Hispanics than for whites. They find support for the first effect but not the second. The signs of both effects are in the expected direction, whereas the difference between the white and minority impacts is significant in the first case (t-statistic: 2.87) but not in the second (t-statistic: 1.14). As noted earlier, this obligation ratio result can also be found in Munnell et al. (1996).

Hunter and Walker interpret this result as support for the cultural-affinity hypothesis. We are not convinced. Even on the surface, the evidence is not very strong. If loan officers are willing to overrule the poor formal qualifications of whites on the basis of informal information, why does this effect show up in only a single coefficient? More importantly, the larger impact of the obligation ratio for minorities than for whites could arise because, as discussed in chapter 6, minorities and whites tend to go to different lenders with different underwriting guidelines, not because individual lenders use different guidelines for minorities and whites.[10]

Overall, lenders may discriminate because of their own prejudice, or they may discriminate because minority status provides information about credit characteristics that cannot be observed directly. The concept of "cultural affinity" does not really add a new hypothesis about the causes of discrimination. The literature on "cultural affinity" has helped, however, to focus attention on the possible link between mortgage discrimination and incomplete information. This link is well worth pursuing in both conceptual and empirical research.

7.2.3 Is Discrimination Likely to Disappear in the Long Run?

Different hypotheses about the causes of discrimination may have different implications for the persistence of discrimination. Consequently, another possible way to test hypotheses about the causes of discrimination is to determine what happens to discrimination over time. Because the Boston Fed Study has not been replicated, credible time-series evidence is not yet available, but future studies might be able to obtain this type of evidence.

This issue was first raised by Becker ([1957] 1971) and Arrow (1973), who argued that prejudice-based discrimination arises when some firms are willing to sacrifice profits to satisfy the prejudice of their owners and that this discrimination is likely to disappear in the long run as unprejudiced firms drive prejudiced firms out of business. Competition has this effect because prejudice induces firms to engage in unprofitable behavior, such as refusing to hire minority workers even if they are more productive, at the margin, than white workers. The point here is not that competition necessarily eliminates discrimination. As Becker (1993b, p. 388) puts it, the impact of competition on discrimination "depends not only on the distribution of tastes for discrimination among potential employers, but also on the nature of firm production functions." Nevertheless, under reasonably general assumptions, competition can be shown to drive out firms that are willing to sacrifice profits for prejudice.

Ferguson and Peters (2000) show that this logic may not carry over to a market, such as the mortgage market, that is characterized by rationing. As discussed in section 3.4.1, lenders sometimes have an incentive to provide loans to some applicants with "marginal" credit qualifications, while at the same time denying loans to other applicants with exactly these same qualifications. Under these circumstances, in other words, a lender's profits are the same no matter which subset of the marginal applicants it provides with credit. As shown by Ferguson and Peters, this result implies that a prejudiced lender might be able to turn down all its minority applicants without lowering its profits. Competition will have no effect on this firm or on the discrimination it practices. As a result, competition does not necessarily imply that prejudice-based discrimination will disappear in the long run, regardless of the distribution of employer prejudice or the nature of firm production functions.[11]

Unlike prejudice-based discrimination, statistical discrimination is associated with higher profits. Specifically, lenders have an incentive to practice statistical discrimination whenever minority status provides information about some credit characteristics that lenders cannot observe directly at some reasonable cost. As pointed out earlier, a lender's perception about the link between minority status and unobserved credit characteristics may or may not be accurate. If it is not accurate, then statistical discrimination is practiced because it is thought to be profitable when, in fact, it is not. In this case, competition may well eliminate statistical discrimination. The first lenders to figure out that standard perceptions about minority applicants are not accurate will make more profits than other lenders and will eventually force them out of business.

Another recent paper, Longhofer and Peters (1998), goes to the heart of Becker's competition argument. Longhofer and Peters consider a model in which lenders use a simple updating process to evaluate creditworthiness.[12] The lender considers both an observed signal and a prior belief concerning the creditworthiness of each group. In equilibrium, this prior belief must be consistent with the creditworthiness of the lender's applicant pool for each group. Longhofer and Peters show that there exists an equilibrium in which prejudice-based discrimination is practiced by some lenders. In their model, competitive forces do not drive the prejudiced lender out of business; instead, minority borrowers separate across prejudiced and nonprejudiced lenders based on information costs and creditworthiness. Moreover, under some circumstances, the existence of prejudiced lenders creates an incentive for nonprejudiced lenders to practice statistical discrimination.

If the standard perception is accurate, statistical discrimination could persist in the long run, because firms that practice it will make more profits than other firms. Even in this case, however, statistical discrimination might disappear over time as information-gathering techniques improve (Greenbaum, 1996). After all, statistical discrimination arises because lenders use minority status as a signal about information that they cannot observe. If this information could be obtained at relatively low cost, then nondiscriminatory behavior would be more profitable than statistical discrimination. This hypothesis is difficult to evaluate, however, because we do not know what type of missing information could lead to statistical discrimination and therefore do not know whether the incentive to practice statistical discrimination could be eliminated by existing information-gathering technology.

Finally, statistical discrimination could be self-perpetuating. Building on the work of Lundberg and Startz (1983) for labor markets, Swire (1995) argues that statistical discrimination by lenders lowers the return that minority households earn from investing in creditworthiness by, for example, paying off credit card debt. As a result, minority households may not invest as much in creditworthiness as white households do. It follows that statistical discrimination may help to perpetuate the minority/white disparities in creditworthiness on which it builds. This argument holds, however, only if the discrimination-induced cutbacks in investment affect measures of creditworthiness that cannot be observed by the lender.

In short, no hypothesis about the causes of discrimination leads to a clear-cut prediction about the trend in mortgage lending discrimination over time. Although there is a widespread perception that prejudice-based discrimination is likely to disappear over time and statistical discrimination is likely to persist, this section shows that one cannot rule out exactly the opposite predictions. Further research on this topic is clearly warranted.

7.3 Discrimination in Loan Terms

Recall from chapter 3 (especially lesson 6) that studies of discrimination in loan approval should account, if possible, for price-setting behavior and that discrimination in loan pricing could be an important phenomenon in its own right. So far as we know, no loan approval study has yet controlled for the price of credit directly, but several studies have examined discrimination in lenders' price-setting behavior. These studies can shed light on the complexity of lender behavior and indicate the potential for bias in loan approval studies that exclude price information.

The importance of studying discrimination in loan pricing has been highlighted by a series of recent lawsuits alleging discrimination in the pricing of automobile loans (Henriques, 2000a, 2000b, 2001a, 2001b):[13]

The accusations of discrimination arise from an auto industry practice that allows a car dealer arranging financing for a customer to quote a higher interest rate for a loan than the lender has set. The lender then buys the loan from the dealer, paying him the cash value of the extra percentage points he added to the consumer's loan. The lender's payment to the dealer, which can be more than $1,000, is variously known as dealer participation, finance commission and dealer markup. (Henriques, 2000b)

These practices allow dealers to negotiate a markup with each buyer and open the door for discrimination against certain groups. The evidence on these practices has not been published, but

[a] statistical study of more than 300,000 car loans arranged through Nissan dealers from March 1993 to last September [2000] ... shows that black customers in 33 states consistently paid more than white customers, regardless of their credit histories.

The gap between black and white borrowers was largest in Maryland and Wisconsin, where the average finance charge paid by blacks was about $800 higher than whites paid. (Henriques, 2001b)

We do not, of course, know whether these accusations are valid,[14] but they provide a potent reminder that loans are a complex business and that lenders have many opportunities to discriminate in loan pricing, as well as in other parts of the loan process, if they decide to do so. This lesson applies not only to car loans but also to mortgage loans.

7.3.1 Discrimination in Overage Practices

Three recent studies of individual lenders have examined discrimination in loan terms.[15] All of these studies focus on "overages," which are defined as the difference between the final interest rate on a particular mortgage and the rate set when the lender first committed to making the loan, a concept that is similar to dealer mark-ups in car loans. One study focuses on the difference between final rates and "lock-in" rates, which are the rates that lenders agree not to exceed. The other two focus on the difference between final rates and the minimum rate a loan officer is allowed to charge. Each lender decides on the minimum interest rate it will accept (for each type of loan in each time period) and then makes a commitment to a borrower not to exceed some lock-in rate when the loan is finalized. Two customers who enter a lender's office on the same day and receive a commitment for the same type of loan face the same policy concerning the minimum allowable rate, but they may not be offered the same lock-in rate and, for a variety of reasons that these studies explore, the final rate could be higher or lower than the lender's "minimum."

Crawford and Rosenblatt (1999) examine final mortgage interest rate differences between whites, Asians, Hispanics, and blacks using information from one national home mortgage lender for 1988 and 1989. They begin with the observation that, near the beginning of the process that leads to a mortgage loan, a lender commits to a certain maximum interest rate, the lock-in rate. Interest rate differences across borrowers arise either because a lender makes commitments that differ from the market rate on the commitment date or because the actual interest rate charged at the time the loan is closed differs from the lock-in rate.[16] If market rates drop in the period after the commitment is made but before the loan is finalized, the borrower may be able to reduce the contractual rate by threatening to switch to another lender. A lender also may be able to take advantage of an increase in market interest rates if some feature of the loan, such as the down payment, changes, an event that generally releases the lender from the commitment.

Based on this analysis, Crawford and Rosenblatt use a regression model to explain the difference between the actual interest rate on a loan and the market rate on the date of commitment, which they call the yield premium, as a function of group membership, loan terms, borrower characteristics, and whether market interest rates changed between the date of commitment and the date of finalization. The loan terms in their data set include LTV and loan amount, and the borrower characteristics include whether the borrower is a first-time homebuyer, whether the loan is for a refinancing, and the borrower's years of education. In the case of conventional loans, they find no significant differences in the yield premium across groups. In the case of government-insured loans, however, they find that the yield premium is about three basis points higher for blacks and Hispanics than for whites, results that are highly significant statistically. They also find some evidence that this difference may arise because blacks and Hispanics have a harder time than whites in negotiating a new, lower rate when market interest rates fall below their lock-in rate.

Crawford and Rosenblatt downplay their results by saying that for the average government-insured loan, three additional basis points add about $1.80 to the monthly payment. Alternatively, one could say that this additional cost comes to roughly $200 over the life of the loan. This average, however, is for all loans in the sample. The impact on an individual borrower who locked in immediately before a substantial rate decline might be quite large. In addition, the average decline in interest rates below the lock-in rate was about six basis points, so one could also say that blacks and Hispanics were only half as successful as whites in negotiating lower rates when market rates declined after the lender's commitment date. Finally, the vast majority of the mortgages granted to blacks and Hispanics are government-insured (Gabriel, 1996), so this result could signal widespread discrimination against black and Hispanic borrowers.

Courchane and Nickerson (1997) report on an investigation conducted by OCC of discrimination in loan pricing at three banks using similar concepts. They begin by pointing out that loan officers work from "loan pricing matrix sheets," which indicate the minimum interest rate they are allowed to charge for each type of mortgage at any given time. They then define an overage as any excess in the actual interest rate charged above the interest rate on these sheets, measured by "rate sheet points," after accounting for legitimate costs in the origination fee. To be precise, the overage, in Courchane and Nickerson, equals the final interest rate on the mortgage (in percentage points) minus the origination fee minus the rate sheet points.

Based on a detailed review of loan files, OCC found evidence of discrimination in overage practices at one of the three banks it investigated. On average, blacks paid an overage of about two points, compared to a one-point overage for whites. Most of this black-white difference arose because of the actions of one black loan officer, but the OCC concluded that the lender contributed to the problem by offering lenders incentives to generate overages without providing guidelines or standards and by defining racially homogeneous territories.

At the second lender, OCC conducted a regression analysis of the overage, measured in basis points, as a function of minority status (black or Hispanic), year of issue, and several loan characteristics, including LTV, loan amount, and loan purpose.[17] This regression indicated that blacks and Hispanics paid a significantly higher overage, but the minority-white difference was relatively small, only 0.176 basis points. This regression also uncovered higher overages for government-insured loans. Since blacks and Hispanics are far more likely than whites to receive these loans, this result could indicate a form of disparate-impact discrimination; after all, legitimate differences in loan costs should be included in rate sheet points, not overages.

OCC also conducted a two-part regression analysis of overage practices by the third lender. The first part looked into the probability that an overage would be charged. It found that both blacks and Hispanics were significantly more likely than whites to be charged overages.[18] The second part addressed the size of the overages, employing control variables similar to those used for the second lender. This regression indicated that, on average, the amount of overage charged was slightly (but significantly) lower for blacks and Hispanics than for whites.[19] This result is suspect, however, because one of the explanatory variables, namely the interest rate on the loan, is clearly endogenous, and the estimated coefficients may be subject to endogeneity bias.[20]

Courchane and Nickerson argue that their results do not indicate disparate-treatment discrimination, because loan officers are equally rewarded for all overages, regardless of the minority status of the borrower. We disagree. If a loan officer takes advantage of the lender's market power to charge a higher overage for groups with fewer options in the market, including minority groups, which is one of the mechanisms Courchane and Nickerson themselves identify, that is an example of applying different rules to different customers, which is the definition of disparate-treatment discrimination.

Also according to Courchane and Nickerson, extensive file reviews by OCC indicated that this evidence of discrimination does not reflect "intentional behavior of the loan officer," but instead reflects "changes in lock dates or close dates." The evidence from the file reviews is not presented, however, so this claim is difficult to evaluate. Moreover, the disparities in overages uncovered by OCC may constitute discrimination even if they are not intentional. Loan officers who base their decisions on unconscious stereotypes are practicing disparate-treatment discrimination. In addition, lenders that allow or encourage practices that result in higher or more frequent overages for minorities without business justification are practicing disparate-impact discrimination. Although one might argue that a lender with market power maximizes profits by encouraging the aggressive assessment of overages on borrowers who appear unlikely to seek out alternative financing, such monopolistic behavior is unlikely to be protected by the standard exception of "business necessity" when the firm's policies have an adverse impact on minorities.[21]

The third study of overages, Black, Boem, and DeGennaro (1999), examines loans sold in the secondary market by one lender. In this study, "the overage depends solely on the amount the loan brings in that market relative to the rate stated on the rate sheet at the time of the loan" (p. 3). The analysis is based on detailed data for the borrower (including credit history), the loan, the property, the branch office, and the loan officer. Minority groups are identified only as group A and group B. Four samples are analyzed.[22] The samples are distinguished by geographic focus (one for a single branch office, the other for branch offices around the country) and by purpose of the loan (one for home purchase, the other for refinancing). The authors do not find a clear pattern. Borrowers in group A are charged significantly higher overages for home purchase loans using the national sample, but significantly lower overages using the local sample. In the case of refinancing loans, borrowers in group B are charged higher overages in the both the national and local samples.

More research is clearly needed to determine whether overage practices (and other practices that affect the cost of a mortgage) simply reflect legitimate business concerns or also include disparate-treatment or disparate-impact discrimination, as the results of these studies seem to imply. In addition, the literature has not adequately addressed the complexity of mortgage pricing. Most existing studies focus on the interest rate as the price variable, but in fact, the price of a mortgage also includes a wide variety of points, charges, and fees that can vary widely across customers and that are not included in the concept of an overage.

Finally, as discussed in chapters 2 and 3, the issue of minority-white differences in credit pricing may be increasing in significance. Many lending industry analysts are now discussing a move away from a system that rations credit by turning down the least qualified borrowers to one that provides credit to almost everyone but sets prices that rise as a borrower's credit qualifications fall. If this type of shift does take hold, the opportunities for discrimination in loan terms will increase, and policymakers will need to have a better understanding of this topic.

7.3.2   Loan Term Differences across Lenders

Avery, Beeson, and Sniderman (1996b) examine loan terms using HMDA data from the Cleveland, Columbus, and Detroit mortgage markets between 1990 and 1992. These data are merged with the advertised interest rates for thirty-year, fixed-rate mortgages from the *National Mortgage Weekly*. Avery, Beeson, and Sniderman find that lenders that lower their rates relative to their normal position in the market attract a larger volume of applicants. In addition, they find that low-rate lenders tend to have lower denial rates. They conclude that lenders post lending terms to signal their eagerness to accept new loan applicants. Furthermore, they suggest that there is substantial risk-sorting across lenders, so that low-rate lenders reject a relatively small number of loans. If this sorting were not taking place, low-rate lenders would have higher denial rates, because these lenders would have to impose higher underwriting standards to achieve the lower default rates in their portfolio that are consistent with their low prices.

Avery, Beeson, and Sniderman's study provides an additional reason to believe that the sorting of borrowers across lenders needs to be considered by studies of lending discrimination. Moreover, the authors suggests one mechanism by which a lender can influence its pool of applicants, namely, marketing and advertising.

7.4   Redlining

Discrimination involves the differential treatment of an individual because of the group to which that individual belongs. Redlining is a form of discrimination based on location instead of group membership. As discussed in chapter 2, there are two different definitions of redlining. The first definition, which focuses on the loan denial process, is that redlining exists when otherwise comparable loans are more likely to be denied when they apply to housing in a minority rather than a white neighborhood. Redlining by this definition is illegal according to ECOA. The second definition, which focuses on lending outcomes, is that redlining exists when minority neighborhoods receive a smaller flow of mortgage funds than comparable white neighborhoods. Redlining by this definition is illegal according to CRA. This section reviews recent studies of redlining by both the process-based and the outcome-based definitions and draws conclusions about the extent of redlining in mortgage markets today.

7.4.1   Process-Based Redlining

The basic approach used by most studies of redlining, employing the process-based definition, is to determine whether the probability that a loan application is denied is higher, all else equal, when the property to be purchased is located in a minority neighborhood than when it is located in a white neighborhood. Thus, studies of redlining face the same key challenge as studies of discrimination, namely, to find a data set with adequate information on loans and

applicants, including applicant credit history. Without this information, inferences about redlining, like inferences about discrimination,
are likely to be subject to severe omitted-variable bias.

The HMDA data, which do not contain information on applicant
credit history, therefore are not adequate for isolating redlining. Indeed, the HMDA data may be particularly unsuitable for studying
redlining because it appears that lenders who are active in minority
and low-income neighborhoods tend to attract applicants with relatively poor credit qualifications, based both on variables that are
observed in the HMDA data and on variables that are not observed
there (see the discussion of Bostic and Canner, 1997, in chapter 6).

In this section we review recent studies of process-based redlining.
The first three studies we review have access to information on
applicants' credit histories, which implies that they are based on the
only data set with such information, namely, the Boston Fed Study's
data set. The final study is based on HMDA data combined with
census tract data and data on house sales by tract.

As discussed in chapter 4, Tootell (1996a) studies redlining using
the Boston Fed Study's data and a standard loan denial equation.
A similar analysis is provided by Hunter and Walker (1996). Both
studies add to this equation explanatory variables that describe both
the risk characteristics and the group composition of the census tract
in which the housing unit is located. After controlling for neighborhood risk, group composition is not statistically significant, and both
studies conclude that there is no evidence of redlining in Boston.[23]

Another study based on the Boston Fed Study's data set, Ross and
Tootell (1998), examines a more complex model in which redlining is
related to the market for PMI. Ross and Tootell examine redlining
based both on the minority composition of a neighborhood and on
the neighborhood's median income. They find evidence of redlining
against low-income census tracts, defined as those census tracts
having a median income at least one standard deviation below that
of the metropolitan-area average, when the applicant did not apply
for PMI. The coefficient estimate was 0.56 (t-statistic: 2.52).[24] They
also find some evidence that applications from low-income tracts are
favored when the applicant applies for PMI. In this case the coefficient estimate was −1.96 (t-statistic: 2.18). They find no evidence,
however, that the probability of denial is higher in tracts with a minority population above 30 percent than in other tracts.

Ross and Tootell suggest that lenders may be meeting their CRA obligations at low risk by encouraging applicants from low-income tracts to apply for PMI. Because low-income tracts are seen as riskier, however, even after accounting for all the variables in the Boston Fed Study's data set, lenders are more likely to deny applications to finance property purchases in those tracts when the applicant does not apply for PMI. Ross and Tootell also conclude that their test for redlining based on minority status has little power in the Boston area. In the Boston Fed Study's data set, the income and minority composition of tracts is highly correlated; in fact, the correlation coefficient between the low-income tract and minority tract variables is 0.7. Moreover, when the cutoff used to define a low-income tract is raised, the minority tract variable is statistically significant. In short, with this data set it is difficult to distinguish between income-based and minority status–based redlining.

Ross and Tootell obtain similar results for many different sets of explanatory variables and for several different models. In one alternative model they exclude cases in which the individual applied for PMI. In another they model the application for and receipt of PMI and allow this outcome to influence the lender's loan denial decision.[25] In both cases, their main result, that lenders practice redlining against low-income neighborhoods, is upheld.

Finally, the Lang and Nakamura (1993) hypothesis is relevant for redlining. As discussed in section 6.2.2.2, this hypothesis says that a greater degree of uncertainty about a neighborhood is associated, all else equal, with a higher probability of denying applications for loans to buy houses in that neighborhood. Lenders gain information by observing house sales, so, controlling for other things, the probability of loan denial for applications to finance home purchases in a particular neighborhood should decline as the number of house sales in that neighborhood goes up. This hypothesis implies that the flow of funds to some neighborhoods, particularly low-income neighborhoods where few house sales take place, may be restricted by a lack of information, which is the type of problem that markets cannot solve. If it is true, therefore, this hypothesis may serve as a justification for CRA, or other policies designed to offset redlining.

As reported in chapter 6, Calem (1996), Ling and Wachter (1998), and Harrison (2001) all find evidence in support of the Lang and Nakamura hypothesis.[26] Specifically, these studies find that the probability of loan acceptance for applications to finance purchases in a particular neighborhood increases with the share of houses in that neighborhood that sell.[27] Although these studies are based on HMDA data, and therefore could be subject to omitted-variable problems, they all support the view that information problems may make it difficult for households in low-income neighborhoods to obtain mortgages. Information problems of this type provide a compelling justification for the Community Reinvestment Act, so further research on this topic is clearly needed.

7.4.2 Outcome-Based Redlining

A review of research on the outcome-based definition of redlining can be found in Schill and Wachter (1993). This section examines one recent study, Phillips-Patrick and Rossi (1996) not covered in that review. This study focuses on outcomes by tract, but, unlike other studies of outcome-based redlining, it also attempts to isolate the role of lenders.

Phillips-Patrick and Rossi initially estimate a single-equation model of mortgage redlining using data on total loan originations by census tract. They begin with a simple equation in which loan originations are a function of racial composition, using a variable that indicates whether more than three-quarters of a tract's residents are black. They find that originations are significantly lower in largely black tracts. They then estimate a more complete single-equation model in which the dependent variable is loan originations divided by salable housing units and in which the explanatory variables include many tract characteristics that might influence underwriting risk. In this revised specification, the racial composition of the tract does not have a significant impact on originations. They conclude that great care must be taken in specifying a redlining equation.

Next, Phillips-Patrick and Rossi estimate a simultaneous-equations model of the demand and supply of mortgages. Their model is in the spirit of the method developed by Maddala and Trost (1982) for applications data (see chapter 4). They measure the demand for loans by the ratio of applications to salable units and supply by the ratio of loan originations to salable units. This approach allows them to separate lenders' role in approving loans from their role in influencing the number of applications (through advertising, branch location, and so on). In this model, they find that largely black tracts have a higher demand for originations after controlling for other tract characteristics. This higher demand masks racial differences in the supply of mortgages to largely black tracts, so that, with their simultaneous-equations framework, Phillips-Patrick and Rossi find that largely black tracts receive a significantly smaller supply of mortgages than other tracts, again controlling for other tract characteristics. These findings lead them to restate their cautions about interpreting any analysis of loan originations.

We agree with one conclusion of Phillips-Patrick and Rossi, namely, that one should be cautious in interpreting studies of outcome-based redlining. This conclusion is not new, however, and is in fact emphasized in Schill and Wachter (1993) and in many of the studies Schill and Wachter review. What is new in Phillips-Patrick and Rossi is the use of a simultaneous-equations framework to study outcome-based redlining. The Phillips-Patrick and Rossi finding that race-based redlining in the supply of loans is revealed when a simultaneous-equations framework is used is an important contribution that is, in our view, downplayed by the authors. This finding suggests that some previous researchers may have failed to uncover race-based redlining because they did not account for this simultaneity. We hope that future work follows up on this suggestion.

7.4.3 Conclusions

Redlining has proven to be a difficult topic to study, both because it has two different definitions and because the underlying behavioral models are difficult to specify. As a result, no strong consensus has emerged in the literature. In the case of process-based redlining, the lack of data with adequate controls for borrowers' credit history makes inferences difficult. The few studies that have examined this topic using the Boston Fed Study's data also yield mixed results. Two studies find no evidence of redlining, but a third, which accounts for the relationship between redlining and PMI, finds redlining against low-income neighborhoods, which are almost all largely black neighborhoods, at least in Boston. Three other studies, all of which may yield biased results because they do not include any credit history information, find evidence that a lack of house sales in some neighborhoods leads to lender uncertainty about future developments there and hence to redlining. In the case of outcome-based redlining, which has received the most attention, most, but not all, of the literature finds some sign of redlining, but there is no consensus on the appropriate methodology for studying the phenomenon. More research on redlining is clearly needed.

7.5   Conclusions

The literature reviewed in this chapter enriches our understanding of the factors that lead to discrimination in mortgage lending and of the range of behaviors in which discrimination might occur. Although the literature does not provide a clear answer to the cause of discrimination in mortgage loan approval, it shows that this type of discrimination could arise for a variety of reasons and that there is no guarantee this discrimination will disappear in the long run. Several existing studies also provide some evidence of discrimination in the setting of mortgage interest rates. This is a difficult topic to study, but the trend in the mortgage market is clearly toward greater use of variation in pricing across loan products, so the possibility of variation in loan pricing across groups of customers clearly deserves more attention. Finally, several studies have found no sign of process-based redlining, which is closely related to group-based discrimination in loan approval. One recent study, however, finds evidence of process-based redlining after the role of PMI is accounted for. More research on this topic is also needed.

8

Using Performance Data to Study Mortgage Discrimination: Evaluating The Default Approach

8.1 Introduction

Lenders measure the performance of a mortgage loan by the events that occur after it has been issued, such as whether the borrower defaults and how much a default ultimately costs the lender.[1] Loan approval decisions and loan performance are thus inextricably linked. Lenders decide which mortgage loans to approve on the basis of expected performance, and past decisions on loan approval heavily influence the performance level in any sample of mortgage loans. As shown in chapters 5 and 6, understanding this linkage is critical for distinguishing among disparate-treatment discrimination, disparate-impact discrimination, and underwriting standards that have a different impact on different groups but are justified on the grounds of business necessity. This linkage also leads to an alternative approach to the study of mortgage discrimination based on intergroup differences in loan performance.[2] This approach, which has come to be known as the default approach, is the subject of this chapter.

The default approach to studying mortgage discrimination has received a great deal of attention in recent years. This attention may reflect the fact that this approach has great intuitive appeal. The basic argument was expressed in a widely read magazine column by Gary Becker (1993a) and in the lecture Becker delivered when he was awarded the 1992 Nobel Prize in Economics (1993b).[3] In Becker's words:

If banks discriminate against minority applicants, they should earn *greater* profits on the loans actually made to them than on those to whites. The reason is that discriminating banks would be willing to accept marginally profitable whites who would be turned down if they were black.[4] (1993b, p. 389, emphasis in original)

The attention given to this approach also may reflect the fact that many of the studies based on it appear to yield results that contradict the widely criticized findings of the Boston Fed Study. In any case, a great deal of research based on the default approach to mortgage lending discrimination has appeared in the last decade. This research is reviewed in this chapter.

Before proceeding, we need to consider two background issues. First, Becker and some other scholars do not simply offer the default approach as an alternative to the analysis of loan approval decisions. As Becker puts it in his Nobel lecture:

Recent studies on whether banks discriminate in their mortgage lending against blacks and other minorities compare the likelihood of getting a loan for minority and white applicants who are similar in incomes, credit backgrounds, and other available characteristics. The conclusion typically has been that blacks but not Asian-Americans are rejected excessively compared to whites of similar characteristics.

Unfortunately, these studies do not use the correct procedure for assessing whether banks discriminate, which is to determine whether loans are more profitable to blacks (and other minorities) than to whites. This requires examining the default and other payback experiences of loans, the interest rates charged, and so forth. (1993b, p. 389)

Becker's magazine column goes even further by claiming that the Boston Fed Study is subject to "serious methodological flaws" because it does not examine loan defaults.

We strongly disagree. Many hypotheses yield more than one prediction. One cannot reject a test concerning one predicted outcome by showing that the same hypothesis makes a prediction for another outcome. Becker's own analysis, along with the more formal models discussed later in this chapter, links discrimination in loan approval with intergroup differences in loan default. Hence, the analysis underlying the default approach inevitably makes predictions about both loan approval and default disparities, and it is illogical to say that tests of one set of predictions are "correct" whereas tests of the other set of predictions are "not correct."

The real issue, it seems to us, is whether the default approach provides a compelling alternative test of the hypothesis that there is discrimination in mortgage lending. If it does, and if studies based on the default approach, unlike loan approval studies, find no sign of discrimination, then scholars must recognize that the evidence for discrimination in mortgage lending is mixed. In other words, the existence of the default approach does not prove that loan approval studies are flawed, but it might provide evidence that contradicts the evidence from those studies. This outcome would, of course, significantly weaken the case that discrimination exists. However, other outcomes are possible as well. Default studies might find higher rates of default among minorities than among whites, all else equal, thereby strengthening the case for discrimination. The default approach also might face insurmountable methodological obstacles. In this case, the evidence from loan approval studies would stand alone as the test for mortgage lending discrimination. The main objective of this chapter is to determine which of these outcomes is most consistent with the available evidence.

The second background issue is that Becker's argument, and indeed virtually the entire default approach literature, is built on the assumption that discrimination takes the form of a higher underwriting hurdle for minority than for white applicants. This assumption, which is discussed by Berkovec et al. (1994), is plausible but has never been tested.

A recent analysis by Ferguson and Peters (2000) reveals the importance of this assumption. The Ferguson and Peters analysis, which was discussed in chapter 7, starts by assuming that there exists a large class of marginal loan applicants, defined as the applicants with the lowest level of creditworthiness that lenders are willing to accept. Under some circumstances, credit will be rationed to this class of applicants so that some members of the class will receive loans and others will be denied despite having exactly the same credit qualifications. As explained in chapter 7, the Ferguson and Peters analysis implies that a lender's profits are the same regardless of which applicants in the marginal class receive loans. Moreover, the expected default rate is the same for every applicant in the marginal class, regardless of whether or not he receives a loan. It follows that the expected default rate of the marginal minority applicant is the same if lenders always discriminate by selecting white applicants before minority applicants or avoid discrimination by selecting applicants at random from the class of marginal applicants. They conclude that "lending discrimination cannot necessarily be detected by examining profits made on loans to marginal borrowers, suggesting that Becker's proposed empirical test is problematical" (p. 33).

Thus, the Ferguson and Peters analysis is noteworthy because it shows that one form for discrimination, namely a credit-rationing process that favors whites, does not result in a lower default rate for the marginal minority borrower than for the marginal white borrower. Ferguson and Peters provide no evidence, however, that their analysis is realistic. In fact, the available evidence seems more consistent with the view that the distribution of creditworthiness is quite spread out, with few applicants at any given level of creditworthiness (see table 5.6). As a result, it seems unlikely that discrimination is confined to the rules governing credit rationing among applicants whose creditworthiness is the same. For the rest of this chapter, therefore, we accept the assumption used by all other studies of the default approach, namely, that lenders discriminate by setting higher underwriting standards for minority than for white applicants.

8.2   The Default Approach to Studying Discrimination

Although analysts disagree about the best way to model many features of mortgage markets, one facet of the mortgage market elicits a clear consensus: Lenders care whether loans are repaid and, all else equal, are unlikely to approve a loan application with a relatively high expected probability of default. This simple premise leads to a number of straightforward conclusions: The sample of approved loans has a lower expected default rate than the sample of rejected loans. The expected default rate in a lender's portfolio depends upon the toughness of its underwriting criteria. Holding the composition of the pool of mortgage applications fixed, a lender that raises underwriting standards will lower the expected default rate in its portfolio of approved loans. Similarly, if a lender raises underwriting standards for a specific group of applications, such as those from minorities or those for houses in minority neighborhoods, the average expected default rate for approved loans in that subsample will decline.

These conclusions have led to the argument that default rates or statistical analysis of defaults can be used to test for the existence of mortgage lending discrimination. In this section, we explore the key

methodological issues involved in studying discrimination by looking at loan defaults and review the existing attempts to implement
this approach using data on defaults for a sample of loans.

8.2.1   Unobserved Underwriting Variables

The most extreme form of the default approach to studying discrimination, which is illustrated by Becker (1993a, 1993b), claims that, in
the presence of discrimination, the average default rate for minorities will be lower than the average default rate for whites. This version of the default approach does not make sense because the
distribution of application "quality," which is another word for
expected loan performance based on applicant, loan, and property
characteristics, is much lower for minority than for white applicants.
Without any discrimination at all, therefore, average realized loan
performance will be lower for minority than for white borrowers.
This point was clearly made twenty years ago by Peterson (1981)
and also appears in Galster (1993a), Ferguson and Peters (1995), and
Tootell (1996b).[5] Based on the Boston Fed Study's data, for example,
minority applicants tend to have larger debt burdens, higher LTVs,
and poorer credit histories than white applications, on average.
Without any discrimination, therefore, the pool of approved minority applications will be of lower quality than the pool of approved
white loans.

This conclusion reflects, of course, a type of omitted-variable bias:
Intergroup comparisons of average default rates give biased results
because they do not control for application quality, as is illustrated
by figure 8.1.[6] The figure's horizontal axis represents the quality of
loan applications, and its vertical axis represents the fraction (or
density) of applications at any given quality level. The distributions
of minority and white loan applications are shown separately, and
the minority distribution is drawn so that minority loan applications
have lower quality than white applications, on average. The quality
cutoff below which loan applications are denied is labeled C. This
cutoff is the same for whites and minorities, which implies that
minority applicants do not face a stricter underwriting standard or,
to put it another way, that underwriting standards do not involve
disparate-treatment discrimination. The average quality of approved
white applications, which is the mean of the white quality distribution above C, is substantially higher than the average quality of

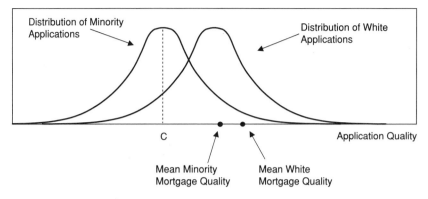

Figure 8.1
Omitted-variable bias in the default approach.

approved minority applications, because so many high-quality white applicants applied for and received mortgages. These high-quality white applicants pull up the average quality of white mortgages and drive down the average actual white default rate. Underwriting discrimination against minorities raises the average quality of accepted minority loans and therefore lowers the average actual minority default rate below the rate with no discrimination. The minority default rate with no discrimination, however, could still be far above the white rate, and discrimination might not lower the minority default rate enough to offset this initial disadvantage. Thus, a lower average default rate for whites than for minorities cannot be interpreted as evidence that discrimination does not exist.

Berkovec et al. (1994) attempt to avoid the problems inherent in examining average default rates by using statistical analysis to examine whether the *marginal* minority applicant is treated the same as the *marginal* white applicant.[7] They attempt to identify the marginal borrower using regression techniques to control for many variables that lenders may consider during the underwriting process. Using a sample of FHA mortgages from 1987 through 1989, they find that minorities are more likely than whites to default, after all the underwriting variables that are available in their data set are controlled for. On the basis of this finding, they reject the hypothesis that minorities encounter discrimination.

Regression analysis controls for variables that are observed by the analyst and compares minority and white treatment based on un-

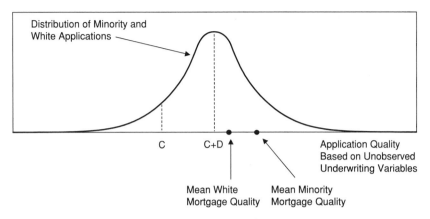

Figure 8.2
The regression-based default approach.

observed factors, which may include borrower characteristics that are observed and used by the lender for underwriting but are not observed by the analyst, henceforth called *unobserved underwriting variables*, along with across-lender differences in underwriting criteria and behavior. Thus, the Berkovec et al. approach essentially replicates the comparison of average default rates, except that the influence of observed underwriting variables has been removed prior to the calculation of intergroup differences in default.

Berkovec et al.'s argument is illustrated in figure 8.2. This figure is constructed in the same way as figure 8.1, except that the horizontal axis now represents the quality of loan applications based on *unobserved* underwriting variables, and, as assumed by Berkovec et al., white and minority applications have the same average quality when only these unobserved underwriting variables are considered. In this case, even if minority loan applications are worse on *observed* underwriting variables, higher underwriting standards for minorities result in a pool of approved minority mortgages that has higher average quality based on *unobserved* underwriting variables than does the pool of white mortgages.

The assumption of equal unobserved loan quality is critical to the Berkovec et al. conclusion. If minority applications have lower quality on the basis of unobserved underwriting variables, figure 8.1 still applies, so long as the horizontal axis is relabeled to be "Loan Quality Based on Unobserved Underwriting Variables." In that case, therefore, average quality can be lower for minority than for white loans even if lenders practice discrimination, and the Berkovec et al. approach cannot determine whether discrimination exists.[8] Thus, the key question is whether this assumption is reasonable. Even on the surface, it does not appear so. If minority applications have lower quality than white applications on the basis of observed underwriting variables, why is it reasonable to assume that they have the same level of quality as white applications on the basis of unobserved underwriting variables?

Moreover, the impact of unobserved underwriting variables on default is the counterpart of the omitted-variable bias problem in an analysis of mortgage application denials. If minority applications are of lower quality based on underwriting variables that are unobserved by the researcher but observed by the lender, a loan denial analysis will indicate a higher likelihood of denial for minorities even if lenders do not discriminate. With omitted underwriting variables, therefore, an analysis of loan denials is likely to overstate discrimination, and an analysis of loan defaults is likely to understate discrimination. A key implication of this point is that any analysis based on loan performance or default must control for the same set of underwriting variables that is used in an unbiased loan denial equation. Otherwise, the loan performance or default analysis may suffer from an omitted-variable bias even if the loan denial equation does not. Unlike the Boston Fed Study, for example, Berkovec et al. (1994) do not control for applicants' credit history. In the Boston Fed Study's data, minority applicants have worse credit histories than white applicants, and the credit history variables are highly significant in predicting denials. These results explicitly contradict the key assumption by Berkovec et al. and undermine their conclusion concerning discrimination.

Only one, recent study, Van Order and Zorn (2001), investigates default on conventional mortgage loans using information on borrower credit history. This study is based on data for about 1.4 million fixed-rate, thirty-year mortgage loans that originated between 1993 and 1995 and were purchased by Freddie Mac. The data set includes information on the well-known FICO credit score, ethnicity, income, age, debt ratio, LTV, loan purpose, census tract income, census tract ethnicity, state, and date of origin. Van Order and Zorn study default using a hazard model, which indicates the probability of default in one period given that has not yet occurred.[9] Two hazard models are estimated. The first contains no neighborhood information. In this model the coefficients for black and Hispanic borrowers are both positive, indicating a higher likelihood of default; the coefficient for black borrowers is not quite statistically significant, but the one for Hispanic borrowers is. The second model adds variables to measure the income level and minority composition of the census tract in which the property is located. In this model, the coefficients for black and Hispanic borrowers are both negative and significant and so are the indicators for largely white neighborhoods.

The Van Order and Zorn study illustrates that the results of a default study may depend not only on the inclusion of a credit history variable but also on the particular set of neighborhood control variables included in the regression. Indeed, even the sign of the minority status variables may not be the same for all sets of control variables. The problem facing Van Order and Zorn is that they do not have very extensive information on census tract characteristics. Their first model is almost certainly subject to omitted variable bias because it does not include any neighborhood variables, but the second is also not very satisfactory because it includes minority composition, which lenders are not allowed to consider when making loan approval decisions. A model with just tract income could be estimated with their data, but this model might yield biased results as well, because it does not include any other legitimate tract characteristics. Even with the high quality of this data set, therefore, definitive results are difficult to obtain. Van Order and Zorn apparently recognize this ambiguity and make no claim about the implication of their finding for discrimination.

8.2.2 Unobserved Borrower Characteristics

So far, we have considered only underwriting variables that are known to the lender but are unobserved by the analyst. As discussed by Brueckner (1996), Galster (1996a), Yinger (1996), and Ross (1996b), however, many factors that determine the likelihood of default (or any other measure of loan performance) are not observed by the lender; we call these variables *unobserved borrower characteristics*. For several reasons, it seems likely that on the basis of these unobserved borrower characteristics alone, minority applicants are less qualified than those of whites. For example, most defaults occur because the borrower experiences an unexpected event, such as a layoff, and discrimination in the labor market may imply that minorities are more likely to experience such negative events. Moreover, the legacy of past discrimination, which takes the form of lower levels of skills and lower wealth for minorities, may imply that minority borrowers are less able to overcome negative events when they do occur.[10] Thus, minority borrowers may be more likely to default than are white borrowers with identical applications. In short, a default analysis might find that blacks are more likely to default than whites even if it controls for all the underwriting variables available to the lender and lenders engage in discrimination.

The proponents of the default approach are correct in saying that holding minorities to a higher standard will decrease the likelihood that minority borrowers will default, but they are not correct in saying that this effect can be seen by comparing minority and white borrowers. The observed likelihood of default for minority borrowers needs to be compared to the likelihood of minority default that would have occurred without discrimination, not to the likelihood of default by white borrowers. This may be the most devastating critique of the default approach. Without knowing the minority-white difference in default likelihood after controlling for all of lenders' underwriting variables, researchers cannot state a null hypothesis to use in a default-based test for discrimination.

Berkovec et al. (1996) counter that the default approach is intended only to test for discrimination caused by lender prejudice. According to this theory of discrimination, an application of the approach in Becker (1971), lenders hold minority applicants to higher standards because loan officers must be compensated for their irrational prejudice against minorities by earning more profits when lending to them. As discussed in chapter 7, an alternative theory of discrimination is that lenders "rationally" (but illegally) use minority status as a signal for unobserved borrower characteristics and therefore hold minority applicants to a higher standard because minority applicants are more likely to default, on average, even after observable credit characteristics have been considered.[11] Berkovec et al. (1996) insist that their approach does not attempt to capture this so-called statistical discrimination.[12]

However, this counter-argument does not address the key issue. Simply stating that one is testing for discrimination caused by one mechanism rather than another does not make the existing group-

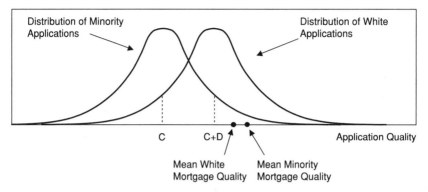

Figure 8.3
The default approach as a sufficient condition for discrimination.

based differences in unobserved borrower characteristics—and in default—go away. Some lenders may practice statistical discrimination, others may discriminate because of their personal prejudice, and others may not discriminate at all. Any interpretation of default results must recognize all these possibilities. One possible way to do so is to say that the default approach tests whether the level of discrimination in the lending industry exceeds the level expected based on "rational" lenders' using minority status as a signal for the likelihood of default. In fact, however, the default approach cannot provide even a test of this limited type. Ross (1996a) shows that if lenders have an incentive to practice statistical discrimination and do so to the extent dictated by their economic interest (ignoring the potential economic costs of violating the law), minority borrowers will still be more likely than observationally equivalent white borrowers to default on loans.

Another approach is taken by Van Order and Zorn (1995), who argue that a lower default rate for minority borrowers is sufficient but not necessary for proving that discrimination exists. Assuming a lower average quality of minority applications (after controlling for observable credit characteristics), minority borrowers could exhibit lower default rates only if minorities were held to a substantially higher underwriting standard, but finding a higher default rate for minorities does not reveal whether or not this type of discrimination exists. In figure 8.3, the cutoff for minority applications is $(C + D)$, where D represent the increased underwriting standard for minorities. The average quality of minority mortgages can exceed the average quality of white mortgages only if D is very large, that is, if substantial discrimination exists in mortgage underwriting. This argument, however, still requires the assumption that minority applications have poorer unobserved credit characteristics, an assumption that Van Order and Zorn cannot test.

8.2.3   Sample Selection Bias and the Default Approach

Several scholars have pointed out that the default approach cannot shed light on discrimination unless some underwriting variables are unobserved (or at least ignored) by the researcher (See Galster, 1996a, and Ross, 1996b). To understand this argument, consider the following highly simplified version. First, suppose that loan applications are evaluated on the basis of the "number of late credit card payments." Second, suppose for now that minority and white applicants have the same distribution of outcomes for this "late payments" variable. Third, suppose that lenders set a higher standard for minority than for white applicants, and in particular, that they deny minority applications if more than two late payments are observed but deny white applications only if more than four late payments are observed. Fourth, suppose that this "late payments" variable is a good predictor of default; for example, people with two late payments (who will all be approved) are more likely to default than people with no late payments. Now if a researcher observes the "late payments" variable and includes it in an equation to explain defaults, he will find that the minority status coefficient equals zero, even though lenders discriminate. In this case, the "late payments" variable fully describes the systematic component of default behavior, and there is nothing left for a minority status variable to explain. The higher hurdle that minority borrowers face in the loan approval decision pushes up their average creditworthiness, according to the "late payments" variable and, indeed, pushes it high enough so that, on average, minority borrowers have better creditworthiness, and hence experience fewer defaults, than do white borrowers.[13] But the impact of this higher hurdle is fully captured by the estimated coefficient of the "late payments" variable combined with the lower value of the "late payments" variable for minority than for white borrowers, a lower value that reflects discrimination.

Now consider what happens if the "late payments" variable is not observed by the analyst. In this case, the method of selecting the sample for a default analysis, namely, restricting it to people who actually receive a loan, introduces sample selection bias. The people who receive a loan have fewer late payments, on average, than people who are denied a loan, and the number of late payments affects whether or not they will default. Thus, the sample selection procedure is correlated with the outcome of interest, in this case, default, which implies that the estimated coefficients will be biased. Ironically, however, this "bias" is what makes the default method work. When the default equation is estimated, now without the "late payments" variable, the minority status coefficient will be negative, because the selected sample of minority applicants has cleared a higher hurdle than the selected sample of white applicants. In other words, the sample selection bias implies that the higher hurdle for minority applicants shows up in the minority status coefficient.

In more formal terms, if a statistical analysis controls for all underwriting variables considered by lenders, the unobserved portion of the denial decision must be entirely due to random differences across banks and across loan officers. The underwriting variables in the analysis completely describe the quality of the mortgage from the lender's perspective, and unobserved borrower characteristics that affect default are unrelated to lender differences in underwriting behavior. Therefore, the underwriting process has no influence on the likelihood of default after controlling for the observed underwriting variables. Under these circumstances, the default approach cannot detect discrimination, regardless of the cause.

This result seems to imply that all one needs to do to ensure the success of the default approach is leave out a few variables. This is not the case, however, because the only variables that can legitimately be omitted are ones that are not correlated with minority status. As pointed out earlier, the default approach yields biased results and is likely to understate discrimination if variables correlated with minority status are omitted from the estimated equation. In the example discussed above, suppose that the "late payments" variable is correlated with minority status, and in particular, that minority applicants have more late payments, on average, than do white applicants. Then even with a higher hurdle for minority than for white applicants in the loan approval decision, minority borrowers, that is, minority applicants who made it over the hurdle, could still have more late payments, on average, than white borrowers. In this case, a default equation that omitted the "late payments" variable would yield a positive minority status coefficient: a reflection of the omitted "late payments" variable and its correlation with minority status, not of reverse discrimination!

One might say that the need to avoid omitted-variable bias and the need to omit some underwriting variables are the Scylla and Charybdis of the default approach. If some variables are not omitted, the default approach will fail for lack of the required sample selection bias, but if variables correlated with minority status are omitted, then default approach will fail because of bias in the estimated coefficients, including the minority status coefficient. Thus, the only credible way to use the default approach is to obtain a data set that contains all underwriting variables that lenders actually use, identify a few of these variables that are not correlated with minority status (if such variables even exist), and omit these variables from the analysis. Existing studies are far from meeting these conditions.[14]

8.2.4 Conventional versus Government-Insured Loans

Berkovec et al. (1994) have been criticized for the use of government-insured (specifically FHA) loans as their sample (see Yinger, 1996, and Galster, 1996a). This issue is important because Berkovec et al. claim to shed light on discrimination in conventional loans, even though their data consist of defaults on FHA loans.[15] They build their case by observing that FHA loans cost the borrower more than conventional loans because they are insured, so low-risk borrowers prefer conventional loans. As a result, they argue, mortgage applications will be sorted into three categories: the lowest-quality applications, which do not receive credit; the highest-quality applications, which receive credit in the conventional market; and the applications in between, which receive credit in the FHA market. With this type of segmentation, discrimination in the conventional sector would force higher-quality minority applicants into the FHA sector, which would result in a lower likelihood of default for approved minority FHA mortgages. The most straightforward application of the default approach would focus on the possibility that only the highest-quality minorities are approved for conventional mortgages. Because of data constraints, Berkovec et al. turn to the FHA sector, arguing that the pool of minority households that cannot receive a conventional mortgage, but qualify for an FHA loan, submit FHA applications

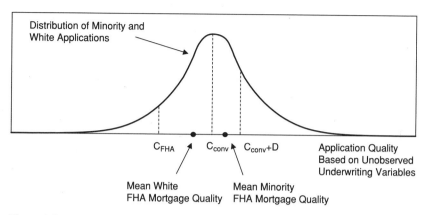

Figure 8.4
The default approach using a sample of FHA loans.

with a higher average quality than does the pool of white FHA applicants. Under this interpretation, any discrimination that pushes up the average performance of loans to minority households will take place in the conventional sector, not the FHA sector. The regressions conducted by Berkovec et al. cannot, of course, distinguish between discrimination in these two sectors, but Berkovec et al. implicitly argue that discrimination is more likely in conventional than in government-insured loans.[16]

This Berkovec et al. argument is illustrated in figure 8.4, which is based on the assumptions that minority and white applications have the same unobserved-quality distribution, conventional mortgages have a higher quality cut-off than FHA mortgages, and lenders practice discrimination in the conventional sector but not the FHA sector. As shown in figure 8.4, discrimination in the conventional sector implies that the upper limit of observed applicant quality in FHA loans is higher for minorities than for whites, and these assumptions lead to the Berkovec et al. conclusion, namely, higher loan quality for minorities in the FHA sector.

This conclusion, however, depends crucially on the assumption that minority and white applications have the same unobserved quality distribution. Without this assumption, the biases illustrated in figure 8.1 could still arise. To be specific, minority FHA loans could have lower quality than white FHA loans despite discrimination in the conventional sector, or minority FHA loans could have higher quality even without discrimination in the conventional

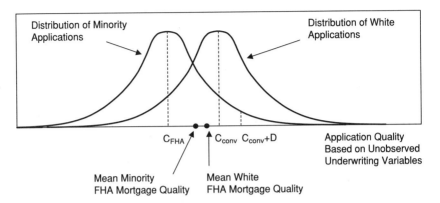

Figure 8.5
Omitted-variable bias with a sample of FHA loans: Failing to find discrimination.

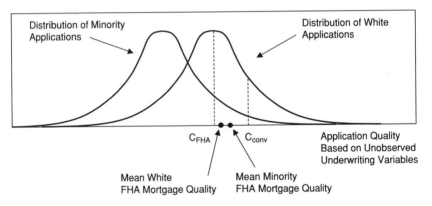

Figure 8.6
Omitted-variable bias with a sample of FHA loans: Detecting discrimination when none exists.

sector. The first of these possibilities is illustrated in figure 8.5, which is based on the same assumptions as figure 8.4, except that the distribution of application quality is now lower for minorities than for whites. In this case the mean quality of the FHA applications, namely, those between the two dotted lines indicating cutoff points, is higher for whites than for blacks, even though blacks face a higher cutoff point in the conventional sector than whites do.

The second possibility is illustrated in figure 8.6, which eliminates both the assumption that minority and white applications have the same quality based on unobserved credit qualifications and the assumption that there is discrimination in the conventional sector. Even though the FHA and conventional cutoff points are the same for both minority and white applications in this figure, the distribution of application quality between these cutoffs, which is, of course, the distribution of quality for FHA loans, has a higher mean value for minorities than for whites. Thus, a higher observed performance for minority than for white loans in the FHA sector is neither necessary nor sufficient to establish that there is discrimination in the conventional sector.

Moreover, it is unlikely that borrowers are perfectly stratified across the three above outcomes. Individuals have imperfect information about the underwriting behavior of lenders when they choose whether to apply for an FHA or a conventional loan. In addition, FHA loans have long been the primary source of credit for minority households (see Gabriel, 1996), and low-quality minority applicants may be pulled into the FHA sector based on this history, just as high-quality minority applicants are pushed into it by discrimination. If so, the sorting assumptions on which the Berkovec et al. analysis depends do not hold, and a finding of higher defaults by minority FHA borrowers, holding constant observable borrower characteristics, does not imply a lack of discrimination in the conventional sector, even if all the problems discussed earlier have been solved.

Ultimately, the default approach can be used to test for discrimination in a given sector of the mortgage market if the data make it possible to ensure that the distributions of unobserved credit characteristics are the same for minority and white applications in that sector. Even in this case, however, the default approach cannot determine the extent to which these distributions are influenced by discrimination in another sector or, indeed, by any other factor.

8.2.5   Other Dimensions of Loan Performance

Finally, several scholars have pointed out that studies based on loan "default" may not capture many relevant aspects of loan performance. In particular, these studies miss the role of lenders in initiating foreclosure proceedings, the possibility that the cost of default may vary across groups, and the possibility that mortgages can be prepaid. In principle, ignoring these issues could lead to biased results.[17]

First, existing "default" studies actually examine foreclosure, not default. In fact, most cases of default, defined as a borrower's being ninety days behind in mortgage payments, do not result in foreclosure by the lender; instead, the borrower sells the house or the borrower and lender negotiate a new payment schedule (see Ambrose and Capone, 1996a, 1996b). Default studies, however, observe only those defaults that turn into foreclosures. This is relevant for studying discrimination because, as we have pointed out elsewhere (Ross, 1996a; Yinger, 1996), the foreclosure process might not be group neutral. For example, lenders may be more willing to work out a new payment schedule, instead of foreclosing, with borrowers in some groups than in others. If lenders are more likely to initiate foreclosure proceedings against black and Hispanic borrowers than against white borrowers, then, at any given level of observable credit characteristics, black and Hispanic borrowers will be more likely to be observed defaulting. This effect works in the opposite direction from the effect of loan approval discrimination on default. If this effect exists, therefore, the default approach will be biased against finding discrimination.

The available evidence indicates, however, that existing default studies are not biased because of their focus on foreclosures instead of defaults. Specifically, Ambrose and Capone (1996b) find, using data on government-insured mortgages originated in 1988 that defaulted at least once, that the probability of foreclosure is not significantly different for minority and white borrowers.[18] To the best of our knowledge, no comparable evidence exists for conventional mortgage loans.

Lenders care about profits, not about defaults as such. For two reasons, the probability of default is not an accurate measure of profitability (even with constant foreclosure policies). First, profits depend on the cost of default when it occurs as well as on its probability, and the cost of default might vary across groups. Second, profits are influenced by prepayments as well as by defaults. If loans to protected classes have lower costs of default or probabilities of prepayment that make them more valuable, then such loans could be more profitable than loans to whites (as expected in a world with discrimination) even if they are more likely to default.

The available evidence on these possibilities is limited. Using data for millions of loans that originated in the mid-1990s and were then purchased by Freddie Mac, Van Order and Zorn (2001) find that the cost to lenders of default is no different for blacks, Hispanics, and whites, after controlling for income and neighborhood characteristics.[19] This evidence indicates that existing default studies are not biased because they ignore the cost of default.

Van Order and Zorn also investigate the role of prepayment. They find that loans to minority borrowers are less likely than loans to whites to be refinanced when mortgage rates decline. This characteristic boosts the profitability of loans to minorities.[20] This result is important because it implies that loans to minorities might be more profitable than loans to whites (as expected in a world with discrimination) even if loans to minorities are more likely to default. In other words, this result implies that ignoring the prepayment option biases the default approach against finding discrimination.

8.2.6   Conclusions

The default approach to studying mortgage lending discrimination has received a great deal of attention in recent years. This approach builds on the simple, intuitively powerful idea that discrimination involves holding minority applicants to higher standards, so that loans given to minorities must perform better, that is, be less likely to default, than loans given to whites. As it turns out, however, this simple idea runs into severe methodological obstacles.

The most fundamental problem is that it is virtually impossible to steer the default approach between two obstacles. The first obstacle is the bias that arises when key underwriting variables are omitted from the analysis. In particular, the default approach yields results that are biased against finding discrimination unless it includes all variables that (1) influence default, (2) are observed by the lender at the time of loan approval, and (3) are correlated with minority status. No existing data set provides all this information.

The second obstacle is that the default approach has no power to detect discrimination when all important underwriting variables are included in the analysis. To be specific, the default approach cannot detect discrimination without omitting some variables that (1) influence default, (2) are observed by the lender at the time of loan approval, and (3) are not correlated with minority status. A researcher obviously can determine which observed variables are correlated with minority status. Even if all variables that influence default and are observed by the lender are available to the researcher, however, there is no guarantee that some of these variables will be uncorrelated with minority status, which is a necessary condition for avoiding the second obstacle. In the more likely case that the researcher does not have access to all this information, there is no way to rule out the (likely) possibility that some of the omitted variables are correlated with minority status, which is a sufficient condition for omitted-variable bias to arise. Thus, it would take extraordinary circumstances, namely, complete data along with some variables that are not correlated with minority status, to overcome these two obstacles—circumstances that are not even close to being met for existing studies.

Even if a researcher could avoid these two fundamental sources of bias, however, she still might not be able to obtain unbiased estimates using the default approach. Perhaps the largest remaining problem is that characteristics of the borrower that are unobserved by the lender and by the researcher also can be a source of bias (generally downward bias) in an estimate of discrimination. Some scholars have argued that these characteristics give lenders a reason to practice statistical discrimination, that is, to use minority status as a signal of poor, unobservable credit characteristics, and that the default approach looks only for discrimination based on prejudice after statistical discrimination has already taken place. This is an enormous concession, because it says that, at best, the default approach can isolate prejudice-based discrimination only by assuming widespread statistical discrimination! As it turns out, however, even this concession does not go far enough: The default approach is biased against finding prejudice-based discrimination even in the presence of "complete" statistical discrimination, that is, of statistical discrimination that fully responds to minority-white differences in expected loan performance.

Finally, some scholars have attempted to connect loan performance in the FHA sector, for which data are available, with discrimination in the conventional sector. We show, however, that evidence from the FHA sector cannot be used to make inferences about discrimination in the conventional sector. The default approach can be used only to study discrimination in the sector to which the data apply, as in Van Order and Zorn (2001), and then only when the methodological problems discussed above have been solved.

8.3   New Versions of the Default Approach

Over the last few years, researchers have explored several new twists on the use of performance data to test for mortgage lending discrimination. We divide this new literature into two parts. The first part consists of studies that attempt to address critiques of the default approach. We examine two studies in this part. The first study uses data on market concentration to insulate a discrimination test against omitted-variable bias. The second study develops a theoretical model in which borrowers respond to discrimination by altering loan terms. The author of this study concludes that under the assumptions in this model, the default approach does not suffer from many of the biases discussed above. The second part consists of studies that combine loan denial and performance data from different sources. We examine two studies in this part. One study performs a simulation analysis, and the other estimates a joint model of loan approval and default.

8.3.1   A Default Test Based on Market Concentration

Berkovec et al. (1998) develop an alternative version of the default approach that may be insulated from the omitted-variable bias that arises because some determinants of default are unobserved by the lender or the researcher and are correlated with minority status. Rather than test directly for differences in default based on minority status, they identify a "proxy" variable that may be related to the level of discrimination but not to minority status and then test whether group-based differences in default are affected by this proxy variable. This is a clever attempt to eliminate one type of omitted-variable bias. Instead of focusing on the coefficient of a minority-status variable, this version of the default approach focuses on the coefficient of an interaction between minority status and the proxy variable—a coefficient that, under certain assumptions, will not be subject to omitted-variable bias.

Recall that under the standard default approach, the expected default rate of minorities relative to whites cannot be specified because the impact of unobserved factors cannot be determined. In other words, this approach fails to provide clear evidence concerning discrimination because it fails to specify a clear null hypothesis, which is the outcome to be expected if there is no discrimination. The new approach in Berkovec et al. (1998) appears to solve this problem because its null hypothesis seems clear: without discrimination, minority status will not influence the relationship between the proxy variable and default, so the coefficient of the interaction term will be zero. A rejection of this hypothesis, they argue, is evidence of discrimination.

To be more specific, Berkovec et al. claim that lenders have a greater ability to discriminate when they operate in an urban area with relatively little competition, as indicated by a highly concentrated lending industry. Moreover, they argue that unobserved credit characteristics, which are the source of the omitted-variable problems, are unlikely to be correlated with the degree to which lenders are concentrated.[21] If so, intergroup differences in default tendencies will not affect the estimated coefficient of the interaction between a borrower's minority status and market concentration, controlling for minority status itself. Using the FHA data in their earlier (1994) default study, Berkovec et al. estimate a default model that includes this interaction variable. They find that minority borrowers are less likely to default in highly concentrated markets, which is consistent with higher levels of discrimination in more concentrated markets, but the estimated coefficient is small in magnitude relative to the minority status coefficient itself and is not statistically significant. They conclude that there is no evidence of discrimination.

Although the estimated coefficient of the Berkovec et al. interaction term is indeed small relative to the minority status coefficient, this result does not establish that the estimated effect is too small to be of economic significance. In particular, one also might ask whether the impact of industry concentration on lenders' ability to discriminate is large relative to its impact on lenders' ability to ration credit more aggressively without regard to race. After all, the market power that comes with concentration could alter the consequences of many lender actions, not just of discrimination. A lender's ability to ration credit in general is indicated by the coefficient of the concentration variable (not interacted with anything) in the Berkovec et al. default equations. This coefficient is statistically significant. In the three years examined by Berkovec et al., the estimated impact of concentration on lenders' ability to ration credit to minorities equals 100, 33, and 66 percent, respectively, of a lender's ability to ration credit in general, which is a large impact even if it is not statistically significant.[22]

It should also be noted that Berkovec at al. interpret this test, like the test in their earlier (1994) work, as a test for the existence of discrimination based on prejudice or, to use their terms, of noneconomic discrimination. They argue that competition may not drive out statistical discrimination, which is based on profit-maximizing behavior. As a result, they concede that statistical discrimination could still exist even if they fail to reject their null hypothesis, that is, even if they find that the treatment of minority applicants does not vary with the degree of competition in the loan industry.

Although it is novel, the Berkovec et al. article also has a more fundamental flaw, namely, that it is built on two assumptions that are essentially contradictory. The first assumption, which is explicit, is that discrimination motivated by prejudice is stronger in locations where the lending industry is more concentrated, that is, when there are fewer lenders to compete against each other. We find this assumption to be plausible; it says, in effect, that lenders are in a better position to allow prejudice to affect their underwriting procedures when they face less competition; as a result, a lack of competition will be particularly hard on minority customers. This assumption has never been tested, however, and it is not tested by Berkovec et al. Given how little is known about the causes of mortgage discrimination, this assumption, or any other for that matter, should treated with considerable skepticism. At best, therefore, this new test for lending discrimination must be seen as conditional on the validity of a so-far untested assumption about discrimination.

The second assumption, which is implicit in the Berkovec et al. argument, is that underwriting standards are not affected by the degree of competition among lenders. Regardless of the degree of concentration, in other words, in the Berkovec et al. model, lenders must always set the same credit standard and place the same weight on each underwriting variable. This assumption all but contradicts the first one: How can a a lack of competition cause lenders to be more aggressive in rationing credit to minorities without causing lenders be more aggressive in rationing credit on other grounds, as well?

Ironically, Berkovec et al. actually test this second assumption. As noted earlier, they include in their default equation the concentration variable itself, not interacted with anything. They find that the level of market concentration lowers the likelihood of default. They interpret this result as support for the view that lenders ration credit more aggressively in more concentrated markets. They fail to see, however, that this result undermines their interpretation of their key interaction variable. In our terms, this result explicitly contradicts the second assumption.

So why is the second assumption necessary for the Berkovec et al. test to be valid? For the sake of illustration, suppose that this assumption is violated in the following way: A higher market concentration raises the quality cutoff for conventional mortgages, but not for FHA mortgages. This effect can be represented by an increase in C_{conv} in figure 8.6. This increase could arise because lenders in areas with high market concentration set a higher standard by using the same weights on all underwriting variables or by placing a higher weight on one or more individual underwriting variables. Given the distributions in figure 8.6, therefore, an increase in market concentration results in the addition of many high-quality white mortgages, based on unobservable underwriting variables, to the FHA sector, compared with only a few high-quality minority mortgages. It follows that an increase in market concentration increases intergroup differences in default, even if such an increase has no impact on discrimination and this new version of the default approach is biased, in this case, away from finding discrimination.

To put it another way, the Berkovec et al. approach cannot distinguish between two different explanations for a change in the minority/white default ratio when market concentration increases. The first explanation is that market concentration facilitates discrimination. The second explanation, which has nothing to do with discrimination, is that market concentration induces lenders to ration credit more aggressively, which changes the composition of successful applicants and in particular alters the average creditworthiness of minority borrowers relative to that of whites. In other words, this second explanation undermines the clarity of the Berkovec et al. null hypothesis.

The assumption that underwriting standards are not affected by competition would be required even in an analysis of defaults in the conventional sector. For the example in figure 8.5, a increase in the cutoff for conventional mortgages drops a large number of low-quality white mortgages and only a small number of low-quality minority mortgages. As before, the relationship between minority status and default increases with market concentration even if market concentration has no impact on discrimination. As a result, the coefficient estimated by Berkovec et al. will be biased toward finding no discrimination. Of course, figure 8.5 is only an example, and a downward bias in this new version of the Berkovec et al. default approach is likely but not guaranteed. If higher concentration leads lenders to be less aggressive in rationing credit based on other factors, for example, the bias could work in the opposite direction. Nevertheless, this analysis shows that the Berkovec et al. revised default approach yields a biased estimate of the key coefficient, the one used to test for discrimination, and there is no way to eliminate or even measure this bias.

The assumption that underwriting standards are unrelated to competition applies not only to the level of creditworthiness that applicants must reach but also to the weights placed on individual underwriting variables. In particular, the revised Berkovec et al. approach is valid only if market power affects the way lenders ration credit to minorities but does not affect credit rationing based on LTV, the housing expense–to–income ratio, the debt-to-income ratio, and possibly a host of other underwriting variables. Any change in the weights placed on these variables will alter the share of minorities among successful applicants and, like a change in the level of creditworthiness, will alter the minority/white default ratio even with no discrimination.

These possibilities describe another kind of omitted-variable bias. Just as omitted underwriting variables bias the minority status coefficient in the standard default model, the omission of variables to capture the impact of market concentration on the use of underwriting variables biases the coefficient of the interaction between market concentration and minority status. In the case of observed underwriting variables, one could solve this problem by interacting all these variables with market concentration and including these interactions in the default equation. If all of these variables prove to be insignificant, then one can conclude that, as required by the second assumption, market concentration does not influence underwriting weights, at least for observed variables. If some of them are significant, however, then the second assumption is violated, and it is necessary to include the new interaction terms as controls. Even though they could have done so, Berkovec et al. do not take this step. As a

result, we cannot determine the magnitude of the bias in the interaction between minority status and market concentration that arises
when these other interactions are omitted.

Including interactions between concentration and observed underwriting variables minimizes this problem but does not eliminate it,
because concentration still might alter the weights lenders place on
unobserved underwriting variables. To put it another way, once
these other interaction variables are included, the required second
assumption needs to refer only to omitted underwriting variables;
that is, the role of unobserved underwriting variables for whites
must not be affected by market concentration. As in the standard
default approach, adding control variables does not alter the nature
of the problem, but it does narrow its scope. Thus, without a complete set of underwriting variables, this version of the default
approach may yield biased results even if it includes interactions
between market concentration and all observed underwriting variables. This problem was first pointed out by Ross (1997), who argues
that the omission of credit history variables may bias the Berkovec et
al. study away from finding discrimination.[23]

Thus, the conditions that must hold for this new version of the
default approach to be valid are very stringent, indeed: Not only
must lenders respond to a lack of competition by increasing discrimination, but they also must refrain from responding to a lack of
competition by altering their underwriting criteria in any other way.
Berkovec et al. undermine their own argument by demonstrating
one important way in which the second condition is violated, and
further investigation of the problem could reveal additional violations. We conclude that Berkovec et. al.'s revised default approach
based on market concentration cannot be interpreted as a test of the
hypothesis that prejudice-based discrimination exists in mortgage
markets.

8.3.2   A Default Test Based on Negotiated Loan Terms

Han (2000) argues that the simple sample selection story behind the
default approach is incomplete, because borrowers who are discriminated against can increase their likelihood of obtaining a loan
by accepting a higher interest rate or a lower loan amount, that is,
by negotiating for approval with less favorable loan terms.[24] Han
examines a two-period model of consumption and borrowing in

which second-period income is uncertain and low second-period income may lead to a borrower default. In this model, Han allows for both prejudice-based and statistical discrimination. Han shows that prejudice-based discrimination results in a lower likelihood of default by minority borrowers, which is the standard result based on sample selection, but also in a higher level of lender loss upon default by minority borrowers, which is opposite to the standard prediction.[25] Han also finds that when minority-white differences in the unobserved determinants of borrower creditworthiness are added to the model and lenders are assumed to practice statistical discrimination to account for these differences, then there is an increase in both the likelihood of default for minority borrowers and lender loss upon default.[26]

This approach allows Han to avoid one of the key flaws in the traditional default approach. To be specific, his test does not rely on the existence of lender underwriting variables that are not observed by the researcher. According to his reasoning, prejudice-based discrimination boosts the minority status coefficient in a loan default model because some rejected minority applicants are willing to accept revised terms that lower the probability of default, not because of selection bias associated with unobserved underwriting variables.

Han estimates a default model using the same FHA data that were used by Berkovec et al. (1994),[27] except that Han does not include any loan terms, such as LTV or debt-to-income ratio. Han argues that loan terms are endogenous and that his predictions apply to a reduced-form model that controls only for borrower and property characteristics. Like Berkovec et al., Han finds a positive relationship between race and default and fails to reject the null hypothesis that there is no prejudice-based discrimination. Han acknowledges, however, that the empirical study is limited because the data do not contain key underwriting variables, such as credit history.

At first glance, it appears as if Han's test would avoid omitted-variable bias if data were available on all borrower and property characteristics observed by the lender. In our view, however, an omitted-variable bias problem remains because of Han's reduced-form specification. Han's argument is that a complete specification should contain all borrower and property characteristics used by the lender but should not include loan terms, which are endogenous. This argument fails to recognize that the lender obtains additional information about the borrower from the loan terms the borrower requests or is willing to accept. If minority applicants have higher LTVs than whites after controlling for applicant and property characteristics observed by the lender, then they will also have a higher default rate after controlling for these variables. Thus, Han's analysis would be more compelling if it included loan terms, treated as endogenous variables.

Finally, although Han's model provides a way to avoid one of the key methodological problems with the standard default approach, it does not solve another key problem, namely, the omitted-variable bias that can arise because of credit characteristics that are unobserved by either the lender or the researcher. As before, it may be tempting to try to resolve this issue by introducing statistical discrimination into the analysis. After all, if minority applications are poorer, on average, because of unobserved credit characteristics, lenders have an incentive to practice statistical discrimination. This statistical discrimination will, in turn, raise the quality of accepted minority applications and might therefore be thought to eliminate this type of omitted-variable bias.

In fact, however, Han comes to the same conclusion as Ross (1996a) on this point. As noted earlier, Han shows that a minority disadvantage on unobserved credit characteristics drives up the minority default rate even if lenders respond to this disadvantage by practicing statistical discrimination. In other words, the Han approach, like the basic Berkovec et al. (1994) approach, does not lead to a clear test for prejudice-based discrimination even under the assumption that lenders practice statistical discrimination whenever they have an economic incentive to do so (again, ignoring costs associated with violating the law). Even with this assumption, minority borrowers could have a higher default rate than white borrowers despite the existence of prejudice-based discrimination. A compelling test for prejudice-based discrimination must compare the estimated minority status coefficient to the minority-white default rate difference that would arise without any prejudice-based discrimination—a difference that is not zero and that no study has yet been able to identify.

8.3.3 A Simulation Analysis of Selection Bias

The default approach builds on the close linkage between the loan approval decision and the performance of approved loans. As discussed in section 8.2, however, the nature of this linkage depends on a variety of unobserved factors with an unknown impact on minority-white default differentials. One way to shed light on this linkage, therefore, is to estimate a default equation, and a minority-white default differential, under various assumptions about these factors. This approach, which is taken by Ross (1997), makes it possible to determine how the parameters of the default equation are influenced by the loan approval process.

To be specific, Ross (1997) simulates samples of loan applications in which information is present on both the loan denial decision and on later default outcomes for approved mortgages. The simulated sample is based on the Boston Fed Study's public-use data and is generated in several steps. First, Ross uses these data to estimate a loan denial model that is similar to the basic version of the third model that we estimated in chapter 5 (that is, to the third entry, row 1, table 5.5). Second, he assumes that the level of prejudice-based discrimination in loan denial is accurately described by the estimated minority status coefficient from this model. Third, he generates 500,000 loan applications by adding a simulated random variable to the actual observable factors in the Boston Fed Data. This random variable accounts for unobservable determinants of loan denial. Since there are roughly 3,000 loans in the Boston Fed Study's sample, this step creates 167 (500,000/3,000) new observations for each original observation, where each of these 167 new observations has a different value for this random variable. Fourth, he simulates the loan denial decision for each new observation based on the estimated coefficients from the loan denial model, the actual values of the variables in the original sample, and the values of the random variable in the simulated sample. This step leads to a sample of borrowers, that is, of accepted applications.

The fifth step brings in default using the FHA foreclosure data, namely, the Berkovec et al. (1994) sample. These data contain most of the underwriting variables used by the Boston Fed Study's data, with the notable exception of borrower credit history. Ross's approach is to calculate an index of applicant credit quality based on the coefficients from the loan approval model, using only those variables that are common to both data sets.[28] This index indicates the probability that a given loan will be approved based on these common credit variables. Ross then estimates a default equation with this index and minority status as the explanatory variables.[29]

The sixth step is to generate another random variable to account for the unobservable determinants of default for each of the approved applications in the 500,000-application sample and then to predict default for each borrower based on the estimated coefficients from the default equation, the value of the credit quality variables, and the value of the random variable. In this simulation, the value of the minority status coefficient is set to zero; that is, the simulation assumes that, after controlling for observable credit quality, minority and white borrowers have the same default rate, on average. This step leads to the final sample, which indicates default for a large sample of mortgages. Ross then investigates several key questions by estimating a standard default model for this sample.[30]

As discussed earlier, discrimination in underwriting can influence the minority status coefficient in a default model only if there exist unobserved underwriting variables that influence both loan denial and the likelihood of default. The presence of these variables is summarized by the correlation between random variables in the two equations, a correlation that is built into the process that generates these variables.[31] Ross compares the values of the minority status coefficient in the default equation estimated with different assumed values for this across-equation correlation. The assumed values of this correlation are 0.00, −0.25, −0.50, and −0.75. These four values result in an estimated minority status coefficient of 0.00, −0.07, −0.19, and −0.45, respectively.

All of these estimates are based on the assumptions that lenders practice prejudice-based discrimination and that intergroup differences in default do not exist, that is, that unobservable factors do not result in a higher default rate for minority than for white borrowers, which is the assumption made by Berkovec et al. (1994). Thus, the negative values of these estimated coefficients support Berkovec et al.'s assertion that minorities will default less frequently when lenders practice discrimination. These estimates also indicate, however, that the default approach may provide a weak test for discrimination when the correlation between unobservable factors in the two equations is 0.25 or below in absolute value. When the across-equation correlation is 0.25, for example, the estimated minority status coefficient is only −0.07 despite extensive (assumed) discrimination in loan approval. As discussed in the next section, the available evidence indicates that this correlation falls into this range in the Berkovec et al sample. (This problem was discussed in section 8.2.1.)

Ross also examines the effect of omitting credit history variables from a default analysis.[32] Again assuming that no intergroup differences in default exist after controlling for all underwriting variables, the estimates of the minority status coefficient are 0.12, 0.04, −0.05, and −0.275 for across-equation correlations of 0.00, −0.25, −0.50, and −0.75, respectively. The positive values of the first two coefficients, along with the small values of the other two, indicate that the omission of credit history variables biases the results of the default approach. Recall that this analysis assumes that discrimination exists at roughly the level identified in the Boston Fed Study. Nevertheless, the default approach leads to the conclusion that discrimination does not exist, as indicated by the positive or negative-but-small effect of minority status on default for minorities, if the correlation between unobservable factors is below −0.5. This problem was discussed in section 8.2.1.

These results cast serious doubt on the usefulness of the default approach as a test for discrimination. On the one hand, if credit history variables are omitted from the default equation, the default approach will probably fail to find discrimination when it exists unless the correlation between unobservable factors in the loan denial and default equations exceeds 0.50 in absolute value, and it probably will understate the role of discrimination substantially even at such high correlations. On the other hand, the default approach is not very powerful if credit history variables are included in the default equation, because including them results in a correlation between the unobservable factors in the two equations that is far below the level needed for the default approach to work. In short, these simulations confirm that the default approach yields misleading answers regardless of whether credit history variables are included or excluded.

Finally, Ross introduces an incentive for lenders to practice statistical discrimination in the form of a higher average default rate for minority borrowers after controlling for observable credit history variables. He then assumes that lenders act on this incentive, that is, he assumes that lenders use minority status as a signal about the propensity to default based on unobservable factors and incorporate this propensity into their loan denial decision. This statistical discrimination comes on top of the prejudice-based discrimination that is already in the simulations. In this case, the default approach breaks down entirely. In particular, the estimated minority status coefficients in the default equation are positive and significant for all four above interequation correlations. Contrary to the assertions of Berkovec et al., in other words, the default equation fails to find a lower default rate for minorities despite the presence of both prejudice-based discrimination and statistical discrimination.

Perhaps the key limitation of Ross's (1997) analysis is its use of two different data sets, one for conventional mortgages in a single urban area and the other for FHA mortgages nationwide. As Ross explains, his analysis depends on the assumption that the underwriting process for FHA applications is the same as, or at least similar to, the underwriting process for conventional mortgage applications. As stated above, the choice to apply for an FHA mortgage is a borrower decision (although this decision could be influenced by other actors in the mortgage market). This choice should not influence the underwriting model unless the decision reveals information about the borrower that both is not observed during the underwriting process and explains default tendencies. An application to FHA is probably influenced by the likelihood of receiving a conventional mortgage, which is based on underwriting variables, and by the cost of a delay in receiving credit when a conventional application is denied, which is probably not correlated with default risk. Thus, if the model controls for most or all key underwriting variables, such as the ones in the Boston Fed Study's data, the approval model for FHA and conventional loans may be similar.

There is some evidence that FHA and conventional underwriting processes are, in fact, quite similar. Rosenblatt (1997) finds that the influence of LTV on loan denial does not vary between the FHA and conventional sectors of the market.[33] In addition, Rosenblatt estimates a model in which an application may be denied for either financial considerations or credit history. The results for loan denials based on financial considerations do not vary between the two sectors. The results for loan denials based on credit history do vary between the two sectors, but Rosenblatt's sample does not contain information on credit history, so his estimates for this model may be severely biased. Avery and Beeson (1998) interact loan-to-income variables with whether an application is for an FHA mortgage and include these variables in a HMDA-based loan denial model. These interactions are found to be insignificant, which suggests a similarity between the approval models in the two sectors.[34] (The use of HMDA data is clearly not optimal for this analysis, but they are the best data currently available).

Overall, therefore, any analysis that combines loan denial information for conventional loans and default information for FHA loans must be interpreted with caution, because this type of analysis requires the assumption that these two sectors have similar underwriting standards. At the present time, however, this is the only way to bring loan denial and default information together, and the limited existing evidence does not suggest major differences in underwriting across these two sectors.

8.3.4 Joint Estimation of Loan Denial and Performance

Ross (2000) estimates a default equation that formally accounts for the selection bias that arises because unobservable factors in the loan approval decision, which determines who receives a loan, are correlated with unobservable factors in default behavior among borrowers. This joint model is not based on the ideal data set, which would involve applications, underwriting decisions, and defaults for the same set of individuals, but instead follows Ross (1997) by combining the Boston Fed Study's public-use data on loan denial and the Berkovec et al. (1994) FHA data on default. The Boston Fed Study's data set is used to estimate the loan denial model. The results of this estimation are then combined with FHA default data in a second-stage analysis of loan default.[35] This second-stage analysis corrects for the influence of the loan denial process on the likelihood of default and provides consistent estimates of the default process under the assumption that this process is the same for the two samples.[36] The resulting estimates provide a relatively complete picture of the likelihood of default for mortgage applications—more complete, at any rate, than the picture in previous research.

This analysis and the analysis described in the previous section both combine the Boston Fed Study's loan approval data with FHA default data. The previous analysis, however, builds a sample of applications based on the Boston Fed Study's data to see how various situations influence the ability of the default approach to uncover prejudice-based discrimination when it exists. In contrast, the analysis in this section combines these two data sets to provide the best possible joint estimation of loan approval and default.

The analysis discussed in this section yields several key results. First, it provides an estimate of the correlation between the unobserved determinants of default and the unobserved determinants of loan denial. A correlation between these sets of unobserved factors can exist only if some underwriting variables are unobserved and excluded from the analysis. The estimated correlation is −0.26 (standard error: 0.04) and −0.18 (standard error: 0.05) using two different specifications.[37] However, the FHA foreclosure sample does not include credit history variables. Ross estimates that the correlation between unobserved factors in the two equations with controls for credit history would be 0.12 (standard error: 0.06) and 0.04 (standard error: 0.06) for his two specifications.[38] These low correlations do not support the view that the Boston Fed Study's data set omits important underwriting variables. Moreover, as discussed above, these results imply that the default approach may not be valid, or at best may only provide a weak test for discrimination, once credit history variables are included in the default model. As noted earlier, any attempt to strengthen the test for discrimination by omitting credit history variables from the default model is likely to cause another serious problem, namely, omitted-variable bias.

Next, Ross explores the possibility that lenders practice statistical discrimination. To do this, he calculates the expected default risk for each observation in the Boston Fed Study's sample using the co-efficients from the FHA regression for common underwriting variables and the coefficient for the minority status variable. He finds that when this variable for expected default is included in a loan denial equation, the estimated difference in loan denial between minorities and whites, controlling for other factors, equals zero. In other words, the unfavorable treatment of minorities in the Boston Fed Study's data can be attributed to the higher default probability of minority applicants after accounting for observable underwriting variables. This is exactly what would happen if lenders practiced statistical discrimination, that is, if they used minority status as a signal for a higher default probability based on factors they could not directly observe.

The minority status coefficient in this loan denial regression can be interpreted as a new test for prejudice-based discrimination. Because this test is based on a loan denial equation, not a default equation, it avoids many of the problems discussed earlier. In particular, this coefficient determines whether lenders are more likely to deny minority than white applications after accounting for the possibility that lenders practice statistical discrimination. The test explicitly models the potential influence of statistical discrimination on underwriting. As a result, the test for prejudice-based discrimination involves only intergroup differences in underwriting above the level implied by statistical discrimination. Moreover, because it focuses on loan denial, not default, this approach does not require omitted underwriting variables to detect prejudice-based discrimination. Finally, the model is somewhat insulated against biases caused by omitted underwriting variables. The omission of these variables will increase the minority status coefficient in both the underwriting model and the default equation, so that any biases in the estimated intergroup differences in underwriting are at least partially offset by intergroup differences in the estimated incentive to discriminate.

Under this interpretation, the insignificant minority status coefficient in Ross's loan denial model leads to a rejection of the hypothesis that there is prejudice-based discrimination. On the surface, this finding appears to be the same as that of Berkovec et al. (1994, 1998). In fact, however, there is a key difference between the findings. Berkovec et al. hypothesize a negative relationship between race and default but find a statistically significant and positive relationship. They conclude that default evidence is inconsistent with the existence of prejudice-based discrimination. In contrast, Ross finds that intergroup differences in underwriting are quite similar in size to those predicted by statistical discrimination, but the standard errors on his estimates allow for the existence of a substantial level of prejudice-based discrimination. This difference in findings between the work of Ross and Berkovec et al. may be due in part to the fact that Ross's analysis avoids many of the problems that bias the default approach away from finding prejudice-based discrimination.

It should be noted, however, that the Ross approach also has some important limitations. First, it requires exclusion restrictions in which certain variables enter the underwriting model only through their influence on the likelihood of default. As Ross discusses, it is difficult to determine the appropriate set of restrictions. In addition, Ross uses the Boston Fed Study's sample of conventional loans and the FHA default data. As discussed in section 8.3.3, this combination of data requires the strong assumption that the underwriting models for conventional and FHA mortgages are very similar. Results from this approach should be interpreted with caution, therefore, until they can be derived from a data set with both loan approval and default information for the same loan applications. Finally, the Ross analysis does not account for the possibility, discussed at length in chapter 6, that different lenders may use different underwriting standards.

8.4 Conclusions

This chapter examines the standard default approach to studying mortgage lending discrimination, along with recent variations and extensions. This approach builds on the simple, intuitively powerful idea that discrimination involves holding minority applicants to a higher standard than whites, so that loans given to minorities must perform better, that is, be less likely to default, than loans given to whites. As it turns out, however, attempting to test this simple idea runs into severe methodological obstacles. Two obstacles are particularly severe. First, the default approach has no power to detect discrimination unless some underwriting variables are excluded from the analysis but yields biased results when any excluded variables are correlated with minority status. No study has identified, and then excluded, underwriting variables that are not correlated with minority status, which would be the only legitimate procedure for correcting this problem. Second, some of the factors that influence default are not observed even by a lender; the omission of these variables can also lead to bias.

Recent studies by Berkovec et al. (1998) and Han (2000) claim to overcome these problems. Instead of asking whether minority applicants are less likely to default, Berkovec et al. ask whether the minority-white default difference is greater in locations where the lending industry is more concentrated, a situation that presumably gives lenders more leeway to indulge their prejudices by discriminating. The new specification that results from this reframing of the question appears to mitigate the omitted-variable problem in previous default studies. It does not save the default approach, however, because it depends on two virtually contradictory assumptions about the impact of market concentration on lender behavior. The first assumption is that if lenders discriminate at all, they discriminate more severely when market concentration is higher. The second is that market concentration does not induce lenders to alter any other aspect of their underwriting procedures. Without the second assumption, which is contradicted by Berkovec et al.'s own evidence, the minority-white default difference across locations with different levels of concentration could reflect variation in underwriting standards, not in discrimination.

Han (2000) shows that the default approach may not require the omission of any underwriting variables. In particular, he shows that prejudice-based discrimination leads to lower default rates for minorities under the assumption that rejected loan applicants can negotiate new credit terms to obtain a mortgage. In other words, this assumption implies that prejudice-based discrimination will result in a lower estimated default rate for minority borrowers even if no credit variables are omitted from the estimation. However, the default model estimated by Han excludes the borrower's credit history, which, as he acknowledges, could lead to omitted-variable bias. Moreover, this model also excludes loan terms, which could lead to more bias from the omission of unobserved borrower characteristics that influence loan terms, and it does not overcome bias that can arise from the omission of credit variables that are not observed by the lender. The Han analysis appears to be worth pursuing with a data set, such as the one in Van Order and Zorn (2001), that can control for credit history and loan terms. Even with such data, however, the key Han assumption would be difficult to test and the results might reflect bias from unobserved borrower characteristics.[39]

The two studies by Ross (1997, 2000) illustrate the possibilities that arise from using specifications that combine underwriting and loan performance data. Ross (1997) provides empirical confirmation for one of the principal methodological flaws in the default approach. For the FHA data considered by Berkovec et al., the omission of credit history data creates a substantial bias away from finding prejudice-based discrimination, and the inclusion of credit history data results in a specification that has no power to detect prejudice-based discrimination.

Ross (2000) provides an alternative test for prejudice-based discrimination using these same two data sets. This test estimates intergroup differences in loan approval after accounting for intergroup differences in default based on unobservable factors, which are the source of lenders' incentive to practice statistical discrimination. It avoids the biases in the default approach because it focuses on racial differences in loan approval, not in default, and explicitly accounts for the possible existence of statistical discrimination in the loan approval decision.

These two articles by Ross demonstrate the advantages of combining loan approval and default information. However, they require the assumption that the loan approval process is the same for both conventional and FHA loans. Moreover, they do not account for the possibility that the loan approval process differs across lenders.

Despite the attention it has received, the default approach to studying lending discrimination faces severe methodological problems that have prevented it from shedding any light on discrimination in mortgage lending in general or on prejudice-based discrimination in particular. As shown by Ross (2000), information on loan performance has great potential to improve tests for discrimination and tests that separate prejudice-based and statistical discrimination. However, the available evidence overwhelmingly supports the proposition that it is difficult, if not impossible, to provide credible evidence about discrimination in mortgage lending based on data about defaults alone.

9

Lender Behavior, Loan Performance, and Disparate-Impact Discrimination

9.1 Introduction

The previous chapters have demonstrated that discrimination in mortgage lending can take the form of disparate treatment or disparate impact. Although these two types of discrimination are conceptually distinct, they may be difficult to untangle in practice. Moreover, one cannot provide a clear interpretation of the Boston Fed Study, or any other study of discrimination in loan approval, without recognizing the possibility that disparate-impact discrimination might exist. The purpose of this chapter is to explore the concept of disparate-impact discrimination in more detail.

We start by explaining why disparate-impact discrimination arises and why it needs to be covered by antidiscrimination legislation. We then turn to two issues that are central to an understanding of discrimination in mortgage lending. The first issue is the possibility that existing credit-scoring models build in disparate-impact discrimination. We explain how disparate-impact discrimination might affect a credit-scoring model and show how a credit-scoring model can be insulated from this problem, that is, how it can be made consistent with fair-lending legislation. We also explore the potential magnitude of this disparate-impact discrimination using the only publicly available loan performance data.

The second issue is how to combine loan performance and loan approval data to distinguish between discrimination, both disparate treatment and disparate impact, and legitimate differences in underwriting standards across lenders. The type of analysis this requires cannot be conducted with any data set that is currently available to independent scholars. The conceptual framework developed in this book can be used, however, to devise an appropriate empirical methodology for addressing this issue should such data become available.

9.2   Why Disparate-Impact Discrimination Should Be Prohibited

The prohibition against disparate-impact discrimination is important because it closes a major loophole in an antidiscrimination program that focuses exclusively on disparate-treatment discrimination. This role is clearly recognized by the courts. According to a federal appeals court, the Supreme Court extended Title VII to cover disparate-impact discrimination because discrimination is often subtle and so "artfully cloaked and concealed in sophisticated language that its true nature does not become obvious."[1]

An insightful analysis of this issue is provided by Lundberg (1991), who shows how disparate-impact discrimination can arise in a labor market. In Lundberg's analysis, employers use test scores to predict workers' productivity. Under the assumption that test scores are a less reliable prediction of productivity for members of group B than of group A, Lundberg shows that employers have an incentive to pay lower wages to members of group B, that is, to practice disparate-treatment discrimination.[2] Because it is based on information about group characteristics, this behavior is a form of statistical discrimination. Lundberg then provides the crucial insight. A law against disparate-treatment discrimination can eliminate group-based wages, but

it will not be self-enforcing. Group membership had provided employers with information about how to interpret individual test scores, and a regulation proscribing its use will result in a greater misallocation of workers to jobs. Employers will thus have an incentive to evade equal opportunity laws. (p. 314)

Lundberg then explains that evasion is possible whenever there exists an observable applicant characteristic that is correlated with group membership but not with worker productivity. Using height as an example of such a characteristic, Lundberg shows that

[p]rior to the enforcement of antidiscrimination laws, employers do not use height as a determinant of wages, since it provides no useful information when group membership is known. Once employers are prohibited from considering group membership, however, height becomes a useful index.... [T]all workers will now be offered a more steeply sloped wage schedule than will short workers. It will be optimal for employers to use height as a sort of

imperfect proxy for the proscribed index, group membership, and so evade the equal opportunity laws. (p. 315)

A law prohibiting disparate-impact discrimination makes this evasion impossible, Lundberg concludes, because it rules out the use of a variable, such as height, that has no legitimate business purpose.

Finally, Lundberg indicates that the same logic applies even if height is correlated with productivity. To be specific, an employer can evade a prohibition of disparate-treatment discrimination by changing the weights placed on various worker characteristics in determining their wages, so that these weights help to predict both group membership and productivity. As Lundberg puts it:

Now consider the imposition of an equal opportunity law, forbidding separate wage schedules based on group membership only. Employers will be able to partially evade this regulation, and its accompanying costs, by exploiting the correlation of group membership and height.... Height will now perform double duty—as a proxy for group and an independent indicator of test reliability [and hence of productivity]. (p. 317)

This is another example of disparate-impact discrimination, because it involves the use of weights that mix the legitimate business purpose (predicting productivity) with the discriminatory business purpose (predicting group membership). Lundberg also points out, however, that a prohibition of disparate-impact discrimination is difficult to enforce in this situation, because it requires enforcement officials to know what the true weight, that is, the true relationship between the worker characteristic and productivity, is.

The Lundberg article focuses on disparate-treatment discrimination (and associated disparate-impact discrimination) that arises when a test provides a less reliable prediction of productivity for one group than for another. In fact, however, the same logic applies to disparate-treatment discrimination that arises for any other reason, as well. Any time employers want to practice disparate-treatment discrimination against a historically disadvantaged group, they have an incentive to evade laws prohibiting such behavior by building disparate-impact discrimination into their employment practices.

This analysis is powerful, because the legacy of this nation's history of discrimination includes large differences across groups in a wide range of social and economic characteristics. An employer would not have to look very far to identify worker characteristics that are correlated with ethnicity and that therefore can be used to "predict" the ethnic group to which an applicant belongs. Under these circumstances, it is a straightforward matter for an employer to transform disparate-treatment discrimination into disparate-impact discrimination.

This conclusion applies directly to lenders, as well, because many of the applicant characteristics they observe are highly correlated with ethnicity. In fact, dramatic illustrations of the possibility for practicing disparate-impact discrimination in loan approval are provided by Buist, Linneman, and Megbolugbe (1999) and Blackburn and Vermilyea (2001), which were discussed in chapters 5 and 6. For example, using the data from the Boston Fed Study, Buist, Linneman, and Megbolugbe show that the outcomes (i.e., loan approval decisions) from an underwriting scheme that involves disparate-treatment discrimination can be replicated with unique underwriting schemes for each lender that place lender-specific weights (some equal to zero) on each underwriting characteristic and that treat every group of applicants identically. As Buist, Linneman, and Megbolugbe explain, variation in these lender-specific weights might or might not reflect legitimate underwriting differences across lenders. Thus, the punch line of their analysis, with which we agree, is that a minority-white disparity in loan approval, as measured by the coefficient of the minority status variable in a loan approval regression, could reflect legitimate underwriting differences across lenders, disparate-impact discrimination, or disparate-treatment discrimination.

The analysis in chapter 6 shows, however, that the first of these explanations is unlikely. Specifically, we show there that the minority status coefficient is largely unaffected by a variety of controls for the possibility that differences in underwriting standards across lenders can be justified on the grounds of business necessity. We are left, therefore, with only two possible explanations for a significant minority status coefficient: disparate-treatment discrimination and disparate-impact discrimination. The analysis by Buist, Linneman, and Megbolugbe and Blackburn and Vermilyea is important in this context because it shows that it is impossible to distinguish between these two explanations. The outcomes of an underwriting system that involves disparate-treatment discrimination can be replicated with an underwriting scheme that involves disparate-impact discrimination. This result highlights the importance of including disparate-impact discrimination in fair-lending legislation.

9.3 Disparate-Impact Discrimination in Automated Underwriting Systems

Credit scores and other forms of automated underwriting are now an established part of the mortgage system in the United States. These schemes do not involve disparate-treatment discrimination, because they do not consider an applicant's membership in a particular racial or ethnic group.[3] As several scholars have pointed out, however, these schemes might involve disparate-impact discrimination; that is, they might involve calculations that impose a disparate impact on loan applicants in certain protected classes without any justification on the grounds of business necessity.[4] This section explores the possibility of disparate-impact discrimination in credit scores and automated underwriting.

Because no publicly available data sets allow an investigation into an actual credit-scoring or automated underwriting scheme, our objective in this section is to provide a clear guide to the conceptual issues: Under what circumstances will one of these schemes involve disparate-impact discrimination? How could a regulatory agency detect disparate-impact discrimination in one of these schemes if it had access to the relevant data? In this section, we present a simple model of loan performance for use in automated underwriting, explore four different ways that automated underwriting schemes might involve disparate-impact discrimination, simulate the potential magnitude for one type of disparate-impact discrimination, and discuss the implications of our results.

9.3.1 Models of Loan Performance and Automated Underwriting Schemes

Credit scores and other automated underwriting systems are designed to predict loan performance. These systems can measure loan performance in a variety of ways. Most existing schemes appear to measure performance with default or delinquency; for example, a scheme might be based on the probability that the borrower will not default in a certain period of time, for example. In principle, however, a scheme could also be based on a more long-run, comprehensive measure of performance, such as the expected profitability of the loan. Our strategy in this section is to specify a general model of loan performance and then analyze automated underwriting systems based on it. We do not formally model the link between any particular system and lender profits, which are the ultimate objective, but instead assume that the better a system's predictions, the higher are the profits of the lenders who use it.[5] In the case of a credit score, a lender obviously wants the best possible prediction of loan performance on the basis of the applicant's credit characteristics; better predictions imply fewer bad decisions on loan approval or on loan terms. In the case of an automated underwriting system, a lending institution wants the most accurate predictions it can obtain on the basis of applicant, property, and loan characteristics, again so that it can design its loan approval and loan-pricing decisions to maximize its profits.

Let P be a measure of loan performance, such as loan profitability or the probability that the applicant will not default. This measure is observed for some time period after a loan is granted. For example, it could be the probability that a particular borrower will not default in the first five years of a mortgage.[6] For the purposes of our analysis, this indicator is always defined so that a higher value implies better performance. In addition, let X_1 to X_N be a set of variables that a lender observes at the time of application. To use the terms from chapter 2, these could be applicant, property, or loan characteristics. To simplify the discussion, we assume that these variables are all defined so that a higher value corresponds to higher loan quality, that is, to a better loan performance.[7] Finally, let M be a variable that indicates whether an applicant belongs to a minority group and ε be a random error.[8]

With these variable definitions, we can write the following general model of loan performance:[9]

$$P = \alpha + \sum_{i=1}^{N} \beta_i X_i + \gamma M + \varepsilon, \qquad (9.1)$$

where α, β_i, and γ are parameters to be estimated. In this context, α is a constant term, β_i indicates the impact of variable X_i on loan performance, and γ measures the impact of unobserved credit characteristics on the average performance of loans to minorities.

Because of this nation's history of discrimination in many markets, the average values of most X variables are lower for minority than for white households. As discussed in chapter 3, for example, minority households are much more likely than white households to face a down payment constraint. It seems reasonable to suppose that minority households also have lower creditworthiness based on *unobserved* credit characteristics, that is, to suppose that γ is negative.[10] The best way to determine whether this is true would be to estimate equation (9.1) and see whether the coefficient of the minority status variable (or variables) does, indeed, have a negative sign. As discussed in chapter 8, however, no existing study provides such a regression with a full set of loan, borrower, and neighborhood characteristics. Without this type of evidence, we believe it is appropriate to explore the characteristics of various automated underwriting schemes under the presumption that γ is negative.

To minimize their risk, lenders want to base their loan approval decisions on the best possible predictions of performance. Suppose that the explanatory variables in equation (9.1) contain all the information available to the lender at the time of application and that the linear specification in this equation is appropriate.[11] In this case, a lending institution that has estimated equation (9.1) with a sample of its past loans can use the estimated coefficients to obtain the best possible predictions for the performance of future applications to it.[12]

These predictions of future performance, which we call loan performance "scores," are based on the estimated coefficients and the values of the explanatory variables at the time a given application is received.[13] In this usage, a score is simply the output of either a credit-scoring scheme or an automated-underwriting system; that is, it is a way of ranking applications. Let a hat ($^\wedge$) indicate an estimated value, based on regression analysis. Then a score, S^1, based on equation (9.1) can be written as follows:

$$S^1 = \hat{\alpha} + \sum_{i=1}^{N} \hat{\beta}_i X_i + \hat{\gamma} M. \qquad (9.2)$$

(This scoring scheme is written with a superscript 1 to distinguish it from other scoring schemes considered later). The most striking feature of S^1 is that it involves disparate-treatment discrimination. Because the estimated value of γ is assumed to be negative, the scheme S^1 implies a lower score for a minority applicant than for a white applicant who is equivalent on all observable characteristics. This type of scoring scheme is clearly illegal under our fair-lending laws, because it treats people unfavorably solely on the basis of their membership in a protected class.[14] As pointed out in chapter 2, this type of disparate-treatment discrimination is called statistical discrimination, because lenders are using minority status as a proxy for unobserved credit characteristics. They can increase their profits by using this proxy, but our fair-lending laws unambiguously declare that it is illegal for them to do so. We have no reason to believe that any lender uses a scheme of this type, but we present it here to provide contrast with other scoring schemes.

To eliminate disparate-treatment discrimination from the scoring scheme, a lender must not consider the impact of M on loan performance. Thus, a nondiscriminatory scoring scheme, called S^2, is as follows:

$$S^2 = (\hat{\alpha} + \hat{\gamma}\overline{M}) + \sum_{i=1}^{N} \hat{\beta}_i X_i, \tag{9.3}$$

where $\overline{M}$ is the share of loans held by minority households and the estimated coefficients are still the ones obtained from a regression analysis of equation (9.1). Unlike S^1, however, this scheme does not differentiate between minority and white applicants, and the constant term is adjusted to account for the average impact of unobservable factors among minority borrowers.

It is also well known that, again under fairly general conditions, a regression analysis produces unbiased estimates of the parameters. In formal terms, the expected values of the estimated parameters equal the true values of those parameters as specified in equation (9.1).[15] Hence, we can write the expected values of these two scoring schemes as follows:

$$E(S^1) = \alpha + \sum_{i=1}^{N} \beta_i X_i + \gamma M, \tag{9.4}$$

and

$$E(S^2) = (\alpha + \gamma\overline{M}) + \sum_{i=1}^{N} \beta_i X_i. \tag{9.5}$$

These expected-value expressions provide a convenient way to summarize what one can expect from each scoring scheme.

9.3.2   *Automated Underwriting Systems and Disparate-Impact Discrimination*

The scoring scheme S^2 does not involve either disparate-treatment or disparate-impact discrimination; the coefficients in this scheme reflect the true impact of each application characteristic on loan performance, and the minority status of the applicant is not considered. Disparate-impact discrimination might arise, however, from other schemes that use the information from equation (9.1) or a similar regression. In this section we explore four of these other schemes and ask whether they involve disparate-impact discrimination.

9.3.2.1   Dropping the Minority Status Variable

The most obvious alternative to scheme S^2 is one based on a regression model in which minority status is ignored altogether. This type of regression model appears to be "group-neutral," because it does not recognize the impact of minority status on loan performance. The question is whether this seemingly neutral appearance hides disparate-impact discrimination.

The model in question is

$$P = \alpha' + \sum_{i=1}^{N} \beta_i' X_i + \varepsilon',\tag{9.6}$$

where the primes indicate that the coefficients (and the error term) will not, in general, be the same as those in equation (9.1). A scoring scheme based on this equation, called S^3, can be written as follows:

$$S^3 = \hat{\alpha}' + \sum_{i=1}^{N} \hat{\beta}_i' X_i.\tag{9.7}$$

To evaluate this scheme, the most important point is to recognize that equation (9.6) is equivalent to a misspecified version of equation (9.1). It is misspecified in the sense that it leaves out a variable, namely, M, that has a clear conceptual link to the dependent variable and is known to have explanatory power. Just like a loan approval regression that omits an applicant's credit history, therefore, a regression analysis of equation (9.6) is subject to omitted-variable bias. The form of this bias is well known. To be specific, the standard omitted-variable bias formula implies that

$$E(\hat{\beta}_i') = \beta_i + \gamma b_i, \tag{9.8}$$

where γ is the parameter associated with M in equation (9.1) and b_i is the correlation between X_i and M.[16] Thus, for any given application characteristic, X_i, the bias increases both with the extent to which minority applicants have unobserved characteristics that lower their loan performance, on average, and with the extent to which this characteristic is correlated with minority status. Given this nation's legacy of past discrimination, we expect that both of these factors are usually negative, that is, that minorities tend to have unfavorable unobserved characteristics and lower average values of observed characteristics. In this case, the bias defined by equation (9.8) is positive, which means that the estimated coefficient is expected to be larger than the value of the true parameter. In section 9.3.3, we provide some examples of the potential magnitude of this bias.

Equation (9.8) makes it possible to compare the expected values of the scoring schemes S^2 and S^3. To be specific,[17]

$$E(S^3) = E(S^2) + \gamma \sum_{i=1}^{N} b_i(X_i - \bar{X}_i). \tag{9.9}$$

This result reveals that the scheme S^3 adjusts the scheme S^2 in two ways: It shifts every applicant's score and changes the weight placed on each application characteristic. The shift depends on the average values of all the X_is, each weighted by γb_i. Moreover, an amount equal to γb_i is added to the weight placed on each characteristic, X_i. As explained earlier, this product is likely to be positive for most characteristics, so this step increases the weight placed on most application characteristics, but it increases the weight the most for the characteristics that are the most highly correlated with minority status. Note that a higher absolute value for γ increases every weight, whereas a higher absolute value for b_i increases the weight only for X_i.

Equation (9.9) implies that when minority applications have poorer unobserved characteristics, that is, when γ is negative, scheme S^3 can differ from scheme S^2 in four different ways. First, application characteristics that have a positive impact on loan performance ($\beta_i > 0$) and are positively correlated with minority status ($b_i > 0$) receive a higher weight in scheme S^3 than in scheme S^2. Specifically, the weight increase equals γb_i. Second, application characteristics that have a positive impact on loan performance ($\beta_i > 0$) and are negatively correlated with minority status ($b_i < 0$) receive a lower weight in scheme S^3 than in scheme S^2.

The other two effects involve changes in the set of variables used in each scheme. Each scheme is based on a regression analysis, and application characteristics that have a coefficient with an expected value close to zero in the relevant regression will not, in general, be included in the scoring scheme. Thus, the third possible difference between the schemes is that variables that have no impact on loan performance ($\beta_i = 0$) but are positively correlated with minority status ($b_i > 0$) may be significant in a regression analysis of equation (9.6) because of the upward bias in their estimated coefficient (γb_i). These are variables that do not influence loan performance according to the equation that provides the best prediction but nevertheless appear in scheme S^3. Thus, scheme S^3 may include variables that do not appear at all in scheme S^2.

This effect can also work in the other direction. Specifically, the fourth possible difference between the schemes arises when a variable has a positive impact on loan performance ($\beta_i > 0$) and has a negative correlation with minority status ($b_i < 0$) that results in a bias in equation (9.6) (γb_i) approximately equal in magnitude (but opposite in sign) to β_i. In this case, the estimated impact of the variable using equation (9.6) has an expected value of zero, and the variable is likely to be dropped from scheme S^3 even though its true impact (β_i) is positive. As explained earlier, most credit characteristics are negatively correlated with minority status, but some may not be. For example, minority applicants might be more likely than white applicants to have private mortgage insurance, a desirable credit characteristic.

The key question, of course, is whether the scoring scheme S^3 involves disparate-impact discrimination. Recall from chapter 2 that the test for disparate-impact discrimination has two main parts. To be classified as disparate-impact discrimination, an action must impose a disparate impact on members of a protected class, and it must have no legitimate business rationale. The second part of this test is sometimes called the "business necessity" defense.

Scheme S^3 clearly satisfies the first part of this test. Suppose only one loan characteristic, say X_j, is correlated with minority status and that this correlation is negative. In other words, suppose that b_j is negative and all other bs equal zero. According to equation (9.9), therefore, applicants with an above-average value of X_j, who are predominantly white, receive a higher score using scheme S^3 than they do using the nondiscriminatory scheme S^2. Applicants with a below-average value of X_j, predominantly minorities, receive a lower score using scheme S^3 than they do using S^2. On average, therefore, a switch from S^2 to S^3 clearly has a disproportionate negative impact on minority applicants. So long as the minority applicants have poorer unobserved credit qualifications than white applicants, the same argument obviously holds for any set of X variables that are correlated with minority status, positively or negatively. In other words, S^3 increases the weights applied to variables on which minority applicants rank relatively poorly, on average, and decreases the weights applied to variables on which minority applications rank relatively well.

This argument also applies to any variables that are added to the list of Xs because of an upward bias in their estimated coefficient in (9.6) or subtracted from the list of Xs because of a downward bias in this estimated coefficient. Adding variables on which minority applicants rate relatively poorly or eliminating variables on which they rate relatively highly obviously has a disparate impact on minorities.

What about the second part of the test for disparate-impact discrimination? Can scheme S^3 be justified as a business necessity? On the surface, the answer to this question might seem to be affirmative, because S^3 does a better job of predicting loan performance than does S^2. After all, the best linear predictor *using just the X variables* comes from equation (9.6), not from equation (9.1), which includes the minority-status variable. Thus, switching from S^2 to S^3 will increase both the accuracy of the predictions and the lender's profits. However, the business-necessity test does not allow an action just because it is profitable. For example, our civil rights laws prohibit the scoring scheme S^1, even though it is more profitable than S^2, because it involves disparate-treatment discrimination.

A deeper look reveals that scoring scheme S^3 cannot be justified on business necessity grounds. The argument supporting this contention can be made in several different ways. First, this supposedly group-neutral scheme brings group membership in through the back door. We have shown that switching from scheme S^2 to scheme S^3 involves changing the weights placed on individual loan characteristics. Moreover, we have shown that the change in the weight placed on characteristic X_i depends both on the impact of a minority group's unobserved credit characteristics on loan performance (γ) and on the correlation between minority status and that characteristic (b_i). This type of information clearly cannot legally be used to define different scoring schemes for different groups, as in S^1, and it should not be allowed to influence a scoring scheme applied to all groups, either. In effect, S^3 can be thought of as the scheme that comes as close as possible to the illegal scheme S^1 without explicitly differentiating among groups. Thus, the change in the weights between schemes S^2 and S^3 serves to approximate the outcome of disparate-treatment discrimination, not to obtain a better prediction of loan profitability based on observable loan characteristics other than group membership, which is what the law calls for.[18] This is precisely the point made by Lundberg (1991).

Note that this argument applies to variables that are included in both equations (9.1) and (9.8), to variables that are included in (9.8) but not in (9.1), and to variables that are included in (9.1) but not in (9.8). As explained earlier, all three of these situations can be described as changes in variable weights. Moreover, all three situations represent attempts to make group distinctions through the nature of the common scoring scheme.

Second, scheme S^3 is less profitable for white applicants than is scheme S^2. As we interpret it, the business necessity test is designed to identify practices that would make sense if group membership were not an issue.[19] It follows that a practice cannot pass this test unless it would be profitable when applied only to a lender's white customers (or to any other group of customers, considered separately). For white customers, the value of M is always zero, so white customers receive the same ranking, regardless of whether a lender uses S^1 or S^2. Moreover, these scoring schemes are the most accurate because they use the most information. Thus, scheme S^3, which makes up for the lack of information on M by placing different weights on applicant characteristics, must be less accurate and therefore less profitable for white customers.

Specifically, scheme S^3 raises the weight the most on the application characteristics that are most correlated with minority status. White customers with relatively high values on these characteristics will receive higher scores, and those with relatively low values will receive lower scores, than they would under S^2. These weight changes arise because of a correlation with minority status, not because of a correlation with profits among white customers, so they result in less accurate scores and lower profits among white applicants. Consequently, these weight changes cannot be justified as a business necessity.

A similar argument can be applied to the pool of minority loans. Suppose one wants to compare the performance of the best 100 minority applications identified by S^2 with the best 100 minority applications identified by S^3. Because the weights in S^3 reflect variables' correlations with minority status, in addition to variables' impacts on loan performance, they will not do as good a job of identifying the best applications as the weights in S^2. Minority applicants with high values of the X_i variables that are highly correlated with minority status will receive scores that are too high, relative to the best prediction of their future performance, and minority applicants with low values for these variables will receive scores that are too low. As a result, the wrong set of minority applicants will be selected.

This discussion leads us to a puzzle and, ultimately, to a third way to explain why S^3 fails the business necessity part of the test for disparate-impact discrimination. The puzzle is this: If a switch from S^2 to S^3 lowers profits among white applicants and does a worse job identifying the best minority applicants, how can this switch be profitable at all? The answer to this question is that S^3 is more profitable because it changes the group composition of a lender's loans. Thanks to unobserved factors, minority applicants are, on average, less qualified than white applicants, so a lender can increase its profits by cutting back the number of minority loans it makes and raising the number of white loans it makes, compared to those granted using S^2. A lender cannot do this directly without practicing disparate-treatment discrimination, but scheme S^3 allows the lender to do this indirectly by changing the weights on application characteristics according to their ability to identify minority applicants. In other words, the profit-based purpose of S^3 is to rule out customers who have the highest chance of belonging to a minority group, as predicted by their observable application characteristics, so as to shift the loan pool away from minority applicants toward white applicants who are more qualified based on unobservable characteristics but no more qualified based on the observable characteristics that the lender is allowed by law to consider.

The use of underwriting weights to predict group membership is directly relevant to the notion of business necessity. It makes no sense to use a business necessity standard that justifies behavior explicitly defined as disparate-impact discrimination. As a result, any standard that validates scoring scheme S^3 must be rejected. Instead, we propose a standard that is based on within-group profitability. To pass this business necessity standard, a scoring scheme must lower the risk (or raise the profitability) of loans to people within each group, holding group composition constant. Scheme S^2 meets this standard, but scheme S^3 does not.[20]

9.3.2.2 Departing from the Statistical Model

Another possibility is that a scoring scheme might depart from the statistical model to decrease the number of minority loans that are accepted. Departing from the statistical model obviously lowers the predictive power of the scoring system, but this cost might be offset by a shift in the group composition of the highest-scoring applications.

The most obvious way to depart from the statistical model is to drop variables that have a significant impact on loan performance.[21] For convenience, let us consider a scoring scheme, S^4, defined by dropping the first credit characteristic, namely X_1, from the non-discriminatory scheme S^2. This scheme can be described as follows:

$$S^4 = (\hat{\alpha} + \hat{\gamma}\overline{M}) + \sum_{i=2}^{N} \hat{\beta}_i X_i$$

$$= S^2 - \hat{\beta}_1 X_1. \tag{9.10}$$

This new scheme uses the same weights as scheme S^2 on all included credit characteristics, but it is less accurate than scheme S^2, because it ignores the impact of X_1 on loan performance. As it turns out, however, this scheme may be more profitable even though it is less accurate. The possibility of added profitability arises whenever X_1 is positively correlated with minority status. Suppose, for example, that the number of late rental payments is a good predictor of default, holding other factors constant, and that applicants in a minority group have fewer late payments (but poorer unobserved credit characteristics) than white applicants.[22] Under these assumptions, leaving the number of late rental payments out of the regression would lower the scores of applicants in the minority group, on average, relative to the scores of white applicants. Moreover, the use of S^4 instead of S^2 would result in less-accurate within-group predictions of loan profitability for both minorities and whites, but such a switch also might increase overall profitability, because it decreases the minority share of the loan pool.[23]

The logic here is similar to our analysis of scheme S^3. Because the presence of X_1 in the statistical model boosts the scores of minority applicants relative to those of whites, removing these characteristics from the scoring scheme lowers the relative scores of minority applicants and therefore could lower their representation in the set of applications above the lender's cutoff point. By lowering minority representation among accepted loans, lenders can lower the impact of unobserved, negative credit characteristics and thereby increase their profits.

As in the case of scheme S^3, this type of scheme clearly involves disparate-impact discrimination. Switching from scheme S^2 to scheme S^4 has a disparate impact on minority applicants. Moreover, because this switch lowers the within-group predictive ability of the model, it cannot be justified on the grounds of business necessity. Furthermore, lenders have many options for designing schemes that build on this logic. As shown by Buist, Linneman, and Megbolugbe (1999) and Blackburn and Vermilyea (2001), lenders may be able, by manipulating the set of Xs (and their weights), to design a group-neutral scheme that essentially replicates the outcomes of a scheme that involves disparate-treatment discrimination.

Another way to express this result builds on a simple decomposition of the profits from any scoring scheme. Let $\bar{P}^i$ be the average profits for a lender who uses scoring scheme i. Moreover, let $\bar{P}^{M,i}$ be the average profits from minority borrowers using scheme i, and $\bar{P}^{W,i}$ be the average profits from white borrowers. As noted earlier, the share of loans given to minorities equals $\bar{M}$, so the share under scheme i can be written as $\bar{M}^i$. Hence, by definition,

$$\bar{P}^i = \bar{M}^i \bar{P}^{M,i} + (1 - \bar{M}^i) \bar{P}^{W,i}. \tag{9.11}$$

This decomposition allows us to compare any two scoring schemes, and in particular, to classify the reasons why two different schemes might lead to different levels of profit. Consider the difference between S^4 and S^2. Using the above formula, this difference can be written as follows:

$$(\bar{P}^4 - \bar{P}^2) = (\bar{M}^4 - \bar{M}^2)(\bar{P}^{M,4} - \bar{P}^{M,2}) + \bar{M}^2(\bar{P}^{M,4} - \bar{P}^{M,2})$$
$$+ (1 - \bar{M}^2)(\bar{P}^{W,4} - \bar{P}^{W,2}). \tag{9.12}$$

The first term on the right side of this equation measures the impact of a change in the minority composition of the loan pool. If loans to minorities are less profitable than loans to whites, on average, and changing schemes results in fewer loans to minorities, then this term is positive; that is, this component implies an increase in profits. The second term on the right-hand side represents the change in the profitability of loans to minorities. Because scheme S^4 uses less information than scheme S^2, it is inevitably less profitable, so this term is negative. The same goes for the third term on the right-hand side, which presents the change in the profitability of loans to whites.

In short, the change from scheme S^2 to scheme S^4 has one positive effect on profits, the first term in equation (9.12), and two negative effects, the last two terms. The switch is profitable to lenders if the first term is larger in magnitude than the other two, that is, if the scheme lowers the minority composition of the loan pool enough to make up for the fact that it lowers the profitability of loans to each group.[24] This switch constitutes disparate-impact discrimination, however, even if it is profitable. It has a disparate impact on minorities because it lowers the minority composition of the loan pool, and it cannot be justified on the grounds of business necessity because it lowers within-group profitability.

9.3.2.3 Selection and Endogeneity Biases
Because loans are given to a selected sample, not a random sample, of applications, performance regressions for a sample of loans may be subject to selection or endogeneity bias. In this section we ask whether these types of bias could result in disparate-impact discrimination.

Selection bias could come from several different sources. One possibility, discussed by Ross (1996b), is that the researcher does not observe some applicant characteristics that the lender does observe and considered. In this case, the sample of borrowers is determined in part by variables that are unobserved (and hence omitted) in the loan performance regression. The result is the coefficients in this regression are biased. This problem cannot arise if the researcher observes all underwriting variables used by the lender. Ross (2000) finds evidence that this type of bias is unlikely to be significant in a default model that controls for the set of variables collected by the Boston Fed Study.

A second possibility, suggested by Rachlis and Yezer (1993), is that selection bias could arise where loan approval decisions are influenced by negotiations between the borrower and the lender. During such negotiations, the lender reveals information about its underwriting standards, and the borrower responds by modifying her requested loan terms. This type of negotiation not only makes the loan terms endogenous in a loan approval regression, an issue discussed in chapter 5, but it also may lead to selection bias in a loan performance regression. Specifically, borrowers willing and able to compromise on loan terms, who are more likely to be approved, may have a different tendency to default than other borrowers. This creates a correlation between the process that selects borrowers and the unobservable variables in the default equation, which is exactly the type of correlation that causes selection bias. As shown in chapter 5, however, there is no evidence, at least not using the Boston Fed Study's data, that this type of negotiation takes place. As a result, this type of selection or endogeneity bias seems unlikely to occur.

Third, endogeneity bias could arise in a scoring scheme based on data for more than one lender if unobserved lender characteristics influence both underwriting and foreclosure behavior. For example, such bias could arise if lenders with certain underwriting standards are more likely to foreclose when a borrower misses a payment. In this case, unobservable lender characteristics in the loan performance equation affect both the dependent variable and some of the explanatory variables, such as LTV, resulting in biased regression coefficients.

Now suppose that lenders specializing in high-LTV loans are more likely to foreclose when a borrower misses a payment. With the probability of avoiding foreclosure in the first five years as the measure of loan performance, this situation results in a downward bias in the estimated coefficient of LTV, which, following the analysis in section 3.4.2, is negative. This bias reflects the positive correlation between LTV and a lender's foreclosure tendency combined with the negative impact of this tendency on the dependent variable. In other words, this bias increases the (negative) weight placed on LTV and therefore lowers the scores of high-LTV borrowers, who are likely to be predominantly minority.

In this example, therefore, endogeneity bias results in disparate-impact discrimination. The bias places minority applicants at a disadvantage, on average. Moreover, the use of a model subject to this endogeneity bias cannot be justified on the grounds of business necessity. After all, a bias implies, by definition, that the regression coefficients are not capturing the true impact of a credit characteristic on loan performance.

It is important to emphasize that this is only an example. Given the lack of data on loan performance, we do not know if this type of bias occurs, and, if it occurs, whether it has a disparate impact on minority loan applicants. Instead, we simply offer this example to show that endogeneity bias might matter and to encourage further research on the topic.

Finally, even if endogeneity bias of this type occurs, it can be minimized through the use of lender dummy variables. Chapters 5 and 6 discuss the role of lender dummy variables in a loan approval regression. Including them in a loan performance regression would eliminate some forms of bias associated with unobserved lender characteristics.[25] As discussed in section 9.4.2.2, lender dummies also prove to be valuable in a test for disparate-impact discrimination by a particular lender.

9.3.3 The Potential for Disparate-Impact Discrimination: A Simulation

As we have pointed out several times, there does not exist a publicly available data set with all the variables needed to estimate equation (9.1) and hence to look for disparate-impact discrimination in loan performance scoring schemes. The best publicly available data with loan performance information is the sample of FHA loans that has been used by several researchers (especially Berkovec et al., 1994, 1996; Ross, 1997, 2000). This data set indicates loan foreclosure along with a wide range of applicant, loan, and property characteristics observed at the time of application, but it applies only to government-insured loans and, as noted in chapter 8, lacks information on applicant credit history. Despite these limitations, this is the

Table 9.1
Variable definitions for loan performance regressions

Variable	Definition
MINORITY	Whether borrower is African American
FEMALE	Whether borrower is female
AGE	Age of borrower exceeds median
COSIGNER	Whether there is a co-signer
MULTI-FAMILY	Whether property is multifamily
FIXED RATE	Whether interest rate is fixed
MARRIED	Whether borrower is married
DEBT-TO-INCOME	Total debt–to–income ratio
EXPENSE-TO-INCOME	Housing expense–to–income ratio
LIQUID ASSETS	Value of liquid assets
LTV	Loan-to-value ratio
TERM	Term of the mortgage
TIME TO DEFAULT	Time between loan origination and default
TIME-2	Square of time to default
NO DEFAULT	Borrower does not default on the loan within the sample period

best available data set for investigating the potential magnitude of disparate-impact discrimination. In this section, we use this data set to conduct simulations designed to reveal the potential magnitude of disparate-impact discrimination from the use of scoring scheme S^3 under two different sets of circumstances.

9.3.3.1 Applications for FHA Loans

To explore the potential magnitude of disparate-impact discrimination from applying scoring scheme S^3 to FHA loans, we begin by estimating versions of equations (9.1) and (9.6) using the public-use FHA foreclosure data. The dependent variable is whether the loan avoids default (and foreclosure) during the sample period. The explanatory variables are defined in table 9.1. One version of the model, which is the analog to equation (9.1), also includes a minority status variable (1 = black; 0 = white); the other version, which is the analog to equation (9.6), does not. The (probit) estimation results are presented in table 9.2. The equations perform as expected. A higher debt-to-income ratio or a higher LTV, for example, lowers the probability that a particular borrower will avoid default; a higher level of liquid assets raises this probability.

Table 9.2
Impact of minority status variable on a loan performance regression

Variable	FHA sample		Simulated sample	
	With minority status	Without minority status	With minority status	Without minority status
MINORITY	−0.893		−1.250	
	(−33.613)		(−23.810)	
FEMALE	−0.485	−0.128	−0.566	−0.088
	(−16.271)	(−4.391)	(−11.373)	(−1.523)
AGE	−0.226	−0.294	0.011	−0.092
	(−9.442)	(−11.282)	(0.227)	(−1.709)
COSIGNER	0.116	0.050	0.104	0.031
	(3.227)	(1.302)	(1.242)	(0.356)
MULTI-FAMILY	−0.114	−0.086	−0.164	−0.040
	(−2.278)	(−1.856)	(−1.713)	(−0.420)
FIXED RATE	4.887	4.713	−4.678	−7.799
	(17.056)	(8.697)	(−5.576)	(−0.225)
MARRIED	0.137	0.094	0.399	0.345
	(4.551)	(2.805)	(5.069)	(4.278)
DEBT-TO-INCOME	−0.958	−1.006	−0.726	−0.621
	(−12.143)	(−14.401)	(−3.017)	(−2.999)
EXPENSE-TO-INCOME	0.943	0.989	0.723	0.617
	(11.772)	(4.134)	(3.031)	(2.996)
LIQUID ASSETS	0.519	0.581	0.310	0.402
	(23.728)	(26.087)	(13.607)	(16.090)
LTV	−0.569	−0.559	0.011	−0.676
	(−5.454)	(−5.793)	(0.086)	(−5.059)
TERM	−0.390	−0.411	−0.381	−0.437
	(−6.092)	(−6.831)	(−4.628)	(−5.383)
TIME TO DEFAULT	−22.384	−22.051	−21.209	−20.283
	(−40.222)	(47.423)	(−14.906)	(−21.385)
TIME-2	25.529	24.627	24.551	22.626
	(31.557)	(37.842)	(11.663)	(17.195)
Intercept	4.889	4.710	13.961	16.937
	(20.018)	(9.010)	(13.927)	(0.489)

Note: All models are estimated with probit analysis. NO DEFAULT is the dependent variable; *t*-statistics are in parentheses. The simulated sample is a randomly drawn subsample of the entire FHA sample that has the same distribution of LTV by minority status as the Boston Fed Study sample.

For both models, we then create a loan performance score based on all the variables except those describing applicant membership in protected classes and the duration variables. The score based on the equation including minority status is analogous to S^2, and the score based on the equation without minority status is analogous to S^3. For each scoring scheme, we then identify three different cutoffs designed to simulate three different underwriting systems. These cutoffs are set to ensure that 25, 50, and 75 percent of the loans, respectively, are approved. Finally, we run the original sample back through each underwriting system to simulate the share of loans that would go to minority borrowers in each case. In other words, we investigate the share of loans that would go to minorities if a sample of applications identical to the loans in the FHA sample were subjected to each of these underwriting systems.

We find that with scheme S^2, the shares of loans made to minority customers are 9.4, 8.9, and 10.7 percent for the three different cutoffs. The shares are similar with scheme S^3, namely, 9.9, 9.5, and 10.2 percent. In this simulation, therefore, we find no evidence of significant disparate-impact discrimination. In fact, scheme S^3 actually results in a higher share of loans to minority applicants when the cutoff is set at 25 or 50 percent of applications, which is the opposite of disparate-impact discrimination.[26] For the other cutoff , disparate-impact discrimination lowers the minority share of loans by only 0.5 percentage points.

9.3.3.2   Applications for Conventional Loans

One likely explanation for the small difference in percentages of loans granted to minority customers between the two scoring schemes in the FHA data is that the loans in these data are not representative of the market as a whole. As explained in earlier chapters, FHA loans tend to be offered to many minority applicants but only to higher-risk white applicants. As a result, differences between minority and white applicants may be much smaller in the FHA loan pool than among conventional loans.

The two most important underwriting variables that exhibit large differences between minorities and whites are probably LTV and credit history. The FHA data set does not contain information on credit history, but it does include LTV and is highly skewed toward high-LTV loans. To simulate disparate-impact discrimination in a sample that looks more like a sample of conventional loans, therefore, we draw a stratified random subsample from the FHA data designed to mimic the distribution of LTV by minority status observed in the Boston Fed Study's data.[27] The product of this exercise is a sample of loans with performance information and with a distribution of LTVs by minority status that is consistent with what one might find in the conventional mortgage market.

We estimate the same two loan performance models for this sample, one with and one without the minority status variable. As before, we then construct a scoring scheme based on each estimated equation and simulate the minority composition of the loans that would be approved under each scheme and under three different cutoff points. The results are dramatically different from the ones based on the entire FHA sample. Using the scheme analogous to S^2, the percentages of approved applications that belong to minority customers are 18.7, 18.9, and 24.0 percent, respectively, for the three cutoffs. When scheme S^3 is used, however, these percentages drop to 11.5, 13.6, and 17.4 percent. Switching to scheme S^3 thereby reduces minority representation by 7.2, 5.3, and 6.6 percentage points, respectively. In these simulations, therefore, the use of scheme S^3 clearly introduces disparate-impact discrimination, and this discrimination is large in magnitude.[28]

9.3.3.3 Conclusions

The simulations presented here cannot provide a definitive answer concerning the magnitude of disparate-impact discrimination in any existing loan performance scoring scheme. Not only are the characteristics of existing schemes unknown, but the FHA sample used for these simulations applies only to government-insured loans and is missing some key underwriting variables. Instead, these simulations reveal that the use of scoring scheme S^3 might or might not introduce disparate-impact discrimination, depending on the characteristics of the applicant pool. Given an applicant pool that resembles the Boston Fed Study's pool, at least in terms of LTV, we find that the use of scheme S^3 could result in substantial disparate-impact discrimination. Further research is needed to determine whether existing scoring schemes are analogous to S^3, whether more complete data sets also find substantial disparate-impact discrimination when this scoring scheme is used, and whether other sources of disparate-impact discrimination exist.

9.3.4   Implications

This analysis has four key implications for discussions about credit-scoring schemes and automated underwriting systems. The first implication is based on our main finding:

1. A credit-scoring scheme or an automated underwriting system based on a statistical procedure that does not explicitly account for group membership is likely to involve disparate-impact discrimination under a wide range of circumstances.

Because the statistical procedures used to devise credit-scoring and automated underwriting schemes are proprietary, we do not know whether existing statistical procedures account for group membership. We suspect, however, that a statistical procedure that does not account for group membership is widely regarded as "group-neutral" and that the implications of omitting group membership variables from such a procedure have not been considered.[29]

We also do not know, of course, the magnitude of the disparate-impact discrimination that is built into existing scoring schemes, even if we are right that they do not include group membership in their underlying statistical procedures. We have shown, however, that this magnitude could be quite large in many cases. This result is not surprising; after all, the legacy of our discriminatory past implies that minority groups fall behind whites on many credit characteristics, both observable and unobservable, which leads to a negative value for γ, to positive values for the b_is, and hence to significant disparate-impact discrimination.

The second implication arises from the observation that the bias in estimated coefficients caused by the omission of group membership variables can result in a scheme that includes the wrong variables:

2. Credit-scoring and automated underwriting schemes may include some variables that are not legitimate predictors of loan performance and exclude other variables that are legitimate predictors of loan performance; either case may introduce disparate-impact discrimination.

Variables that are not legitimate predictors of loan performance, which, by definition, have a β_i equal to zero, may be included in a credit-scoring or automated underwriting scheme because their estimated coefficients in equation (9.8) have an expected value of γb_i and are biased upward from zero. Similarly, some variables that have a positive β are positively correlated with minority status, so that b_i is positive, γb_i is negative, and the estimated coefficient in equation (9.8), with an expected value of $(\beta_i + \gamma b_i)$ could be biased toward zero. In either case, the scoring scheme treats minority applicants less favorably for reasons that are unrelated to within-group profitability, which, as shown above, invalidates the business necessity defense.

A third implication concerns the rules for evaluating any change in a credit-scoring or automated underwriting scheme. The institutions that devise these schemes want them to raise profits, so they may want to select any change in a scheme that increases their profits, or, in our terms, that increases their ability to predict loan performance. As we have seen, however, some changes increase profits by bringing discrimination in through the back door. Thus,[30]

3. Even if it raises profits, a change in a credit-scoring scheme that has a disproportionate impact on minority applicants cannot satisfy the business necessity test unless it increases profits *within* each group of customers (as defined by race, ethnicity, or gender), holding constant the number of loans each group receives.

The use of scheme S^3 or, under some circumstances, S^4, instead of S^2 increases a firm's profits, but only by shifting the composition of loans away from minorities toward whites. In fact, the ranking of both minority and white applications on the basis of predicted performance is clearly less accurate with the scheme S^3 or S^4 than with scheme S^2. No firm should be able to justify a change in a credit-scoring scheme simply by showing that it increases the accuracy of predicted loan performance; instead, it should be required to show that the change boosts accuracy within each group of applicants.

The fourth implication concerns what we do not know:

4. Disparate-impact discrimination could enter a credit score or other aspects of automated underwriting systems through selection bias in the underlying regression equation and perhaps through other routes that have not yet been identified; more research is needed to ensure that subtle forms of disparate-impact discrimination do not arise in these systems and hence in the loan approval process.

The lack of publicly available loan performance data implies that little is known about the nature of existing automated underwriting schemes. However, well known methodological problems, such as selection or endogeneity bias, could lead to disparate-impact discrimination even when the designers of one of these systems are trying hard to avoid it. Scholarly access to loan performance data and careful research are needed to shed further light on these issues. As a starting point, our analysis indicates that some of these methodological problems can be minimized by including lender dummy variables in the regression equations on which these schemes are based (but not in the loan performance scores themselves).

It is important to reemphasize that this material should not be interpreted as an analysis of any particular credit-scoring or automated underwriting scheme. Because the formulas for existing schemes are not known, it is possible that they all are analogous to S^2, not to S^3 or S^4, and that none of them are affected by selection bias or some other methodological problem. Moreover, even if many or most existing schemes are analogous to S^3, the values of γ and of the b_is may be so close to zero that the disparate-impact discrimination in these schemes is too small in magnitude to be worth worrying about. Given the evidence of discrimination in other aspects of lending, however, and the ease with which disparate-impact discrimination can be incorporated into one of these schemes, intentionally or unintentionally, we think that federal fair-lending enforcement agencies should place a high priority on determining whether these schemes are consistent with existing fair-lending legislation.[31]

The need for fair-lending enforcement agencies to pay attention to disparate-impact discrimination is reinforced by the possibility that this type of discrimination could arise for reasons other than profitability. This chapter focuses on disparate-impact discrimination motivated by a search for higher profits, which is a form of statistical discrimination, but people designing or implementing automated underwriting schemes also might alter underwriting weights or change the set of underwriting variables because they are prejudiced against people in certain groups and wish to exclude them from credit. We do not know, of course, the extent to which this type of discrimination occurs. As shown in section 7.2.3, however, regulators cannot count on competition to eliminate all forms of prejudice-based discrimination. In addition, disparate-impact discrimination obviously could arise, intentionally or unintentionally, in underwriting schemes that are based, to some degree, on judgment instead of on statistics.

9.4   Blending Performance and Loan Approval Data

Throughout this book we have stated that the frontier for studying mortgage lending discrimination involves blending loan approval and loan performance data. Unfortunately, neither we nor any other scholars have been able to obtain such data, at least not for recent years. As a result, we conclude this chapter with a discussion of some of the key conceptual issues that scholars will have to confront when this type of data becomes available. Specifically, we explain how to test for the presence of discrimination when both loan performance and loan approval data are available and show how this type of test can account for variation in underwriting standards across lenders.

9.4.1   Testing for Discrimination in Loan Approval when Loan Performance Data Are Available

The existing methods for studying discrimination, namely, loan approval regressions and the default approach, face difficult methodological challenges and have proven to be controversial. This section asks whether less controversial methods would be available if both loan approval and loan performance information were available. We present a basic framework and develop a new test for discrimination in loan approval.

9.4.1.1   A Framework for Loan Performance and Approval Data
The starting point of any analysis of loan approval and performance must be the observation that, in a world without discrimination, any lender attempting to maximize profits will base its loan approval decisions solely on predicted loan performance. Some lenders predict loan performance based on an automated underwriting scheme; others use a less formal method for obtaining predictions. For our purposes, it is sufficient to say that a lender attempting to maximize profits will base its approval decision on a loan performance score, say S^i; that is, a profit-maximizing lender will use the following decision rule when considering loan applications:

approve if: $S^i \geq S^*$,

deny if: $S^i < S^*$.   (9.13)

where S^* is the lender's minimal acceptable performance.[32]

Discrimination could enter this analysis in two ways. First, the formal or informal scoring scheme could involve disparate-impact discrimination. This type of discrimination arises if the underwriting weights used in a lender's scoring system depart from those in the nondiscriminatory scheme, S^2.[33] Second, lenders may practice disparate-treatment discrimination; that is, they may use different underwriting standards for applicants from different groups.

A framework for thinking about these two types of discrimination in loan approval was presented in chapter 2. To be specific, we showed in equations (2.8) and (2.10) that a loan approval model containing both disparate-impact and disparate-treatment discrimination by lenders has three components. The first component is the best available estimate of the relationship between loan profitability and applicant, loan, and property characteristics.[34] This component is equivalent to the best-predicting nondiscriminatory scoring scheme, S^2. The second component reflects differences, if any, in underwriting standards between minority and white applicants (or between minority and white neighborhoods). It can be written as a shift in the underwriting decision for minority applicants, $D(M, N)$, where N indicates a minority neighborhood. This component, which is measured by the coefficients of minority status and neighborhood variables, captures disparate-treatment discrimination, including statistical discrimination. The third component measures differences, if any, between the underwriting standards used by the lender and the best available estimate of the relationship between profits and application characteristics. This component is equivalent to the difference between the underwriting rules used by the lender and the nondiscriminatory scoring scheme. Any disparate-impact discrimination that exists will appear in this component.

Let X stand for the set of X_i variables. Then, using the terminology presented earlier in this chapter, this general loan approval model can be written as follows:

approve if: $S^2(X) - D(M, N) + [S^i(X) - S^2(X)] \geq S^*$,

deny if: $S^2(X) - D(M, N) + [S^i(X) - S^2(X)] < S^*$.   (9.14)

One important example of this equation arises when a lender uses scoring scheme S^3. In this case, equations (9.9) and (9.14) imply that the model is

$$\text{approve if:}\quad S^2(X) - D(M,N) + \left(\gamma \sum_{i=1}^{N} b_i X_i\right) \geq S^*,$$

$$\tag{9.15}$$

$$\text{deny if:}\quad S^2(X) - D(M,N) + \left(\gamma \sum_{i=1}^{N} b_i X_i\right) < S^*.$$

In this example disparate-impact discrimination shows up as a change in the weights of the individual underwriting variables away from their weights in the nondiscriminatory scoring scheme.

The fact that the actual underwriting weights differ from the weights in the best-predicting nondiscriminatory scheme does not prove, of course, that a lender practices disparate-impact discrimination. After all, these differences in weights might not place minority applicants at a disadvantage. In other words, these differences in weights are necessary but not sufficient for the conclusion that disparate-impact discrimination exists. Such a conclusion cannot be supported without additional evidence that significantly fewer loan applications from minority households are approved under the actual underwriting scheme, equation (9.14) or (9.15), than would be approved under a scheme that granted the same number of loans but relied exclusively on the best-predicting nondiscriminatory scoring scheme.[35]

9.4.1.2 A New Test for Discrimination in Loan Approval

Although equation (9.14) provides a helpful framework for thinking about disparate-treatment and disparate-impact discrimination, a regulator with information on loan performance does not have to estimate this equation to determine whether discrimination exists. In fact, estimating this equation is not the best way to examine discrimination in loan approval. This section develops these two points (in reverse order).

If loan performance data are available, estimating equation (9.14) is not the best way to examine discrimination in loan approval, because this step requires strong assumptions that will inevitably cast doubt on the results. Consider the case of equation (9.15). This equation literally cannot be estimated as written. The loan performance score, S^2, is based on the set of X variables, so these two elements of the equation are perfectly correlated, and the b coefficients cannot be estimated. One way out of this dilemma would to estimate a simplified version of (9.15) with the X variables but without S^2 and then to compare the estimated coefficients of the X variables with the coefficients obtained in the loan performance equation, (9.1). This type of comparison cannot be made, however, without several strong assumptions about the functional forms of these two equations.[36]

Although equation (9.14) is more general, it, too, cannot be estimated without strong assumptions. Specifically, to estimate equation (9.14), a researcher must make assumptions about the way both S^2 and the X variables affect the loan approval decision; for example, the equation is based on the assumption that S^2 has a linear impact on loan approval. This reliance on assumptions that are difficult, if not impossible, to test is problematic because it could influence the magnitude and significance of the X variables' coefficients and hence influence the equation's implications concerning discrimination. Conclusions about discrimination should not depend on arbitrary and untestable assumptions about functional forms.

Another specification issue is that the apparent ability of equation (9.15) to distinguish between disparate-treatment and disparate-impact discrimination is an illusion. Building on the work of Buist, Linneman, and Megbolugbe (1999) and Blackburn and Vermilyea (2001), we show in section 9.3.2.2 that lenders may be able to devise a group-neutral underwriting scheme that replicates a set of loan approval decisions based on disparate-treatment discrimination. In other words, there may exist an underwriting scheme containing disparate-impact discrimination that can duplicate loan approval decisions based on disparate-treatment discrimination. It follows that a significant minority status coefficient in a loan approval regression could reflect either disparate-treatment or disparate-impact discrimination that is not captured by the functional form used to estimate the regression. To put it another way, one cannot be confident that a loan approval regression correctly distinguishes between these two types of discrimination unless one is confident that the regression correctly specifies the underwriting procedures actually used by lenders.[37]

Now we can address the first point, namely, that a regulator (or researcher) with information on loan performance does not have to estimate equation (9.14) to determine whether lenders practice discrimination in loan approval. Both disparate-treatment and disparate-impact discrimination imply that minority applicants are less likely to be approved with the underwriting system a lender actually uses than they would be under a system based entirely on the best-predicting nondiscriminatory scoring system. Thus, all a regulator has to do is to compare the actual minority and white denial (or approval) rates for all the applications that would be approved using a scoring system equivalent to S^2.[38] This calculation not only captures disparate-treatment discrimination, it also encompasses both parts of the test for disparate-impact discrimination. It includes the first part of that test because it identifies cases in which a lender's loan approval process places minority applicants at a disadvantage. It includes the second part of the test because S^2 fully accounts for all legitimate credit characteristics; in other words, any disparate impact on minority applicants found through this type of calculation must be the result of a deviation from the best-predicting nondiscriminatory scheme and therefore cannot be justified on the grounds of business necessity.

More formally, to determine whether a lender is practicing discrimination, a regulator must take the following steps:

1. Obtain a sample of applications to a lender and observe how many applications are approved (say, A).

2. Obtain loan performance data and estimate equation (9.1) with a sample of loans drawn from the same pool as those of the lender under investigation (with careful attention to relevant methodological problems).[39]

3. Use the estimated coefficients from equation (9.1) and the characteristics of the applications obtained in step 1 to calculate a loan performance score for each application.

4. Rank the applications by their loan performance score, and identify the highest-ranking A applications.

5. Compare the minority composition of the highest-ranking A applications with the minority composition of actual loans (that is, of approved applications). This difference is a measure of discrimination.

Its significance can be determined with a standard difference-of-means test.

This is a nonparametric test, so it does not require any assumptions about specification and is therefore very general. Moreover, the test simply involves a difference in minority composition, which is easy to calculate and easy to understand. For the sake of exposition, let us use the terms "high-quality" applications for all the applications that are among the highest-ranking *A* applications according to the "true" performance model and "low-ranking" applications for all others. For this test to conclude that discrimination exists, the underwriting process must have two features: It must reject a significant number of the high-ranking minority applications, and it must accept a significant number of the low-ranking white applications. Neither one of these features is sufficient by itself. For example, a rejection of high-ranking minority applications could be accompanied by an acceptance of low-ranking minority applications, which changes the quality of minority loans but does not constitute discrimination. Similarly, the acceptance of low-ranking white applications could be accompanied by a rejection of high-ranking white applications, with no impact on opportunities for minority applicants.

With loan performance data, therefore, the key statistical issue is how to estimate equation (9.1). Because discrimination can be identified through a direct examination of loan approval decisions, there is no need to estimate equation (9.14). Moreover, the lesson from Buist, Linneman, and Megbolugbe (1999) and Blackburn and Vermilyea (2001) still applies: Neither the direct procedure presented here nor the estimation of equation (9.14) can determine whether any discrimination that is found takes the form of disparate-treatment discrimination or disparate-impact discrimination.

This approach could be extended to determine whether discrimination takes the form of a higher hurdle for minority than for white applicants or simply involves the denial of minority applications, regardless of their quality.[40] This analysis of the form of discrimination is valuable both because it provides guidance to fair-lending enforcement officials and because it provides a test of a key assumption behind the default approach to studying lending discrimination. As discussed in chapter 8, the default approach assumes that discrimination takes the higher-hurdle form.

In addition, this approach can be extended to study the causes of discrimination in loan approval.[41] This is potentially an important extension; as discussed in chapter 7, no consensus has emerged about the causes of mortgage discrimination, and a better understanding of these causes could be of great value to fair-lending enforcement officials. Moreover, our analysis reveals that it may not be possible to distinguish between disparate-treatment and disparate-impact discrimination. For example, statistical discrimination has traditionally been thought of as a type of disparate-treatment discrimination, but we find that lenders may be able to replicate the outcomes from disparate-treatment discrimination by treating all groups equally while manipulating the underwriting weights, that is, by implementing a cleverly designed scheme of disparate-impact discrimination. As a result, studies of the causes of discrimination may benefit from separating the incentives that lead to discrimination from the factors that determine the form discrimination takes.

9.4.2 Accounting for Legitimate Variation in Underwriting Standards across Lenders

It is now time to bring the discussion full circle, that is, to merge our analysis of loan performance with our earlier discussion of variation in underwriting standards across lenders. In this section, we review the possible reasons for variation in underwriting standards across lenders and devise appropriate ways to account for this variation in a loan performance regression. We do not consider the role of this variation in a loan approval regression, which was addressed in chapter 6, because we have just shown that the best way to identify discrimination in loan approval does not involve a regression of this type.

In chapter 3, we argued that differences in loan performance models across lenders, and hence in the underwriting standards based on these models, can arise for many reasons, only some of which would be considered legitimate in the sense that they can be justified on the grounds of business necessity. This analysis is summarized in lessons 4 and 5 in that chapter. Lesson 4 stresses the importance of accounting for variation in underwriting standards across lenders, and lesson 5 explains that these differences could involve discrimination. This section begins with some examples designed to illustrate these two lessons. We then show how to bring legitimate across-lender variation in underwriting standards, that is, variation that does not involve disparate-impact discrimination, into a test for discrimination in loan approval.

9.4.2.1 Sources of Variation in Underwriting Standards across Lenders

Lenders that serve different pools of borrowers obviously could have different experiences with loan performance. In formal terms, differences across borrower pools result in different estimated underwriting weights, from equation (9.1). Underwriting weights might be different in different regions, for example, and they might be different for prime versus subprime loans and for home purchase versus refinancing loans.[42]

Geographic variation in underwriting standards also could be misused by a lender who wants to avoid lending in some parts of its service area, which is, as discussed in chapter 2, a violation of its obligations under CRA. This issue is of concern here because a lender that has been avoiding loans in low-income or minority neighborhoods, in violation of its CRA obligations, may have in its portfolio a sample of loans that are quite different from those that would have appeared for properties in those neighborhoods had the lender served them. As a result, a model of loan performance estimated from the lender's existing portfolio may involve weights (i.e., estimated coefficients) that are not appropriate for applications from low-income and minority neighborhoods and could even have a disparate impact on these applications.

Underwriting standards also could vary across lenders because lenders differ in liquidity, risk aversion, or cost of capital. As explained in chapter 3, different risk preferences could lead to different foreclosure policies, and borrowers might sort across lenders based on these policies and on borrower characteristics that the lenders cannot observe. The resulting systematic difference in unobserved borrower characteristics across lenders could result in variation in underwriting weights across lenders, as determined by equation (9.1). This type of variation can persist in a full-information, perfectly competitive environment and is therefore justified on the grounds of business necessity.

A final example is that underwriting standards could vary across lenders because some lenders are able to take advantage of poor borrower information. As shown in chapter 3, underwriting differences of this type could not be sustained if borrowers had good information, which is a requirement for fully competitive markets. Moreover, actions based on noncompetitive behavior, even if they are profitable, cannot be justified on the grounds of business necessity.[43]

The potential importance of asymmetric information is highlighted by two examples presented earlier in this book: overages and predatory lending. The discussion in chapter 7 of overages, that is, of the flexible portion of mortgage interest rates, reveals that discrimination in overages could arise because of intergroup differences in leverage during negotiations. If minority applicants believe that they have fewer options than do white applicants, they may be more willing to accept a relatively high overage. If loan officers use minority status as a signal for poor leverage, this discrimination takes the form of disparate treatment. However, loan officers also could devise bargaining rules designed to identify any customer with poor leverage, so this discrimination also could take the form of disparate impact. In either case, discrimination arises because loan officers are able to take advantage of asymmetric information in a way that places minority applicants at a disadvantage.

Predatory lending, which was discussed in chapter 2, provides the extreme case of what can happen when some lenders convince borrowers to accept loans on far worse terms than they could obtain from other lenders.[44] Predatory lending is obviously far from the norm, but its persistence reminds us that markets operating with poor information often do not work very well and suggests that loan performance models that reflect predatory lending may not be valid tools to use in the search for lending discrimination. In fact, if the predatory lending examples in chapter 2 are any guide, the impact of poor information on borrowers is likely to be correlated with minority status, so basing a business necessity defense on a loan performance model that could not be sustained with perfect borrower information could be nothing more than another way to let disparate-impact discrimination in through the back door.

Overall, therefore, we conclude that regulators and researchers concerned about variation in underwriting standards across lenders face a serious dilemma when estimating a loan performance model such as equation (9.1). Underwriting standards clearly can vary across lenders for legitimate business reasons. It is entirely appropriate to account for this type of variation in a loan performance

model. However, variation in underwriting standards across lenders
could also reflect lender policies involving disparate impact or violations of CRA obligations. In addition, it is not possible to determine on conceptual grounds which observed types of variation in
underwriting standards across lenders are legitimate and which
are examples of discrimination. Fortunately, however, our approach
provides a way out of this dilemma.

9.4.2.2 Accounting for Variation in Underwriting Standards without Introducing Disparate-Impact Discrimination

By taking four simple steps, a regulator or researcher can build a
test for lending discrimination that accounts for legitimate variation in underwriting standards across lenders without introducing
disparate-impact discrimination or violations of CRA. The first step
is to make sure that the sample used to estimate the loan performance model is consistent with the CRA obligations of the lenders in
the sample. Lenders who totally neglect to serve some portion of
their service area should be dropped from the estimation, and their
behavior should be evaluated on the basis of the loan performance
model estimated for the other lenders, that is, the lenders that meet
their CRA obligations. In cases of less extreme neglect, loans in
underserved neighborhoods in a lender's portfolio should be re-
weighted so that the effective sample resembles the sample that
would be drawn if that lender served all neighborhoods equally.

The second step is to introduce lender dummy variables into the
loan performance model, equation (9.1). These variables go a long
way toward accounting for variation in underwriting standards
across lenders and cannot introduce any disparate-impact discrimination.[45] Moreover, they do not change in the test for discrimination
by a single lender.[46]

The third step is to identify variables associated with sources of
variation in underwriting standards that appear to be legitimate and
to introduce these variables into the loan-performance model. Variables to measure region or loan purpose, for example, could help to
identify cases in which different lenders face different pools of borrowers. Following Ambrose, Buttimer, and Capone (1997), the average time between default and foreclosure could be used as a measure
of a lender's foreclosure policy, and hence of the type of borrowers
that it attracts. To capture variation in underwriting standards, these

variables must be interacted with standard credit characteristics, that is, the X variables in equation (9.1). The basic point of this step is to determine whether the underwriting weight, that is the estimated coefficient, of a given credit characteristic, varies systematically with region, loan type, foreclosure policy, or some other variable.

The fourth step is to use the test presented in section 9.3.4 to make certain that none of the significant variables found in step 3 introduce disparate-impact discrimination. This test is simple: No variable, including the interaction variables defined in step 3, should be included in a loan performance regression unless it improves the within-group predictions of loan performance. This step is critical; indeed, it is the only way to rule out the possibility that across-lender variation in a particular underwriting weight involves disparate-impact discrimination.[47]

Once a loan performance model based on these four steps has been estimated, the discrimination test developed in section 9.4.1.2 can be directly applied. This test applies to a single lender, so it should make use of the underwriting weights for that lender, which will differ from the underwriting weights of other lenders if any of the interaction terms from step 3 are statistically significant and pass the test in step 4.[48] The question is whether there is a significant difference between the minority composition of the highest-scoring applications received by a lender, as determined by that lender's underwriting weights, and the minority composition of that lender's actual loans.

In short, the discrimination test proposed in this section is general and easy to understand, and it is easily expanded to consider the possibility that legitimate underwriting standards vary across lenders. Regulators and researchers do not need to rely on controversial loan approval regressions or the problematic default approach to determine whether a lender practices discrimination in loan approval. Instead, they need to obtain data sets that provide information on both loan performance and loan approval, carefully estimate loan performance equations that account for legitimate variation in underwriting standards across lenders, and then compare the minority composition of the lender's actual loans to the minority compositions of the applications submitted to that lender that have the highest loan performance scores based on estimated underwriting weights for that lender.

9.5 Conclusions

The recent literature on discrimination in mortgage lending focuses on two critical issues confronting loan approval regressions in general and the Boston Fed Study in particular: (1) They do not distinguish among disparate-treatment discrimination, disparate-impact discrimination, and legitimate variation in underwriting standards across lenders, and (2) they do not consider loan performance. This chapter builds on the analysis of these issues in previous chapters to show how pervasive disparate-impact discrimination might be and how to incorporate loan performance into an analysis of discrimination in mortgage lending. Our analysis brings together the findings in previous chapters by showing how performance data can be used to measure discrimination after accounting for legitimate differences in underwriting standards across lenders.

We begin by demonstrating that disparate-impact discrimination can be built into many types of loan performance models and associated loan performance scores, including several that appear to treat different groups of applicants equally. For example, loan performance scores based on a regression analysis that explains loan performance on the basis of credit characteristics but includes no variables to indicate a borrower's minority status are very likely to involve disparate-impact discrimination.

In effect, these scoring schemes, and many others, exploit the correlation between many credit characteristics and minority status to create underwriting weights that serve to help identify minority applicants, not just to measure the impact of credit characteristics on loan performance. We show that the only way to rule out disparate-impact discrimination is to make sure that every element of a scoring scheme improves the ability of the scheme to predict the performance of the applicants within a group (among whites, for example). More research is needed to determine whether the elements of existing scoring schemes meet this test, but we use existing default data to show that disparate-impact discrimination generated by these schemes could severely limit minority households' access to credit under some circumstances.

Our next step is to explore the possibilities for combining loan approval and loan performance information. More specifically, we incorporate loan performance information into a test for discrimination in loan approval. This test differs substantially from both a loan approval regression (the approach used by the Boston Fed Study) and the default approach (which has been offered as an alternative approach) and avoids the main problems with both of these approaches. It compares the minority composition of the applications that have the highest predicted performance based on a loan performance regression with the minority composition of a lender's actual loans. The difference between these minority compositions is a measure of the extent to which the lender's underwriting procedures work against minorities compared to a procedure based entirely on predicted loan performance; in other words, this difference is a measure of discrimination. This approach can also be adapted to study the causes of discrimination in loan approval and to determine whether discrimination strikes all types of minority loan applications or just minority applications with relatively low credit quality.

This measure of discrimination is based on a loan performance regression but does not require the estimation of a loan approval regression. Moreover, it picks up both disparate-treatment and disparate-impact discrimination. In fact, we show that it may not be possible to distinguish between these two types of discrimination in the mortgage context; the available evidence indicates that a set of loan approval decisions based on disparate-treatment discrimination could be replicated using disparate-impact discrimination, that is, by manipulating the weights in an underwriting procedure.

Finally, we show that the new approach presented in this chapter to studying discrimination in loan approval can easily accommodate the possibility that different lenders use different underwriting standards. To be specific, the loan performance regression on which this approach is based can easily be modified to determine whether the impact of applicants' credit characteristics on performance varies across lenders. We also show, however, that variation in loan performance scoring systems across lenders could hide disparate-impact discrimination. As a result, no across-lender variation in the impact of credit characteristics should be introduced into a loan performance model unless it can be shown that this variation meets the test devised earlier for any scoring system element: Specifically, it must improve the ability of the model to predict performance within each group of borrowers.

Overall, the analysis in this chapter resolves several crucial issues in the literature on mortgage lending discrimination and points the way for future research:

• Automated underwriting systems do not involve disparate-treatment discrimination, but they can involve disparate-impact discrimination and may even be able to replicate the exact set of decisions that disparate-treatment discrimination would produce.

• Using the data on which it is based, any existing credit-scoring or automated underwriting system could easily be checked for disparate-impact discrimination.

• A data set combining information on loan approval and loan performance would make it possible to measure discrimination in loan underwriting (and test hypotheses about its causes) without using either of the methods that have generated so much controversy, namely, a loan-approval regression or the default approach.

• A data set combining information on loan approval and loan performance also would make it possible to measure discrimination using a model that formally accounts for legitimate differences in underwriting standards across lenders.

10 Implications for Fair-Lending Enforcement

10.1 Introduction

So far, this book has been about research, but the results in the book also have profound implications for fair-lending enforcement. This chapter explores these implications. We focus on enforcing the laws against discrimination in loan approval, although our discussion has implications for other types of discriminatory behavior as well.

Existing antidiscrimination legislation raises a variety of complex legal issues, particularly when disparate-impact discrimination is involved. We begin, therefore, with a review of the court decisions and regulations associated with this legislation. Because existing regulations apply to discrimination in employment, not lending, we then develop some principles and procedures to guide the development of the regulations that are required for mortgage lending. Most importantly, we develop two new enforcement procedures that make it possible to identify loan approval discrimination in the vast majority of cases, without generating false positives, defined as cases in which discrimination is "found" even though it does not, in fact, exist. These tools pick up both disparate-treatment and disparate-impact discrimination. Finally, we show that one of these new tools can be extended to consider discrimination in automated underwriting systems (even before they are used to make underwriting decisions) and in lenders' interest rate–setting behavior.

Next, we turn to a description of the enforcement procedures currently used by the fair-lending enforcement agencies. We demonstrate that these procedures are not consistent with existing legal doctrines and indeed are incapable of identifying many, if not most, instances of discrimination in loan approval. This situation cries out for reform.

10.2   The Legal Basis for Fair-Lending Enforcement

FaHA and ECOA explicitly outlaw disparate-treatment discrimination in mortgage lending, which is, of course, the use of different
underwriting standards for people in different groups. As explained
in chapter 9, lenders can evade a prohibition against disparate-
treatment discrimination by practicing disparate-impact discrimination. The implications of FaHA and ECOA for disparate-impact
discrimination are not straightforward, however, so we begin our
analysis of fair-lending policy with a review of the legal standards
and regulations that have been developed for disparate-impact discrimination cases.

10.2.1   Legal Standards in Disparate-Impact Cases

A prohibition against disparate-impact discrimination was introduced through a series of U.S. Supreme Court decisions involving
Title VII of the Civil Rights Act of 1964, which is directed toward
discrimination in labor markets. This prohibition is not explicitly
written into FaHA or ECOA, and the Supreme Court has never
indicated whether these two acts cover disparate-impact discrimination. However, the language in FaHA and ECOA is similar to that in
Title VII, so it is reasonable to conclude, as have many lower courts,
that these acts made it illegal to practice disparate-impact discrimination in mortgage lending (see Schewemm, 1994; Kushner, 1995;
Mahoney, 1998). Moreover, during the debate over the 1988 amendments to FaHA, members of Congress explicitly recognized the court
precedents concerning Title VII and decided that there was no need
to make explicit reference to disparate-impact discrimination in these
amendments (Schwemm, 1994).

Because the rules for determining disparate-impact discrimination
are not settled, even for Title VII, and because court precedents for
considering this type of discrimination in lending are so limited, no
clear standards exist for determining when a lender is practicing
disparate-impact discrimination. As one scholar puts it, "Decades
after statutory enactment, courts, federal agencies charged with enforcing the Fair Housing Act and the ECOA, and commentators have
failed to produce a reliable rule for determining liability" under a
disparate-impact standard (Mahoney, 1998, p. 411).

Drawing on the analysis in Mahoney (1998), this section reviews the current state of legal doctrine concerning disparate-impact discrimination and the applicability of this doctrine to FaHA and ECOA. Any case involving disparate-impact discrimination has three steps, each of which is reviewed in this section:

1. Determine whether a practice has a disparate impact on a legally protected class of people.

2. Determine whether the practice can be justified on the grounds of business necessity.

3. Determine whether there exists an alternative practice that achieves the same business objectives without the same disparate impact.

Disparate-impact discrimination is said to exist if (a) a practice has a disparate impact on a protected group and either (b) the practice cannot be justified on the grounds of business necessity or (c) the practice can be justified by business necessity, but its disparate impact can be avoided through the use of an alternative policy that achieves the same business objectives.

One of the most critical issues in any disparate-impact case is determining whether a policy meets the business necessity criterion. Regulations for making this and other determinations have been written by the Equal Employment Opportunity Commission (EEOC) for Title VII cases. These regulations are examined in section 10.2.2.

10.2.1.1   Does a Practice Have a Disparate Impact on a Protected Class?

The first step in any disparate-impact case is showing that some business practice has a disparate impact on the members of a legally protected class. If it does, then the plaintiff has established what is known as a "prima facie case" for discrimination. This step has three parts: identifying the offending practice, selecting the proper pool for comparison, and establishing causation.

As the U.S. Supreme Court put it in *Watson v. Fort Worth Bank & Trust*, "[t]he plaintiff must begin by identifying the specific employment practice that is challenged."[1] This is called the particularity requirement. There is an exception to this requirement, however, that appears to be important for fair lending. To be specific, "if the complaining party can demonstrate to the court that the elements of a respondent's decisionmaking process are not capable of separation for analysis, the decisionmaking process may be analyzed as one employment practice."[2] This exception is designed to prevent employers from formulating their decision-making processes in such a way as to make it impossible to evaluate them. As Senator John Danforth put it in defending the Civil Rights Act of 1991:

> For example, if employment decision-makers cannot reconstruct the basis for their employment decisions, because uncontrolled discretion is given to a respondent's employment decision-makers, then the decision-making process may be treated as one employment practice and need not be identified by the complaining party as discrete practices. Similarly, if a complaining party proves to a judge that it is impossible for whatever reason to reconstruct how practices were used in a decision-making process, then the decision-making process is incapable of separation for analysis and may be treated as one employment practices and challenged and defended as such.[3]

According to one expert, "there is some indication that courts in FaHA cases will permit an exception to the particularity requirement in cases in which plaintiffs allege that the 'practice' causing disparate impact consists of a defendant's delegation to its employees of subjective decision-making authority" (Mahoney, 1998, p. 464). Moreover, this exception appears to be directly relevant for underwriting schemes, which reveal the outcome but not the weights placed on each variable considered in the scheme. In fact, most credit-scoring or other automated underwriting schemes are regarded as proprietary, which implies that these weights are hidden from the customer (and the fair-lending enforcement official) and therefore cannot be evaluated for disparate impact.[4] Even when the weights are known, however, the impact of a particular weight on the outcome, namely loan approval or denial for a given loan application, is difficult, if not impossible, to establish, so the logic of the particularity exception still applies.[5]

The second part of step 1 involves sample selection. Any disparate-impact case involves a claim that some practice or practices have a disproportionate impact on a set of people in a protected class compared to a set of people not in this protected class. The courts require that this comparison be made between sets of people who are in similar situations. According to Mahoney (1998),[6]

> the few FHA or ECOA cases that have addressed the issue suggest that, in these cases, the proper pool is the group of protected class members who

were actually adversely affected by the challenged policy. Recent lending discrimination cases support the view that the proper pool of applicants for measurement of statistical disparities is the group of financially qualified protected class members that actually applied for financing and were rejected. (p. 467)

The final part of step 1 is offering proof of causation. As the Supreme Court put it in *Watson,*

Once the employment practice at issue has been identified, causation must be proved; that is, the plaintiff must offer statistical evidence of a kind and degree sufficient to show that the practice in question has caused the exclusion of applicants for jobs or promotions because of their membership in a protected group. (p. 994)

The courts have not provided much guidance on the nature of the required proof. In Title VII cases, several courts have argued that the proof must take the form of statistical significance. According to Mahoney (1988), "there is a paucity of guidance on the measure of statistical significance courts should use in FHA and ECOA cases" (pp. 466–467).

10.2.1.2 Can the Practice Be Justified on the Grounds of Business Necessity?

If the defendant establishes that a practice or set of practices has a disparate impact on a protected class, a disparate-impact case moves on to step 2. In this step the issue is whether the challenged practice has a legitimate business justification. Four questions arise in this step: Who has the burden of proof? How strong must be the connection to business objectives? What type of evidence is required? What types of business objectives are "legitimate"?

Although the burden of proof has shifted over the years, the legal standard at this point is that this burden falls on the defendant (Mahoney, 1998, p. 469). In other words, once a prima facie case for disparate impact has been made, it is up to the defendant to prove that the challenged practice has a legitimate business justification.[7]

The most critical question in step 2 concerns the standard of proof that the defendant must meet. This question has been addressed in many Supreme Court decisions and was explicitly considered in the Civil Rights Act of 1991. In *Griggs v. Duke Power Co.* (1971), the Court declared that practices must be "demonstrably a reasonable measure of job performance."[8] This link to job performance has been weakened, however, in several subsequent decisions. In *Wards Cove Packing Co. v. Atonia* (1989), for example, the Court ruled that "there is no requirement that the challenged practice be 'essential' or 'indispensable' to the employer's business for it to pass muster."[9]

The Civil Rights Act of 1991 attempted to clarify what is required of a defendant to establish that a practice has a legitimate business justification but, according to most commentators, did not succeed (Mahoney, 1998; Lye, 1998). This act requires practices to be "consistent with business necessity." As several courts have pointed out, however, the "consistent" part of this language is much weaker than the "necessity" part, and Congress's intention is not clear. Recent court cases seem roughly consistent with the view that this act requires a business to prove that the challenged practice is "reasonably necessary to achieve an important business purpose" (Mahoney, 1998, p. 473). This interpretation seems closer to *Wards Cove* than to *Griggs*.

This question has not been addressed in many housing or lending cases. As pointed out by Mahoney (1998, p. 477), a recent federal appeals court decision in a housing case, *Mountain Side Mobile Estates V. HUD* (56 F.3d 1243, 10th Cir. 1995), uses language that is very similar to that in *Wards Cove*. The business necessity standard for lending cases is also addressed in a congressional committee report prepared in conjunction with the 1988 amendments to FaHA:

The Committee does not intend that those purchasing mortgage loans be precluded from taking into consideration factors justified by business necessity ... which relate to the financial security of the transaction or the protection against default or diminution in the value of the security.[10]

This language seems closer to *Griggs* than to *Wards Cove* but certainly cannot be said to make the required standard clear.

The existing cases and regulations involving FaHA or ECOA focus on a standard defined by "legitimate business interests." One court declared, for example, that the "Fair Housing Act's prohibition against denying a loan based upon the location of the dwelling does not require that a lender disregard its legitimate business interests or make an investment that is not economically sound."[11] Moreover, according to Mahoney (1998, p. 482), the regulations devised by HUD to implement the 1988 amendments to FaHA "echo" the language of the congressional committee report cited above. Finally, the commentary prepared by the Federal Reserve Board to accompany its regulations implementing ECOA say that "[t]he act and regulation may prohibit a creditor practice that is discriminatory in effect ... unless the creditor practice meets a legitimate business need."[12]

A related question in step 2 concerns the nature of the proof required to establish the legitimate business necessity of a particular practice: Once a standard has been selected, what kind of evidence is needed to show that a business practice meets this standard? In general, the courts have not required that the proof take any particular form:

> However, in a large number of cases, particularly those involving tests administered by employers for the purpose of hiring or promotion, courts have very nearly required defendants to provide proof that tests are, in the words of *Griggs*, "demonstrably a measure of job performance." Thus, in cases that involve employer-administered tests, "the business justification that the employer must show is that the test is job related." (Mahoney, 1998, p. 475).

In these cases, therefore, the nature of the required evidence appears to push the business necessity standard back toward one based on job performance. In other words, when job performance is clearly the issue, as it is with a test upon which a hiring decision is based, the courts appear to be comfortable with a performance-based standard backed up with formal evidence concerning performance.

The final question in step 2 concerns the meaning of the word "legitimate," which accompanies the term "business justification" in many court decisions. In our judgment, the use of this term raises two issues. First, it is obviously not "legitimate" for an employer (or a lender) to use a practice that replicates the outcomes of disparate-treatment discrimination, even if this practice is profitable. Indeed, this is precisely the reason courts have developed a disparate-impact standard: No economic agent should be able to use an indirect method to accomplish objectives that are illegal when pursued directly. In the case of mortgages, no lender should be able to use underwriting variables or weights that serve to predict group membership instead of loan performance. The trouble with such an assertion, of course, is that courts have never clearly explained what type of evidence is needed to separate practices that are legitimate in this sense from those that are not.

Second, some legal scholars have argued that only those practices that can be sustained in a competitive environment are considered to be "legitimate" (Ayres, 2001). Practices that draw on a firm's market power, in other words, cannot meet the business necessity test. Recall from section 2.3.2 that the FFIEC guide to fair lending says that lending practices must be justified on the basis of "cost or profitability." This "competitive practices" qualification indicates that, in some cases at least, cost-based arguments are likely to have more validity than profit-based tests.

10.2.1.3   Are Less-Discriminatory Alternatives Available?
If the defendant convinces the court that the practice or practices in question have a sufficient business justification, then the ball goes back into the plaintiff's court for the final step in a disparate-impact case. Specifically, the plaintiff can prevail despite the defendant's success in step 2 if she can show that there exists an alternative practice that meets the defendant's business needs but does not have a disparate impact on the relevant protected class. Although this issue has rarely arisen in cases involving FaHA or ECOA, "the accumulated wisdom from federal regulatory and enforcement agencies, court decisions involving private defendants, and the legislative history provides support for the reading of the less discriminatory alternatives standard that is emerging in the post-1991 Act Title VII case decisions" (Mahoney, 1998, p. 490).

Two issues are particularly important in this final step. First, a plaintiff must show that an alternative business practice (a) is equally effective in meeting the defendant's legitimate business interests, (b) is not significantly more costly than the challenged policy, and (c) has a significantly smaller disparate impact on the protected class in question. Clear rules for the type of evidence needed to satisfy this requirement have not yet been developed by the courts (Mahoney, 1998).

This issue has not arisen in any court cases involving ECOA. However, the Federal Reserve Board's Regulation B, which implements ECOA, states that a credit-scoring system is not "qualified" to be counted as a legitimate business practice unless it is "[d]eveloped for the purpose of evaluating the creditworthiness of applicants with respect to the legitimate business interests of the creditor utilizing the system (including, but not limited to, minimizing bad debt losses and operating expenses in accordance with the creditor's business judgement)." As Mahoney (1998) puts it, this language implies that "for an offered substitute to be considered a true 'alternative,' it must achieve economic results that are at least roughly equal to the results obtained by using the challenged practice" (p. 495).

The second issue is that the plaintiff must show that the defendant has refused to adopt the less discriminatory alternative that exists. This issue has great symbolic importance, because it introduces a hint of discriminatory intent into a disparate-impact case. As the Supreme Court put it in its *Wards Cove* decision,

[i]f respondents, having established a prima facie case, come forward with alternatives to petitioners' hiring practices that reduce the racially disparate impact of practices currently being used, and petitioners refuse to adopt these alternatives, such a refusal would belie a claim by petitioners that their incumbent practices are being employed for nondiscriminatory reasons. (pp. 660–661)

10.2.2 Regulations to Implement Title VII

Any case involving Title VII raises many practical issues, such as how to determine disparate impact and how to determine whether a challenged practice can be justified on the grounds of business necessity. In the case of employment discrimination, detailed regulations to deal with these issues were developed in 1978 by the EEOC and other federal agencies (EEOC, 1978). These regulations, the *Uniform Guidelines on Employment Selection Procedures*, have been cited by many courts. As explained by Mahoney (1998, p. 513), many courts have paid deference to the *Uniform Guidelines* as reflective of the administrative expertise of the agency charged with enforcing Title VII, but the Supreme Court has not always required defendants to follow these guidelines.

No such guidelines have been developed for FaHA or ECOA cases. As Mahoney (1998) puts it, "While there may be some useful general guidance in the Regulation B language, it cannot be relied upon as establishing a regulatory standard similar to the Uniform Guidelines, for example, in terms of validating a testing mechanism under the Fair Housing Act or the ECOA" (pp. 518–519). Thus "to provide any complete analogy from Title VII to FHA cases and ECOA cases, it helps to have a rudimentary understanding of what the Uniform Guidelines expect employers to do in validating employment tests" (p. 513).

The *Uniform Guidelines* deal with many, if not most, of the issues addressed by the courts in disparate-impact cases. In this review, we discuss four elements of these guidelines that are particularly important for our purposes.

First, the *Uniform Guidelines* give some guidance on the particularity requirement in disparate-impact law. Specifically, the guidelines say that if the information collected for a particular employer

shows that the total selection process does not have an adverse impact, the Federal enforcement agencies, in the exercise of their administrative and prosecutorial discretion, in usual circumstances, will not expect a user to evaluate the individual components for adverse impact, or to validate such individual components, and will not take enforcement action based on the adverse impact of any component of that process. (pp. 125–126)

This rule is directly related to the congressional testimony cited earlier with respect to the Civil Rights Act of 1991. Employers should not be able to hide disparate-impact discrimination by making it impossible for regulators to observe individual practices or to evaluate their decision-making processes, just as regulators should not focus on individual practices when the total selection process can be observed.

Second, the *Uniform Guidelines* explain how to build a prima facie case that disparate-impact discrimination is being practiced. Using the term "adverse impact," which is a synonym for "disparate impact," the guidelines define something commonly referred to as the "four-fifths rule," which says that

[a] selection rate for any race, sex, or ethnic group which is less than four-fifths (or eighty percent) of the rate for the group with the highest rate will generally be regarded by the Federal enforcement agencies as evidence of adverse impact. Smaller differences in selection rate may nevertheless constitute adverse impact, where they are significant in both statistical and practical terms or where a user's actions have discouraged applicants disproportionately on grounds of race, sex, or ethnic group. Greater differences in selection rate may not constitute adverse impact where the differences are based on small numbers and are not statistically significant, or where special recruiting or other programs cause the pool of minority or female candidates to be atypical of the normal pool of applicants from that group. (p. 126)

The four-fifths rule is designed to identify practices that have a large negative impact on the selection rates of a protected class. It does not formally deal with the issues of the appropriate pool for comparison or the determination of causation, but it implicitly recognizes that these issues must be considered when evaluating an employment practice. For example, the rule indicates that the pool of job applicants may not be the appropriate choice for comparison if the employer's actions have influenced the set of people who apply.

Third, the *Uniform Guidelines* offer a set of standards for determining when an employment practice is valid according to the business necessity test. Several different types of analysis are discussed in the guidelines. The most relevant of these for our purposes is a "criterion-related" study, which addresses the relationship between a practice and some measure of job performance (the criterion). As the guidelines put it,

Evidence of the validity of a test or other selection procedure by a criterion-related validity study should consist of empirical data demonstrating that the selection procedure is predictive of or significantly correlated with important elements of job performance. (p. 127)

The guidelines make this more explicit by referring to statistical standards:

Generally a selection procedure is considered related to the criterion, for the purposes of these guidelines, when the relationship between performance on the procedure and performance on the criterion measure is statistically significant at the 0.05 level of significance. (p. 132)

Fourth, the *Uniform Guidelines* declare that a practice cannot be justified as a legitimate business necessity if it is found to be "unfair." The guidelines acknowledge that "[t]he concept of fairness or unfairness of selection procedures is a developing concept" (p. 133), but still provide a formal definition:

When members of one race, sex, or ethnic group characteristically obtain lower scores on a selection procedure than members of another group, and the differences in scores are not reflected in differences in a measure of job performance, use of the selection procedure may unfairly deny opportunities to members of the group that obtains the lower scores. (p. 133)

This fairness doctrine is specifically invoked in the guidelines only when an employer uses "validity studies not conducted by the user." The guidelines also say, however, that "all relationships between selection procedures and criterion measures investigated should be reported for each relevant race, sex, and ethnic group and for the total group" (p. 139), which suggests that fairness is an issue in any validation study.

10.3   Toward Uniform Guidelines for Underwriting Decisions

The purpose of this section is to develop some principles that could be used by regulators in the preparation of "Uniform Guidelines for Underwriting Systems." Such guidelines are urgently needed. They would serve the same function for FaHA and ECOA cases that the *Uniform Guidelines on Employment Selection Procedures* (EEOC, 1978) serve for Title VII cases. We first present some general guidelines for fair-lending regulations and then present specific procedures that could be used to identify mortgage lending discrimination, regardless of whether it takes the form of disparate treatment or disparate impact.

10.3.1   *Guidelines for Fair-Lending Regulations*

This section discusses several of the key principles that must be addressed in any formal regulations for fair-lending enforcement. These principles draw on the *Uniform Guidelines on Employment Selection Procedures* but also modify these employment-based guidelines in several important ways to make them applicable to fair lending. Most of these modifications flow from the fact that our guidelines for fair lending focus on a single type of behavior, underwriting, with a clear structure, whereas the *Uniform Guidelines* are designed to cover a wide range of employment practices. As a result, our guidelines can be more precise than the guidelines developed for employment cases.[13] This issue is discussed by Mahoney (1998), who points out that the *Uniform Guidelines* must devote a great deal of attention to the selection of appropriate job performance measures:

These concerns probably will not prove material in validating selection devices under the FHA or the ECOA. Creditors and insurers rely upon much more objective factors in constructing and applying their selection criteria. In most cases, "performance" is measured by a stark, objective and singular result: Was a loan or other obligation paid as agreed? The scoring tests used in credit and other financial market are constructed almost exclusively to measure this or other statistical outcomes. This suggests that the "performance criteria" used in most selection devices that may be tested under the FHA or the ECOA will prove much more amenable to cogent validation than the selection devices used in the employment area. (p. 521)

The relative clarity of the performance objectives in underwriting systems leads to several key principles for fair lending regulations.

First, fair-lending regulations should rely on the exception to the particularity principle that has been developed by the courts. The discussion of this exception in the *Uniform Guidelines* appear to be reasonable, consistent with legal precedents, and directly applicable to underwriting. In the case of underwriting, an individual "practice" could be thought of as the weight placed on an individual underwriting variable and the "process" as the set of underwriting weights that lead to the final decision concerning loan approval. Because underwriting is, by definition, a multivariate procedure, the impact of a single weight on the final outcome cannot be determined. Therefore, even though a lender could, in principle, reveal the weight it places on an individual underwriting variable, the impact of this weight on the final decision (or on disparate impact in the final decision) cannot be determined without considering the role of all the other weights. In short, the rule in the *Uniform Guidelines* concerning the particularity principle can be preserved and even strengthened in the case of underwriting. All parties to an analysis of disparate-impact discrimination in underwriting should focus on the impact of the underwriting system as a whole, not on the impact of individual underwriting weights.

Second, fair-lending regulations should set a high standard for establishing a prima facie case that an underwriting system involves discrimination, and in particular, should set a standard that requires a multivariate procedure. Specifically, the appropriate way to establish a prima facie case against a particular underwriting system is to show that under that system, members of a protected class are less likely to be approved than are whites after controlling for all observable, legitimate characteristics of the applicant, loan, and property. We develop two such procedures in the following section.

The *Uniform Guidelines*, and specifically the four-fifths rule, do not provide much guidance on this issue. The four-fifths rule is a compromise designed to apply to a wide range of employment practices, many of which are not amenable to formal analysis. The analog to the four-fifths rule for underwriting would be to say that a plaintiff can establish a prima facie case for disparate-impact discrimination simply by showing that the approval rate for a protected class is only 80 percent of the approval rate for whites. Under such a standard, however, a prima facie case for disparate-impact discrimination could be built against the majority of lenders in the nation. It would be unfair to lenders (and a waste of enforcement funds) to charge so many lenders with discrimination. Moreover, this analog to the four-fifths rule implies that lenders who attract applications from highly qualified members of a protected class would never face a prima facie case, even if they practice disparate-impact discrimination. Because straightforward multivariate procedures are available to assess lending practices (in contrast to the lack of such procedures for assessing employment practices), an approximate procedure such as the four-fifths rule is neither desirable nor necessary for evaluating an underwriting system.

Third, fair-lending regulations should draw on the relatively strict business necessity standards that have been applied to employer-administered tests. To paraphrase the language courts have used in employment cases, the business justification that the lender must show is that the underwriting system is related to loan performance. Moreover, the clarity of the performance objectives in lending has been enhanced by the growing use of credit scoring and other forms of automated underwriting. After all, any automated underwriting system is explicitly designed to determine the impact of observable characteristics (of applicants, loans, and/or properties) on some measure of loan performance. The clear logic of such a system activates the stronger court standards for proving business necessity.

As noted in section 10.2.2, the *Uniform Guidelines* call for a defendant in a case involving employment discrimination to show that "the selection procedure is predictive of or significantly correlated with important elements of job performance." We believe that this standard can be much more precise in the underwriting context. Specifically, a proof of business necessity should require a multivariate, performance-based analysis. Requirements for such an analysis are discussed in the next section.

Finally, guidelines for proving business necessity in fair-lending cases should include a fairness principle designed to rule out the possibility of disparate-impact discrimination. The fairness principle in the *Uniform Guidelines* captures some forms of disparate-impact discrimination in underwriting. This principle will correctly declare an underwriting system to be unfair if it alters the set of credit characteristics, or the weights placed on them, in a manner that is not consistent with statistically based evidence and that is unfavorable to minority applicants.[15] If, for example, a lender increases the weight placed on, say, down-payment capacity beyond what is justified by a performance-based statistical analysis, and people in some protected class tend to have lower down-payment capacity than whites, then loans made to people in the protected class will perform better than their (innacurate) loan performance scores indicate. The fairness principle in the *Uniform Guidelines* declares such an outcome to be unfair.

This fairness principle does not correctly identify disparate-impact discrimination, however, when it is associated with credit characteristics that the lender cannot observe.[15] Consider the case discussed in chapter 9 in which the members of some protected class have poorer unobservable characteristics than do whites.[16] This is a plausible outcome in mortgage markets. As explained earlier, people in some historically disadvantaged groups have lower average creditworthiness on many characteristics, only some of which lenders can observe. In that case, lenders have an incentive to set higher underwriting standards for member of such a class, that is, to practice disparate-treatment discrimination. Because such disparate treatment is illegal and relatively easy to observe, the lender may turn to disparate-impact discrimination instead. As discussed in chapter 9, lenders can approximate the outcome of disparate treatment by altering the underwriting weights on variables that are correlated with group membership, that is, by practicing disparate-impact discrimination. In this case, the outcome is an underwriting system that gives lower scores to members of the protected class (because they have relatively low values of characteristics that the system overweights) and that *accurately* predicts average group performance. Such an underwriting system, defined to include disparate-impact discrimination, explicitly passes the fairness standard in the *Uniform Guidelines*. A revised standard is therefore clearly needed for fair lending. As explained in chapter 9, it should not be permissible to use a business necessity standard to justify behavior explicitly defined as disparate-impact discrimination.

A general principle of fairness was declared by the Supreme Court in the *Griggs* decision: "[A]ny tests used must measure the person for the job and not the person in the abstract" (p. 436). In other words, it is entirely legitimate for an employer (or, by inference, a lender) to rely on observable characteristics of an applicant to the extent that they are related to the relevant performance objective, but it is not appropriate for the applicant's membership in a protected class to affect the decision in any way. A specific fairness principle consistent with this formulation was developed in section 9.3.4. According to this principle, the fairest test is the one that does the best job of predicting performance *within a group*. In other words, such a test is designed to ensure that underwriting weights are based solely on a link to performance, not to the likelihood that a person belongs to a particular group. Like the fairness principle in the *Uniform Guidelines*, our principle recognizes that a test is unfair to the extent that it deviates from performance-based underwriting weights (or sets of credit variables) in a way that places a protected class at a disadvantage. Because within-group comparisons cannot be influenced by average differences across groups, however, this new principle, unlike the principle in the *Uniform Guidelines*, captures disparate-impact discrimination associated with across-group differences in performance based on characteristics that cannot be observed. Thus, this new principle captures all forms of disparate-impact discrimination.

A point worth emphasizing is that our proposed fairness standard is designed to identify practices with group-neutral outcomes, not procedures that ignore group membership. As shown in chapter 9, a statistical analysis of loan performance that ignores a borrower's minority status may result in a scoring system that has disparate-impact discrimination built into it. The only way to ensure that the estimated coefficients of credit variables do not reflect minority status is to include minority status as a separate variable. Fairness cannot be achieved by assuming, incorrectly, that minority status has no effect on a statistical procedure. Instead, fairness requires taking steps to ensure that minority status has no impact, direct or indirect, on a scoring system. In most cases, people designing underwriting systems must statistically control for minority status (and then exclude minority status from the score calculation) to ensure that this standard is met.

10.3.2 New Fair-Lending Enforcement Tools

The central question in any set of regulations to enforce FaHA and ECOA is how to determine whether a given underwriting system has a disparate impact on a protected class after accounting for all legitimate business considerations. In this section we present two new tools that build on the above principles to provide answers to this question. In our judgment, these tools integrate many aspects of the legal standards that have developed for disparate-impact cases.

They show what is required (1) for an enforcement official to build a prima facie case of discrimination, with explicit attention to the appropriate pool, and of causation; (2) for a lender to establish that an underwriting system can be fully justified on the grounds of legitimate business considerations; and (3) for an enforcement official or lender to determine whether an underwriting system meets the fairness principle presented in the previous section. Although these aspects are treated separately in most legal discussions, the multivariate nature of the problem requires, in our judgment, that they be treated in an integrated manner. Moreover, the tools developed in this section are designed to capture disparate-treatment discrimination as well as disparate-impact discrimination.

These new tools build on the analysis presented in chapters 6 and 9. One tool is a type of loan approval regression, and the other is based on loan performance data. Our focus is on tools for uncovering discrimination in loan approval, but we also show how the loan performance tool could be applied to unmasking discrimination in other types of lender behavior.

10.3.2.1 Pooled Loan Approval Regressions with Lender-Specific Estimates of Discrimination

The first new enforcement tool developed here is a loan approval regression designed to capture both disparate-impact and disparate-treatment discrimination. In this section, we describe this tool in detail and illustrate how it works using the data from the Boston Fed Study.

This tool builds on several key conclusions from our earlier analysis. First, even if some lenders use idiosyncratic underwriting standards that are not linked to loan performance, the average standards observed for a set of lenders are likely to predict loan performance quite well. Second, legitimate variation in underwriting standards across lenders is likely to be associated with variation in portfolios among lenders; as a result, such legitimate variation can be captured by interacting underwriting variables with portfolio characteristics. Thus, the tool we propose is a regression that explains loan approval decisions for a sample of lenders as a function of applicant, loan, and property characteristics and portfolio interactions.

To be more specific, this tool is distinguished by four key characteristics:

1. It uses a sample of loan applications consisting of all the applications by minority households for a given loan product, region, and time (or a random sample, if the number of such applications is very large) plus a random sample of white applications at the same institutions.[17] The sample of white applications should be at least as large as the sample of minority applications. Lenders with only a few minority applications (less than ten, say) would be dropped from the sample.

2. It includes the types of interactions among loan terms that were discussed and estimated in section 6.3.2.[18] One such interaction, for example, is an interaction between the debt-to-income ratio and all other credit characteristics. This type of interaction is important to separate nonlinearities in an underwriting model that is common across lenders from differences in underwriting across lenders that are associated with a lender's portfolio.

3. It includes interactions between key characteristics of a lender's portfolio and credit characteristics, such as those discussed and estimated in section 6.3.3. The average debt-to-income ratio for a lender's loans, for example, might influence its underwriting weights. Including this type of interaction is important to separate legitimate differences in underwriting standards across lenders from differences that impose a disparate impact on applicants from protected classes.

4. It includes both lender-specific fixed effects and interactions between these effects and minority status.[19] These interactions result in an estimate of the minority status coefficient (and hence of discrimination) for each lender in the sample.

This type of regression model provides an estimate of discrimination for each lender, namely, the coefficient of the minority status variable interacted with that lender's fixed effect.[20] If this coefficient is negative and statistically significant, indicating that the lender is less likely to approve minority applications than equivalent white applications, then it is appropriate to conclude that the lender is practicing discrimination. In legal terms, this type of finding builds a prima facie case that discrimination exists, as discussed in section 10.2.1.1.

Specifying the regression model in this way is intended to allow underwriting standards to vary across lenders in ways that are associated with lenders' portfolios. Following the analysis in earlier chapters, any remaining intergroup differences in loan approval for a single lender can legitimately be attributed to either disparate-treatment discrimination by that lender or to idiosyncratic features of that lender's underwriting standards that have an adverse impact on minority applicants without any clear business necessity, that is, to disparate-impact discrimination.

This approach taken in this model does not, of course, directly control for the link between underwriting standards and loan performance and therefore does not directly address the business necessity issue. Instead, it builds on the view that elements of a lender's underwriting standards that are justified on the grounds of business necessity will appear in two places: the average underwriting weights in a sample of lenders and variation in underwriting weights associated with a particular lender's portfolio. Any unfavorable treatment of minority applicants that remains after controlling for these two factors is considered to be discrimination.

Because it does not involve performance information, this approach to interpreting underwriting standards is not exact. For example, it could miss disparate-impact discrimination that is built into average underwriting standards or that is correlated with a particular lender's portfolio. Moreover, some legitimate variation in underwriting standards across lenders could be incorrectly classified as disparate-impact discrimination if the regression does not control for the relevant features of a lender's portfolio. Nevertheless, we believe that *this approach provides the best possible way to identify both disparate-treatment and disparate-impact discrimination when loan performance information is not available.* It is entirely appropriate for building a prima facie case, which requires only presumption, not proof.

Our analysis of this approach places us at odds with several scholars who have rejected a loan approval regression that pools observations for many lenders on the grounds that the huge differences in underwriting standards across lenders cannot possibly be captured by a pooled regression (Courchane, Nebhut, and Nickerson, 2000; Stengel and Glennon, 1999). Lenders may, indeed, have very different underwriting standards from each other, and the standards of individual lenders may have idiosyncratic elements that are difficult to incorporate into a pooled regression model. However, idiosyncratic underwriting standards are exactly the type of standards that cannot be justified on the grounds of business necessity and that cannot be sustained in a full-information, competitive environment. Legitimate differences in underwriting standards are those associated with differences in the characteristics of the loans that lenders attract, and these are the differences that are captured through interactions between underwriting variables and portfolio characteristics.

Scholars who reject the type of loan approval regression we are advocating here defend separate loan approval regressions for each lender on the grounds (1) that such an approach is the best way to isolate disparate-treatment discrimination and (2) that disparate-impact discrimination cannot be definitively isolated without performance information. We think these arguments miss the point. Fair-lending enforcement officials are charged with finding all forms of discrimination, not just discrimination that takes the form of disparate treatment. Moreover, the distinction between disparate-treatment and disparate-impact discrimination is quite misleading in mortgage lending, in which these two forms of discrimination can be regarded as close substitutes for one another. In addition, the literature on mortgage markets reveals that legitimate variation in underwriting standards cannot be random or idiosyncratic but must instead be related to the types of loans a lender attracts. Enhancing controls for the unique features of a lender's underwriting standards, the advantage of separate regressions, is therefore roughly equivalent to introducing variation in underwriting standards that are unlikely to have a legitimate business justification. Thus we reject separate regressions, which are based on the presumption that all lender underwriting standards are legitimate (or, equivalently, that disparate-impact discrimination is not worth investigating), in favor of pooled regressions, which are based on the presumption that legitimate differences in underwriting standards across lenders are associated with differences in lenders' loan portfolios.

In our judgment, therefore, a negative, significant minority status coefficient for a lender in the regression model we have outlined establishes a prima facie case that the lender is practicing either disparate-treatment or disparate-impact discrimination. This is a much stricter standard for a prima facie case than the four-fifths rule or its lending analog. Instead of simply demonstrating a disparity in loan approvals, it formally accounts for the "pool" and "causation" requirements in the Supreme Court's standards through an appropriate multivariate statistical procedure.

This type of finding should shift the burden of proof to the lender. Once a prima facie case for the existence of discrimination has been made using the tool described in this section, the charge that a particular lender discriminates should not be removed unless it can be countered with loan performance information. Specifically, to escape the charge of discrimination, a lender must provide a business necessity defense for any idiosyncratic differences that are determined to exist between its underwriting practices and those observed in the market as a whole.[21] This defense must include a demonstration that these differences promote the accuracy of the lender's within-group loan performance predictions. This is, of course, the fairness principle presented earlier.

A loan approval regression based on applications to a single lender cannot be used to overrule a prima facie case based on this approach; that is, it cannot be used to prove that a particular lender's practices are justified by legitimate business considerations. A loan approval regression for a single lender can determine only whether that lender uses the same rules for applicants from a protected class and other applicants. Such a regression cannot determine whether a lender's underwriting scheme is accurately linked to loan performance. In other words, a lender-specific regression cannot identify disparate-impact discrimination. Allowing a lender to show business necessity on the basis of such a regression is therefore equivalent to declaring that lenders can practice disparate-impact discrimination with impunity.

The sampling procedure for this new tool differs from the one used by the Boston Fed Study, because it selects white applications only from lenders with at least a minimum number of minority applications. This change in sampling strategy from the one used in the Boston Fed Study, which is designed to ensure that a minority status coefficient can be estimated for each lender in the sample, has four important advantages.

First, because it is based on all lenders with applications from at least a few minority households (or on a random sample of the applications to these lenders), this sampling procedure ensures that all lenders who practice discrimination have a nonzero probability of ending up in the sample. For example, lenders who attract relatively high-quality applications from the members of a protected class but who then discriminate against these applicants will not be exempt from examination, as they would be under an analog to the four-fifths rule in the *Uniform Guidelines*.

The procedure also generates a sample that includes applications to some nondiscriminating lenders. This is entirely appropriate. Any system that exempts certain lenders from examination before their discriminatory behavior can be observed makes it possible for discriminating lenders to avoid an investigation by changing behavior that is related to the examination decision but not to discrimination. The same principle applies in many other settings, so, for example, random audits have long been a part of the income tax enforcement system. Moreover, the presence of nondiscriminating lenders in the sample implies that the underwriting weights, which are, of course, crucial for isolating discrimination, are estimated for a representative sample of lenders. This increases the credibility of these estimates and therefore increases the credibility of the conclusions about discrimination that are drawn from the results of the regression.

The advantage resulting from the inclusion of nondiscriminating lenders in the sample studied would be preserved even if budgetary concerns restricted the study to a random sample of minority applications, instead of all such applications. With a random sample, of course, some discriminating lenders would be excluded from the regression. Because selection is random, however, no discriminatory lender would be able to influence the probability that it would be examined—or caught. As a result, the use of a random sample would preserve the integrity of the enforcement system.

In our judgment, the combination of a random sample and a multivariate procedure is also entirely consistent with the "appropriate pool" requirement developed by the courts. The key purpose of this requirement is to make certain that across-group differences in treatment based on differences in group characteristics that a lender can legitimately consider are not mistaken for disparate-impact discrimination. The use of a random sample ensures that applications from different groups are all drawn in the same way from the pool of applicants, and the use of statistical controls for applicant, loan, and property characteristics ensures that across-group differences in these characteristics have been fully accounted for.

Second, by pooling data for many lenders, this sampling procedure increases the sample size available for a regression analysis and therefore results in more precise estimates of the underwriting weights employed by lenders.[22] This advantage obviously complements the first advantage. The more precisely the underwriting weights are estimated, the more likely it is that a regression analysis will accurately distinguish between discrimination and differences in treatment across groups that are associated with differences in groups' average credit characteristics.

The expansion of sample size also helps to address a concern raised by Calem and Canner (1995), Calem and Longhofer (2000), and Stengel and Glennon (1999), namely, that some underwriting variables appear in so few loan files that they cannot be incorporated into a regression analysis of one lender's loan approval decisions. Even if it is rare for a single lender, any legitimate underwriting variable is likely to appear often enough in a large across-lender sample of loans that its underwriting weight can be estimated. Indeed, if it does not appear often enough to be included in a regression, it is difficult to understand how a lender could determine its impact on loan performance, which is a requirement for giving it a legitimate weight in underwriting decisions.

Third, our approach makes it possible to draw conclusions about discrimination by lenders that do not have enough loan applications to support a lender-specific regression. It is not, of course, possible to estimate discrimination for lenders with only a few applications from minority households.[23] However, the number of observations required to estimate a separate minority-status coefficient for a lender is far less than the number of observations needed to estimate coefficients for all the variables in the loan approval regression.

Fourth, this approach makes it possible for different fair-lending enforcement agencies to pool their efforts. Many loan products are offered by lenders regulated by different agencies, so these agencies can take advantage of economies of scale, such as more precise coefficients and lower personnel requirements, that come from considering in the same regression all the lenders that offer a particular loan product in a given region at a given time.

We do not have access to a sample of loan applications drawn using the sampling procedures developed above. For the sake of illustration, however, we can make use of the Boston Fed Study's data, which was collected using a sampling strategy that is similar in some ways to the one we propose for our enforcement tool. To be specific, the Boston Fed Study began by drawing all minority applications from the pool, which is the same as the first step of our proposed procedure, and then added a random sample of white applications from all lenders in the original pool, which differs from our procedure in that it does not restrict the sample of white applications to lenders that receive minority applications. As a result, the Boston Fed Study sample may have few white applications for some lenders that receive minority applications, thereby making it difficult to estimate a separate minority status coefficient for these lenders. Moreover, as discussed in chapter 6, we were not able to identify the lenders for some of the applications in the Boston Fed Study's sample. This limits still further our ability to estimate separate, lender-specific minority status coefficients.[24]

Our matching procedure identified 115 lenders in the Boston Fed Study's data. We had enough minority and white observations to estimate a separate minority status coefficient for twenty-seven of these lenders. These twenty-seven lenders, which accounted for 448 out of the 561 total applications by minority households, included the ten lenders with the largest number of applications but also included eight lenders with twenty-five or fewer applications.[25] The remaining eighty-eight lenders and 113 minority applications were combined; that is, we estimated a single minority status coefficient for this group.

On the basis of our analysis in chapter 6, we estimate a loan approval model in which underwriting characteristics are interacted with the debt-to-income ratio and with the difference between the lender's average debt-to-income ratio and debt-to-income ratio for the applicant. In this model, the estimated minority status coefficient was negative and statistically significant for two of the twenty-seven lenders.[26] These lenders were two of the largest lenders, with 104 and 37 minority applications, respectively. This result, which does not appear to depend on the precise specification we used, builds a strong prima facia case for discrimination by these two lenders.[27] The estimated minority status coefficients are similar in magnitude, but not statistically significant, for eight smaller lenders.[28] These eight lenders account for an additional forty-five minority applications in the sample. Moreover, the estimated minority status coefficients are negative for twenty-three of the twenty-seven lenders. More precise estimates, but not necessarily more signs of discrimination, undoubtedly could be obtained with the sampling plan described earlier (and, of course, with more complete identification of lenders).

Finally, we also estimated a minority-status coefficient for the set of applications received by the remaining 88 lenders. This coefficient was close to zero and not statistically significant. This finding helps to put the above results (and, indeed, the results of the Boston Fed Study) in perspective. Minority-white differences in underwriting in the Boston Fed Study's sample clearly come from within-lender comparisons of minority and white applications. There is no sign that estimated minority-white differences in loan approval reflect a denial of minority applications by one set of lenders compared to an approval of comparable white applications by a different set of lenders.

10.3.2.2   A Performance-Based Tool to Find Discrimination in Loan Approval

The second type of fair-lending enforcement tool that we propose involves the use of loan performance information. Up to now, the fair-lending enforcement agencies have not employed loan performance information in their investigations, although collecting such information is clearly within their authority. In this section, we present a performance-based tool for evaluating discrimination in loan approval and show how it could be adapted to test for redlining. The following section modifies this tool for use in investigating discrimination in other types of lender behavior.

As explained in chapter 9, the availability of loan performance data makes it possible to test for discrimination in loan approval without estimating a loan approval regression. Moreover, the approach developed there picks up discrimination regardless of whether it takes the form of disparate treatment or of disparate impact.

In an enforcement setting, the test developed in chapter 9 has five steps. The first step is to select a sample of loans and to gather all the information in the files for the loans in that sample. A random sample of loans from a single lender could be used, if the sample size is large enough. However, pooling loans across lenders could greatly increase the precision of the estimates without introducing any methodological difficulties, so long as all the lenders in the sample use the same loan performance criterion (e.g., default) and draw from the same broad pool of applicants. If possible, the data set extracted from the loan files should include all the information available to lenders.

The second step is to estimate a loan performance model. The dependent variable in this model is a measure of loan performance, and the explanatory variables are applicant, loan, and property characteristics observed at the time of loan application, plus lender fixed effects, if the sample is pooled across lenders.[29] The explanatory variables in the model should also include indicators of group membership. The model should consider all of the methodological issues that arise in this setting, such as the choice of functional form and the possibility of selection bias. The objective of the model is to obtain the best possible explanation of loan performance based on information in loan files.

The third step is to select a sample of applications to a particular lender that come from the same applicant pool as the loans selected in step 1. There is no need to combine data across lenders for this step, because from here on, the test proceeds one lender at a time.

The fourth step is to calculate a loan performance score for each application in the sample selected in step 3 based on the estimated coefficients from the loan performance model. The coefficients of the minority status variables obviously are not included in this calculation.

The fifth and final step is to compare the minority composition of the applications actually approved by the lender with the minority composition of the applications that have the highest loan performance scores. If A applications were actually approved, then the highest-ranking A applications are used for this calculation. The appropriate test statistic is a simple difference-of-means test. A significantly higher minority composition for the highest-ranking applications than for actual loans is an indication of discrimination.

One great advantage of this test is that it does not require the investigator to know anything about a lender's actual underwriting procedures. Instead, it requires information on loan performance and some understanding of the factors that influence loan performance. Of course, a lender's underwriting procedures are likely to be related to performance, and they can be consulted when specifying the loan performance regression. An investigator using this test need only be concerned, however, with finding the best-predicting nondiscriminatory loan performance regression and need not worry about whether this regression accurately describes a lender's actual underwriting standards. The objective is accurate prediction of performance, not accurate replication of a lender's procedures.

Another advantage of this test is that it automatically picks up both disparate-treatment and disparate-impact discrimination, although it does not distinguish between them. Both types of discrimination operate by lowering the number of minority applications that are accepted compared to the number that would be accepted based on group-neutral business considerations alone. As explained earlier, the ability to capture both types of discrimination is particularly important in the context of mortgage lending, because the available evidence suggests that the distinction between these two forms of discrimination is difficult to make and, indeed, that lenders may be able to accomplish the same loan approval outcomes by practicing either form.

A significant difference in mean treatment between minorities and whites under this test establishes a prima facie case for discrimination. As with all other tests used to establish the existence of discriminatory practices, a lender who is found to be discriminating using this test should be given the opportunity to provide evidence in its defense. In this case, such evidence would have to take the form of a comparable test that (1) is based on an alternative specification of the loan performance model that boosts within-group predictability compared to the investigator's specification and (2) finds no significant difference between the minority compositions of actual loans and of the highest-scoring applications.[30] (The first of these criteria is, of course, the fairness principle derived earlier).

Another striking feature of this test is that it automatically provides information relevant for the third step in a disparate-impact discrimination case, namely, establishing whether alternative, less discriminatory practices exist. A finding of disparate-impact discrimination involves a comparison of outcomes from a statistical analysis prepared by the regulator to those that actually occurred using the underwriting practices of the lender. The regulator's statistical analysis produces loan approval scores that could be used to make loan approval decisions. This statistical analysis is therefore equivalent to an alternative underwriting system. A finding of disparate-impact discrimination implies that this alternative system exists and is less discriminatory than the system actually used by the lender.[31]

Finally, this test could also be applied to redlining. For this application, the last step should compare the share of high-scoring applications that are linked to houses in minority neighborhoods with the share of loans actually offered to purchase properties in minority neighborhoods. A finding that a significantly higher share of the high-scoring applications than of actual loans are in minority neighborhoods would be an indication of redlining. As before, a lender found to be practicing redlining by this test should be given the opportunity to refute the charge, but only with performance-based information, and only by showing that its underwriting scheme boosts the accuracy of performance predictions within a neighborhood type relative to the scheme estimated by the investigators.

10.3.2.3 Performance-Based Enforcement Tools for Other Types of Discrimination

The performance-based tests for discrimination in loan approval discussed in section 10.3.2.2 can be modified to look for discrimination in credit-scoring or other automated underwriting systems and to look for discrimination in loan pricing.[32] Consider, first, an automated underwriting system. The procedure in 10.3.2.2 applies to underwriting decisions based on an automated underwriting system, but it cannot be applied to an automated underwriting system itself, that is, to the scores it produces. Our performance-based tool can readily be adapted, however, to a situation in which scores, but not underwriting decisions, are observed. In this case, the highest-ranking applications based on the investigator's loan performance model should be compared to the highest-ranking applications based on the automated underwriting system. A finding that the minority percentage is higher for the first set of applications than for the second is a sign of discrimination. Such an adaptation requires some cutoff point or points. If, for example, the automated underwriting system classifies A applications as "automatic accepts" (or places them in some other desirable category), then the highest-ranking A applications from the two ranking schemes could be compared. Alternatively, the test could compare the minority compositions of the highest-ranking half of the applications under the two schemes.[33]

Note that this test can be conducted even if the investigator does not know anything about the (presumably proprietary) formula that defines the automated underwriting system. All the investigator needs to perform the test is the loan performance score for each application in the sample based on that system and data on the variables that went into it. A finding that the automated underwriting system results in fewer highly rated minority applications than does the investigator's regression creates a prima facie case that the system involves discrimination. The institution responsible for the system can escape this charge by showing that there is a justification, based on loan performance and backed by statistics, for the composition of its formula. As in other cases, the institution must show that, compared to the investigator's loan performance regression, its formula boosts within-group predictive power.

Another important question that can be addressed with the tests developed here is whether lenders practice discrimination in setting mortgage interest rates. As noted throughout this book, this question is becoming more important over time as lenders switch from rationing credit to pricing credit according to risk. One way to address this question is to ask whether minority and white borrowers with the same predicted loan performance are charged different interest rates. Such an approach can look at all elements of interest rates that are reflected in the final mortgage contract, including overages, points, and certain fees. Although such an approach provides a more comprehensive look at discrimination in interest rate–setting behavior than the clever studies of overages that were discussed in chapter 7, it must, like those studies, find a way to control for market conditions at the time of application.[34]

More formally, a test to determine whether lenders practice discrimination in setting mortgage rates has the same structure as the performance-based test for discrimination in loan approval. The steps in the test are as follows:

1. Select a sample of loans for a given product/market/time for which performance can be observed.

2. Estimate a loan performance model for the sample.

3. Select a sample of applications from the same pool.

4. Calculate the predicted performance of each approved application in the second sample, assuming an average interest rate.

5. Estimate a regression model with the actual interest rate (including points and, perhaps, selected charges) as the dependent variable and predicted performance, minority status, and various other factors as the explanatory variables.

This test differs in several ways from the test for discrimination in loan approval. First, the loan performance model can include the actual interest rate and other variables, such as the housing payment–to–income ratio, that depend on it. These variables cannot be included in the regression for the loan approval test, because the actual interest rate is observed only for accepted loans, and step 4 would be impossible for applications that were not accepted.[35]

Second, loan performance is predicted just for accepted applications, not for all applications. Note, however, that the predicted loan performance in step 4 of this new test must be calculated on the basis of variables that reflect an average interest rate, not a loan's actual interest rate. A lender's average interest rate should be used in calculating each loan's housing payment–to–income ratio, for example. After all, the point of this test is to determine whether the interest rate charged to a customer is justified on the basis of the loan's predicted performance as determined by factors other than the interest rate. It makes no sense to justify a higher interest rate because a high interest rate drives up the housing payment–to–income ratio!

Third, the regression in the test's final step is designed to determine whether the trade-off between interest rate (price) and predicted performance (risk) is the same for minority and white customers. This regression need not be linear in form. It could, for example, include predicted performance and predicted performance squared as explanatory variables, should they both prove to be statistically significant. The key point is simply to determine whether interest rates are higher for minority applicants than for white applicants after controlling for the price-risk trade-off. Specifically, a finding that the coefficient of the minority status variable is positive and significant implies that the lender is practicing discrimination in its rate-setting behavior.[36]

Finally, the regression in the fifth step does not contain just predicted performance and minority status as explanatory variables, but also includes controls for market conditions and perhaps other factors, such as loan characteristics associated with higher origination costs. Variables to account for market conditions could be just dummy variables for the time of application, such as one variable for each week or, if there are enough observations, for each day. Indicators of average interest rates in the region at the time of application also could be used.

Any additional factors included in the regression must be selected with great care, however. Longhofer and Calem (1999) argue that an analysis of discrimination in loan pricing needs to control for factors that affect the cost of the mortgage and for the bargaining skills of the lender and of the potential borrower. We do not find this argument compelling. Rate-setting behavior clearly might depend on loan costs as well as on the probability of default. The right way to address this possibility, however, is to use a measure of loan performance, such as profitability, that includes costs, so that costs are incorporated into the loan performance regression and the associated calculations for predicted performance. In this case, adding cost variables to the interest rate regression would be redundant. Using loan default as the measure of loan performance and including cost variables in the interest rate regression is clearly an inferior solution, because the link between these variables and costs is not observed and must instead be assumed. As a result, this approach makes it impossible to rule out the possibility that the "cost" variables are simply tools for disparate-impact discrimination.[37]

In our view, variables to measure negotiating skill also should not be included in an enforcement-based interest-rate regression. Suppose a regulatory agency conducts an interest rate regression without these variables and finds a disparate impact, that is, finds that minority borrowers are charged significantly higher interest rates. Because variables to measure negotiating skill are likely to be correlated with minority status, including them in the regression could change this result, and, in particular, could eliminate the significant minority status coefficient. The question is whether a finding of this type could be interpreted as a sign that no discrimination exists. This question is equivalent to asking whether practices that allow a lender to take advantage of some borrowers' poor negotiating skills can be justified on the grounds of business necessity; after all, the only way to counter a finding of disparate impact is to show that it results from practices that meet this justification. In fact, however, a lender cannot gain a negotiating advantage over some borrower without asymmetric information and hence imperfect competition, and, as discussed earlier, the business necessity defense does not extend to noncompetitive practices.

The most obvious way to use the type of interest rate equation recommended in the test's fifth step is to determine whether a single lender discriminates in setting interest rates. Another possible use is to determine whether the process by which minorities and whites are linked to lenders results in higher rates for minorities than for whites after accounting for the trade-off between price and risk. This more exploratory application of this tool, which requires pooling data across lenders, cannot produce conclusions about discrimination by a particular lender. Nevertheless, even for the same loan product, minority and white borrowers appear to patronize lenders with different interest rate policies, at least in some markets. Moreover, the available evidence about predatory pricing indicates that some lenders use particularly aggressive rate-setting rules with minority customers. Fair-lending enforcement officials could determine the magnitude of the resulting interest rate disparities, and hence the urgency of the need for solutions, by regressing actual interest rates on minority status and on predicted loan performance.

There is, of course, a precedent for concern about disparate outcomes that are not necessarily connected with discrimination by individual lenders, namely, CRA. To be specific, a lender may not be able to meet the credit needs of all the neighborhoods in its lending territory, which is its obligation under CRA, simply by eliminating discriminatory behavior. If not, then CRA declares that the goal of equal access to credit is so important that the lender must take additional steps. Similarly, eliminating discrimination in interest rate–setting behavior may not be sufficient to eliminate disparities in interest rates between equally qualified minority and white borrowers. If not, the federal government may want to pass legislation that gives lenders incentives to work toward the elimination of these disparities while protecting their legitimate business interests.[38] After all, if they exist, disparities of this type would constitute a major barrier to homeownership for minority households.

An analysis of interest rate disparities could proceed in several stages. The first stage would be to estimate a regression without any lender fixed effects or interactions. This regression would indicate whether minorities face higher rates than whites, controlling for the average price-risk trade-off. The next stage would be to add lender fixed effects. A finding that this addition eliminates estimated minority-white differences in interest rates from the first stage (if any) would indicate that minorities face relatively high interest rates at a given risk level because they tend to patronize lenders with relatively high rates. The third stage would be to add interactions between lender fixed effects and loan performance. A finding that adding these variable eliminates estimated minority-white differences in interest rates from the second stage (if any) would indicate that minorities face relatively high interest rates because they tend to patronize lenders with a relatively harsh trade-off between interest rates and risk. These types of findings would be invaluable guides to the development of policies for eliminating minority-white interest rate disparities.

10.4 Current Fair-Lending Enforcement Procedures

As explained in chapter 2, the federal responsibility for fair-lending enforcement is shared by the financial regulatory agencies, the FTC, HUD, and the Department of Justice. The first line of enforcement at depository lenders comes from the financial regulatory agencies, which have many oversight responsibilities other than those involving fair lending.[39] These agencies have jointly developed a set of enforcement procedures, which are presented in a guide published by the Federal Financial Institutions Examination Council (FFIEC, 1999). Several enforcement agencies also have developed additional regression-based procedures for use in fair-lending enforcement, which are discussed below.

A particularly concise and helpful description of these enforcement procedures, as implemented by the Federal Reserve, is provided by Calem and Canner (1995).[40] We begin our analysis with a review and discussion of this article, which covers both traditional enforcement methods and new regression-based procedures. Alternative procedures developed by OCC, as described by Stengel and Glennon (1999) and Courchane, Nebhut, and Nickerson (2000), are also discussed to the extent that they differ from the procedures of the Federal Reserve.

10.4.1 *Traditional Enforcement Methods*

Calem and Canner (1995) begin by describing what they call "the traditional fair-lending enforcement method," which is essentially the method describe in the FFIEC (1999) manual.

Both traditionally and now, fair lending examinations generally begin with a review of a lender's written loan policies and procedures, and with interviews of lending personnel. In this way, examiners determine the underwriting standards used by the creditor. There are two reasons for undertaking this review: to confirm that the policies and procedures are not inherently discriminatory, and to provide a basis for assessing whether loan policies are applied consistently across applicants.

To help assess the consistency of underwriting decisions, examiners traditionally have applied a technique known as "comparative loan file review"
or "matched-pair analysis." Essentially, this procedure can be described as
follows. The examiners begin by selecting a sample of applications. Next,
they note on "Applicant Profile Worksheets" the key factors considered
in the underwriting decision, and the disposition of each application. The
examiners then evaluate the information on these spreadsheets to identify
potential instances of disparate treatment of similarly qualified applicants.
This review for unequal treatment covers possible disparities in loan disposition, credit terms, or the process by which decisions were reached. The
examiners then go back to any specific loan files where analysis of spread-
sheet data suggests a problem. They more closely examine these particular
files and seek explanations from bank management before making any final
determination as to discriminatory treatment. (pp. 118–119)

Calem and Canner then proceed to discuss various problems with
this approach. Our own evaluation, which is presented below, builds
on this analysis. According to Calem and Canner:

The traditional matched-pair examination procedure suffers from two important limitations. First, it is difficult for examiners to find applicants that
are perfect, or even close, matches; some differences in underlying financial
or property related characteristics nearly always remain.

Such differences in creditworthiness make it difficult to identify cases of
unequal treatment. Even if there exist close matches among an institution's
files, it may be difficult for an examiner to find them through manual effort
alone. Moreover, in some instances, there may not be many close matches
among the pool of applicants.

The second difficulty with the traditional matched-pair approach is that
even if some differences in treatment are detected, it is hard to determine
whether these are isolated events that do not result from discrimination, or
the result of a pattern or practice of discrimination. Differences in treatment
observed for a particular "matched pair" could be a purely random outcome
of the underwriting process.

For instance, purely by chance, the minority applicant in question may
have been assigned to a loan underwriter who applied the institution's
underwriting standards more rigidly. Furthermore, some of the institution's
non-minority applicants may have been treated similarly, but they may not
have been included among the files examined. In other words, the traditional approach was not well-suited to developing a statistical basis for
documenting a fair-lending complaint. (p. 119)

The crux of the two limitations Calem and Canner discuss in the
above quotation is that it is difficult to find one or more loan files
submitted by a white household that are truly comparable to any
given loan file submitted by a minority household. Without a comparable file, an investigator cannot determine whether a particular

minority file is treated differently simply because it comes from a minority applicant. In other words, comparability is critical for accurately identifying disparate-treatment discrimination. If no file comparable to a particular minority file is found, the investigator cannot shed any light on the possibility that this type of discrimination exists (the first limitation), and any file that is declared to be "comparable" on the basis of some credit characteristics might differ from the minority file in some other way that explains any differences in treatment between the two files (the second limitation).

Another way to express these limitations is to say that it is difficult, if not impossible, to make judgments about the use of a multivariate procedure, such as loan underwriting, employing just one pair of observations. A multivariate procedure is one in which a decision is based on the weighted values of several different variables. In the case of underwriting, a comparison of one minority and one white application yields valid inferences about the treatment of that minority applicant only if those two applications are both comparable on all applicant, loan, and property characteristics and representative of other loans with those characteristics. This is an extremely demanding standard. Moreover, any procedure that does not meet the two above conditions could run into several problems not mentioned by Calem and Canner. For example, a case in which a minority applicant is expected to meet a higher standard could be mistaken for a case in which "comparable" minority and white applications are both approved.

10.4.2 The Use of Regression Procedures by Fair-Lending Enforcement Agencies

Several of the fair-lending enforcement agencies have supplemented traditional enforcement procedures with regression analysis for individual large lenders. This approach has been used, for example, by the Justice Department (Siskin and Cupingood, 1996), OCC (Stengel and Glennon, 1999; Courchane, Nebhut, and Nickerson, 2000), and the Federal Reserve Board (Calem and Canner, 1995; Avery, Beeson and Calem, 1997; Calem and Longhofer, 2000).

We begin by following the discussion of Calem and Canner (1995), who explain that these regression-based procedures were developed at the Federal Reserve in an attempt to overcome the limitations of traditional enforcement techniques. The Federal

Reserve's regression-based technique involves supplementing HMDA data for a sample of loan applications, both minority and white, submitted to a particular lender with data from the loan files for those applications.[41] The procedure calls for a sample of about 100 applications from both minorities and whites and is not attempted if the available number of applications falls far short of this target. According to Calem and Canner, "[o]f the roughly 1,000 commercial banks supervised by the Federal Reserve System, about 500 are subject to HMDA and of these, about 100 have a sufficient volume of loan applications to be evaluated under the new statistical technique" (p. 121).

Once the data from the 200 (or so) applications have been collected, the next step in the procedure is to estimate a loan approval regression with logit analysis. In the words of Calem and Canner,

[t]o gauge the effect of applicant race on the disposition of loan applications, examiners, in consultation with Reserve Bank economists, construct a statistical model of the lender's underwriting decisions. This model is developed on the basis of information gathered from the bank's written underwriting guidelines and from interviews with loan officers. Factors considered important to the decision of whether to approve an application are included as explanatory variables in the model of loan disposition. (p. 121)

The next step involves interpreting the results of this regression. Calem and Canner describe this step in some detail:

If the results of the statistical analysis indicate that the race of the applicant is a statistically significant predictor of loan disposition, then this is viewed as an initial indication that a pattern or practice of discrimination may exist.

However, the statistical model is necessarily an abstraction that can only partially replicate the loan approval process. Each and every factor that might reasonably influence an underwriting decision cannot possibly be incorporated into a model. Therefore, the statistical results alone are not considered definitive. In order to more fully evaluate the discrimination issue, examiners select specific loan files for closer review. (p. 123)

The loan files selected for further review are minority-white pairs "matched with respect to key underwriting variables" (p. 123) These are not random pairs, but instead are pairs thought to be ones in which disparate-treatment discrimination, if it exists, is likely to show up. More specifically,

The computer program identifies minority applicants who have been denied credit and who appear as well qualified as, or better than, white applicants who were approved. The program can also identify white applicants who are denied who appear to have been as well, or better qualified than, minority applicants who were approved. These are the cases for which a more intensive review are the most appropriate. (p. 123)

Once the loan files are selected for further review, the examiners try to identify any explanation for observed differences in treatment between comparable minority and white files that might have a legitimate business purpose. As Calem and Canner (1995) put it:[42]

As a result of this review, examiners may find that factors omitted from the model may account for these decisions.

For example, examiners may find that the property being purchased failed to meet zoning requirements or that the applicant was unable to document all reported income. Similarly, examiners may find that the model specification failed to adequately represent the true underwriting process. For example, the credit history variables specified in the model may not account for nuances in underwriting such as a distinction between revolving debt and installment debt in scoring late payments. (p. 124)

A similar discussion appears in Calem and Longhofer (2000), which provides examples of factors that arose in file reviews conducted as part of a fair-lending investigation of a particular lender—and after a regression analysis. In their words:

Other factors contributing to denial appeared to be more idiosyncratic in nature. These included, for instance, reliance on rental income coupled with a very-high back-end ratio, and issues pertaining to the adequacy of collateral coupled with a high loan-to-value ratio. Such factors, because they are unusual, cannot feasibly be controlled for in a statistical model. Again, examiners relied on a judgmental analysis to determine whether these reasons for rejection had been applied in a non-discriminatory manner.[43] (p. 16)

A similar argument is made by Stengel and Glennon (1999), who assert that "[a] statistical model cannot possible capture every single provision" (p. 325).

Calem and Canner's summary of this new technique emphasizes an issue that has been central to the analysis in this book, namely, that different lenders may have different underwriting standards. In particular, they argue that the postregression review of loan files is critical to ensure that lenders are not prevented from exercising their judgment:

The Federal Reserve's new fair-lending examination technique seeks to achieve a reasonable balance between bringing more statistical power to fair lending examinations and retaining examiner judgment. One concern in employing a statistical model to assess fair lending performance is that creditors may feel pressured to base their actual credit decisions strictly on an automated underwriting system, thus abandoning flexibility in their credit evaluations. The inherent flexibility in current underwriting decisions is desirable, as humans can bring to underwriting decisions the discretion and judgment that will allow individuals who might not appear credit-worthy to receive home loans. Lenders must be aware, however, that dis-cretion brings with it the increased possibility of unfair treatment. (p. 125)

Horne (1995) also emphasizes the advantages of preserving lender flexibility.

The regression-based procedures undertaken by the OCC appear to place more weight on the statistical analysis than do those devel-oped by the Federal Reserve.[44] First, OCC recognizes that

[a]ccurately and thoroughly documenting how transactions are processed and underwritten is important in any fair lending examination, but doing so *early* in the examination is particularly important when a statistical model is used, since the variables collected from the files will determine (and limit) the model tested.... Typical sources of information on the bank's under-writing process consist of the underwriter interview, written underwriting manuals, and subsequent conversations with the bank's staff. (Courchane, Nebhut, and Nickerson, 2000, p. 285; emphasis in the original)

This description emphasizes the importance of collecting all relevant information early in the process. The practical significance, of this statement is unclear, however, because OCC and the Federal Reserve both use underwriting documents and interviews to guide their data collection efforts. In principle, at least; both agencies agree that ex-tensive, early data collection efforts are needed.

Second, OCC uses statistical procedures to look at the influence of unusual observations, often called outliers, on any findings of disparate treatment.[46] OCC also appears, however, to allow non-statistical considerations to enter as well. Specifically, the OCC pro-cedures include an "examination of the exceptions files" and give the lender an opportunity to "account for" any statistically based find-ings of disparate treatment. As before, therefore, it is not clear whether the OCC and Federal Reserve procedures are significantly different in practice.

10.4.3 Using HMDA Data to Improve the Cost-Effectiveness of Fair-Lending Investigations

Another recent innovation in fair-lending enforcement by the Fed-eral Reserve Board is an attempt to use the HMDA data to guide fair-lending enforcement efforts, and in particular to ensure that these efforts are as cost-effective as possible. This innovation raises several additional issues that need to be considered in evaluating the current fair-lending enforcement system and its alternatives. A detailed explanation of this innovation is provided by Avery, Beeson, and Calem (1997):

The new system has two goals. One is to determine which institutions and which loan products or markets served by the institution show statistically significant evidence of disparities in the disposition of loan applications by race (or some other protected characteristic) that cannot be explained with the limited set of explanatory variables available in HMDA. The second is to provide examiners with a specific list of matched files to pull in those cases where detailed follow-up review is to be conducted. A special computer-based program has been created for the new system to accomplish both tasks. The new procedures are designed to replace only the file-sampling components of fair lending exams; examiners will continue to examine institutions' procedures and policies as before. (p. 12)

The first of these goals is addressed by comparing the approval rates of minority applicants with those of similar nonminority applicants. As Avery, Beeson, and Calem describe it:

Each minority application is matched to *all* nonminority applications filed with the same lender for the same product, same market, same quarter of action date (for large institutions), with the same number of applicants (single or joint), and *similar* income and loan amount. Ideally, *similar* would mean identical income and loan amount. In practice, if the average of the absolute amounts of the income and loan amount differences is less than 8%, the applications are deemed to be "matched." The disposition of the minority application is then compared with the *average* disposition of all nonminority applications matched to it. This comparison is averaged over all minority applications in the institution (or the institution's market/product subcategories). Minority applications that cannot be matched to any nonminority applications are not included in the analysis. (p. 13, emphasis in original)

The results of this calculation are then used

to determine which institutions warrant detailed further review. In short, detailed further investigation is warranted if the difference in the matched-pair denial rates for the institution as a whole, or for any of its major product areas or markets, is sufficiently large.... Institutions are sorted into three categories: (1) those where no detailed further review is indicated, (2) those with product or market areas where there are enough applications from minorities and nonminorities (including a reasonable mix of approvals and denials) to warrant further *statistical* review, and (3) those where the institution as a whole (or a particular product or product/market area) shows evidence of a substantial disparity but where no individual product or market area has enough applications from minorities or nonminorities or both to qualify for further statistical analysis. For the third set of institutions, detailed qualitative, but not statistical, analyses of loan files are conducted. (p. 13, emphasis in original)

The key point in this discussion is that the Federal Reserve does not use its new regression procedure to investigate discrimination at a particular lending institution unless that lender has a statistically significant disparity in its loan denial rates between blacks and whites *with similar incomes and loan amounts*. For a given loan product, time, and location, no other applicant, loan, or property characteristics are used to select the minority and white loans for comparison.

As explained by Courchane, Nebhut, and Nickerson (2000), a comparable new OCC procedure, also based on HMDA data,

identified statistically significant differences in denial rates by race—whether a group has enough applications to support more sophisticated statistical analyses or has the prohibited bases, products, and decision centers where statistically meaningful analysis can be conducted. (p. 280)

If this initial information reveals large denial disparities that could meaningfully be examined, the OCC analysts then matched minority denials and up to three white approvals by loan amount, income, and geography to identify apparent disparities" (p. 280). As a result, this procedure is similar to the Federal Reserve procedure, except that it compares files based on the basis of geography, not just on the basis of income and loan amount.

The second goal of the new Federal Reserve procedure is to select loan files for further investigation. As Avery, Beeson, and Calem (1997) put it:

Each minority applicant to the institution (or selected market/product areas) is paired with its closest nonminority applicants, using the preceeding [*sic*] criteria. Up to three matches are allowed with replacement (i.e., the same nonminority can be matched to several minorities). If the number of minorities is too large for the resources at hand, a random sample of pairs is taken. (p. 14)

The point to emphasize here is that, for a given loan type, location, and time, the nonminority applications that are brought into the analysis through this procedure are matched to a minority application based solely on the basis of income and loan amount. Other factors affecting underwriting decision are not considered. If there are enough pairs, the sample of minority and nonminority applications developed through this process is then examined using the regression procedure outlined in the previous section.

OCC follows a totally different procedure for selecting loan files to be reviewed. Specifically, it uses stratified random-sampling techniques to ensure a representative sample in all outcome/group categories (see Courchane, Nebhut, and Nickerson, 2000; Giles and Courchane, 2000).

10.5 Evaluation of Current Enforcement Procedures

The new regression and file review procedures used by the Federal Reserve Board and OCC are valuable contributions to the fair-lending enforcement system. Moreover, they are consistent with the first two guidelines for fair-lending regulations developed in section 10.3.1: they recognize that an evaluation of underwriting must rely on the exception to the particularity rule and that building a prima facie case for discrimination requires a multivariate procedure. Even with these new procedures, however, the fair-lending enforcement system retains two serious limitations: It misses many instances of disparate-treatment discrimination, and it fails to look for disparate-impact discrimination at all.

10.5.1 Obtaining an Accurate Estimate of Disparate-Treatment Discrimination

It is self-evident that fair-lending enforcement officials should use procedures that measure disparate-treatment discrimination as accurately as possible. The procedures used by the Federal Reserve, and similar procedures used by some other enforcement agencies, fall short of meeting this criterion for two reasons: They fail to recognize the problems that arise when file reviews are allowed to overrule a multivariate procedure, and they fail to recognize that a two-variable matching procedure can yield seriously misleading results. The next two subsections deal with these two issues.

10.5.1.1 The Need to Rely on a Multivariate Procedure
According to the official interagency definition, discrimination in loan approval exists when, among other things, lenders "use different standards in determining whether to extend credit" to people in

a legally protected class than those used for determining whether to extend credit to other applicants (FFIEC, 1999, p. ii). The underwriting standards to which this definition applies depend upon many applicant, loan, and property characteristics. These standards cannot be directly observed but must instead be inferred from the actions taken by lenders. The scholarly work reviewed in this book recognizes the complexity involved in this and provides a way to make this type of inference, namely, a multivariate statistical procedure. Moreover, a multivariate procedure is entirely consistent, in our view, with the legal requirements for a case involving disparate-treatment discrimination. As noted throughout this book, a lender is said to practice disparate-treatment discrimination if it is less likely to approve loans for minority than for white applicants, controlling for all the applicant, loan, and property characteristics that the lender considers in making its underwriting decisions. Because of the complexity inherent in this definition, the only way to determine the impact on an underwriting decision of any one characteristic is to hold all the others constant, that is, to use a multivariate statistical procedure.

The new regression procedures used by certain fair-lending enforcement agencies represent a significant step in the right direction, because they recognize this principle. Compared to traditional file reviews, in other words, these regressions lead to a process that is more likely to find discrimination when it exists and less likely to find discrimination when it does not exist. As they are currently designed, however, the new file review procedures associated with this regression analysis appear to forget this principle and therefore have the potential to undermine the gains that accrue from employing the regressions. The problem here lies not with file reviews as such, but instead with the way some enforcement agencies use information from file reviews.

To be specific, information from postregression file reviews can be used in two ways. The first way, which is the one built into the Federal Reserve procedure, is to search for "information that would legitimately account for the divergent credit decisions" disclosed by the results of the regressions (Calem and Canner, 1995, p. 124), that is, for benign explanations for cases in which minority applicants appear to have been treated less favorably than comparable whites.[46] Unfortunately, however, this approach runs into exactly the same problems as traditional file reviews, namely, that it may be difficult to identify comparable files and that any two files identified as comparable may still differ in important ways. Calem and Canner acknowledge this when they note that their new procedure "is very similar to the 'matched-pair' technique traditionally used by examiners" (p. 123). They go on to argue, however, that the new approach is better than the traditional matched-pair technique because "the statistical model guides the identification of matched pairs for review" (p. 123). It is no doubt true that the quality of the matches is improved through the use of the statistical model, but a model cannot eliminate the problem. Even if two matched files have identical values for all "key underwriting variables," they are bound to differ on some other characteristics, and, as explained earlier, it is not logically possible for a file review to determine the impact of these differences on the underwriting decision. In short, a file review cannot provide an alternative test for the hypothesis that discrimination exists.

The second way that information from postregression file reviews can be used is to improve the regression specification or to do tests for the robustness of the results. The OCC procedures follow this approach. This second way of using the information is consistent with principle that underwriting discrimination cannot be identified without a multivariate procedure. Consider the examples provided by Calem and Canner (1995). If some applicants to a particular lender are unable to document all reported income, then regulators should reestimate the regression for that lender with an "unable to document" variable.[47] If certain underwriters make a distinction between revolving debt and installment debt in scoring late payments, then regulators investigating those underwriters should estimate a regression that incorporates this distinction. These revised regressions would make full use of the information in the file reviews without giving up the regression's multivariate structure.

Another way to put this is that file reviews may be able to identify underwriting factors that were missed in an initial regression, but they cannot determine the weights placed on these underwriting factors. As explained earlier, these weights cannot be directly observed but instead must be inferred using multivariate statistics. It is not logically possible to determine whether a newly identified underwriting factor can explain a minority rejection without estimating the weight placed on this factor by the lender—and controlling for other factors.[48]

Moreover, focusing on cases in which a minority application was denied and a "comparable" white application was not could lead to a significant understatement of discrimination. After all, underwriting factors identified in the file reviews may explain white denials as well as minority denials. If many of the white denials are explained by factors not incorporated in the regression, then the relative probability of minority denials might be severely understated.

In some cases, of course, a file review may turn up an explanation for a minority denial that has nothing to do with the lender's underwriting standards. Another example from Calem and Canner falls into this category, namely, the case of a property that fails to meet zoning requirements. Presumably a loan denial in this case, to either a minority or a white applicant, cannot reveal anything about a lender's underwriting standards. Thus, it is appropriate for a regulator to identify legitimate reasons for a loan denial that have nothing to do with underwriting and to exclude from a statistical analysis any applications that were clearly denied for one of these reasons. The main lesson here, however, is that all the data for a loan approval regression need to be carefully checked and rechecked; the example of an application rejected for a property's failure to meets zoning requirements does not provide a justification for rejecting the results of a regression analysis on the basis of file reviews.

A procedure that checks and corrects only matched pairs in which the minority application was denied and the white was approved also could be a source of understatement in the estimated resulting minority status coefficient. After all, data errors, such as missing a failure to meet a zoning condition, could result in many incorrectly classified white denials, a mistake that would bias the minority status coefficient toward zero. As discussed in chapter 5, this type of unbalanced—and inappropriate—data correction was practiced by some of the critics of the Boston Fed Study.[49] In the context of a fair-lending enforcement system, it obviously makes no sense at all to complete a partial data-checking exercise. If a data error is found in one type of matched pair, such as those in which the white is approved and the minority is not, then examiners must check for and correct this error in all the applications used in the regression. Any other approach could lead to biased results.

The lesson from this analysis is that a formal test for disparate-treatment discrimination requires a multivariate underwriting model estimated with a carefully determined specification and carefully collected data. The specification of this model should reflect, as fully as possible, a lender's stated underwriting standards, and it should, to the extent possible, incorporate lessons learned from interviews or file reviews.

The problem that Calem and Canner (1995), Stengel and Glennon (1999), and Calem and Longhofer (2000) struggle with is that, from the investigator's point of view, estimating a complete, careful model like this may not be possible. To be specific, the investigator may not be given the time or resources necessary to estimate another specification that has been modified in response to file reviews or to recheck all the data after file reviews have uncovered a new type of error. As Stengel and Glennon (1999) put it, "It can be difficult to find and verify all the necessary data" (p. 326). Moreover, even if these steps have been taken, a new underwriting variable discovered in file reviews may show up in so few loan files—one or two, say— that its underwriting weight cannot be estimated without obtaining a larger sample, which requires even more time and expense.[50]

The most obvious way out of this dilemma is to collect sufficient information at the beginning of the process so that there will be no reason to revise the regressions later. This is what the OCC procedures attempt to do (Courchane, Nebhut, and Nickerson, 2000). The second-best approach is to respond to any postregression findings by checking the files of all the loans in the sample used in the regression for problems uncovered by the file review and rerunning the regressions with the new (complete) information.[51] The Federal Reserve Board does not appear to follow either of these approaches, perhaps because they are thought to be too costly or too intrusive. As a result, investigators at the Federal Reserve are sometimes left with the difficult, if not impossible, task of trying to guess the weight placed on a newly discovered underwriting factor or to guess the impact on the minority status coefficient of a newly found data error.

Moreover, the guidance given to Federal Reserve investigators who face this dilemma seems inappropriate to us. As explained in section 10.4.2, investigators are asked to examine matched loan applications, one of which was approved and one of which was denied, and to judge whether "factors omitted from the model may account for these decisions." According to the examples in Calem and Canner (1995) and Calem and Longhofer (2000), an investigator is empowered to reject the regression model if it does not "account for nuances in underwriting" or if the file contains variables that appear to be "contributing to denial" but are too "idiosyncratic" to be included in a regression model. This approach encourages investigators to overlook a minority denial whenever any factor that might plausibly be linked to that denial can be identified, without worrying about whether the lender's underwriting standards give that variable enough weight to explain the denial decision, or even whether that variable is ever consulted in evaluating white applications.[52]

In our judgment, the guidance given to Federal Reserve investigators inappropriately leans over backwards to avoid finding discrimination. Indeed, it is very difficult for regression analysis or any other procedure to sustain a charge of disparate-treatment discrimination, no matter how strong the evidence, if a lender or an investigator can refute the charge simply by finding a variable in the file of each rejected minority applicant that is not considered in the regression but that has some plausible connection to the denial decision. A more appropriate starting point would be to say that a significant, negative minority status coefficient in a loan approval regression establishes the presumption that the lender practices disparate-treatment discrimination. An investigator should not be able to overturn this presumption without providing clear evidence that (1) the regression did not consider a variable (or variables) that appears in the rejected minority loan files, (2) this variable has an impact on underwriting decisions for many applications, not just the rejected ones, and (3) this impact does not depend on the minority status of the applicant. The OCC procedures describe by Courchane, Nebhut, and Nickerson (2000) appear to move in this direction.

We conclude that the procedures described by Calem and Canner (1995), Stengel and Glennon (1999), and Calem and Longhofer (2000) are likely to understate disparate-treatment discrimination, perhaps severely.[53] Detailed file reviews may indeed find that the regression analysis used to evaluate a particular lender's practices has left out an important element of that lender's underwriting standard (or missed a data problem), but the appropriate response to such a finding is to incorporate this element into the regression analysis (or correct all the data), not to reject the regression approach altogether. As discussed by Courchane, Nebhut, and Nickerson (2000), regulators also can minimize this type of problem by expanding their efforts to identify all relevant underwriting variables at the beginning of a fair-lending investigation.

Moreover, because disparate-treatment discrimination cannot formally be identified without a multivariate procedure, investigators should begin with the presumption that the regression provides the right answer, as recent OCC procedures appear to do (Courchane, Nebhut, and Nickerson, 2000). This presumption should not be overturned using information in loan files unless this information provides clear evidence that legitimate underwriting factors influencing many loan decisions, but not included in the regression analysis, are responsible for many of the minority denials and not for many of the white denials.

Because a regression analysis inevitably involves judgments, a lender should, of course, be allowed to comment on a regression analysis that finds it practices disparate-treatment discrimination. In our view, a thoughtfully conducted loan approval regression with a significant negative coefficient for the minority status variable establishes a prima facie case for disparate-treatment discrimination and therefore shifts the burden of proof onto the lender.[54] In such a situation, the lender can escape the charge of discrimination only if it can show that an alternative regression specification that is consistent with its expressed underwriting policies (and with principles of regression methodology) yields a minority status coefficient that is not negative and significant.

10.5.1.2 Problems with Two- or Three-Variable Sampling Procedures

The second major problem with recent enforcement procedures is that they select lenders for further investigation based on minority/white denial ratios after accounting for only a few variables.[55] As explained in section 10.4.3, the Federal Reserve examines a lender's loan files in detail only when that lender has a large disparity in minority/white denial ratios in applications matched by income and loan amount. The OCC procedure adds matching based on geography to this list. If the lender has enough applications to make regression analysis feasible, this examination takes the form of a regression analysis; otherwise it consists of detailed file reviews.

It is certainly reasonable to try to narrow the set of lenders that are subjected to a detailed file review and to avoid a simplistic solution such as the four-fifths rule. Since the HMDA data are the only available source of information, it also seems reasonable to use these data to help identify the lenders that need to be investigated.

We do not think it is appropriate, however, to rely exclusively on a procedure for selecting the lenders to be investigated further that controls for only a few variables. Disparate-treatment discrimination in loan approval can take many forms other than a higher denial rate for minorities than for whites with similar incomes and loan amounts, even when they want to buy houses in the same locations. Moreover, as many scholars have pointed out, including the researchers who developed the Federal Reserve procedure (Avery, Besson, and Calem, 1997), a loan approval decision depends on many characteristics that are not observed in the HMDA data, such as an applicant's credit history, and no minority-white comparison based solely on income and loan amount can provide a credible indication of discrimination. Thus, such procedures are bound to identify some lenders that do not discriminate as worthy of further investigation and to let other lenders that do discriminate escape investigation altogether.[56]

The first of these two possibilities is not so serious, because the regression analysis will exonerate lenders who do not discriminate. The findings of Bostic and Canner (1997) imply, however, that these procedures are likely to place a relatively high enforcement burden on minority-owned lenders, which attract a relatively large number of low-qualified minority applicants. Careful regression procedures would ensure that none of these lenders is unfairly accused of discrimination, but it is still inappropriate for them to bear a disproportionate share of the enforcement costs.

In contrast, the second of the possibilities constitutes a serious gap in the federal government's fair-lending enforcement system.[57] Specifically, the use of the limited information in HMDA to identify lenders for fair-lending investigations allows some lenders to discriminate without fear of the consequences. This is, of course, exactly analogous to the problem that arises with the four-fifths rule. Moreover, lenders may be able to use the publicly available HMDA data to determine whether they face the risk of a fair-lending examination.

The problem, of course, is that federal regulators cannot investigate every lender and need some mechanism that will help them make their enforcement efforts more cost effective. In this setting, some use of the HMDA data, which cover most lenders, is certainly reasonable.[58] To ensure that no lenders are exempt from a fair-lending investigation, however, the Federal Reserve and OCC procedures for selecting loan files and lenders for review need to be supplemented with a random sample of lenders. Alternatively, these procedures could be replaced with stratified random sampling, in which the probability of a particular lender's being selected as part of the sample is proportional to its minority-white denial ratio, after accounting for income, loan amount, and geography.

10.5.2   The Need to Look for Disparate-Impact Discrimination

Both the traditional enforcement policies and the regression-based policies developed by the Federal Reserve and OCC also have another major flaw: They are incapable of identifying most cases of disparate-impact discrimination. In fact, as stated in Avery, Beeson, and Calem (1997), Stengel and Glennon (1999), and Courchane, Nebhut, and Nickerson (2000), the explicit purpose of the regression-based procedures is to identify disparate-treatment discrimination alone. As Avery, Beeson, and Calem put it, "In any statistical analysis of discrimination (parametric or nonparametric), the goal is to determine whether or not the treatment of an individual would have been different had the individual been of a different minority status" (p. 14). This is a textbook definition of disparate-treatment discrimination, and it completely ignores behavior that has a disparate impact on member of a minority group.[59]

Moreover, Courchane, Nebhut, and Nickerson (2000) explicitly reject regressions that pool information across lenders, such as those proposed in section 10.3, on the grounds that pooling is a poor technique for isolating disparate-treatment discrimination:[60]

It is the examination of an institution under its own standards, accompanied by an examination of those standards, that can best indicate the extent and scope of the disparate treatment at a particular institution. (p. 278)

The problem we see here is not in the logic of this statement, which is fine, but in the choice of objective, which is not. The fair-lending enforcement agencies are responsible for identifying both disparate-treatment and disparate-impact discrimination, and it makes no sense for them to rely, for purposes of enforcement, exclusively on methods that hide disparate-impact discrimination from view.

The analysis in this book demonstrates that disparate-impact discrimination can enter a loan approval regression in two ways. First, it can show up in the estimated minority status coefficient, if the regression specification does not exactly accurately reflect a lender's actual underwriting standards. Second, it can show up in the estimated coefficients of the credit characteristics and therefore will not be recognized as discrimination in a loan approval regression. This analysis also shows that a lender may be able to disguise disparate-treatment discrimination by transforming it into disparate-impact discrimination.

The first of these two possibilities needs to be considered because it helps to show why looking for disparate-impact discrimination is so important. As explained in chapters 5 and 6, disparate-impact discrimination may show up in the minority status coefficient whenever the lender's underwriting standards contain elements that are not reflected in the specification of the loan approval regression. Hence, an investigator following the Federal Reserve procedures (or a lender responding to them) might be able to reduce apparent discrimination, as indicated by the minority status coefficient, by adding these elements to the specification of the regression. In particular, this step could shift the effect of disparate-impact discrimination from the minority status coefficient to the coefficients of credit characteristics, where it will not be observed. Thus, the search for the "correct" specification, that is, the specification most accurately portraying a lender's underwriting criteria, a search that is central to the logic of the Federal Reserve's regression procedure, can be seen as a way to ensure that disparate-impact discrimination is ignored.

The problem runs even deeper than this, however. As shown in such a compelling fashion by Buist, Linneman, and Megbolugbe (1999) and Blackburn and Vermilyea (2001), lenders may be able to hide disparate-treatment discrimination by transforming it into disparate-impact discrimination. In this case, the Federal Reserve's regression procedure could miss discrimination altogether, even when it is severe. Indeed, we believe it is inappropriate—if not irresponsible—for these agencies to use a procedure that violates the Inter-Agency Fair Lending Examination Procedures (Federal Financial Institutions Examination Council, 1999) by assuming that disparate-treatment discrimination is the only kind worth looking for.

10.6   Conclusions and Recommendations

In our judgment, the current fair-lending enforcement system is seriously inadequate. As demonstrated by several high-profile cases against large lenders, this system does uncover some cases of discrimination in loan approval that take the form of disparate treatment (see Siskin and Cupingood, 1996; Lee, 2001). The analysis in this chapter shows, however, that this system also is likely to miss other cases of loan approval discrimination that take the form of disparate treatment and is incapable of identifying loan approval discrimination that takes the form of disparate impact. In addition, little is known about the application of this system to automated underwriting systems or to the setting of interest rates. These limitations could all be overcome with relatively straightforward procedures.

The problems in the current enforcement system can be traced to the way enforcement agencies select lenders for further investigation and to the way they use statistical procedures. The selection methods employed focus on only a subset of possible discrimination indicators and therefore insulate some discriminating lenders from further investigation, which is clearly an inappropriate outcome. Moreover, these methods may have the ironic consequence of placing an unfair enforcement burden on minority-owned lenders.

The federal financial regulatory agencies have recently improved the fair-lending enforcement system by introducing multivariate statistical procedures. The current use of these statistical procedures causes two sorts of problems, however. First, at the Federal Reserve, these procedures are often treated as an initial test for discrimination that can be overruled by the subsequent judgment of investigators based on limited information from selected file reviews. In this setting, there is no reason to believe that investigators can accurately distinguish between discriminatory and nondiscriminatory denial of minority households' loan applications. More satisfactory approaches include investing more in the initial data collection and study design phase, as the OCC has done, or treating file reviews as sources of information to be incorporated into the statistical procedures.

Fair-lending laws require lenders to use the same underwriting standards for all applicants, regardless of their group membership. Allowing lenders to evaluate applications on the basis of idiosyncratic factors and to place unobservable weights on these factors in making their underwriting decisions would eviscerate these laws, because such a step would make it impossible to determine whether common standards are applied to all applicants. Thus, fair-lending laws cannot be enforced unless each lenders is held to a standard of equal treatment based on an available and objective method, namely, a multivariate analysis of the lender's loan denial decisions.

Second, the existing statistical procedures at all fair-lending enforcement agencies, along with the less formal enforcement procedures, are explicitly designed to find only disparate-treatment discrimination. This is a serious problem, because disparate-impact discrimination may be quite common. It can easily be built into an underwriting system, for example, even when that system is based on seemingly group-neutral statistical procedures. In addition, lenders may be able to transform disparate-treatment discrimination, which might be detected by the existing procedures, into disparate-impact discrimination, which will escape detection altogether under those procedures. The laws pertaining to fair lending outlaw discrimination whether it takes the form of disparate treatment or of disparate impact, and we can think of no justification for an enforcement system that ignores one of these forms altogether.

We propose four steps for improving the fair-lending enforcement system. These steps are designed to be consistent with existing legal requirements for disparate-impact discrimination cases. Moreover, they all could be codified in a set of regulations for enforcing fair-lending legislation.

1. The fair-lending enforcement agencies should come up with the resources needed to make certain that they are not missing a large share of existing disparate-treatment discrimination. In selecting lenders to investigate, they should develop new strategies that do not rule out large classes of potential discriminators. They also should provide enough resources so that multivariate regressions conducted to identify discriminators can be based on virtually complete information and loan file reviews can be treated as a method for improving regression analysis, not overruling it.

2. The fair-lending enforcement agencies should implement the new enforcement tool developed in section 10.3.2.1, namely, a loan approval regression based on applications submitted to a large sample of lenders. This tool, which recognizes both the complexity of underwriting standards and the possibility that these standards vary across lenders, makes it possible to estimate the extent of discrimination by each lender in the sample, regardless of whether that discrimination takes the form of disparate impact or of disparate treatment. The courts have made it clear that FaHA and ECOA prohibit disparate-impact discrimination as well as disparate-treatment discrimination, and it is irresponsible for the fair-lending enforcement agencies to use procedures that ignore one of these forms.

Moreover, because it is based on a large, random sample, this tool does not exempt any discriminating lenders from investigation, provides precise estimates of the weights placed on a wide range of underwriting variables, yields an estimate of discrimination even for lenders that are too small for current regression procedures, and eliminates the arbitrary separation of lenders based on the agency that regulates them. In short, this tool provides the best possible lender-specific estimate of discrimination that is available without loan performance information and is an ideal way to determine if there is a prima facie case for discrimination for any lender in the sample. The standards required to establish a prima facie case using this method are, of course, much more stringent than the standards implicit in the four-fifths rule used in employment cases.

3. The fair-lending enforcement agencies should also implement the new enforcement tool developed in section 10.3.2.2, namely, a performance-based analysis of loan approval decisions, to supplement the first tool. This tool requires an enforcement agency to estimate a model of the factors that determine loan performance. More specifically, this tool compares the minority composition of the applications that have the highest predicted loan performance based on this loan performance model with the minority composition of the applications a lender actually approves. Discrimination exists if more minority applications would be approved on the basis of predicted performance than are actually approved on the basis of the lender's underwriting standards. This tool requires loan performance information, which the fair-lending agencies have, so far, been reluctant to obtain, but it does not require the investigator to know the details of a lender's underwriting standards, and it could easily be implemented if the required data were available. This tool, like the other one we propose, captures both disparate-impact and disparate-treatment discrimination.

This second enforcement tool would yield more precise answers about discrimination than the first one, but it would obviously be more costly to implement. Loan performance is observed by the institution servicing a loan, which may not be the same as the institution that issued the loan. To examine discrimination in under-writing, therefore, regulators must develop procedures that link loan performance information with information about the issuing lend-er.[61] This issue arises even for large lenders that originate and then continue to service many loans. After all, these lenders also sell some of their loans on the secondary market, and the sample of loans they retain is not a random sample of the loans they originate.

In the short run, therefore, we recommend that regulators collect loan performance information from institutions that service a large number of loans, including information on the lenders that origi-nated the loans. These data should then be used to estimate loan performance models for various types of loans, such as conventional home purchase loans. These loan performance models will provide the basis for an evaluation of discrimination at any of the lenders that originated a significant number of loans in the sample. The lenders to be investigated could be determined randomly, perhaps with sampling weights based on minority/white denial ratios or other information from HMDA.

In the long run, we recommend a new Home Mortgage Disclosure Act for Loan Performance Information (HMDA-LP). This act would require all institutions servicing loans to report to the federal gov-ernment on certain standardized performance indicators, loan char-acteristics, and originator identifiers. Just as the HMDA data provide a foundation for a detailed analysis of loan approval, these HMDA-LP data could provide a foundation for a detailed analysis of loan performance. Specifically, samples of various types of loans could be drawn from these data, and further information on applicant, loan, and property characteristics could then be collected for each sample. This HMDA-LP data set, supplemented with additional information, would make it possible for regulators to estimate a loan performance model for each type of loan. In the final step, the results of these models could be used to test for discrimination by a (weighted) ran-dom sample of the lenders represented in the HMDA-LP data for each type of loan.[62]

Although our second and third recommendations would require lenders to provide information from their loan files, they are de-signed, in part, to protect lenders from unwarranted charges of dis-criminatory behavior. Recall that we recommend stringent standards for establishing a prima facie case for disparate-impact discrimina-tion, based on a multivariate procedure. Regulators should make it clear that the random selection of a lender for further investigation, even if that selection is guided by weights based on an adjusted minority/white denial ratio, does not imply that the regulator has already built a prima facie case for discrimination by that lender. Just as an income tax audit does not imply that a taxpayer has cheated on his taxes (even if it is guided by variables correlated with cheating), a lending investigation does not imply that a lender has practiced discrimination. Instead, a lender is charged with discrimination only if a statistical procedure finds a minority-white disparity after controlling for all legitimate underwriting variables. With these procedures, a lender who does not discriminate has nothing to worry about.

4. *The fair-lending enforcement agencies should develop performance-based tools designed to test for discrimination in the scores that come out of automated underwriting systems and in loan pricing.* To the best of our knowledge, these agencies have paid little attention to discrimination in these types of behavior. This neglect is unfortunate. Automated underwriting systems are now a central element of the mortgage market, and pricing according to risk is replacing credit rationing in many settings. Moreover, in some cases, lenders may be able to increase their profits by discriminating in the design of automated underwriting systems or loan-pricing policies. Such discrimination is not likely to take the form of disparate treatment, but disparate-impact discrimination can impose just as serious a burden on minority borrowers. It is imperative that the fair-lending enforcement agencies develop tools that recognize the possibility of discrimination in these activities and are capable of recognizing discrimination regardless of the form it takes. The tools we propose in this chapter fulfill these requirements. Moreover, these tools do not require the release of proprietary information about the formulas that define an automated underwriting system.

For some reason, unknown to us, the fair-lending enforcement agencies have decided not provide the public with any credible evidence on the current extent of discrimination in mortgage underwriting.[63] As a result, neither we nor anyone else knows how much of this type of discrimination still exists. According to the best available evidence, however, extensive underwriting discrimination existed in 1990, and there is no more recent evidence to show that this discrimination has gone away. Moreover, black and Hispanic households continue to have homeownership and loan approval rates far below the rates attained by white households, even after controlling for income and other factors.

Under these circumstances, this nation cannot begin to live up to the important principles embodied in its fair-lending laws without actively searching for mortgage discrimination in all its possible forms using the most accurate tools possible. The current fair-lending enforcement system does not even come close to meeting this standard.

It does not have to be this way. More comprehensive and accurate enforcement tools that build on a large body of scholarly research and are consistent with legal standards are readily available. We strongly urge the fair-lending enforcement agencies to make these tools a regular part of their enforcement activities. We also urge interested citizens, community groups, academics, lenders and other participants in the mortgage market, and public officials to work for improvements in the fair-lending enforcement system. Every American household should be able to enter the mortgage market without fear of discrimination.

Appendixes

A   Technical Appendix

A.1   Introduction

This appendix serves two purposes. First, it provides an intuitive explanation of the main statistical concepts on which this book relies. This material, which is directed toward readers without any training in econometrics, is presented in section A.2. Second, it contains equations and other material to further explain the book's estimation and analysis. This material is directed toward readers who want to know more technical details than can be presented in the text. After section A.2, the headings in this appendix make links to the appropriate chapters and sections in the text.

A.2   Econometric Concepts

This section presents a brief review of some key econometric theorems. For a far more complete and precise discussion of these theorems, see an econometrics textbook, such as Greene (2000).

The fundamental empirical tool used by the research reviewed in this book is regression analysis, which is designed to estimate a behavioral relationship based on the information in a data set. In this context, a data set contains numerical values for a series of variables and a sample of observations. In a regression analysis, a dependent variable, say Y, is expressed as a function of a set of explanatory variables, say X, and a random error term, say e (in equation form, $Y = a + bX + e$, where a and b are the coefficients to be estimated). The data set provides information on Y and X for each of the observations in the sample. This information is used to estimate a and b.

If there are many X variables, then b represents a set of coefficients, not a single one. Each b coefficient indicates the impact of one of the X variables on the dependent variable. In some cases two different X variables, say X_1 and X_2, are multiplied together, or interacted, to form a new explanatory variable. An interaction term of this type indicates whether the impact of X_1 on the dependent variable depends on the value of X_2 (and vice versa).

Standard regression techniques provide estimates of a and b for a sample of observations. The overall explanatory power of a regression is summarized by an R^2, which indicates the percentage of the variance in the dependent variable that is explained by the model. When Y is a yes-or-no variable, such as whether a loan was accepted or denied, the expression $(a + bX)$ can be interpreted as the probability that an event (such as loan denial) will occur. In this case, the well-known logit or probit models are often used to estimate a and b. These models focus on an underlying latent variable, under the assumption that the dependent variable takes on a value of one if the latent variable exceeds a certain value. A standard R^2 does not apply to logit and probit models, but researchers can use pseudo R^2, which indicates the share of the variance in the latent variable explained by the model (Laitila, 1993).

Scholars are interested in both the magnitude and statistical significance of the estimated values of b. An estimate that is large in magnitude indicates that the associated X variable has a large impact on the dependent variable. An estimate that is statistically significant is very unlikely to have arisen by chance, so a scholar can be confident that the impact of the X variable on the dependent variable is real. Statistical significance is measured with a t-statistic, which is the ratio of the coefficient estimate to its standard error, which indicates the likely range of the coefficient if it were estimated many times with different values for the random error term. The conventional indicator of statistical significance for a reasonably large sample is a t-statistic above 1.96, which indicates that the probability that the estimated coefficient simply reflects random factors is less than 5 percent. This is a so-called two-tailed test, which is appropriate if the estimated coefficient could, in principle, be either positive or negative. If the estimated coefficient can only be positive (or only negative), then a one-tailed test is appropriate. In this case, statistical significance at the 5-percent level is indicated by a t-statistic above 1.65.

Regression analysis is based on several assumptions about the nature of the random error term. When those assumptions are satisfied, the estimated values of a and b can be shown to be accurate in the sense that they are close to the true behavioral parameters. In some cases, a violation of one or more of these assumptions will result in biased estimates, that is, in estimated values of a and b that differ systematically from their true values. Many of the methodological problems in this report involve issues of bias.

One key source of bias is an omitted variable. If the true behavioral relationship involves a variable, but this variable is omitted from the regression analysis, then the estimated coefficients of variables that are included in the analysis may be biased. Such bias arises because one of the basic regression assumptions is violated, namely, the assumption that all explanatory variables are uncorrelated with unobserved factors, that is, with the error term. In general the amount of bias depends on the true coefficient of the omitted variable and the correlation between the omitted variable and the included variable. Intuitively, some of the impact of an omitted variable on the dependent variable may be incorrectly assigned to one or more of the included variables. The solution to this problem is to obtain data on all key variables and to include them in the regression; otherwise one cannot rule out the possibility of biased results.

The basic regression model also assumes that all variables are exogenous, which means that they are determined by factors that are not part of the behavior under investigation. Estimated coefficients may be biased if some of the explanatory variables are endogenous. Endogeneity can arise either if some unobserved variable affects both an explanatory variable and the dependent variable or if the dependent variable has a causal impact on the explanatory variable. In either case, the regression coefficients may not simply reflect the direct impact of an explanatory variable on the dependent variable but may also pick up indirect effects or effects flowing from the dependent variable. As in the case of omitted variables, the problem here is that, in violation of the basic assumptions, the explanatory variables are correlated with unobserved factors. This type of problem can be solved with a simultaneous-equations procedure, in which the explanatory variable is "cleansed" of its endogenous component. The cleansed variable is then used in the regression, and the estimated coefficient reflects only the desired direct impact of the explanatory variable on the dependent variable.

In general, a simultaneous-equations procedure requires the use of instruments, which are variables that do appear in the basic regression themselves but are related to the endogenous explanatory variable. A good instrument should (1) make conceptual sense, (2) be significant in a regression to explain the endogenous explanatory variable, and (3) not have explanatory power in the regression of interest (when the potentially endogenous variable is also included). In principle, one can estimate a simultaneous-equations model so long as one has one instrument for each endogenous explanatory variable. In practice, however, a high correlation among instruments may make it difficult to sort out the effects of more than one endogenous variable, and better results can often be obtained with more instruments than endogenous variables.

In a study of mortgage lending discrimination, instruments that meet these tests are often difficult to find, because all the variables observed by the researcher are also observed by the underwriter and could, in principle, influence the denial decision. In practice, however, lenders collect a huge array of information during the application procedure and, to keep the process manageable, they must simplify this information using broad indicators of the likelihood of default, such as a credit score or LTV. Our search for instruments focuses on variables that may not be directly considered by lenders because they are summarized in a broader indicator that lenders are known to use.

A.3　Modeling the Endogeneity of "Unable to Verify" and "Meets Guidelines" (Section 5.2.3)

A.3.1　A Simple Model of Endogeneity in the Loan Denial Equation

This section presents a model to account for endogeneity in "unable to verify." The same model can be used to account for endogeneity in "meets guidelines." Let y_v be a binary variable equal to one when the loan officer is "unable to verify" certain information. The value of this variable is determined by a latent variable, marked with an asterisk, which is, in turn, influenced by a set of exogenous variables, labeled X:

$$y_v = \begin{cases} 1 & \text{if } y_v^* \geq 0 \\ 0 & \text{if } y_v^* < 0 \end{cases}, \quad \text{where } y_v^* = \beta_v X + \varepsilon_v. \tag{A.1}$$

In addition, let y_d be a binary variable equal to one when a loan application is denied. The value of this variable is determined by a latent variable, also market with an asterisk, which is, in turn, influenced both by X and by y_v:

$$y_d = \begin{cases} 1 & \text{if } y_d^* \geq 0 \\ 0 & \text{if } y_d^* < 0 \end{cases}, \quad \text{where } y_d^* = \beta_d X + \gamma y_v + \varepsilon_d. \tag{A.2}$$

We estimate this model using a bivariate probit with recursion. Note that the influence of "unable to verify" or of "meets guidelines" on the latent variable for denial is identified without exclusion restrictions because these variables are not continuous. See Amemiya (1974) and Sickles and Schmidt (1978).

A.3.2 A Complex Model of Endogeneity in "Meets Guidelines"

Let y_{m1} be a binary variable to indicate whether the original loan officer believes a loan application meets the guidelines of the lender the loan officer represents. It is driven by a latent variable, marked with an asterisk, that is a function of a set of exogenous variables, X (a different set of variables than the one in the previous model). The actual binary variable is not observed, but we can write

$$y_{m1}^* = \beta_{m1} X + \varepsilon_{m1}. \tag{A.3}$$

Now let y_{m2} be a binary variable that equals one when the bank official filling out the HMDA form for a loan application indicates that the applicant meets the lender's guidelines. It is driven by a latent variable, marked with an asterisk, and is influenced by the same factors that influence the original loan officer's "meets guidelines" decision and loan denial decision:

$$y_{m2} = \begin{cases} 1 & \text{if } y_{m2}^* \geq 0 \\ 0 & \text{if } y_{m2}^* < 0 \end{cases}, \quad \text{where } y_{m2}^* = \gamma_1 y_{m1}^* + \gamma_2 y_d + \varepsilon_{m2}. \tag{A.4}$$

Finally, let us modify the model of loan denial given earlier by introducing into it the original loan officer's latent variable for "meets guidelines":

$$y_d = \begin{cases} 1 & \text{if } y_d^* \geq 0 \\ 0 & \text{if } y_d^* < 0 \end{cases}, \quad \text{where } y_d^* = \beta_d X + \gamma_3 y_{m1}^* + \varepsilon_d. \tag{A.5}$$

We cannot estimate equation (A.3) because the latent variable for y_{m1}

is not observed, but we can substitute equation (A.3) into (A.4) and (A.5). The result:

$$y_{m2} = \begin{cases} 1 & \text{if } y_{m2}^* \geq 0 \\ 0 & \text{if } y_{m2}^* < 0 \end{cases}, \quad \text{where } y_{m2}^* = (\gamma_1 \beta_{m1})X + \gamma_2 y_d + \varepsilon_{m2} + \gamma_1 \varepsilon_{m1}.$$

$$(A.6)$$

$$y_d = \begin{cases} 1 & \text{if } y_d^* \geq 0 \\ 0 & \text{if } y_d^* < 0 \end{cases}, \quad \text{where } y_d^* = (\beta_d + \gamma_3 \beta_{m1})X + + \varepsilon_d + \gamma_3 \varepsilon_{m1}.$$

$$(A.7)$$

We estimate equations (A.6) and (A.7) using a bivariate probit model with recursion. In estimating these equations, the parameter γ_1 is not identified and is initialized to one. In addition, the variances of the error terms are not identified, and the variance of the reduced-form error terms in equations (A.6) and (A.7) are also both initialized to one.

As an econometric matter, the relationship between the latent "meets guidelines" variable for the actual loan officer and loan denial can be identified only if there exists a variable that influences "meets guidelines" but does not have any direct influence on loan denial. The standard criteria for determining whether a variable passes this test is that it must be significant in explaining the first dependent variable ("meets guidelines") but insignificant in explaining the second dependent variable (loan denial) when the first dependent variable is included in the specification. The consumer credit history variable appears to pass this test. Past mortgage payment history is probably closely related to future payment, and defaults that appear in an applicant's record undoubtedly result in a stigma that alters the entire underwriting process. To keep their decision process manageable, however, lenders may not refer to individual credit history variables once they have been incorporated into the decisions about whether an applicant meets the lender's guidelines. As it turns out, the consumer credit history variable is highly significant in explaining "meets guidelines" but has no explanatory power, as indicated by a t-statistic of 0.15, for the denial variable when "meets guidelines" is included in the equation. Once consumer credit history has been used to determine whether an application meets the lender's credit history standards, consumer credit history has no additional influence on the underwriting decision.

A.4 The Annuity Formula (Section 5.3.3)

The present value, A_{PV} of a \$1 annuity stream that lasts T periods with an interest rate i can be written as follows:

$$A_{PV} = \frac{1}{i}\left(1 - \frac{1}{(1+i)^T}\right). \tag{A.8}$$

If all the other terms are known, (A.8) can be used to solve for the interest rate.

A.5 Modeling the Endogeneity of Loan Terms (Section 5.6.1)

The model for the endogeneity of loan terms proposed by Rachlis and Yezer (1993) is as follows. Let y_l stand for LTV. Then, using the notation defined earlier,

$$y_l = \beta_l X + \gamma_l y_d^* + \varepsilon_l \tag{A.9}$$

and

$$y_d = \begin{cases} 1 & \text{if } y_d^* \geq 0 \\ 0 & \text{if } y_d^* < 0 \end{cases}, \quad \text{where } y_d^* = \beta_d X + \gamma_d y_l + \varepsilon_d. \tag{A.10}$$

Substituting equation (A.10) into (A.9) results in

$$y_l = \frac{\beta_l + \beta_d \gamma_l}{1 - \gamma_d} X + \frac{\varepsilon_l + \gamma_l \varepsilon_d}{1 - \gamma_d} = \hat{\beta}_l X + \hat{\varepsilon}_l. \tag{A.11}$$

Hence, a regression of LTV on a set of exogenous variables can be interpreted as a reduced form of equation (A.9). We employ a reduced form of this type to obtain an "instrument" for LTV, that is, to correct for the possible endogeneity of LTV in a loan denial equation.

A.6 Bias in a Default Test Based on Market Concentration (Section 8.3.1)

As noted in the text, market concentration may affect credit rationing on many underwriting variables, including credit history, which is omitted from Berkovec et al.'s (1998) analysis. Lenders in highly concentrated markets will hold applicants to higher standards on credit history variables. So just as omitted credit history variables bias the race coefficient in the default model, the relationship between credit rationing and market concentration biases the coefficient for the interaction between race and market concentration.

The path of the bias is complex but can be untangled (see Ross, 1997). First, we consider the bias a default analysis based on a sample of conventional mortgages. The omission of credit history variables biases the race coefficient upward in a default model. More stringent credit rationing in highly concentrated markets should weaken the relationship between credit history and default in the sample of approved mortgages for highly concentrated markets. Therefore, the bias in the race coefficient should be smaller in more concentrated markets, which would create a negative relationship between market concentration and the size of the race coefficient. This bias is consistent with Berkovec et al.'s negative estimate for the coefficient on the interaction between market structure and race and biases the default approach toward finding discrimination. Since Berkovec et al. did not find statistically significant evidence of discrimination, this bias would not be a problem for their results if the results were based on conventional mortgages.

For a sample of FHA mortgages, the problem is even more complex. First, the effect of omitting credit history variables on the relationship between race and defaults for FHA mortgages is unknown. The omission of credit history variables lowers the quality of the distribution of minority applications on unobserved underwriting variables. At first glance, a leftward shift in the distribution of black applications relative to white applications will increase racial differences in default, because many low-quality FHA mortgages are falling below the cutoff and out of the FHA sample. This assumes, however, that the FHA and conventional cutoffs are fixed, but these cutoffs are for application quality based on unobserved underwriting variables. The nature of this quality measure changes when credit history variables are omitted. Most white applications are for loans in the conventional sector, and most of those applications are approved. So most white applications have acceptable credit history, other things equal, and omitting credit history variables may actually shift the FHA and conventional cutoffs to the left relative to the distribution of white mortgage applications. Therefore, the omission of credit history variables shifts both the cutoffs and the distribution of minority applications to the left, and it is uncertain whether omitting credit history increases or decreases racial differences in default for an FHA sample. Moreover, the effect of market concentration on the relationship between credit history and default is unknown. For conventional loans, more aggressive underwriting filters out lower-quality applications, decreases the variance in the sample, and reduces the strength of the relationship between credit history and default. More aggressive underwriting by conventional lenders, however, shifts more mortgages into the FHA sector, which may increase the variance in the FHA sample and increase the relationship between credit history and default. No conclusions can be drawn concerning the direction of the omitted-variable bias when the default approach is pursued with a sample of FHA mortgages.

A.7 Disparate-Impact Discrimination and the Minority-Status Variable (Section 9.3.2.1)

The analysis in section 9.3 considers two regressions [equations (9.1) and (9.6)] and three associated scoring schemes [equations (9.2), (9.3), and (9.7)]. The expected value of the second scoring scheme is given by equation (9.5). The expected value for the third scheme is

$$E(S^3) = E(\hat{\alpha}') + \sum_{i=1}^{N} E(\hat{\beta}'_i) X_i. \tag{A.12}$$

To compare the expected values of the last two schemes, we must evaluate this expected-value expression.

Consider first the constant term. The estimated value of the constant term in any regression equals, by definition, the mean value of the dependent variable minus the sum of the mean values of the explanatory variables, each weighted by its estimated coefficient. As a result,

$$\hat{\alpha} = \bar{P} - \sum_{i=1}^{N} \hat{\beta}_i \bar{X}_i - \hat{\gamma} \bar{M}. \tag{A.13}$$

Because the expected values for the estimated coefficients on the right side of this expression are estimated without bias using equation (9.1), this equation leads directly to an expression for the expected value of the estimated constant term:

$$E(\hat{\alpha}) = \alpha = \bar{P} - \sum_{i=1}^{N} \hat{\beta}_i \bar{X}_i - \gamma \bar{M}. \tag{A.14}$$

The formula behind equation (A.13) also yields an expression for the constant term in equation (9.6):

$$\hat{\alpha}' = \bar{P} - \sum_{i=1}^{N} \hat{\beta}'_i \bar{X}_i. \tag{A.15}$$

Using equations (A.12) and (9.8), the expected value of this constant can be derived as follows:

$$E(\hat{\alpha}') = \bar{P} - \sum_{i=1}^{N} E(\hat{\beta}_i)\bar{X}_i$$

$$= \bar{P} - \sum_{i=1}^{N} (\beta_i + \gamma b_i)\bar{X}_i$$

$$= \alpha - \gamma \sum_{i=1}^{N} b_i\bar{X}_i + \gamma\bar{M} \tag{A.16}$$

Finally, equations (A.12) and (A.16) make it possible to derive an expression for the expected value of the scoring scheme in equation (9.7). To be specific,

$$E(S^3) = E(\hat{\alpha}') + \sum_{i=1}^{N} E(\hat{\beta}'_i)X_i$$

$$= \alpha - \gamma \sum_{i=1}^{N} b_i\bar{X}_i + \gamma\bar{M} + \sum_{i=1}^{N} (\beta_i + \gamma b_i)X_i$$

$$= E(S^2) + \gamma \sum_{i=1}^{N} b_i(X_i - \bar{X}_i). \tag{A.17}$$

This is the formula presented in the text.

A.8 Extensions of a Performance-Based Test for Discrimination in Loan Approval (Section 9.4.1.2)

In this section we consider two extensions to the test for discrimination in loan approval that is made possible by a combination of loan approval and loan performance data. The first extension examines the form of discrimination, and the second makes it possible to test hypotheses about the causes of discrimination.

A.8.1   The Form of Discrimination

To determine the form of discrimination present in a sample, loan applications must be ranked by their loan performance score and then divided into quantiles. The top quantile consists of the x percent of applications with the highest scores, where a smaller value for x simply defines a more detailed distribution of scores. The final step is to calculate the difference between the minority and white denial rates (or approval rates) in each quantile. The "higher hurdle" view of discrimination predicts that this ratio will be higher in lower quantiles than in higher quantiles. A finding that this ratio is roughly the same in all quantiles would therefore lead to a rejection of the higher-hurdle view in favor of the view that all minority applicants are at risk of encountering discrimination, regardless of their credit quality. A standard difference-of-means test can be used to determine the significance of both the difference between the minority and white denial rates within a quantile and the difference in this difference across quantiles.

A parametric test also could be used to shed more light on the form of discrimination. The test we have in mind begins with a simplified loan approval regression that does not require any assumptions about specification other than the basic logit or probit framework. The basic regression explains loan approval as a function of only two variables, the best-predicting nondiscriminatory loan performance score and minority status. (A third variable, the minority composition of the neighborhood, could be used to test for redlining. This variable is not considered here.) The coefficient of the minority status variable measures all discrimination, regardless of whether it is composed of disparate treatment or disparate impact. As explained in the text, it is not possible to distinguish between these two types of discrimination, but it is possible to measure their net impact. Moreover, the exclusion of the other variables in equation (9.14) is not a source of bias in the estimated coefficient of the minority status variable. If these other variables are correlated with minority status, then any impact they have on loan approval is a source of disparate-impact discrimination and is appropriately measured by the minority status variable. If, on the other hand, these variables are not correlated with minority status, then they cannot be a source of bias in the minority status coefficient. As a result, this simplified regression framework avoids the specification problems that plague equation (9.14).

Introducing a new variable, namely, an interaction between minority status and the best-predicting nondiscriminatory score, into this regression provides a way to study the form of discrimination. (Other forms for this interaction variable are, of course, possible. For example, minority status could be interacted with a variable indicating that the application's score falls above some threshold.) The higher-hurdle view predicts that the coefficient of this variable will be positive; the minority-white disparity in loan approval declines as the loan performance score increases. The alternative view, namely, that discrimination affects minority loans of all credit qualities, predicts that the coefficient of this variable will be zero.

A.8.2 The Causes of Discrimination

These new nonparametric and parametric tests for discrimination in loan approval also could be extended to test hypotheses about the causes of this discrimination. In the nonparametric approach, the measure of discrimination is the difference between the minority composition of the highest-scoring loan applications and the minority composition of actual loans. A hypothesis about the causes of discrimination identifies circumstances under which this measure is expected to be relatively large. Following Kim and Squires (1998), for example, the hypothesis that discrimination is driven by the prejudice of loan officers predicts that discrimination decreases with the minority concentration among a lender's employees. To test for statistical discrimination, a researcher must identify circumstances under which unobserved characteristics of minority applicants have a particularly large negative impact on performance. A loan performance regression could determine, for example, whether the negative impact of minority status on loan performance is higher when the average debt-to-income ratio of minority applications is higher, as suggested by a result in chapter 6. If it is, then the incentive to practice statistical discrimination is higher for loans with a higher debt-to-income ratio, and the statistical-discrimination hypothesis predicts that discrimination increases with the debt-to-income ratio.

With a sample of lenders, hypotheses like these can be tested by regressing the measure of discrimination for each lender on the variables associated with various hypotheses about the causes of discrimination, such as the minority composition of the lender's workforce and the average debt-to-income ratio of the lender's loans. In this framework, it is not possible to test for statistical discrimination unless the incentives to practice it vary across lenders. This variation in incentives can be observed in the loan performance regression, equation (9.1), by determining whether the impact of minority status depends on any credit characteristics. Statistical discrimination could still exist even if the incentive to practice it does not vary across lenders, but in this case the discrimination regression discussed in the text cannot be used to look for it.

As noted in the text, the hypothesis tests proposed here do not distinguish between disparate-treatment and disparate-impact discrimination. Because lenders may be able to replicate the outcomes from disparate-treatment discrimination through a cleverly designed scheme of disparate-impact discrimination, a test for a hypothesis about the causes of discrimination should identify circumstances under which discrimination is likely to occur without specifying the mechanism, disparate treatment or disparate impact, through which this discrimination is implemented.

Finally, the simplified loan approval regression described above could also be used to test hypotheses about the causes of mortgage discrimination. In this case, each variable associated with one of these hypotheses, such as the minority composition of a lender's employees, must be interacted with minority status. The coefficient of this interaction variable provides a test of the hypothesis.

A.9 Introducing Disparate-Impact Discrimination through Across-Lender Variation in Underwriting Standards (Section 9.4.2.2)

This section shows that introducing variation across lenders into a loan performance model could result in disparate-impact discrimination, even if the estimated coefficients of the relevant variables are highly significant statistically. As explained in the text, the relevant variables are interactions between credit characteristics and variables thought to be associated with variation in underwriting standards, such as a measure of a lender's foreclosure policy or the characteristics of a lender's portfolio. The problem is that the coefficients of these interaction terms also might reflect intergroup differences in the impact of various credit characteristics on loan performance instead of, or in addition to, variation in underwriting standards across lenders.

To be more precise, unobserved credit characteristics of minority borrowers, which are the focus of the discussion in section 9.3, might influence the coefficients of the credit variables, the β_is in equation (9.1), as well as the constant term. We showed that a loan performance scoring scheme involves disparate-impact discrimination if it accounts, directly or indirectly, for the average impact of these unobserved characteristics on loan performance. The same lesson applies to a loan performance scheme that accounts, directly or indirectly, for the impact of these unobserved characteristics on the βs. Moreover, if, as seems likely, the variables designed to capture credit rationing or foreclosure policy are correlated with the minority composition of a lender's loans, then the interaction terms defined earlier might pick up the effect of minority status, not the effect of credit rationing or foreclosure policy. This effect could be a source of disparate-impact discrimination.

In formal terms, this is another example of omitted-variable bias. Consider a simple case in which the coefficient of one of the credit characteristics included in equation (9.1), say X_1, is affected by both unobserved credit characteristics of minority borrowers and some lender trait, say Z. The logic of this example extends to more complex cases in which many coefficients are affected. In this example, equation (9.1) must be modified as follows:

$$P = \alpha + \sum_{i=1}^{N} \beta_i X_i + \gamma M + \delta_1 X_1 M + \delta_2 X_1 Z + \varepsilon, \qquad (A.18)$$

where the δs are the coefficients of the new interaction terms between X_1 and both M and Z.

The best-predicting nondiscriminatory scoring scheme based on this equation must not consider minority status. In other words, this scheme must set the minority status variable at its mean value for all applications. Thus, this scheme can be written as follows:

$$S^2 = (\hat{\alpha} + \hat{\gamma}\overline{M}) + \sum_{i=1}^{N} \hat{\beta}_i X_i + \hat{\delta} X + \hat{\delta}_1 X_1 \overline{M} + \hat{\delta}_2 X_1 Z. \qquad (A.19)$$

The expected value of this scheme is therefore

$$E(S^2) = (\alpha + \gamma\overline{M}) + \sum_{i=1}^{N} \beta_i X_i + \delta_1 X_1 \overline{M} + \delta_2 X_1 Z. \qquad (A.20)$$

Now suppose that a lender employs a model of loan performance that recognizes the direct role of minority status, as measured by γ, but ignores the indirect role of minority status through the first interaction term, as measured by δ_1. Then this lender's model can be written

$$P = \alpha' + \sum_{i=1}^{N} \beta_i' X_i + \gamma M + \delta_2' X_1 Z + \varepsilon'. \tag{A.21}$$

A scoring scheme based on this model that does not involve disparate-treatment discrimination takes the following form:

$$S^3 = (\hat{\alpha}' + \hat{\gamma}\overline{M}) + \sum_{i=1}^{N} \hat{\beta}_i' X_i + \delta_2' X_1 Z. \tag{A.22}$$

Because the first interaction term in (A.18) is left out of (A.21), the δ_2 coefficient is estimated with bias. Using the standard omitted-variable bias formula, this bias is given by

$$E(\hat{\delta}_2') = \delta_2 + \delta_1 c, \tag{A.23}$$

where c is the correlation between $X_1 M$ and $X_1 Z$, which can be obtained by regressing the second of these variables on the first. Equation (A.23) implies that the expected value of the scheme in equation (A.22) is

$$E(S^3) = E(S^2) + \delta_1 X_1 (cZ - \overline{M}). \tag{A.24}$$

The last term in equation (A.24) represents a departure from the best-predicting nondiscriminatory scheme and therefore could introduce disparate-impact discrimination. In the extreme case defined by a perfect correlation between Z and M (that is, by $c = 1$), the scheme in equation (A.24) is equivalent to a scheme in which the underwriting weight on X_1 is altered only for minority applicants, which is an example of disparate-treatment discrimination. Less extreme cases obviously could still lead to schemes that have a disparate impact on minority applicants without a business justification.

In sum, any scoring scheme based on a regression with interactions between lender characteristics and application characteristics could involve disparate-impact discrimination. To rule out the possibility that such discrimination is present, no interaction term should be included unless it can be shown to boost the within-group predictability of the model.

B

Data Appendix

Bo Zhao

This data appendix explains how the data from the Boston Fed Study (Munnell et al., 1996) were matched with the HMDA data. The purpose of this matching process is to identify the lender associated with each loan in the Boston Fed Study's data. This matching procedure closely follows the procedure in Day and Liebowitz (1996).

The first step in the procedure was to turn the raw public-use data set from the Boston Fed Study into a SAS data set. (SAS is a trademark of the SAS Institute Inc.; it is a widely used computer program.) This set contains 2,932 observations (applications) and sixty variables. Of these applications, 685 came from black or Hispanic households. We identified the variables used in the Boston Fed Study and corrected any miscoded observations we noted.

The second step was to create a SAS data set for the 1990 HMDA data for the Boston metropolitan area. This data set contains 51,586 observations (applications) and twenty-three variables. We then corrected the miscoded observations and deleted all loans that were not for the purchase of a home, that were insured by the government, or that were not received from white, black, or Hispanic households. These actions reduced the size of data set from 51,586 to 20,399 observations. Finally, we removed applications from lenders with fewer than twenty-five loans, which reduced the sample size to 19,032, including 1,365 minority applications. These applications were submitted to 344 different lenders.

The third step was to match the two data sets using nine variables: loan action, race/ethnicity and sex of applicant and coapplicant, income, loan amount, if and by whom the loan was purchased, and whether the applicant intended to occupy the home. To avoid incorrect matches, we first identified sets (usually pairs) of observations in either data set that contained exactly the same values for each of these variables. All these observations were deleted. This procedure reduced the HMDA sample to 16,389 observations and the Boston Fed Study sample to 2,833 observations. Then we identified all observations in the Boston Fed Study sample that had the same value for all nine of these variables as an observation in the HMDA sample. We were able to match 2,369 observations using this procedure.

The fourth step was to add HMDA information on lenders to the Boston Fed Study–matched sample. The matching process resulted in the identification of 115 different lenders in the Boston Fed Study's sample, resulting in 115 lender dummy variables to use in estimating lender fixed effects. We then calculated the mean characteristics of the applications and mortgages for each lender based on the HMDA data and added the resulting variables to the Boston Fed Study data. The variables we added are average applicant income, average loan size, average loan-to-income ratio, percentage of applications from black households, percentage of applications that were approved, percentage of the lender's conventional mortgages that were sold to Fannie Mae or Freddie Mac, and a dummy variable to control for missing income information.

These matched data, with lender dummy variables and average lender characteristics from HMDA added to observations in the Boston Fed Study data, are used to estimate the loan approval regressions in chapter 6.

Notes

Chapter 1

1. Wolff (1995) reports, for example, that in 1989 a principal residence constituted two-thirds of total wealth for households in the bottom 90 percent of the wealth distribution. Moreover, Hurst, Luoh, and Stafford (1998) show that most households hold the vast majority of their nonpension wealth in the form of equity in their home and that over one-third of total household nonpension wealth is in housing.

2. Much has been written, for example, about the sorting of high-income people, who are predominantly homeowners, into high-service jurisdictions. For a review of this literature, see Ross and Yinger (1999d).

3. These data come from the Home Mortgage Disclosure Act data, which is discussed in more detail below. Additional home-related mortgage applications in 2000 included 6.5 million for refinancing and 1.3 million for home improvements (FFIEC, 2001b, tables 4-3 and 4-4).

4. Throughout this book, the term "minority" is used to mean African American or Hispanic, and the term "white" is used to mean non-Hispanic white. "Black" is used as a synonym for African American. This usage of "white" is a shorthand, because many Hispanic Americans have "European" or "white" backgrounds. In addition, we believe it is appropriate to treat distinctions between these groups as "ethnic" distinctions because they have social origins (Patterson, 1997; J. Milton Yinger, 1994). To be consistent with the literature, we occasionally use the term "race," which we consider to be a synonym of "ethnicity."

5. For the 1983 to 1993 period, homeownership rates are available for non-Hispanic blacks but not for all blacks. To keep the figures consistent, figure 1.1 therefore presents homeownership rates for non-Hispanic blacks from 1994 to 2001. The black/white gap in homownership is higher for all blacks (the text) than for non-Hispanic blacks (figure 1.1) throughout this period, with the largest difference, 0.8 percentage points, in 2001. Not surprisingly, these black/white differences in homeownership are accompanied by large and persistent black/white differences in wealth. According to Wolfe (2001), the mean wealth of black families in 1994 was only 18 percent of the mean wealth of white families, and black median wealth equaled only 2 percent of white median wealth. These ratios were the same in 1984.

6. The series (Dedman, 1988) obviously inspired the title of this book. As explained in the next chapter, community groups can challenge mergers and other actions by a lender who does not meet the credit needs of all neighborhoods in its service area. The

"Color of Money" series followed an unsuccessful attempt by the Atlanta Community Reinvestment Alliance to challenge a merger by an Atlanta lender, apparently after someone working with this alliance gave the documents challenging the merger to the *Atlanta Journal-Constitution* (see Robinson, 1992). The results of this series are updated to 1996 by Wyly and Holloway (1999), who find little change from the patterns of 1988 (despite the addition of data on independent mortgage companies).

7. The articles following the "Color of Money" series include Blossom, Everett, and Gallagher (1988) and Brenner and Spayd (1993). A more scholarly follow-up on redlining, which is defined in chapter 2, was provided by Bradbury, Case, and Dunham (1989).

8. For a more detailed discussion of the data and reporting requirements in the HMDA amendments, see Canner and Gabriel (1992) and Scheessle (1998). Before 1989, HMDA reporting requirements applied to all depository urban lenders with assets over $10 million and their subsidiaries. The 1989 amendments extended coverage to unaffiliated nondepository lenders with at least $10 million in assets. Smaller lenders are now covered as well, thanks to legislation passed in 1991 and effective in 1992. According to Scheessele, HMDA now covers between 80 and 90 percent of the mortgage loans in the country. The main gaps in its coverage are loans by lenders who specialize in nonmetropolitan areas and by small lenders.

9. For more on the legislative history of HMDA and its amendments, see Dreier (1991) and Fishbein (1992).

10. For a detailed history of this investigation, see Ritter (1996).

11. According to the acknowledgments in the original version (Munnell et al., 1992), the methodology for the Boston Fed Study was widely discussed with researchers in several federal financial regulatory agencies, in HUD, and in universities before and after the study was carried out. The acknowledgments in the final version (Munnell et al., 1996) are more cryptic.

12. For alternative reviews of this literature, see Goering and Wienk (1996) and Ladd (1998).

13. All the 2000 HMDA information in this section comes from FFIEC (2001b).

14. See note 8.

15. It should be noted, however, that intergroup income differences might help to explain these results. For example, the higher black/white denial ratio in the highest income class might reflect the fact that the black/white income gap is higher in this class than in lower classes. In any case, an accurate analysis of the role of income must await the multivariate methods discussed later in this book.

16. The studies commenting on the Boston Fed Study are reviewed in detail in chapter 5.

17. A more formal definition of redlining is provided in chapter 2.

Chapter 2

1. More technically, thrifts are usually said to include both savings and loan associations and savings banks, similar institutions that operate under slightly different regulations.

2. Follain and Zorn (1990) discuss the origins of this unbundling, and LaCour-Little (2000) discusses recent trends in these four services.

3. Collateralized mortgage obligations rearrange the cash flows from a pool of mortgages into different bondlike securities, called tranches. The uncertainty in payments falls into a residential tranche that is held by the issuer. See Clauretie and Sirmans (1999, pp. 136–141, 194–195). See also Raines (2000).

4. Fannie Mae, Freddie Mac, and Ginnie Mae were all originally federal government agencies, but Fannie Mae and Freddie Mac have since been privatized (see Lea, 1996). The federal government retains some regulatory authority even for the privatized agencies, however, and all three institutions are often lumped together as "government-sponsored enterprises" (GSEs).

5. Information on the activities of all these regulatory agencies can be obtained through the Web site for the Federal Financial Institutions Examination Council ⟨http://www.ffiec.gov⟩.

6. For the latest limits, see the relevant Web site ⟨http://www.fanniemae.com⟩ or ⟨http://freddiemac.com⟩.

7. Information on these restrictions and other features of the roles played by Fannie Mae and Freddie Mac can be found at their Web sites, as cited in the previous note. Some new, special programs now involve mortgages with loan-to-value ratios of 0.97 or even 1.0.

8. Subprime borrowers need not be low-income, however. See Pennnington-Cross, Yezer, and Nichols (2000).

9. Subprime lenders either accept a substantially reduced price for their mortgages on the secondary market, or else they divide their mortgages into primary and subordinated debt. The primary debt is sold on the secondary market and has first claim on the borrowers' equity in case of default, and subordinated debt is held in the lender's portfolio. As a result subprime lenders often hold onto a substantial portion of the default risk (Royer and Kriz, 1999). Moreover, subprime lenders face substantial uncertainty in selling nonconforming mortgages. In fact, during the Asian financial crisis in the late 1990s, investors became unwilling to purchase securities based on nonconforming mortgages, and many subprime lenders were forced into bankruptcy.

10. No data source directly identifies either subprime loans or lenders that specialize in subprime lending. Existing studies focus on lending by subprime specialists, which are identified by combining a variety of information on types of loans issued, denial rates, and other factors. See Canner and Passmore (1999, appendix B).

11. Because the purchasers of manufactured houses tend to have low incomes and low wealth, mortgage loans for the purchase of manufactured houses tend to be relatively high risk and to involve relatively high interest rates. As a result, some sources, including U.S. Department of Housing and Urban Development (1997), Scheessele (1999), and FFIEC (1998), combine subprime lending with lending for manufactured homes. The share of conventional home purchase loans from lenders in either the subprime or the manufactured home category rose from 5.1 percent in 1993 to 14.1 percent in 1998 (Canner and Passmore, 1999).

12. For extensive discussion of both points of view, see the testimony in U.S. House of Representatives (2000).

13. In addition Cincotta (2000) says that "the Illinois Attorney General found that 76% of borrowers from the subprime lender First Alliance belonged on the prime market and were steered into predatory loans."

14. Large banks and mortgage companies can issue their own MBSs, which are made up of loans that do not conform to the standards of the major secondary mortgage market institutions.

15. For more on these data issues, see Scheessele (1998).

16. "Affiliated institutions" are mainly mortgage bankers affiliated with a depository institution, usually a commercial bank. "Other purchasers" include nonaffiliated mortgage bankers, federal credit agencies, and, to a lesser extent, state and local credit agencies, life insurance companies, and pension funds.

17. For further discussion of these tools, see Mester (1997), Avery, Beeson, and Sniderman (1996a), or Straka (2000).

18. The three main private credit bureaus are Equifax, Experian, and Trans Union. These credit bureaus calculate credit scores using software from a credit-scoring company. The best known such company is FairIsaac, which developed the well-known FICO score. The factors that go into a FICO score reflect past payment history, amount of credit, length of time credit has been established, the frequency of searching for and acquiring new credit, and the type of credit established. See the FairIsaac Web site ⟨www.fairisaac.com⟩.

19. Most analysts reserve the term "credit score" for a default prediction based exclusively on the characteristics of the applicant; others use a broader definition that allows information about the property and the loan to be considered. See Mester (1997).

20. For example, the Desktop Underwriter used by Fannie Mae considers the following factors in addition to credit report factors: equity and loan-to-value ratio, liquid reserves, debt-to-income ratio, loan purpose, loan type, loan term, property type, number of borrowers, and whether the borrower is self-employed. See the Fannie Mae and Freddie Mac websites cited earlier.

21. This issue was emphasized by Bradbury, Case, and Dunham (1989).

22. These disparities also have increased significantly since 1993, when only about 2 percent (5 percent) of home purchase (refinancing) loans were from subprime specialists, even in predominantly minority neighborhoods. See Joint Center for Housing Studies (2000).

23. No multifamily, refinancing, or nonoccupant loans were included.

24. Zorn et al. (forthcoming) also demonstrate the improved predictive power that results from switching from traditional underwriting to the Freddie Mac Loan Prospector system.

25. For more discussion of these issues, see Avery et al. (1999).

26. Another linkage that has not been addressed in the literature (and that will not be considered in this book) is that discrimination in loan approval against some group of applicants might be influenced by a lender's knowledge about the way it will treat defaults by that group relative to defaults by other groups. If a lender believes it can boost its profits through an aggressive foreclosure policy toward some minority

group, for example, then it might be less inclined to discriminate against that group in the loan approval decision.

27. In addition, the Civil Rights Act of 1866 outlaws racial discrimination in any form of contract, including a mortgage. This act has been widely used as a tool to combat discrimination in housing (see Yinger, 1995) but has not been applied extensively to lending.

28. The fair-lending enforcement procedures employed by these agencies are explored in detail in chapter 10.

29. For examples of recent enforcement actions taken by one of these institutions, see Board of Governors (1998). This document is available on the Board of Governors' Web site ⟨http://www.bog.frb.fed.us⟩. The Web sites for the other financial regulatory agencies describe fair-lending procedures and regulations but say little or nothing about enforcement actions.

30. This document is available at the FHA Web site ⟨http://www.fairhousing.com/legal_research/fha/3605.htm⟩.

31. For a more detailed discussion of the enforcement duties of these two agencies, see Schwemm (1994) or Yinger (1995). Recent enforcement actions by Justice are described in Lee (2001).

32. For more on these overlapping responsibilities and their potential for producing interagency conflict, see Yinger (1995).

33. For more on CRA and the regulations that are used to enforce it, see the FFIEC Web site ⟨http://www.ffiec.gov⟩, along with the links on that site to the federal financial regulatory agencies.

34. This point is important for full understanding of the example given in the previous section of behavior that left protected classes at a disadvantage without violating antidiscrimination laws. In that example, the lenders involved were nondepository lenders, that is, mortgage bankers. If they had been depository lenders, then the actions in the example would probably be covered by CRA.

35. For a more detailed analytical discussion of these two types of redlining, see Barth, Cordes, and Yezer (1979) or Bradbury, Case and Dunham (1989).

36. A lending institution is in the business of maximizing the profitability of its loan portfolio, but individual actors in a lending institution may have different objectives. An individual loan officer, for example, may have an incentive simply to avoid defaults over some relatively short time horizon. Some examples of this type of behavior are considered later in this book.

37. In fact, of course, a lender's choice is more complex than just to accept or reject. He can make a counteroffer, for example. More complex decisions are analyzed in later chapters.

38. Predicting expected profitability also raises some difficult technical issues, but a few studies explore alternative possible approaches (Thomas, 2000).

39. Similarly, lenders planning to sell their mortgages on the secondary market are given significant discretion in meeting the guidelines of the secondary mortgage market institutions, such as Fannie Mae and Freddie Mac. They must be careful, however, not to abuse their discretion so badly that many of their loans default, because then

they might then lose access to the secondary market; in other words, Fannie Mae and Freddie Mac may refuse to buy loans from lenders with poor track records.

40. For example, lenders may actually influence default. As Quercia and Stegman (1992, p. 343) put it, "although it is the borrower who stops payments, it is the lender who decides if default has occurred by choosing whether to work with the borrower or to foreclose." A credit-scoring system that does not recognize this possibility could yield biased results. In addition, credit scores are often based on an applicant's consumer credit history, which may not be very closely correlated with his or her propensity to default on a mortgage loan. Avery et al. (2000, p. 524) also point out that in the calculation of these scores, "typically no adjustment is made for local economic conditions (such as regional recession) that may have affected the history of loan repayment in a local area but may be unrelated to future patterns of repayment." A similar point is made by Thomas (2000). Finally, Thomas points out that credit-scoring systems tend to focus on a short time horizon, because a long horizon "leaves the system open to population drift in that the distribution of the characteristics of a population change over time, and so the population sample may be significantly different from that the scoring system will be used on" (p. 153). As a result, credit-scoring schemes may not be accurate for predicting defaults after the first few years.

41. The characteristics in the π function actually used by a lender need not be the same as those in the "true" function, but we will save that complication for a later chapter.

42. Even lenders that face the same regulations may have different costs of capital because the impact of those regulations may vary by region or by market segment. In addition, imperfect competition in the mortgage market implies that lenders in different segments of the market may be able to extract different rates of return on their investments. We return to these issues in chapters 3 and 6.

43. This framework employs a linear form for simplicity, but this form is not necessary.

44. For example, Lindsey (1995) argues that credit scoring will eliminate disparate-treatment discrimination but does not recognize that it might boost disparate-impact discrimination. In contrast, the trade-off between these two types of discrimination is clearly recognized by Yezer (1995), Buist, Linneman, and Megbolugbe (1999), and Avery et al. (2000). We discuss these issues in detail in chapters 6 and 9.

45. In chapter 10, we show one way to address this issue.

46. This concept was first applied to discrimination in labor markets. See Arrow (1973), Phelps (1972), and Cain (1986).

47. As in the case of equation (2.8), we select a linear form for simplicity, but the concepts do not depend on this form.

48. The conflict between Becker's statement and the law is discussed by Swire (1995). As one of us has remarked elsewhere (Yinger, 1995), Becker's statement is also inconsistent with the work of most other scholars (see the review in Cain, 1986). It is even inconsistent with Becker's own influential book (1971), in which the prejudice of customers or workers can give an unprejudiced firm an incentive to discriminate in order to protect its profits. Thus, there is a broad consensus that discrimination can be defined without reference to its causes and can even arise without prejudice on the part of the discriminator.

Chapter 3

1. Marital status and family structure naturally have a large effect on the choice between owner-occupied and rental housing. Therefore, household formation decisions also might be relevant (see Börsch-Supan and Pitkin, 1988).

2. The increase in low-down-payment mortgages in recent years may have loostened the down-payment contraint for many households while at the same time tightening the income constraint.

3. Hendershott, LaFayette, and Haurin (1997) do not examine the effect of income constraints in explaining racial differences in homeownership rates.

4. Alternatively, racial differences in income may explain this difference in the influence of being credit constrained. Owner-occupancy increases rapidly with income, and as a result, rental markets are usually quite thin for households with high demand for housing (2,000 square feet or larger). Therefore, high-income but credit-constrained households, which tend to be white, may accept less housing and remain in the owner-occupied market because the choices are so limited, but low-income, credit-constrained households may refuse to accept less housing, because there are many rental options available that meet their housing desires.

5. Sheiner (1995) investigates the relationship between the influence of housing price and household characteristics, such as income, age, and education, but does not test for racial differences in the influence of housing price on savings behavior.

6. The presence of intermediaries does not, of course, guarantee efficient outcomes. See Yinger (1981) and Wachter (1987) for a discussion of some of the problems that can arise in the market for real estate brokerage, including those related to market power.

7. Yinger (1997) did not separate the last two steps in figure 2.1. In his model, the third step is merged with the second or fourth.

8. To be more precise, they were told that nothing was available only 3.0 percent of the time, and they learned about a single unit 32.9 percent of the time, about two units 16.1 percent of the time, about three units 19.4 percent of the time, and about four or more units 28.6 percent of the time (Yinger, 1995, table 6.1). HDS provides information on marketing behavior by housing agents, with a focus on discrimation. It makes use of a matched-pair or audit research technique, see Yinger (1995).

9. The racial dimension of housing search is only one dimension of the broader question of racial residential segregation. On this broader question, see Cutler, Glaeser, and Vigdor (1999), Galster (1992), Massey and Denton (1993), and Yinger (1995).

10. These differences are all statistically significant. See Yinger (1995).

11. As discussed earlier, the preapplication stage of the mortgage process has increasingly become integrated with the borrower's housing search. Many real estate agents refer prospective home buyers to lenders to be prequalified for a mortgage or even prequalify the buyer themselves.

12. For evidence from other pilot audit studies, see Galster (1993b) and Lawton (1996).

13. The flip side of this point is that a high LTV lowers the cost of default for the borrower. See section 3.4.2.

14. These fractions can vary by lender or by loan program, with higher-cost lenders or programs accepting higher ratios.

15. In the 1970s, market interest rates rose above the FHA/VA interest rates. As a result, substantial discount points were routinely charged on FHA/VA interest rates, but federal policy required that these points be paid by the seller of the house. See Lea (1996).

16. Posey and Yavas (2001) also suggest that borrowers may sort between ARM and FRM mortgages based on default risk, with high default risk borrowers opting for ARMs.

17. Alternatively, the shortage of supply may be addressed by providing all borrowers with less credit than they request. Stiglitz and Weiss do not address this possibility.

18. We do not claim, of course, that this is the only explanation for recent growth in subprime mortgages. Deregulation provides another possible cause, for example. See Mansfield (2000).

19. For some evidence that lenders ration credit (or do not offer different interest rates based on observable characteristics, which is the same thing), see Duca and Rosenthal (1994). The data for Duca and Rosenthal's study come from 1981–1983, so they refer to a period before the appearance of the subprime market.

20. As an alternative, Calomiris, Kahn, and Longhofer suggest moral hazard as a rationale behind credit rationing. Specifically, a borrower can affect the value of her house, and therefore the value of the default option, through maintenance decisions. A high interest rate increases the value of the default and prepayment options, resulting in loan return curves that are very similar to those shown in figures 3.2, 3.3, and 3.4.

21. We return to the Van Order and Zorn paper in chapter 8.

22. Also see Van Order (1996) on adverse selection in the secondary market for mortgages. Van Order also discusses the possibility of moral hazard in this market. Specifically, originators may relax overall underwriting standards to increase payments for servicing mortgages.

23. For a comparison of public and conventional mortgages, see Chinloy (1995).

24. A correlation between the error term and an explanatory variable can also arise in the case of "simultaneous" equations in which a dependent and an explanatory variable influence each other. In chapter 5, we explore two cases in which a simultaneous-equations procedure must be used to analyze the loan approval decision.

25. If these factors are known to have no influence on underwriting, they can be omitted from the specification without causing any bias. In that case, they would be appropriate instruments for estimating a simultaneous-equations model of loan approval and loan terms.

26. Lenders might, for example, specialize in different neighborhoods, and the degree of lender risk might vary by neighborhood. In such a case, a loan approval regression must control for neighborhood characteristics.

27. This mechanism for the endogeneity of loan terms was first suggested by Rachlis and Yezer (1993).

28. This form of selection differs from previous suggestions that mortgage performance suffers from selection bias due to the application process. In fact, this bias may be more severe than the bias from the application process, because a correlation between unobservables in the application and default processes is unlikely to arise in a well-specified statistical model of loan approval. If a loan approval model contains all of a lender's underwriting variables, no mechanism exists to create the correlation between the approval and default unobservables.

29. Some scholars have argued that because of variation in lender underwriting standards, it makes no sense to pool applications across lenders. See, for example, the comments by Glenn Canner in Bogdon and Bell (2000, p. 40). We will return to this issue in later chapters.

30. This idea has been made explicit in the new automated underwriters developed by FannieMae and FreddieMac. If a mortgage passes through the automated underwriting systems of a particular GSE, that GSE guarantees that it will purchase the mortgage.

31. Figure 3.5 builds on a result in section 6.3.2, namely, that the negative influence on loan performance of an applicant's debt-to-income ratio is smaller when the lender's average debt-to-income ratio is higher. For the sake of simplicity, the figure draws this relationship as linear; the same principles apply to any other reasonable shape.

32. Several models based on imperfect information are discussed in chapter 6. See, for example, Lang and Nakamura (1993), which shows how imperfect information can lead to redlining.

33. A similar problem of interpretation arises with housing audits, although the situation is reversed (See Yinger, 1995, chap. 2). Existing audit studies are based on a sample of advertisements and therefore capture the discrimination that would be encountered if minorities applied (and were qualified for) a typical ad. These studies do not capture the discrimination that is encountered by the typical minority household. HDS finds, however, that discrimination does not depend in a significant way on the characteristics of the auditor or the unit, so in the case of housing, at least, there is no reason to think that these two measures of discrimination are very different.

34. However, the Boston Fed Study (Munnell et al., 1996) did look at the extent to which discrimination varied with various lender characteristics and found little variation. For example, the amount of discrimination was found to be no different for lenders who did and did not specialize in loans to minorities.

35. One approach that appears to avoid this problem is provided by Charles and Hurst (forthcoming), who estimate a loan approval regression using credit characteristics from the Panel Study of Income Dynamics, a data set that is, of course, not directly influenced by lender actions. Even in this case, however, household characteristics could be influenced by anticipated lender discrimination.

Chapter 4

1. We do not review early studies on outcome-based redlining, such as Bradbury, Case, and Dunham (1989). For a review of these studies, see Schill and Wachter (1992).

2. We return to the Peterson study in chapter 8, however, because it was the first to make several key points about studies of loan default.

3. The authors also dropped a few applications that were withdrawn by the applicant before the lender made a decision.

4. The 1993 figure is the earliest one available. The comparable figure for 1998 is 12.0 percent. The rejection rate for applications to subprime lenders was 43.4 percent (56.0 percent) in 1993 (1998), but this rate is not comparable to the rate in Black, Schweitzer, and Mandell because subprime mortgage loans did not exist in 1977. Note also that Black, Schweitzer, and Mandell offer several explanations for their low rejection rate but do not consider the possibility that lenders with high rejection rates decided not to participate in their survey—a potential source of selection bias.

5. Black, Schweitzer, and Mandell (1978) recognize that various loan terms are interdependent, so that every loan term should be treated as endogenous in a study of loan terms (p. 187), and two of the authors (Black and Schweitzer, 1985) later estimated a simultaneous model of loan terms. Neither the 1978 article nor the 1985 article, however, discusses the possibility that loan terms should be treated as endogenous in a study of loan approval.

6. As one would expect, King's results are similar, although somewhat weaker, if this flawed credit history variable is included. See the discussion in chapter 5.

7. King also omits applications that were withdrawn before a final decision or that had missing data.

8. King also replicates his loan denial regressions using logit analysis. The results are very similar to those from the OLS regressions.

9. King recognizes that the loan-to-value ratio might be endogenous in a loan denial regression, but then he makes loan terms exogenous by assuming that they are set after the approval decision is made.

10. Although recognizing the complexity of the loan decision is an important contribution, one might question Schafer and Ladd's use of multinomial logit analysis, which assumes that the choice between any two alternatives is unaffected by the introduction of a third alternative (see Börsch-Supan, 1987). This assumption seems implausible in this case. For example, surely the choice between approval and denial is affected by the possibility of a counteroffer with different terms. Alternative techniques that do not make this assumption, such as nested logit analysis, are available.

11. Although Schafer and Ladd describe their key loan terms variable as the borrower's requested loan amount, this amount might be influenced by the lender, through advice or negotiation, for example. See chapter 3.

12. Schafer and Ladd (1981, table 5.19) also report that the black/white denial ratio was 0.00 and significantly different from one in one metropolitan area.

13. In one urban area, Bakersfield, California, Hispanics encountered a significantly lower denial probability than did whites.

14. A list of all the variables for which they collected data can be found in Munnell et al. (1996, table 1). Detailed definitions of the variables in table 4.4 can be found in the appendix to Munnell et al. (1996).

15. Munnell et al. excluded withdrawn applications from their sample. To test the view that applications are sometimes withdrawn because of discouraging comments made by the lender, they estimated a multinomial model similar to that in Schafer and

Ladd (1981), with withdrawals as a third alternative. They found that withdrawals were influenced by totally different factors than denials and that there was no racial difference in number of applicants making withdrawals. These findings support their decision to exclude these cases.

16. Tootell (1996a) draws on an unpublished manuscript by all the authors of the Boston Fed Study, namely Munnell et al. (1993).

17. Additional analyses of process-based redlining using the Boston Fed Study's data are examined in chapter 7.

Chapter 5

1. This chapter draws on Ross and Yinger (1999b), which was prepared for the Urban Institute under a contract from HUD's Office of Policy Development and Research. Many of the empirical results presented in this chapter were originally presented in this report, but the conclusions have been extensively revised.

2. The original version of the Boston Fed Study was released as a working paper in 1992 and the final version was published in 1996. Because many of the critics focused on the original version and were published in 1994 or 1995, Munnell et al. (1996) includes considerable material responding to the critics. Subsets of the authors of the Boston Fed Study also have published additional responses. See Browne and Tootell (1995) and Tootell (1996b).

3. A discussion of these potential flaws draws on several econometric theorems. A brief discussion of the key econometric concepts is provided in section 2 of the appendix A.

4. Another variable is considered by Hunter and Walker (1996), who argue that loan denial may depend on how "thick" an applicant's file is, as measured by whether there are two or more credit checks in the file. This variable proves to be insignificant.

5. This effect was described to us in correspondence with Geoffrey Tootell. Our regressions do not include lender dummies because, to protect confidentiality, they are not included in the public-use data set. Because they omit these variables, our regressions overstate the minority status coefficient by 20 percent. The public-use data set, however, also does not, for the same reason, include census tract dummies, which raise the estimated minority status coefficient. By coincidence, these two effects almost exactly offset each other, so our estimate of the minority-white denial gap using the methodology that is closest to the Boston Fed Study's, 7.7 percentage points, is almost the same as the Boston Fed Study's estimate, 8.2 percentage points. In chapter 6, we use the HMDA data to identify a large subset of the lenders in the Boston Fed Study's data set and estimate some models with lender dummy variables.

6. This list is similar to the set of variables in the baseline estimation of Munnell et al. (1996), except that it substitutes census tract characteristics for tract dummies and excludes lender dummies (See table 4.4). Munnell et al. could not reject the hypothesis that a separate coefficient for black applicants was the same as one for Hispanic applicants.

7. As discussed in section 2 of the Technical Appendix, the pseudo R-squared is the percentage of the variance in the underlying latent variable that is explained by the

model. This is a better measure of explanatory power than the percent of observations correctly classified, which is used by Zycher and Wolfe (1994) in their critique of the Boston Fed Study.

8. For simplicity, the text of this chapter presents only the absolute values of t-statistics.

9. In a probit model (as used here) or the similar logit model (in Munnell et al., 1996), a percentage impact is determined by comparing the average predicted probability for all observations at two different values of the variable in question. In this case, we compare the average predicted probabilities of denial for minority applications with the minority status coefficient set to zero and to its estimated value.

10. This technique is called a bivariate probit with recursion. Equations describing the model are presented in section 3.1 of the appendix A.

11. A high value for this correlation also might reflect omitted variables.

12. To make them comparable with the simultaneous-equations procedures in appendix A, the single-equation results we present here and elsewhere are based on bivariate probit models, not the related logit models used by Munnell et al. Logit and probit results for comparable equations are, however, similar.

13. The reader may be puzzled by the fact that the minority status coefficient is larger in the first specification, but the percentage impact on loan denial is smaller. This apparent contradiction arises because predicted probabilities from a two-equation model reflect not only the estimated coefficients but also the estimated correlation between unobserved factors across equations.

14. An alternative response to these results would be to include "unable to verify" and treat it as endogenous. We implemented this alternative approach for many of the models discussed later in this chapter and found that the results are very similar to those using the simple approach of dropping this variable altogether. Consequently, we present only the results from the simpler approach.

15. The equations for this model, along with a discussion of econometric issues it raises, including the identification of the model, can be found in section 3.2 of appendix A.

16. The estimated correlation between the errors in these two equations is 0.0316, with a standard error of 0.4538.

17. We also pointed out earlier that a control variable for "lender toughness" has no impact on the minority status coefficient and that the Boston Fed Study's regressions already include lender dummies.

18. We are grateful to Geoffrey Tootell for suggesting this example to us.

19. As discussed in chapter 3 (lesson 7), this type of information gap not only requires controls for lenders (or at least for lender characteristics) but also subtly changes the interpretation of the minority status coefficient. If this type of gap exists, then this coefficient reflects discrimination by the lenders to which minorities apply, not discrimination by a random sample of lenders or even by the lenders to which whites apply.

20. The simplified procedure at the very end of this section implies that the Boston Fed Study overstates discrimination by 37.5 percent $[(7.7 - 5.6)/5.6]$.

21. To be specific, Munnell et al. (1996) find that the minority status coefficient is virtually the same for the sample of lenders that specialize in dealing with minority applicants as for the sample of other lenders. Moreover, Browne and Tootell (1995) show that the minority status coefficient is literally unaffected if one excludes two large minority lenders that together account for half the minority applications in the Boston Fed Study's sample.

22. Another possibility is that the cases under II.B.2 arise from different underwriting standards for minority and white applicants, on average. However, Munnell et al. (1996) and Hunter and Walker (1996) find little evidence that individual underwriting variables receive different weights for minority and white applicants. One exception, which is discussed in section 5.5, is in Hunter and Walker, which finds that the minority status coefficient is larger at a high obligation ratio than at a low one.

23. As noted earlier, several studies have documented discrimination in lender pre-application procedures or loan marketing, but no study has determined whether this results in a mismatch between minority borrowers and the lenders they select.

24. There is some disagreement between Horne and the Boston Fed Study's authors about the extent to which they are making the same corrections. Munnell et al. (1996) cite an unpublished paper by Horne, which, after revisions, became Horne (1994). Tootell (1996b) cites another unpublished paper by Horne, which, after revisions, became Horne (1997). The last word, so far, is in Horne (1997).

25. They also remove observations on the exceptions list that were identified as problematic by Horne (1994).

26. Note that the baseline estimate presented here is lower than the estimates reported above because Day and Liebowitz also alter the data by removing the observations that Horne (1994) claims are misclassified. This issue is discussed in the next section.

27. Results for models that drop multifamily applications and drop applications with low LTVs are presented later in this chapter.

28. This formula is presented in section 4 of appendix A.

29. Stengel and Glennon perform other regressions that qualify this finding. See the discussion in section 5.5.1.

30. The statistically significant results are as follows: In 1977, downward modification was less likely for blacks than for whites in three areas and more likely for Hispanics than for whites in one area (Schafer and Ladd, 1981, table 5.21). In 1978, downward modification was more likely for blacks in two areas, less likely for blacks in one area, and less likely for Hispanics in one area (table 5.21).

31. Although difficult to interpret, the New York results also do not give comfort to the view that the Boston Fed Study's results are driven by its treatment of counteroffers. To be specific, counteroffers are significantly more likely for blacks than for whites in two of the metropolitan area/lender type combinations, are significantly more likely for Hispanics than for whites in only three of these combinations, and are significantly less likely for Hispanics than for whites in one other combination (Schafer and Ladd, 1981, table 7.8).

32. As noted in chapter 4, the use of multinomial logit analysis in the pioneering work of Schafer and Ladd requires an implausible assumption. Alternative estimating

techniques, such as nested logit models, that avoid this problem have not yet been applied to these loan choices.

33. Hunter and Walker's argument is motivated by a theory about the causes of lending discrimination. We return to this topic in chapter 7.

34. Munnell et al. (1996) also find that self-employed minority applicants are less likely than other minority applicants to encounter discrimination. The impact of minority status on loan denial does not vary with any of their other explanatory variables.

35. Stengel and Glennon (1999) is a revised version of a working paper that came out several years earlier: Glennon and Stengel (1994b). As discussed in chapter 6, the line of argument presented in Stengel and Glennon also is taken up in several studies that have appeared since the original Glennon and Stengel piece, including Buist, Linneman, and Megbolugbe (1999) and Courchane, Nebhut, and Nickerson (2000).

36. Chapter 6 reviews several more-recent studies that investigate whether the minority status coefficient is lower for minority-owned lenders or for lenders with many minority employees. These include Black, Collins, and Cyree (1997), Bostic and Canner (1997), and Kim and Squires (1998).

37. The coefficient is 0.98 (*t*-statistic: 2.84) for lenders with many minority loans and 0.91 (*t*-statistic: 2.22) for other lenders. See Munnell et al. (1996, table 5).

38. As we show in chapter 8, a similar confusion arises in several studies that use the so-called default approach to mortgage lending discrimination.

39. The equations defining Rachlis and Yezer's model are presented in section 5 of the appendix A.

40. Phillips and Yezer estimate this model with conditional bivariate probit analysis, which controls for the selection of applicants into special programs.

41. Phillips and Yezer (1996) also estimate a model in which the first decision is the lender's loan denial decision and the second decision is whether the borrower accepts the lender's offer. This model, estimated with conditional probit, has a key technical flaw. The authors do not have any new exogenous variables to "identify" the model, so they identify it by making different assumptions about the functional forms of the two equations, but using the same set of explanatory variables. If these untested assumptions are not correct, their procedure yields biased estimates. Moreover, the estimated correlation between unobservable factors in the two equations is implausibly high, −0.997, and the authors indicate that many alternative specifications did not converge; that is, they could not find a solution for the underlying econometric formulas.

42. Munnell et al. (1996) also examined the PMI variable. They found that the minority status coefficient in the loan denial equation was not affected by dropping this variable or by dropping all applications that were denied PMI from the sample.

43. Although the validity of an instrument can be tested by including it in the regression of interest, instruments found to be valid are not included in the final form of this regression, but are instead used to cleanse the relevant explanatory variable of its endogenous component.

44. Rachlis and Yezer (1993) totally reject the use of instrumental variables in this case because any variable that explains LTV is likely to be used by lenders during the

underwriting process, that is, to be correlated with denial. We agree that one must use caution in selecting instruments in this case but also believe that it is possible to identify acceptable instruments.

45. To be specific, we estimated a loan approval model in which the LTV dummy variables are replaced with LTV itself and which includes income, house price, liquid assets, and all three pairwise interactions as explanatory variables. The coefficients of house price and on all three pairwise interactions are small and statistically insignificant (t-statistics of about 0.5 or lower). We also can reject the hypothesis that this set of variables is statistically significant in the loan denial equation. In particular, the chi-square ratio for the appropriate likelihood ratio test is below 1.3 for all three models in table 5.5; the 5-percent critical value for this test is 9.5.

46. Missing values for income, house price, and liquid assets required the deletion of nineteen observations, resulting in a sample size of 2,912. In addition, we dropped sixteen observations in which the application's LTV is 1.5 or greater. We estimate LTV using OLS and use the predicted LTV as a regressor in a probit analysis of loan denial. For the specification with the "meets guidelines" variable when applications with extreme LTVs are not eliminated, the R^2 is 0.10 for the LTV models, but when the outliers are dropped, the R^2 is 0.25. Moreover, the magnitude of the coefficient on the LTV variable is only −0.304 (t-statistic: 3.09) when the outliers are not eliminated, but the coefficient is −0.971 (t-statistic: 3.97) when the outliers are dropped. Similar results arise for the other two specifications. In addition, making LTV endogenous requires us to alter the model in which "meets guidelines" is treated as endogenous, because LTV was treated as an (exogenous) instrument in that model. In particular, LTV is replaced as an instrument for the "meets guidelines" variable with the instruments used to identify LTV.

47. Our procedure is to obtain a predicted value of LTV using the exogenous instruments and then to include this predicted value in the probit regression for loan denial. The coefficients (t-statistics) of actual LTV in the loan approval models are −0.804 (3.06), −0.744 (2.25), and −0.971 (3.97), whereas the coefficients of predicted LTV are −0.777 (1.01), −1.334 (1.86), and −1.114 (1.59). Thus, treating LTV as endogenous has little impact on its coefficient in the loan approval equation, except in the second model. These results for the second model support the prediction by Yezer, Phillips, and Trost (1994) that LTV has a coefficient that is biased downward when it is treated as exogenous.

48. As an additional check on the validity of these instruments, we also estimated four new versions of our second model, that is, of the model that treats "meets guidelines" as endogenous. In each version we dropped one of the four instruments, leaving the other three. In every case the minority status coefficient is larger than when all four instruments are used. Our results are thus not driven by the use of too many instruments.

49. We are grateful to Anthony Yezer for pointing this out to us.

50. This relationship is presented in section 4 of appendix A, in the section on errors in the explanatory variables.

51. The coefficients (t-statistics) of LTV in the three models are −0.665 (0.49), −1.99 (1.51), and −0.602 (0.52), and the coefficients (t-statistics) of the housing expense–to–income ratio are −0.017 (0.54), −0.041 (1.32), and −0.011 (0.41). As in note 47, these results for the second model support Yezer, Phillips, and Trost (1994).

52. Recall that Rachlis and Yezer (1993) doubt that enough acceptable instruments can be found to estimate a loan denial model with several endogenous variables. We disagree: Our variables meet all three criteria for a good instrument. One possible explanation for the lower impact of minority status in model 2, however, is that this model involves one more endogenous variable ("meets guidelines") than the other models without any additional instruments; without sufficient instruments, a simultaneous-equations model may be unable to sort out the impacts of various endogenous variables. Future loan denial studies should pay close attention to the collection and testing of potential instruments.

53. To be specific, these correlations (*t*-statistics) are 0.843 (7.70), 0.917 (13.59), and 0.911 (13.35).

54. When the ratio of loan to assessed value is replaced with the traditional loan-to-value ratio (based on the minimum of assessed value and house price), the estimated correlation moves even closer to one, and two of the models do not converge, probably because the ratio of loan to house price is so similar to the traditional loan-to-value ratio. The only model to converge is the one that includes the "meets guidelines" variable. The results for that model are similar to the model that uses the ratio of loan amount to appraised value. These problems are similar to the problems experienced by Phillips and Yezer (1996) in trying to estimate a joint model of lender and borrower choice. See note 41. These problems did not arise in Phillips and Yezer's simultaneous-equations model of loan denial and special-program choice, because they used far fewer explanatory variables than we do, yielding more left over in the "unobserved" factors. With many explanatory variables, the small differences between the ratio of loan amount to assessed value and the ratio of loan amount to house price do not provide enough new information to sort out the direct impact of special-program choice on loan denial from the unobserved factors that influence both special-program choice and loan denial.

55. To be specific, the correlations (*t*-statistics) for our three models are −0.462 (1.86), −0.467 (1.80), and −0.508 (2.10).

56. As we will see in chapter 6, several studies find disparate-treatment discrimination by one or by a few lenders.

Chapter 6

1. This section draws on Ross and Yinger (1999c), although the material is significantly reorganized, revised, and expanded.

2. See Ritter (1996) for a detailed discussion of this case. Black (1995) argues the Siskin and Cupingood study is flawed because it does not account for the endogeneity of loan terms or explore enough alternative specifications. In our judgment, these extensions, if made, are unlikely to alter the study's main result.

3. The evidence of discrimination against blacks by Decatur Federal was not confined to these regression results. For example, Decatur Federal's market share was much lower in black than in white census tracts, even though Decatur Federal was a large-volume lender with an ability to compete throughout the Atlanta area. Moreover, Decatur Federal had a history of closing branches in black neighborhoods, and the criteria it stated as justification for closing a branch were not the same in black and white neighborhoods. Finally, Decatur Federal solicited referrals primarily from real

estate agents whose business was concentrated in white neighborhoods. In fact, a former Decatur Federal account executive told investigators that she was instructed not to solicit loans south of Interstate 20, where many of Atlanta's black neighborhoods were located. See Ritter (1996), Siskin and Cupingood (1996).

4. This study also did not deal with the simultaneity issues raised in chapter 5, but, as in the case of the Boston Fed Study, it seems unlikely that a simultaneous equations procedure would alter the study's main conclusions.

5. The Federal Reserve Board's investigation procedures are considered in detail in chapter 10.

6. These OCC procedures are examined in detail in chapter 10.

7. Stengel and Glennon also present another set of results obtained after "deleting a number of denied files with certain ambiguous characteristics" (p. 314). The results are very similar. See their table 2.

8. Again, Stengel and Glennon also estimate their models with various other samples to explore the impact of potential data errors; the results are similar. See their tables 3–5.

9. Strictly speaking, Stengel and Glennon do not test this hypothesis. See Ross and Yinger (1999c).

10. See Giles and Courchane (2000) for the econometric procedures used to adjust for the stratified sample design.

11. In both cases, the lenders were referred to the Department of Justice, and the resulting legal proceedings led to out-of-court settlements that entailed substantial penalties for the lenders and compensation for the victims, that is, for the minority applicants who had been denied loans.

12. More formally, Buist, Linneman, and Megbolugbe use a computer algorithm to identify the set of underwriting weights that replicates the actual decisions of lenders, calculate a "score" for each applicant based on these weights, and then show that the minority status coefficient in a loan approval equation is no longer statistically significant when this score is included as an explanatory variable.

13. In addition, the implicit "meets guidelines" variable equals zero for 265 of the 410 denied applications in their sample. This variable therefore effectively explains these observations and eliminates their influence on any of the other estimated coefficients, including the minority status coefficient. In other words, their procedure is equivalent to a substantial decrease in effective sample size. As a result, the impact of this variable on the minority-status coefficient could simply reflect the decline in sample size, not a real behavioral effect.

14. We do not review loan approval studies that rely on HMDA data and that do not explore variation in underwriting standards across lenders. These studies include Rosenblatt (1997) and Myers and Chan (1995). Each of these studies is a clever, but ultimately unsatisfactory, attempt to make use of the HMDA variable indicating whether a loan was "denied due to poor credit," which is similar to the credit history variable available to King (1980). For example, Myers and Chan estimate, for all denied loans, the relationship between this variable and observable characteristics of the borrower, loan, and location. The estimation results are then used to calculate a predicted credit risk variable for all applications. This variable is then used as a proxy

for the missing credit history information in a loan denial equation. We do not believe that this is an adequate patch for the problem of missing credit history information, because "denied due to poor credit" is available only for denied applications. Moreover, this approach does not address the problems that arise when a variable that reflects the lender's judgment is used as an explanatory variable. These problems were discussed in chapter 5. Rosenblatt is reviewed in Ross and Yinger (1999c).

15. This paper is also discussed in section 6.2.2.3.

16. This paper is also discussed in sections 6.2.2.3. and 6.3.3.1.

17. As discussed in chapter 5 (see, especially, the discussion of Day and Liebowitz, 1996), lender dummies are preferred to lender characteristics for the purpose of estimating the minority status coefficient. They may not be preferred for other purposes.

18. This hypothesis should be of interest to policymakers, because it implies that the flow of funds to some neighborhoods, particularly low-income neighborhoods where few house sales take place, may be restricted by a lack of information, which is the type of problem that markets cannot solve. If it is true, therefore, this hypothesis may serve as a justification for the CRA or other policies to offset redlining.

19. Calem uses national HMDA data and proxies for transactions using the number of households that are owner-occupants and moved into their residence in 1989. Ling and Wachter and Harrison use HMDA data for Dade (Miami) and Pinellas (St. Petersburg) counties in Florida, respectively, and data on house sales and sales prices from the Florida Department of Revenue. Ling and Wachter and Harrison also examine the relationship between housing appreciation rates and loan approval.

20. Bostic and Canner also find that the share of Asian applications was higher at Asian-owned banks, all else equal, as was the share of white applications at white-owned banks.

21. We also cannot be certain that we have accounted for every relevant feature of a lender's portfolio.

22. In performing this matching, we follow the Day and Liebowitz procedure very closely. We are grateful to Bo Zhao for carrying out these calculations, which are described in the appendix B.

23. For more on this issue, see Day and Liebowitz (1996).

24. More formally, the evidence reviewed in chapter 5 rules out the possibilities in case I of table 5.4. The most crucial distinction for the remaining cases is between explanations that involve differences in underwriting based on business necessity (the cases under II.B.2), none of which involve discrimination in loan approval, and all other cases, each of which involves some type of discrimination in loan approval or in evaluating loan files. Thus, after controlling for legitimate differences in underwriting standards, the estimated coefficient of a cleaned "meets guidelines" variable must be capturing discrimination that would otherwise appear in the coefficient of the minority status variable. To make sure that discrimination is confined, as it should be, to the coefficient of the minority status variable, the best specification in this case is to drop the "meets guidelines" variable altogether.

25. The results for this regression are not included in table 6.1.

26. Other results for this regression are not reported here.

27. Recall from table 5.1 that a higher value for the credit history variable indicates more credit history problems.

28. Note that the specification shown in columns 3 and 4 does not include an interaction between race and consumer credit history. This interaction is not significant when it is included; that is, the specification containing such an interaction is not statistically different from the specification presented.

29. We reached this conclusion using a nonnested hypothesis test in which the debt-to-income interaction model and one other interaction model are compared to a composite model including both sets of interactions. With the exception of the consumer credit history specification, all other specifications were rejected in favor of the debt-to-income specification. Note that a composite model containing both debt-to-income and credit history interactions yields results that are almost identical to those using the specifications shown in table 6.2.

30. This approach also has the disadvantage that it makes sense only for the subset of lenders with more than a few loans in the data set.

31. This approach is also supported by the finding, discussed in section 6.3.2, that many different sets of applicant-level interactions are significant and that some of them provide results that are qualitatively similar to those of the preferred debt-to-income interactions.

32. To be more precise, each set is significant based on a comparison to the specification that includes only the appropriate set of applicant-level interactions.

33. This result is not surprising. These two variables have a correlation of 0.76.

34. The specification that includes the difference between the applicant's ratio and the mean ratio has higher explanatory power than the specification that simply controls for the mean ratio. We are unable, however, to estimate a model that provides a formal test of the hypothesis that this difference specification is superior to the mean-ratio specification.

35. The direct evidence for statistical discrimination is less powerful in this case. Specifically, the coefficient for the interaction between application-level consumer credit and minority status is negative, as expected by the statistical-discrimination hypothesis, but the coefficient is not statistically significant. Moreover, a specification based on the difference between the applicant's credit history and the mean credit history for the lender does not improve the fit of the regression.

36. We find that the basic debt-to-income ratio interaction model in section 6.3.2 is rejected in favor of this model. In addition, this model cannot be rejected relative to a complete model that interacts all variables with both applicant-level debt-to-income ratio and the difference between the applicant-level and portfolio-level debt-to-income ratio.

37. To be more precise, our sample here includes all lenders who have at least ten rejected applications in the subset of the Boston Fed Study's sample for which the lender can be identified.

38. The specification in which underwriting requirements are the same across lenders is rejected in favor of the more general specification at the 0.001 level.

39. Surprisingly, the underwriting weight on LTV has the wrong sign (positive) for the first lender but has the right sign (negative) for all the other lenders.

40. The minority status coefficient could still understate discrimination if average underwriting weights have a disparate impact on minority applicants without a business justification. In chapter 9, we show how this possibility could be explored with loan performance data.

41. Recall that our third model and the analysis of Blackburn and Vermilyea (2001) both indicate that the minority status coefficient cannot be explained by idiosyncratic variation in the weights placed on standard variables.

Chapter 7

1. The material in this chapter draws on Ross and Yinger (1999c).

2. See Cain (1986) for a review of the literature on statistical discrimination in labor markets.

3. Ondrich, Ross, and Yinger also find that "for blacks, but not for whites, a unit is more likely to be shown if its value is below that of the advertised unit. This result suggests that real estate agents expect blacks, but not whites to request more expensive units than they can afford." This is, of course, another example of statistical discrimination.

4. Hunter and Walker (1996) present a third explanation, which does not, in our view, make sense. They point out that loan officers see many more white than minority applications and conclude that loan officers may therefore have more accurate predictions about the impact of less formal factors on outcomes for whites. As they say, "it is quite possible for factors other than credit history to matter for whites, possibly mitigating the impact of a weak credit history, while at the same time credit history may continue to play a dominant role in the accept/reject decision for minorities" (p. 67). This begs the question, because it does not explain why loan officers feel the need to treat black and white loan applicants any differently: Why can't their experience with white applicants be applied to black applicants?

5. The notion of statistical discrimination based on the variance in unobservable factors goes back to Phelps (1972).

6. Prejudice has long been recognized as a cause of discrimination. In the economics literature, this link was emphasized by Becker (1971).

7. For more on this point, refer to the discussion of figure 1.4.

8. Specifically, this effect is positive and statistically significant in two of five areas for commercial banks, three of five areas for savings and loans, and one of two areas for mortgage brokers. Only two areas were observed for mortgage brokers because of data limitations. In one case (commercial banks in Atlanta) the effect was negative and significant. See Kim and Squires (1998, table 5). The five areas are Atlanta, Boston, Denver, Milwaukee, and San Francisco.

9. Specifically, this effect was positive and significant in one of five areas area for savings and loan associations and positive in two of three areas for mortgage brokers. It was also negative and significant in one area (Milwaukee) for commercial banks. See Kim and Squires (1998, table 5).

10. Indeed, this effect could arise because of something even simpler, such as a non-linearity in the relationship between the obligation ratio and loan denial.

11. This conclusion does not apply to the models of credit rationing by Besanko and Thaker (1987) or Calem and Stutzer (1995), which were discussed in chapter 3. In these models, the lender cannot impose a differential rate of credit rationing by group without affecting the composition of minority applicants over unobservable creditworthiness. Any shift in the unobservable creditworthiness of applicants imposes real economic costs on lenders.

12. Technically, they assume a Bayesian updating process.

13. Evidence of discrimination in car loans by some dealers is also provided by Kissinger and Richardson (2001).

14. These accusations have been disputed by Nissan. See especially Henriques (2001a).

15. Early studies of discrimination in loan terms include King (1980), Schafer and Ladd (1981), and Black and Schweitzer (1985). King found little evidence of discrimination in interest rates or LTVs. Using the same data described in chapter 3, Schafer and Ladd found that black and Hispanic borrowers were charged higher interest rates and higher loan fees than white borrowers, all else equal, in several of their study areas. Black and Schweitzer also found some evidence that blacks are charged higher interest rates than whites.

16. Crawford and Rosenblatt use a complex (and appropriate) definition of interest rate, or yield, that accounts for points and the prepayment option.

17. Unlike the Crawford and Rosenblatt regressions, the OCC regression for this lender does not control for a change in the interest rate between the date of commitment and the date of closing. It also does not control for the market interest rate at the lock-in date, but instead controls only for the year.

18. In addition, women were more likely than men to be charged overages.

19. The OCC regressions for the third lender control for an interest rate, but Courchane and Nickerson do not indicate whether the regressions use the actual interest rate for the individual loan or the average market rate, and they do not indicate whether the rate is measured at the lock-in date or the closing date. The regression coefficients may contain endogeneity bias if this variable was defined either as the individual loan rate or as the market rate at closing.

20. No clear definition of the interest rate used as an explanatory variable is given, but it appears from context to be the final interest rate on the loan, which includes, of course, the overage, if any. This problem can be avoided by following Crawford and Rosenblatt, who use the market interest rate at the lock-in date, as well as the change in the market rate between lock-in and closing.

21. See Ayres (2001). We return to this issue in chapter 10.

22. These samples are analyzed using Tobit analysis, which is an appropriate technique when the dependent variable is limited (in this case to be positive). See Greene (2000).

23. The results in Tootell's study are particularly compelling because he controls for the perceived risk to owners of home equity in a neighborhood, using variables that are not in the public-use version of the Boston Fed Study's data.

24. This coefficient and the following one are based on logit analysis. Ross and Tootell estimate several different models; these results are from the most complete one.

25. This simultaneous-equations model, which was estimated with bivariate probit analysis, is discussed in chapter 5. As noted there, this model yields little evidence that the receipt of PMI is endogeous to the loan denial decision.

26. Harrison also tests directly for process-based redlining. In his regression with lender fixed effects (the one we prefer), he finds that the probability of loan approval declines significantly as the minority population (in percent) in a neighborhood increases. The t-statistic is -2.46. However, this regression does not control for applicant credit history, so the result may be subject to omitted-variable bias.

27. Ling and Wachter (1998) also find that the probability of loan acceptance increases with the rate of increase in housing prices in a given neighborhood. As they point out, an increase in sales in a particular neighborhood could signal an upward shift in the demand for housing in that neighborhood, so that this result is consistent with the view that lenders see less risk in neighborhoods where housing demand is on the rise.

Chapter 8

1. This chapter is a revised version of Ross and Yinger (1999a).

2. A performance-based approach to studying discrimination has been used in other markets, too. See Ayres (forthcoming).

3. This argument also appeared in several other columns, including Brimelow (1993), Brimelow and Spencer (1993), and Roberts (1993).

4. Here is the comparable quotation from the magazine column (Becker, 1993a, p. 18): "The theory of discrimination contains the paradox that the rate of default on loans approved for blacks and Hispanics by discriminatory banks should be lower, not higher, than those on mortgage loans to whites."

5. Peterson (1981) addresses mortgage discrimination against women, not against blacks or Hispanics, but Peterson clearly makes the conceptual point that a comparing average default rates across groups cannot reveal anything about discrimination.

6. A comparable figure (and argument) can be found in Quigley (1996).

7. Recall from the earlier discussion of Ferguson and Peters (2000) that discrimination does not imply a lower default rate for the marginal black applicant than for the marginal white applicant if it takes the form of a credit-rationing rule that favors whites over blacks.

8. A clear exposition of this argument is provided by Brueckner (1996). See Berkovec et al. (1996) for their views on this conclusion (and on some of our others). These two citations are both part of a special issue of the journal *Cityscape* on the default approach (Goering, 1996).

9. In a hazard model the dependent variable is the probability that an action will occur in one period given that it has not yet occurred in previous periods. See Greene (2000). This type of model differs from a logit or probit model, therefore, because the dependent variable has a time dimension. The explanatory variables do not have a time dimension, however, at least not in Van Order and Zorn, so this approach provides another legitimate way to study the impact of application characteristics on the probability of default.

10. For example, Charles and Hurst (forthcoming) find that blacks are far less likely than whites to receive help from their families in coming up with a down payment for their first home purchase. It seems reasonable to suppose that blacks are also far less likely to come up with financial support from their families when some unfortunate event puts them in danger of defaulting on their mortgage.

11. The term "rationally" is in quotation marks to indicate that lenders may be following an economic incentive to discriminate but they are still breaking the law, which may, of course, be irrational (not to mention wrong) given the associated penalties.

12. Recall that statistical discrimination was discussed in chapters 2 and 7.

13. This outcome depends on the assumption that the "late payments" variable has the same distribution for minority and white applicants. Without this assumption, it could be true that there are so many white applicants with no late payments that the average white applicant has fewer late payments than the average minority applicant, even with the higher hurdle for minority applicants. We return to this issue below.

14. Even if they did meet these conditions, they could still be biased because of omitted borrower characteristics that the lender does not observe. See section 8.2.2.

15. The study by Van Order and Zorn (2001) obviously avoids this problem by looking directly at loans in the conventional sector.

16. Other scholars have used the assumption of no discrimination in the FHA sector, presumably because the federal oversight in that sector is thought to make discrimination more difficult. See, for example, Barth, Cordes, and Yezer (1979) and Shear and Yezer (1985). As shown in chapter 1 (figure 1.3), however, the HMDA data reveal that minority/white denial ratios are almost as high in the FHA sector as in the conventional sector. This finding is consistent with, but certainly does not prove, the view that there is just as much discrimination in the FHA sector as elsewhere.

17. Recall that a detailed review of the literature on default, prepayment, and foreclosure is provided in chapter 3.

18. However, neither Ambrose and Capone nor any other study of which we are aware rules out the possibility that foreclosure policies involve disparate-impact discrimination.

19. However, the cost of default is significantly lower for loans to other minority groups than for loans to whites.

20. As discussed by Van Order and Zorn, a lower probability of prepayment in a time of rising interest rates could make a loan less valuable to a lender. Van Order and Zorn find that loans to minorities are less likely to be repaid in both circumstances (rising and falling interest rates). The net effect on loan value depends on the pattern of interest rates over time, but Van Order and Zorn's simulations indicate that the prepayment effects always make loans to minorities at least as valuable as loans to whites.

21. This assumption is offered without any evidence. One can certainly imagine a contrary situation in which the economic conditions that influence the quality of mortgage applications are correlated with regional-level variables, such as state banking laws, that influence the degree of concentration in the lending industry. In more formal terms, the issue is whether the interaction between minority status and

industry competition is correlated with minority-white differences in unobserved credit qualifications. Here again, one can imagine a contrary situation in which regions with a high (or low) degree of concentration are also regions with relatively large minority populations where minorities have relatively high (or low) credit qualifications, even if concentration and credit qualifications are not themselves correlated. In short, some evidence to back up this assumption would be helpful.

22. Comparing the coefficient of the interaction term with the coefficient of the minority status variable also is suspect because, as shown earlier, the coefficient of the minority status variable is biased upward by omitted variables. This bias is, of course, exactly the problem that Berkovec et al. are trying to avoid.

23. A discussion of the potential bias can be found in section 6 of the appendix A.

24. As discussed in chapter 5, a rejected borrower often negotiates with the lender to find terms that are acceptable to both. The argument that this alters the quality of accepted minority applications relative to accepted white applications is not supported, however, by the finding in chapter 5 that the minority status coefficient in a loan denial model is unaffected by the inclusion of a negotiation variable.

25. This conclusion is based on a theoretical result that the relationship between default (lender loss) and prejudice-based discrimination should be the same as (opposite of) the relationship between loan amount and interest rates. Han estimates the relationship between per capita mortgage originations and market interest rates and finds a negative relationship for FHA borrowers with incomes less than $70,000 per year. Following his theoretical result, this empirical result implies that prejudice-based discrimination increases lender loss. Of course, any bias in the empirical estimates could affect this conclusion.

26. Following logic similar to that described in the previous footnote, this conclusion is based on a theoretical result and the empirical relationship between interest rates and default or lender loss. As discussed below, this finding is consistent with the conclusion of Ross (1996a), namely, that statistical discrimination by profit-maximizing firms will not completely eliminate the racial differences in default that arise from unobservable borrower characteristics.

27. Unlike most default studies using FHA data, Han's draws conclusions about discrimination in the FHA sector alone. This follows from his use of the FHA data to calibrate his theoretical model (see the previous two footnotes).

28. Ross's initial loan approval regression also leaves out credit history variables. As discussed below, however, these variables are included in a test for omitted-variable bias.

29. Ross also includes a variable that is in the FHA data but is not relevant to the Boston Fed Study, namely, the number of years since the mortgage was issued. He also enters this variable and the credit quality index in quadratic form. See Ross (1997, table A.2). Note also that this default equation is used to determine only two parameters in the simulations, namely, the constant term and the coefficient for the credit quality index in the determination of default.

30. To be more precise, he estimates each default model fifty times, with fifty different draws for the random variables, and presents results based on the average coefficient from these fifty regressions.

31. More formally, these two random variables are drawn from a bivariate normal probability density.

32. For this simulation, Ross estimates the initial loan denial equation with credit history variables included. Then he calculates an expanded credit quality index that includes the impact of credit history variables, weighted by their estimated coefficients. To bring this new index into the default model, he assumes that the impact of this credit quality index on loan default equals the impact of the simpler credit history index, which does not include credit history variables. This assumption makes it possible for him to obtain new predictions of default that reflect credit history, even though credit history is not included in the FHA sample used to estimate the default model.

33. Further discussion of the Rosenblatt study can be found in chapter 7.

34. Interactions between income variables alone and FHA are significant in the Avery and Beeson analysis. However, income does not provide a good basis for comparing approval models in the HMDA data because it is correlated with key unobserved underwriting variables, such as credit history, LTV, and nonhousing debt–to–income ratio.

35. Ross uses a two-stage approach because he employs separate samples for estimating the denial and default models. These two samples can be combined because they contain most of the same underwriting variables, with the notable exception of applicant credit history, which, as noted earlier, is not in the default data. Boyes, Hoffman, and Low (1989) estimate a default model for consumer credit that does not require a two-stage approach. Their approach cannot be applied to default on mortgages because, also as noted earlier, no existing data set contains both denied applications and default information on approved mortgages.

36. This procedure is similar to the technique called the Heckman two-step (Heckman, LaLonde, and Smith, 1999), which corrects for sample selection in a simple linear regression. The key difference is that here the dependent variable in the second-stage model (default) is discrete. As a result, the analysis must control for the heteroscedasticity caused by the selection process. See Ross (2000).

37. One specification assumes that only the total debt-to-income ratio influences default and therefore omits from the default equation variables reflecting housing debt alone. The other specification assumes that the source of income does not influence default and therefore omits variables describing the sources of income. These assumptions represent alternative ways of identifying the model, which is a requirement of the estimating procedure. See Ross (2000).

38. These calculations use the percentage of the variance in loan denial that is explained by the non–credit history variables to calculate the portion of the covariance across equations that is explained by these variables. See Ross (2000).

39. Despite this limitation, a study of this type might meet a key legal standard for discrimination developed for disparate-impact cases. This standard says, in effect, that a practice is "unfair," and therefore legally suspect, if people in one group have a higher performance (in this case less default) than their test scores (in this case, predicted default based on factors other than group membership) would predict. We discuss this standard in detail in chapter 10.

Chapter 9

1. *Huntington v. Huntington* 844 F2d 926, 935 (2d Cir.) *aff'd per curiam*, 488 U.S. 15 (1988).

2. More formally, Lundberg assumes that the mean innate ability and test-taking ability are the same in the two groups, but group A has a relatively high variance in innate ability and group B has a relatively high variance in test-taking ability. Under these assumptions, employers will have an incentive to pay higher wages to members of group A at any given test score, or, to use Lundberg's words, to have a more steeply sloped wage schedule for group A than for group B.

3. Of course, lenders who make use of one of these schemes could still practice disparate-treatment discrimination by using different thresholds for minority and white applicants or by amending these schemes in different ways for different groups.

4. See Avery et al. (1996, 2000), Buist, Linneman, and Megbolugbe (1999), Straka (2000), and Yezer (1995).

5. Although formal models of lender profits could be developed, we believe that this step would complicate the analysis considerably without adding additional insight into the key issues addressed in this section. We return to this issue in section 9.4.

6. The choice of variable could result in disparate-impact discrimination, too. If, for example, minorities are most likely to default in the first two years of holding a mortgage and whites are most likely to default in the third and fourth years, then an analysis that examines only the first two years after loan approval obviously will have a disparate impact on minorities and will not have a clear business purpose. We do not pursue this issue in this chapter, but it would be an ideal subject for empirical analysis.

7. This assumption facilitates the presentation but is totally inconsequential for the results.

8. Specifically, $M = 1$ for an applicant who belongs to a minority group and $M = 0$ for a white applicant. This analysis obviously could be extended to consider several minority groups.

9. To simplify the presentation, this model is assumed to be linear. However, the measures of performance and the explanatory variables could themselves be nonlinear functions, such as logarithms, and the explanatory variables could include interaction terms. An extension to additional dimensions of nonlinearity would not change the general principles derived from our specification.

10. As reported in section 3.3.2, for example, Charles and Hurst (forthcoming) find that 27 percent of whites, compared to only 10 percent of blacks, cover some of their down payment with family funds. These results suggest that black borrowers are also much less likely than white borrowers to receive help from their families when they fall behind on their mortgage payments. Whether family financial help is available under these circumstances is, of course, a key unobserved borrower characteristic.

11. It is well known that, under fairly general assumptions, regression analysis provides the best linear, unbiased predictions for any dependent variable based on the explanatory variables included in the regression. However, our argument does not rely on linearity. Indeed, most performance models focus on a discrete dependent

variable, default, and use a nonlinear method such as logit or probit. Instead, our argument relies on the notion that methodological considerations generate a best method for predicting loan performance. One important caveat to this theorem is that the regression must be free of selectivity bias. This may not be the case in a sample of loans, because the loans in the sample were selected from a larger pool of applications. We return to this issue in section 9.3.2.3.

12. This assumes, of course, that future loans are drawn from an application pool with the same characteristics as the pool that produced past loans. We return to this issue in section 9.4.

13. The term "score" is most often associated with a credit score, which is based only on an applicant's credit characteristics, but some analysts also talk about "application scores" or "origination scores," which are based on applicant, loan, and property characteristics.

14. This analysis could easily be extended to consider other forms of disparate-treatment discrimination. For example, a lender could estimate an equation in which all the β coefficients were allowed to differ across groups. This step might increase the predictive power of the regression, but it would result in a scoring scheme that used different weights for minority and white applicants—a clear violation of civil rights laws. Because our main focus here is on disparate-impact discrimination, we do not pursue these possibilities.

15. An expected value is the average value one can expect for the estimated parameters from a large number of estimated regressions, each with a different draw for the random-error term, ε. For further discussion, see section 2 of appendix A. Again, the assumption of linearity is not important for this discussion.

16. The value of b_i can be obtained from the following regression

$X_i = a + b_i M + e$

where a and b_i are parameters to be estimated and e is a random error term.

17. This relationship is formally derived in section 7 of appendix A.

18. Looking ahead to the discussion of court decisions in chapter 10, it is interesting to note that scheme S^3 is illegal even if the lender did not design it as a way to discriminate.

19. A detailed discussion of the legal standards associated with the business necessity test is provided in chapter 10.

20. Note that if γ is positive, which seems unlikely given our nation's history, a switch from S^2 to S^3 will disproportionately *favor* minority applicants. This switch still cannot be justified on business necessity grounds, however, because it also requires the use of underwriting weights that diverge from the true impact of characteristics on loan performance. In fair-employment law, adjustments to test scores that are analogous to schemes S^1 and S^3 with a positive γ have sometimes been accepted by the courts as part of remedial programs to address past discrimination by a firm (Hartigan and Wigdor, 1989). Some observers (Larson, 1992) have concluded that the Civil Rights Act of 1991, which prohibits group-based adjustments of "employment-related tests," closed the door on schemes of this type. Other observers (Belton, 1993), however, argue that adjustments of this type are still permissible when a test can be shown to be "invalid," that is, a poor predictor of performance, for people in some groups. Under

these circumstances, a test is said to have "differential validity." So far, the U.S. Supreme Court has not addressed these issues, and, to the best of our knowledge, they have never arisen in a fair-lending case in any court.

21. It is also possible to depart from the statistical model by adding variables that are not statistically significant. Lundberg's (1991) example of height in an employment context provides one example of such a variable.

22. This example comes from an early draft of Avery et al. (2000), but does not appear in the published version.

23. If lenders rely on loan profitability, not default, as a measure of performance, another example of this type of disparate-impact discrimination is provided by PMI, which minority applicants, with their relatively high LTVs, might be more likely to buy than white applicants. Because PMI lowers the cost of default to a lender, it could have a negative and significant coefficient in a version of equation (9.1) with loan profitability as the dependent variable.

24. This same framework can be applied to all of the cases in sections 9.3.2.1 and 9.3.2.2, which also lower minority concentration and decrease the accuracy of within-group predictions.

25. Lender dummy variables cannot eliminate all possible forms of selection bias. For example, some lenders may have unobserved traits that influence both loan approval and their propensity to foreclose *on loans with certain characteristics*. An elaborate sample selection model would be needed to eliminate bias in this situation.

26. Following the argument in section 8.2.4, this result may reflect the possibility that unobserved credit characteristics actually favor minorities in the FHA sample ($\gamma > 0$), so that switching from scheme S^2 to scheme S^3 has a disproportionately positive impact on minorities. Because the FHA sample does not observe all the variables considered by lenders, however, we cannot test for this possibility.

27. To be specific, we divided the Boston Fed Study's data into cells based on LTV and minority status and computed the share of applications in each cell. Then we divided the FHA data into the same cells and randomly drew observations from each cell until the share in each cell was the same as in the Boston Fed Study's data.

28. In this simulation, disparate impact arises from a bias in the estimated coefficient of LTV. This coefficient is small and insignificant in the estimated version of equation (9.1) but substantially larger and significant in the estimated version of equation (9.6). See table 9.2.

29. For example, Straka (2000) writes that "[s]ound AU [automated underwriting] ignores an applicant's minority status" (p. 218).

30. This implication does not cover cases of disparate-impact discrimination that directly affect the measure of loan performance. Suppose that foreclosure is the measure of loan performance, for example, and that foreclosure policies are particularly harsh in default situations that are more common among minority than among white borrowers, even though a harsher foreclosure policy in these circumstances does not increase a lender's profits. Then using (lack of) foreclosure as the dependent variable in a loan performance regression builds discrimination into the results.

31. For example, HUD is developing statistical procedures to evaluate existing scoring systems and to create a new scoring system for FHA loans, but the discussion in

Bunce, Reeder, and Scheessele (1999) makes it appear that these procedures do not include minority status variables.

32. Equation (9.13) is analogous to equation (2.6), where S^i has the same meaning as π^E. Estimated versions of equation (9.13) [or of equation (2.6) or of equations (9.14) and (9.15)] obviously add a stochastic element to the left side of the equation.

33. As explained earlier, this assumes that the regression equation on which S^2 is based has been corrected, if necessary, for selection bias.

34. In chapter 2, we denoted this relationship by $\pi(L, A, P)$, where L, A, and P stand for loan, applicant, and property characteristics, respectively.

35. Recall that any test for disparate-impact discrimination has two parts: Does the practice have a disparate impact on minorities, and can the practice be justified on the grounds of business necessity? The structure of equations (9.14) and (9.15) implies that any departure from the best-predicting nondiscriminatory scoring system that has a disparate impact on minorities automatically fails the second part of the test; after all, deviations from the best-predicting score cannot be justified as a business necessity.

36. Specifically, this comparison requires the assumptions that the X variables affect the loan performance measure and the loan approval measure in a linear fashion and that the loan performance score affects the loan approval measure in a linear fashion. These are very strong assumptions.

37. This point also applies to tests concerning the causes of discrimination. Because a disparate-impact scheme can be designed to mimic disparate-treatment discrimination, statistical discrimination, which is usually thought of as a form of disparate-treatment discrimination, could be implemented through a group-neutral underwriting scheme with disparate-impact discrimination built into it.

38. Although he does not propose any particular test, Galster (1996b) also argues that a loan performance model (or, as he calls it, a mortgage scoring model) could be a powerful research and enforcement tool for identifying disparate-impact discrimination.

39. The need to make the pools consistent is emphasized by Avery et al. (2000).

40. A discussion of this extension can be found in section 8 of appendix A.

41. A discussion of this extension can be found in section 8 of appendix A.

42. Avery et al. (2000) point out that a loan performance equation estimated across regions should control for region-specific economic circumstances but then not include variation in these circumstances in loan performance scores. As they put it, "by not controlling for local economic factors, ... scoring models assign the same risk level to a person who performs poorly during a recession as a person with similar performance during better times" (p. 526).

43. We return to this point in chapter 10.

44. As discussed in chapter 2, predatory lending involves offering loans with hidden terms that are very unfavorable to the borrower. Most, if not all, borrowers who accept these loans would be eligible for other loans on more favorable terms.

45. More technically, these dummy variables eliminate bias in the underwriting weights that arises because buyers with different unobserved credit characteristics

select different types of lenders, assuming that these unobserved characteristics affect equation (9.1) in a linear fashion. As pointed out in section 9.3.2.3, these dummy variables also eliminate the most basic kinds of selection bias in equation (9.1), which arise when unobserved buyer characteristics also are correlated with a lender's loan approval behavior.

46. Another way to put this is that in conducting a discrimination test for a single lender, a regulator can ignore both the estimated constant term and the estimated coefficient of the lender's dummy variable. Neither of these coefficients affects the ranking of the lender's applications.

47. As shown in section 9 of appendix A, disparate-impact discrimination can arise even with types of variation in underwriting standards that appear to have a solid theoretical justification.

48. More specifically, the underwriting weight for characteristic i and lender j equals the estimated coefficient of characteristic i plus the estimated coefficient of the interaction between characteristic i and lender characteristic k multiplied by the value of characteristic k for lender j. Thus the differences in the weights across lenders depend on the estimated coefficients of the interaction terms and the across-lender differences in the variables designed to capture differences in underwriting standards.

Chapter 10

1. 487 U.S. 977 (1988), p. 994.

2. This quotation comes from the Civil Rights Act of 1991 (42 U.S.C. 2000e-2(k)(1)(B)(i)) (1998). A similar quotation comes from the congressional report prepared as an explanation for this act: "When a decision-making process includes particular, functionally-integrated practices which are components of the same criterion, standard, method of administration, or test . . . , the particular, functionally-integrated practices may be analyzed as one employment practice" (137 *Congressional Record* S15276, October 25, 1991).

3. Statement by Senator John Danforth, 137 *Congressional Record* S15484 (October 30, 1991).

4. Mahoney (1998, p. 465) argues that a lender accused of discrimination can force the plaintiff to focus on particular practices by using a statistically based underwriting procedure and revealing the weights placed on each variable. We do not think this strategy would work, both because lenders (or the designers of automated underwriting schemes) will be reluctant to reveal their formulas and because it does not recognize that the particularity requirement does not apply to practices that are "functionally integrated," as are the elements of a statistically based underwriting procedure. We return to this issue in discussing the EEOC guidelines in section 10.2.2.

5. This argument is also supported by the fact that the Supreme Court has ruled that statistics in general and regression analysis in particular are legitimate evidence in labor market discrimination cases. See Ashenfelter and Oaxaca (1987).

6. To avoid confusion, note that Mahoney uses the acronym FHA for the Fair Housing Act, whereas we use FaHA (to distinguish this act from the Federal Housing Authority).

7. A defendant can also attempt to rebut the prima facie case for disparate impact. As pointed out by Mahoney (1998), however, attempts at rebuttal are generally more effective and less risky if they occur during step 2 of a disparate-impact case.

8. 401 U.S. 424 (1971).

9. 490 U.S. 659 (1989).

10. H.R. Rept. 100-711, 100th Congress, 2nd Session (1988).

11. *Cartwright v. American Savings and Loan Ass'n*, 880 F. 2d. 912 (7th Cir. 1989), at 923, cited in Mahoney (1998, p. 481).

12. Cited in Mahoney (1998, p. 483).

13. The *Uniform Guidelines on Employment Selection Procedures* apply to all types of employment practices. We focus exclusively on underwriting systems. A general set of "Uniform Guidelines for Lending Procedures" obviously would have to consider many issues that are not addressed here.

14. Lundberg (1991) argues that "disparate impact is realistically limited to allowing or disallowing the use of specific worker qualifications in setting wages" (p. 318). In other words, it is difficult to identify disparate-impact discrimination when it takes the form of a change in the weight placed on a legitimate employment (or credit) variable. In the case of underwriting, at least, this limitation does not apply. Because, as discussed earlier, underwriting has relatively clear business objectives, simple techniques for identifying legitimate business-based weights are available. Some such techniques are discussed in the next section.

15. As explained in chapter 8, measuring discrimination in the default approach to the lending decision also founders on its failure to adequately consider unobserved credit characteristics.

16. The fairness principle in the *Uniform Guidelines* might be intended in part to deal with cases in which minority applicants have *better* unobserved performance characteristics than whites. As indicated in note 20 of chapter 9, the situation is sometimes called "differential validity," but it is not disparate-impact discrimination. Moreover, the Civil Rights Act of 1991 appears to overrule the application of such a fairness standard to such a case when the tests in question are shown to be valid predictors of performance.

17. A simple random sample of the white applications from those lenders would be acceptable, but stratified-sampling techniques might increase the precision of the estimates obtained from a given sample size. Stratification techniques for drawing white applications from a single lender are discussed by Giles and Courchane (2000).

18. These interactions are included, of course, only if they are statistically significant. This point applies to the interactions in the third characteristic of this approach, as well.

19. This regression does not include any interactions between a lender's portfolio characteristics and minority status. This type of interaction variable would undermine a test for discrimination. In principle, it is possible to estimate the level of discrimination for a lender as a function of its values for the portfolio variables that are interacted with minority status. However, these variables are picking up the average impact of portfolio variables on the treatment of minorities across all lenders at each

value of each variable. Any such estimation procedure therefore assumes that all lenders with a particular value for the portfolio variable treat minorities in exactly the same way. This type of inferences seems to us to be inappropriate. Just as it is not legal for a lender to assume that every minority applicant has negative, unobserved credit characteristics, it is not appropriate for an investigator to assume that all lenders with the same value of, say, the average debt-to-income ratio in their portfolio of loans treat minority applicants in the same way (even though, in both cases, the assumption is right, on average).

20. Logit and probit analysis are the most obvious methods for estimating this regression model. As discussed in Courchane, Golan, and Nickerson (2000), alternative techniques are available, and these techniques might improve the accuracy of discrimination estimates.

21. As explained above, the lender does not have to justify differences between its underwriting standards and those of the average lender if those differences can be explained by composition of the lender's portfolio. Instead, it only has to justify "idiosyncratic" differences in standards, which are the ones that remain after accounting for portfolio differences.

22. Strictly speaking, this statement assumes that different lenders share at least some underwriting standards. If all lenders differ on every underwriting weight, then a pooled approach does not increase precision.

23. Of course, financial regulatory agencies should make certain that a lack of applications to a particular lender from minority households does not reflect that lender's failure to meet its CRA obligations, but this is a separate issue from discrimination in loan approval.

24. The fact that we cannot identify all lenders does not, however, magnify our findings of discrimination. As shown in chapter 6, there appears to be considerable discrimination in the sample of loans for which the lender could not be identified.

25. Here we are focusing on the number of applications in the Boston Fed Study's sample, not the total number of applications a lender received overall.

26. The minority status coefficient was also positive and statistically significant for one other lender. Of all the twenty-seven lenders, this one received the highest percentage of its applications from minority households.

27. To determine whether this result is robust, we also estimated two other models with lender-specific minority status coefficients, one with no interaction terms and another with just the interaction terms based on the applicant's debt-to-income ratio. These two estimations plus the one in the text produce three sets of minority status coefficients for the twenty-seven lenders. The coefficients for the two large lenders were negative and significant in all three cases. We also looked at the correlations among these three sets of coefficients. The first set was not highly correlated with the other two. Specifically, the correlations between the coefficients in the simple model and the other two were 0.256 and 0.023, respectively. On the other hand, the correlation between the last two models was 0.878. At least for this example, accurate estimates of discrimination for individual lenders require controls for potential complexities in the pooled underwriting model but do not depend heavily on controls for systematic underwriting differences across lenders.

28. These results for smaller lenders indicate that the significant minority status coefficients for two large lenders in the sample should not be interpreted as support for the

hypothesis that large lenders are more likely than small lenders to discriminate. See the discussion of this issue in section section 6.3.3.2.

29. This regression should exclude any explanatory variables that are based on data collected after the application is submitted. The objective of the regression is to obtain the best possible explanation of loan performance based on information available at the time of application, and including postapplication information would undermine this objective.

30. Of course, a lender also could counter a claim of discrimination by pointing to a methodological error in the investigator's test, such as the use of loan and application samples drawn from very different pools.

31. It also follows that any lender who can establish that its practices are justified on the basis of business necessity, using the test described above, also rules out the possibility that an alternative, less discriminatory set of practices exists.

32. As in the case of loan approval, this performance-based test for discrimination in automated underwriting or loan pricing could be adapted to consider redlining.

33. Many other cutoff points obviously could be used. Moreover, it might prove useful to divide the applications into quantiles (as indicated by scores) and compare each quantile under the two schemes. Discrimination would be found to exist if the higher-ranking quantiles have a higher minority composition using the investigator's scoring scheme than using the scores based on the automated underwriting system.

34. Longhofer and Calem (1999) assert that "[w]hen regulators test for compliance with fair-lending laws, they typically conduct statistical analyses to see whether lenders systematically charge minority borrowers a higher price than they do whites. In doing so, they control for other factors that may affect the pricing of mortgage loans, many of which are correlated with race." One of the factors they list is "market conditions." We are not aware of any published material on this type of enforcement-based statistical analysis, however.

35. Housing payment–to–income ratios can be included in this procedure, of course, if they are calculated on some consistent basis that does not require information on the final mortgage interest rate, such as the average regional mortgage interest rate at the time of application.

36. As pointed out by Longhofer and Calem (1999), a depository lender typically holds some loans with rates that were set by mortgage brokers, so there is some question about the extent to which the depository lender should be held responsible for any observed minority-white interest-rate disparity. We think it is appropriate to hold both the depository lender and the relevant mortgage brokers that issued them responsible in this case; after all, both of these parties have a role in providing credit on discriminatory terms. Longhofer and Calem argue that the depository lender should not be held responsible for actions by mortgage brokers, just as FannieMae and FreddieMac should not be held responsible for discrimination by lenders whose loans they purchase.

37. To be more precise, suppose the "cost" variables are correlated with minority status and the lender uses them to help set interest rates even though they have no link to costs whatsoever, which is, of course, an example of disparate-impact discrimination. In this case, the regression will find significant coefficients for these variables, and the investigator will mistakenly interpret these coefficients as a "control" for variation in loan costs.

38. Designing the appropriate policies to accomplish this goal is beyond the scope of this book. For a discussion of some related fair-lending policies, see Yinger (1995).

39. Nondepository institutions, such as mortgage brokers, fall under the jurisdiction of the FTC but are not subject to the regular examinations that depository institutions must submit to. For proposals to enhance fair-lending enforcement for mortgage brokers, see Longhofer and Calem (1999) and Yinger (1995).

40. This discussion is repeated, almost verbatim, in Avery, Beeson, and Calem (1997, p. 12).

41. Calem and Canner emphasize that "[t]he process of creating applicant profiles is labor-intensive and costly. However, it should be noted that even under the traditional examination approach to fair lending enforcement, Federal Reserve examiners create applicant profiles to use in their matched-pair analysis, although these latter profiles typically are less extensive than those created for the statistical model" (p. 122).

42. Calem and Canner also point out that file review can find subtle forms of discrimination in other types of lender behavior. "For example, a review of loan files and supporting documentation may indicate that lenders fail to provide all applicants equal opportunity to explain apparent flaws in job or credit history" (pp. 124–125). As discussed in section 3.3.1, this issue is also raised by Siskin and Cupingood (1996).

43. The "back-end ratio" is the ratio of the total debt payment to income.

44. This information on OCC procedures comes from Courchane, Nebhut, and Nickerson (2000), which describes procedures that were put in place after the OCC procedures described in Stengel and Glennon (1999).

45. One interesting application of this step is to distinguish between a pattern and practice of discrimination and "isolated instances of discrimination" (Courchane, Nebhut, and Nickerson, 2000, p. 26). A statistically significant difference across groups in the estimated model is interpreted to be evidence of a pattern and practice of discrimination, unless this result is "driven only by unique files" (p. 26).

46. At another point, Calem and Canner say that the file reviews search for "explanations that would dispel concerns raised by the statistical analysis" (p. 125).

47. As pointed out in section 5.2, a variable of this type should not be used if it reflects the lender's efforts to obtain complete documentation.

48. For a similar view, see Browne and Tootell (1995).

49. See, especially, the discussion of Horne (1994, 1997) and Day and Liebowitz (1996) in section 5.4.

50. If a variable appears only once or twice in a large sample of loan files, one might ask whether it is a legitimate underwriting variable in the first place. By definition, a variable cannot be part of an underwriting "standard" if it has never been encountered before. Moreover, it is not possible to estimate the impact of rarely encountered variables on loan performance, so allowing underwriters to place weights on these variables could be equivalent to allowing them to transform disparate-treatment discrimination into disparate-impact discrimination, an issue discussed at length in section 9.3.

51. This second-best approach appears to have been followed by the Justice Department in the Decatur Federal case (Siskin and Cupingood, 1996).

52. As indicated in section 10.4.2, Calem and Longhofer (2000) say that examiners are asked "to determine whether these reasons for rejection had been applied in a nondiscriminatory manner" (p. 16), but they do not indicate how this question can be answered when the variable appears only in the minority file, which is always the case. Moreover, as noted in section 10.4.2, Calem and Canner (1995) and Horne (1995) go so far as to argue that allowing regulators to overrule regression results preserves lenders' "flexibility" in evaluation each application. In fact, however, the procedure to which these authors refer only examines minority denials, not minority approvals, and allowing a regulator to overrule the regression-based conclusion that a minority denial is due to discrimination is equivalent to giving lenders the flexibility to approve loans to whites while denying applications from minorities that are comparable in terms of all the variables the regulator can observe and include in a regression. Allowing this form of flexibility would totally undermine fair-lending legislation.

53. Ironically, Longhofer (1996b) appears to come to the same conclusion in another article, in which he says "Not surprisingly, paired file reviews rarely uncover any but the most egregious cases of illegal discrimination."

54. We are not lawyers, so this is a claim about the logic of the argument, not about the standards that would hold up in court. This same qualification applies to other uses of the term "prima facie case" in this chapter.

55. The use of a two-variable matching procedure to select the sample of nonminority loans for the Federal Reserve's regression procedure also should receive closer scrutiny. Avery, Beeson, and Calem (1997) argue that this procedure is not a source of bias if the loan approval model is correctly specified. This statement is formally correct, but it ignores the possibility that the sample selection procedure creates such a high correlation between minority status and variables other than income and loan amount that the role of minority status will be difficult to estimate with precision. Specifically, the vast majority of minority-white pairs with equal incomes and loan amounts could involve lower values for the minority application on most other credit characteristics. An analysis of the Boston Fed Study's data by Avery, Beeson, and Calem is consistent with this possibility; the estimated minority status coefficient is smaller and less significant with a matched-pair sample than with a random sample (table 13, p. 37). A formal analysis of alternative stratified sample designs for a loan approval regression is provided by Giles and Courchane (2000).

56. Black (1995) makes a similar point about the use of HMDA as a screen for further inquiries: "discrimination may not occur even if rejection rates were widely different, and may occur if rejection rates were identical" (p. 148).

57. Avery, Beeson, and Calem (1997, p. 15) recognize that poor matching could lead to estimates that are not "robust," but they argue that "the HMDA data offer high potential for matching" because it is easy to find nonminority applications that match minority applications on the few available characteristics. We find this argument totally unconvincing. Matching is "easy" in these circumstances only because it considers just two variables; the quality of the match on all relevant underwriting variables is still likely to be poor.

58. One way to make this practice even more reasonable would be to collect more information for the HMDA data, such as loan terms or the applicant's FICO score (and, of course, to check FICO scores for disparate-impact discrimination).

59. Stengel and Glennon (1999) even go so far as to say that they "are concerned solely with the particular type of post-application discrimination known as disparate-

treatment—the differential application of a bank's underwriting guidelines across racial categories" (p. 301).

60. A similar argument was made by Glenn Canner, a senior advisor to the Federal Reserve Board of Governors, at a recent conference on fair lending. According to the conference transcript:

Canner reported that the Federal Reserve does examine lending data for individual institutions on a regular basis using statistical methodologies such as logit analysis. However, there is no single market model that works for all institutions. In his view, the most effective way to enforce the law is to focus on building models that are specific to a particular lender. Therefore, they do not require a market study but routinely require investigations of individual lenders. (Bogdon and Bell, 2000, p. 40)

61. One possible way to keep track of a loan's originator is to require the loan servicer to keep a copy of the original HMDA submission sheet for the loan.

62. This HMDA-LP data also might help improve the targeting of enforcement activities compared to targeting based on HMDA alone. As noted earlier, current HMDA-based targeting might inappropriately select lenders that specialize in providing credit to minorities, because these lenders have relatively high minority/white denial ratios. If loan performance data were available, regulators might find that some of these lenders also have relatively high minority/white default ratios. Such a finding would suggest that a high denial ratio reflects a lender's tendency to accept minority applications with marginal creditworthiness, not a tendency to discriminate, so that the lender is a poor target for further investigation. Van Order and Zorn (1995) provide an example of how HMDA and performance data could be combined to explore intergroup differences in underwriting.

63. These agencies, along with the secondary mortgage market institutions, also have not provided data to independent scholars for investigation of this issue, although they certainly have the authority to do so.

References

Ambrose, Brent W., R. J. Buttimer, and Charles A. Capone. 1997. "Pricing Mortgage Default and Foreclosure Delay." *Journal of Money, Credit, and Banking*, 29(3) (August): 314–325.

Ambrose, Brent W., and Charles A. Capone. 1996a. "Cost-Benefit Analysis of Single-Family Foreclosure Alternatives." *Journal of Real Estate Finance and Economics*, 13(2) (September): 105–120.

Ambrose, Brent W., and Charles A. Capone. 1996b. "Do Lenders Discriminate in Processing Defaults?" *Cityscape: A Journal of Policy Development and Research*, 2(1) (February): 89–98.

Amemiya, Takeshi. 1974. "Multivariate Regression and Simultaneous Equation Models When the Dependent Variables Are Truncated Normal." *Econometrica*, 42(6) (November): 999–1012.

Arrow, Kenneth. 1973. "The Theory of Discrimination." In Orley Ashenfelter and Albert Rees, eds. *Discrimination in Labor Markets*. Princeton, NJ: Princeton University Press, pp. 3–42.

Artle, Roland, and Pravin Varaiya. 1978. "Life Cycle Consumption and Homeownership." *Journal of Economic Theory*, 18(1) (June): 38–58.

Ashenfelter, Orley, and Ronald Oaxaca. 1987. "The Economics of Discrimination: Economists Enter the Courtroom." *American Economic Review*, 77 (May): 321–325.

Avery, Robert B., and Patricia E. Beeson. 1998. "Neighborhood, Race, and the Mortgage Market: Evidence from HMDA Data." Paper presented at the Annual American Economic Association/National Economic Association Meetings, Chicago, January.

Avery, Robert B., Patricia E. Beeson, and Paul D. Calem. 1997. "Using HMDA Data as a Regulatory Screen for Fair Lending Compliance." *Journal of Financial Services Research*, 11(2) (April): 9–42.

Avery, Robert B., Patricia E. Beeson, and Mark S. Sniderman. 1996a. "Accounting for Racial Differences in Housing Credit Markets." In John Goering and Ron Wienk, eds., *Mortgage Lending, Racial Discrimination, and Federal Policy*. Washington, DC: Urban Institute Press, pp. 75–142.

Avery, Robert B., Patricia E. Beeson, and Mark S. Sniderman. 1996b. "Posted Rates and Mortgage Lending Activity." *Journal of Real Estate Finance and Economics*, 13(1) (July): 11–26.

Avery, Robert B., Patricia E. Beeson, and Mark S. Sniderman. 1999. "Neighborhood Information and Mortgage Lending." *Journal of Urban Economics*, 45(2) (March): 287–310.

Avery, Robert B., Raphael W. Bostic, Paul S. Calem, and Glenn B. Canner. 1996. "Credit Risk, Credit Scoring, and the Performance of Home Mortgages." *Federal Reserve Bulletin*, 82(7) (July): 621–648.

Avery, Robert B., Raphael W. Bostic, Paul S. Calem, and Glenn B. Canner. 1999. "Trends in Home Purchase Lending: Consolidation and the Community Reinvestment Act." *Federal Reserve Bulletin* (February): 81–102.

Avery, Robert B., Raphael W. Bostic, Paul S. Calem, and Glenn B. Canner. 2000. "Credit Scoring: Statistical Issues and Evidence from Credit-Bureau Files." *Real Estate Economics*, 28(3) (Fall): 523–547.

Ayres, Ian. Forthcoming. *Pervasive Prejudice? Unconventional Evidence of Race and Gender Discrimination*. Chicago: University of Chicago Press.

Ayres, Ian. 2001. "Expert Report." Case No. 3-98-0223, *Cason v. Nissan*, U.S. District Court for the Middle District of Tennessee, May 25.

Ayres, Ian, and Peter Siegelman. 1995. "Race and Gender Discrimination in Bargaining for a New Car." *American Economic Review*, 85(3) (June): 304–321.

Barth, James R., Joseph J. Cordes, and Anthony M. J. Yezer. 1979. "Financial Institution Regulations, Redlining, and Mortgage Markets." In *The Regulation of Financial Institutions*. Conference Series No. 21. Boston: Federal Reserve Bank of Boston, pp. 101–143.

Becker, Gary S. 1971. *The Economics of Discrimination*. 2nd ed. Chicago: University of Chicago Press. (Original work published in 1957.)

Becker, Gary S. 1993a. "The Evidence against Banks Doesn't Prove Bias." *Business Week*, April 19, p. 18.

Becker, Gary S. 1993b. "Nobel Lecture: The Economic Way of Looking at Behavior." *Journal of Political Economy*, 101(3) (June): 385–409.

Belton, Robert B. 1993. "The Unfinished Agenda of the Civil Rights Act of 1991." *Rutgers Law Review*, 45(4) (Summer): 921–941.

Ben-Shahar, Danny, and David Feldman. 2001. "Signaling-Screening Equilibrium in the Mortgage Market." Working paper, Arison School of Business, The Interdisciplinary Center, Herzliya, Israel.

Bergsman, Steve. 1999. "Reexamining Subprime Insurers." *Mortgage Banking* (May): 24–29.

Berkovec, James A., Glenn B. Canner, Stuart A. Gabriel, and Timothy H. Hannan. 1994. "Race, Redlining, and Residential Mortgage Loan Performance." *Journal of Real Estate Finance and Economics*, 9(3) (November): 263–294.

Berkovec, James A., Glenn B. Canner, Stuart A. Gabriel, and Timothy H. Hannan. 1996. "Response to Critiques of 'Mortgage Discrimination and FHA Loan Performance.'" *Cityscape: A Journal of Policy Research*, 2(1) (February): 49–54.

Berkovec, James A., Glenn B. Canner, Stuart A. Gabriel, and Timothy H. Hannan. 1998. "Discrimination, Competition, and Loan Performance in FHA Mortgage Lending." *Review of Economics and Statistics*, 80(2) (May): 241–250.

Berkovec, James A., and Peter Zorn. 1996. "How Complete Is HMDA? HMDA Coverage of Freddie Mac Purchases." *Journal of Real Estate Research*, 11(1): 39–55.

Besanko, David, and Anjan V. Thakor. 1987. "Collateral and Rationing: Sorting Equilibria in Monopolist and Competitive Credit Markets." *International Economic Review*, 28(3) (October): 671–689.

Black, Harold A. 1995. "HMDA Data and Regulatory Inquiries Regarding Discrimination." In Anthony M. Yezer, ed., *Fair Lending Analysis: A Compendium of Essays on the Use of Statistics*. Washington, DC: American Bankers Association, pp. 147–154.

Black, Harold A., Thomas P. Boem, and Ramon P. DeGennaro. 1999. "Overages in Mortgage Pricing." Unpublished manuscript. Department of Finance, University of Kentucky, Lexington, KY.

Black, Harold A., M. Cary Collins, and Ken B. Cyree. 1997. "Do Black-Owned Banks Discriminate against Black Borrowers?" *Journal of Financial Services Research*, 11(2) (April): 189–204.

Black, Harold A., and Robert L. Schweitzer. 1985. "A Canonical Analysis of Mortgage Lending Terms: Testing for Discrimination at a Commercial Bank." *Urban Studies*, 22(1) (February): 13–19.

Black, Harold A., Robert L. Schweitzer, and Lewis Mandell. 1978. "Discrimination in Mortgage Lending." *American Economic Review*, 68(2) (May): 186–191.

Blackburn, McKinley, and Todd Vermilyea. 2001. "Racial Discrimination in Home Purchase Mortgage Lending among Large National Banks." Unpublished manuscript. Moore School of Business, University of South Carolina, Columbia, SC.

Bloom, David E., Beth Preiss, and James Trussell. 1983. "Mortgage Lending Discrimination and the Decision to Apply: A Methodological Note." *Journal of the American Real Estate and Urban Economics Association*, 11(1) (Spring): 97–103.

Blossom, Teresa, David Everett, and John Gallagher. 1988. "Detroit Banking: The Race for Money." *Detroit Free Press*, July 24, p. 27.

Board of Governors of the Federal Reserve System. 1998. *85th Annual Report*. Washington, DC: Federal Reserve System.

Bogdon, Amy S., and Carol A. Bell, eds. 2000. *Making Fair Lending a Reality in the New Millennium: Proceedings, June 30, 1999*. Washington, DC: FannieMae Foundation.

Börsch-Supan, Axel. 1987. *Econometric Analysis of Discrete Choice*. Berlin: Springer-Verlag.

Börsch-Supan, Axel, and John Pitkin. 1988. "On Discrete Choice Models of Housing Demand." *Journal of Urban Economics*, 24(2) (September): 153–172.

Bostic, Raphael W. 1996. "The Role of Race in Mortgage Lending: Revisiting the Boston Fed Study." Working paper, Division of Research and Statistics, The Federal Reserve Board of Governors, Washington, DC, December.

Bostic, Raphael W., and Glenn B. Canner. 1997. "Do Minority-Owned Banks Treat Minorities Better? An Empirical Test of the Cultural Affinity Hypothesis." Unpublished manuscript. Washington, DC. Board of Governors of the Federal Reserve System.

Boyes, William J., Dennis L. Hoffman, and Stuart A. Low. 1989. "An Econometric Analysis of the Bank Credit Scoring Problem." *Journal of Econometrics*, 40(1) (January): 3–14.

Bradbury, Katherine L., Karl E. Case, and Constance R. Dunham. 1989. "Geographic Patterns of Mortgage Lending in Boston, 1982–87." *New England Economic Review* (September/October): 3–30.

Brendsel, Leland C. 2000. "Written Statement." Hearings before the Subcommittee on Capital Markets, Securities, and Government Sponsored Enterprises, Committee on Banking and Financial Services, U.S. House of Representatives, May 16. Available online at http://financialservices.house.gov/banking/51600wit.htm.

Brenner, Joel Glenn, and Liz Spayd. 1993. "A Pattern of Bias in Mortgage Loans: Statistics Show Blacks at a Disadvantage." *Washington Post*, June 6, p. A1.

Brimelow, Peter. 1993. "Racism at Work?" *National Review*, April 12, p. 42.

Brimelow, Peter, and Leslie Spencer. 1993. "Mortgage Lending: Surprise! The Evidence Suggests that Banks are Color-Blind When It Comes to Mortgage Lending." *Forbes*, 151(1), January 4, p. 48.

Browne, Lynn E., and Gregory M. Tootell. 1995. "Mortgage Lending in Boston: A Response to the Critics." *New England Economic Review* (September/October): 53–78.

Brueckner, Jan K. 1986. "The Downpayment Constraint and Housing Tenure Choice: A Simplified Exposition." *Regional Science and Urban Economics*, 16(4) (November): 519–525.

Brueckner, Jan K. 1996. "Default Rates and Mortgage Discrimination: A View of the Controversy." *Cityscape*, 2(1): 65–68.

Buist, Henry, Peter Linneman, and Isaac F. Megbolugbe. 1999. "Residential Lending Discrimination and Lender Compensation Policies." *Journal of the American Real Estate and Urban Economics Association*, 27(4) (Winter): 695–717.

Bunce, Harold L., Debbie Gruenstein, Christopher E. Herbert, and Randall M. Scheessele. 2001. "Subprime Foreclosures: The Smoking Gun of Predatory Lending?" In Susan M. Wachter and R. Leo Peene, eds., *Housing Policy in the New Millennium Conference Proceedings*. Washington, DC: U.S. Department of Housing and Urban Development, pp. 257–272. Available online at http://www.huduser.org/publications/pdf/brd/12Bunce.pdf.

Bunce, Harold L., William J. Reeder, and Randall M. Scheessele. 1999. "Understanding Consumer Credit and Mortgage Scoring: A Work in Progress." Paper presented at Fannie Mae Foundation Roundtable "Making Fair Lending a Reality in the New Millennium," Washington, DC, June 30.

Cain, Glen G. 1986. "The Economic Analysis of Labor Market Discrimination: A Survey." In Orley Ashenfelter and Richard Layard, eds., *Handbook of Labor Economics*. Amsterdam: North-Holland, pp. 693–785.

Calem, Paul S., and Glenn Canner. 1995. "Integrating Statistical Analysis into Fair Lending Exams: The Fed's Approach." In Anthony M. Yezer, ed., *Fair Lending Analysis: A Compendium of Essays on the Use of Statistics*. Washington, DC: American Bankers Association, pp. 117–126.

Calem, Paul S., and Michael Stutzer. 1995. "The Simple Analytics of Observed Discrimination in Credit Markets." *Journal of Financial Intermediation*, 4(3) (July): 189–212.

Calem, Paul S. 1996. "Mortgage Credit Availability in Low- and Moderate-Income Minority Neighborhoods: Are Information Externalities Critical?" *Journal of Real Estate Finance and Economics*, 13(1) (July): 71–89.

Calem, Paul S., and Stanley D. Longhofer. 2000. "Anatomy of a Fair-Lending Exam: The Uses and Limitations of Statistics." Unpublished manuscript. Washington, DC, Board of Governors of the Federal Reserve System.

Calomiris, Charles W., Charles M. Kahn, and Stanley D. Longhofer. 1994. "Housing-Finance Intervention and Private Incentives: Helping Minorities and the Poor." *Journal of Money, Credit, and Banking*, 26(3) (August/Part 2): 675–678.

Canner, Glenn B., and Stuart A. Gabriel. 1992. "Market Segmentation and Lender Specialization in the Primary and Secondary Mortgage Markets." *Housing Policy Debate*, 3(2): 241–329.

Canner, Glenn B., and Wayne Passmore. 1999. "The Role of Specialized Lenders in Extending Mortgages to Lower-Income and Minority Homebuyers." *Federal Reserve Bulletin*, 85(11) (November): 709–723.

Canner, Glenn B., and Dolores S. Smith. 1991. "Home Mortgage Disclosure Act: Expanded Data on Residential Lending." *Federal Reserve Bulletin*, 77(11) (November): 859–881.

Card, David. 2000. "The Causal Effect of Education on Earning." In O. C. Ashenfelter and D. Card, eds., *Handbook of Labor Economics*, vol. 3A. Amsterdam: North-Holland, pp. 1801–1864.

Carr, James H., and Isaac F. Megbolugbe. 1993. "The Federal Reserve Bank of Boston Study on Mortgage Lending Revisited." *Journal of Housing Research*, 4(2): 277–313.

Chamberlain, Gary. 1980. "Analysis of Covariance with Qualitative Data." *Review of Economic Studies* 47(1) (January): 225–238.

Charles, Kerwin Kofi, and Erik Hurst. Forthcoming. "The Transition to Home Ownership and the Black-White Wealth Gap." *Review of Economics and Statistics*.

Chinloy, Peter. 1989. "The Probability of Prepayment." *Journal of Real Estate Finance and Economics*, 2(4) (December): 267–283.

Chinloy, Peter. 1995. "Public and Conventional Mortgage and Mortgage-Backed Securities." *Journal of Housing Research*, 6(2): 173–196.

Chinloy, Peter, and Isaac F. Megbolugbe. 1994. "Hedonic Mortgages." *Journal of Housing Research*, 5(1): 1–21.

Cincotta, Gale. 2000. Testimony before the U.S. House of Representatives Committee on Banking and Financial Services, May 24. Available online at http://financialservices. house.gov/banking/52400wit.htm.

Clauretie, Terrence M., and Stacy G. Sirmans. 1999. *Real Estate Finance: Theory and Practice*, 3rd ed. Upper Saddler River, NJ: Prentice Hall.

Courant, Paul N. 1978. "Racial Prejudice in a Search Model of the Urban Housing Market." *Journal of Urban Economics*, 5(3) (July): 329–345.

Courchane, Marsha, Amos Golan, and David Nickerson. 2000. "Estimation and Evaluation of Loan Discrimination: An Informational Approach." *Journal of Housing Research*, 11(1): 67–90.

Courchane, Marsha, David Nebhut, and David Nickerson. 2000. "Lessons Learned: Statistical Techniques and Fair Lending." *Journal of Housing Research*, 11(2): 277–296.

Courchane, Marsha, and David Nickerson. 1997. "Discrimination Resulting from Overage Practices." *Journal of Financial Services Research*, 11(1–2) (April): 133–151.

Crawford, Gordon W., and Eric Rosenblatt. 1999. "Differences in the Cost of Mortgage Credit: Implications for Discrimination." *Journal of Real Estate Finance and Economics*, 19(2) (September): 147–159.

Cutler, David M., Edward L. Glaeser, and Jacob L. Vigdor. 1999. "The Rise and Decline of the American Ghetto." *Journal of Political Economy*, 107(3) (June): 455–506.

Cutts, Amy C., Robert A. Van Order, and Peter M. Zorn. 2001. "Adverse Selection, Licensing, and the Role of Securitization in Financial Market Evolution, Structure and Pricing." Working paper, Freddie Mac, Washington, DC.

Day, T., and Stan J. Liebowitz. 1996. "Mortgages, Minorities, and HMDA." Paper presented at the Federal Reserve Bank of Chicago, April.

Dedman, B. 1988. "The Color of Money." *Atlanta Journal-Constitution*, May 1, p. 4.

Deng, Yongheng, and Stuart Gabriel. 2002. "Modeling the Performance of FHA-Insured Loans: Borrower Heterogeneity and the Exercise of Mortgage Default and Prepayment Options." Unpublished manuscript. Unicon Research Corporation, Santa Monica, CA, February.

Deng, Yongheng, John M. Quigley, and Robert Van Order. 2000. "Mortgage Terminations, Heterogeneity and the Exercise of Mortgage Options." *Econometrica*, 68(2) (March): 275–307.

Deng, Yongheng, Stephen L. Ross, and Susan M. Wachter. 1999. "Job Access, Residential Location, and Homeownership." Unpublished manuscript. Los Angeles: University of Southern California.

Diamond, Peter A. 1982. "Aggregate Demand Management in Search Equilibrium." *Journal of Political Economy*, 90(5) (October): 881–894.

Dietrich, Jason. 2001. "Missing Race Data in HMDA and the Implications for the Monitoring of Fair Lending Compliance." Economic and Policy Analysis working paper no. 2001-1, Office of the Comptroller of the Currency, Washington, DC.

DiPasquale, Denise, and Edward L. Glaeser. 1999. "Incentives and Social Capital: Are Homeowners Better Citizens?" *Journal of Urban Economics*, 45(2): 354–384.

Dreier, Peter. 1991. "Redlining Cities: How Banks Color Community Development." *Challenge* (November/December): 15–23.

Duca, John V., and Stuart S. Rosenthal. 1994. "Borrowing Constraints and Access to Owner-Occupied Housing." *Regional Science and Urban Economics*, 24(3) (June): 301–322.

Dunn, K. B., and J. J. McConnell. 1981. "Valuation of Mortgage-Backed Securities." *Journal of Finance*, 36(3) (June): 599–616.

Dunn, K. B., and Chester S. Spatt. 1988. "Private Information and Incentives: Implications for Mortgage Contracts Terms and Pricing." *Journal of Real Estate Finance and Economics*, 1(1): 47–60.

Engelhardt, Gary V. 1994. "House Prices and the Decision to Save for Down Payments." *Journal of Urban Economics*, 36(2) (September): 209–237.

Engelhardt, Gary V., and Christopher J. Mayer. 1998. "Intergenerational Transfers, Borrowing Constraints, and Savings Behavior: Evidence from the Housing Market." *Journal of Urban Economics*, 44(1) (July): 135–157.

Equal Employment Opportunity Commission (EEOC). 1978. *Uniform Guidelines on Employment Selection Procedures*. Code of Federal Regulations, Title 41, Volume 1, Part 60-3. Washington, DC: U.S. Government Printing Office.

Federal Financial Institutions Examination Council (FFIEC). 1998. Press release, August 6. Available online at http://www.ffiec.gov.

Federal Financial Institutions Examination Council (FFIEC). 1999. "Interagency Fair Lending Examination Procedures." Available online at http://www.ffiec.gov.

Federal Financial Institutions Examination Council (FFIEC). 2001a. "Annual Report, 2000." Available online at http://www.ffiec.gov.

Federal Financial Institutions Examination Council (FFIEC). 2001b. "HMDA Aggregate National Reports." Available online at http://www.ffiec.gov.

Federal Financial Institutions Examination Council (FFIEC). 2001c. "Nationwide Summary Statistics for 2000 HMDA Data." Available online at http://www.ffiec.gov.

Ferguson, Michael F., and Stephen R. Peters. 1995. "What Constitutes Evidence of Discrimination in Lending?" *Journal of Finance*, 50(3) (June): 739–748.

Ferguson, Michael F., and Stephen R. Peters. 1997. "A Symmetric-Information Model of Credit Rationing." Unpublished manuscript, University of Cincinnati, Cincinnati, OH.

Ferguson, Michael F., and Stephen R. Peters. 2000. "Is Lending Discrimination Always Costly?" *Journal of Real Estate Finance and Economics*, 21(1) (July): 23–44.

Figlio, David N., and Joseph W. Genshlea. 1999. "Bank Consolidations and Minority Neighborhoods." *Journal of Urban Economics*, 45(3) (May): 474–489.

Fishbein, Allen J. 1992. "The Ongoing Experiment with 'Regulation from Below': Expanded Reporting Requirements for HMDA and CRA." *Housing Policy Debate*, 3(2): 601–636.

Follain, James R. 1990. "Mortgage Choice." *American Real Estate and Urban Economics Association Journal*, 18(2) (Summer): 125–144.

Follain, James R., and Peter M. Zorn. 1990. "The Unbundling of Residential Mortgage Finance." *Journal of Housing Research*, 1(1): 63–89.

Foster, Chester, and Robert Van Order. 1984. "An Option-Based Model of Mortgage Default." *Housing Finance Review*, 3(4) (October): 351–372.

Gabriel, Stuart A. 1996. "The Role of FHA in the Provision of Credit to Minorities." In John Goering and Ron Wienk, eds., *Mortgage Lending, Racial Discrimination, and Federal Policy*. Washington, DC: Urban Institute Press, pp. 183–250.

Galster, George C. 1992. "Research on Discrimination in Housing and Mortgage Markets: Assessment and Future Directions." *Housing Policy Debate*, 3(2): 639–683.

Galster, George C. 1993a. "The Facts of Lending Discrimination Cannot Be Argued Away by Examining Default Rates." *Housing Policy Debate*, 4(1): 141–146.

Galster, George C. 1993b. "Use of Testers in Investigating Discrimination in Mortgage Lending and Insurance." In Michael Fix and Raymond Struyk, eds., *Clear and Convincing Evidence*. Washington, DC: Urban Institute Press, pp. 287–334.

Galster, George C. 1996a. "Comparing Loan Performance between Races as a Test for Discrimination." *Cityscape: A Journal of Policy Development and Research*, 2(1) (February): 33–39.

Galster, George C. 1996b. "Future Directions in Mortgage Discrimination Research and Enforcement." In John Goering and Ron Wienk, eds., *Mortgage Lending, Racial Discrimination, and Federal Policy*. Washington, DC: The Urban Institute Press, pp. 679–716.

Galster, George C., Fred Freiberg, and Diane Houk. 1987. "Racial Differences in Real Estate Advertising Practices: An Explanatory Analysis." *Journal of Urban Affairs*, 9(3): 199–215.

Gensler, Gary. 2000. Statement before the House Banking and Financial Services Committee, May 24. Available online at http://financialservices.house.gov/banking/52400wit.htm.

Giles, Judith A., and Marsha J. Courchane. 2000. "Stratified Sample Design for Fair Lending Binary Logit Models." Econometrics working paper no. 0007, University of Victoria. Department of Economics, Victoria, Canada.

Glennon, Dennis, and Mitchell Stengel. 1994a. "An Evaluation of the Federal Reserve Bank of Boston's Study of Racial Discrimination in Mortgage Lending." Economic and Policy Analysis working paper no. 94-2, Office of the Comptroller of the Currency, Washington, DC.

Glennon, Dennis, and Mitchell Stengel. 1994b. "Evaluating Statistical Models of Mortgage Lending Discrimination: A Bank-Specific Analysis." Economic and Policy Analysis working paper no. 95-3, Office of the Comptroller of the Currency, Washington, DC.

Goering, John M., ed. 1996. "Race and Default in Credit Markets: A Colloquy." *Cityscape: A Journal of Policy Development and Research*, 2(1) (May).

Goering, John M., and Ron Wienk, eds. 1996. *Mortgage Lending, Racial Discrimination, and Federal Policy*. Washington, DC: Urban Institute Press.

Goldberger, Arthur D. 1984. "Reverse Regression and Salary Discrimination." *Journal of Human Resources*, 19(3) (Summer): 293–318.

Green, Richard K., and Michele J. White. 1997. "Measuring the Benefits of Homeowning: Effects on Children." *Journal of Urban Economics*, 41(3) (May): 441–461.

Greenbaum, Stuart I. 1996. "Twenty-Five Years of Banking Research." *Financial Management*, 25(2) (Summer): 86–92.

Greene, William H. 2000. *Econometric Analysis*, 4th ed. Upper Saddle River, NJ: Prentice Hall.

Gyourko, Joseph, Peter Linneman, and Susan Wachter. 1999. "Analyzing the Relationships among Race, Wealth, and Home Ownership in America." *Journal of Housing Economics*, 8(2) (June): 63–89.

Han, Song. 2000. "The Economics of Taste-Based Discrimination in Credit Markets." Unpublished manuscript, University of Mississippi, Jackson, MS, March 20.

Harding, John. 1997. "Estimating Borrower Mobility from Observed Prepayments." *Real Estate Economics*, 25(3) (Fall): 347–371.

Harrison, David M. 2001. "The Importance of Lender Heterogeneity in Mortgage Lending," *Journal of Urban Economics*, 49(2) (March): 285–309.

Hartigan, John A., and Alexandra K. Wigdor, eds. 1989. *Fairness in Employment Testing: Validity Generalization, Minority Issues, and the General Aptitude Test Battery*. Washington, DC: National Academy Press.

Haurin, Donald R., Patric H. Hendershott, and Susan M. Wachter. 1996. "Expected Home Ownership and Real Wealth Accumulation of Youth." Working paper no. 5629, National Bureau of Economic Research, Cambridge, MA. Available online at http://www.nber.org.

Heckman, James J., Robert J. LaLonde, and Jeffrey A. Smith. 1999. "The Economics and Econometrics of Active Labor Market Programs." In O. C. Ashenfelter and D. Card, eds., *Handbook of Labor Economics*, vol. 3A. Amsterdam: North-Holland, pp. 1865–2097.

Hendershott, Patric H., William C. LaFayette, and Donald R. Haurin. 1997. "Debt Usage and Mortgage Choice: The FHA-Conventional Decision." *Journal of Urban Economics*, 41(2) (March): 202–217.

Henriques, Diana B. 2000a. "Extra Costs on Car Loans Draw New Legal Attacks." *New York Times*, October 27.

Henriques, Diana B. 2000b. "New Front Opens in Battle against Race Bias in Loans." *New York Times*, October 22.

Henriques, Diana B. 2001a. "Nissan Says It Can Refute Report of Bias in Car Loans." *New York Times*, July 12, p. A17.

Henriques, Diana B. 2001b. "Review of Nissan Car Loans Finds that Blacks Pay More." *New York Times*, July 4, pp. A1, A11.

Horne, David K. 1994. "Evaluating the Role of Race in Mortgage Lending." *FDIC Banking Review* (Spring/Summer): 1–15.

Horne, David K. 1995. "Testing for Discrimination in Mortgage Lending." In Anthony M. Yezer, ed., *Fair Lending Analysis: A Compendium of Essays on the Use of Statistics*. Washington, DC: American Bankers Association, pp. 127–138.

Horne, David K. 1997. "Mortgage Lending, Race, and Model Specification." *Journal of Financial Services Research*, 11(1–2) (April): 43–68.

Huck, Paul. 2001. "Home Mortgage Lending by Applicant Race: Do HMDA Figures Provide a Distorted Picture?" *Housing Policy Debate*, 12(4): 719–736.

Hunter, William C., and Mary Beth Walker. 1996. "The Cultural Affinity Hypothesis and Mortgage Lending Decisions." *Journal of Real Estate Finance and Economics*, 13(1) (July): 57–70.

Hurst, Erik, Ming Ching Luoh, and Frank P. Stafford. 1998. "The Wealth Dynamics of American Families, 1984–94." *Brookings Papers on Economic Activity*, 1: 267–329.

Joint Center for Housing Studies. 2000. *The State of the Nation's Housing: 2000*. Cambridge, MA: Author.

Jones, Lawrence D. 1993. "The Demand for Home Mortgage Debt." *Journal of Urban Economics*, 33(1) (January): 10–28.

Kahn, Charles M., and Abdullah Yavas. 1994. "The Economic Role of Foreclosures." *Journal of Real Estate Finance and Economics*, 8(1) (January): 35–51.

Kau, James B., and Donald C. Keenan. 1995. "An Overview of the Option-Theoretic Pricing of Mortgages." *Journal of Housing Research*, 6(2): 217–244.

Kau, James B., Donald C. Keenan, and Taewon Kim. 1993. "Transaction Costs, Suboptimal Termination, and Default Probabilities." *American Real Estate and Urban Economics Association Jounal*, 21(3) (Fall): 247–263.

Kau, James B., Donald C. Keenan, and Taewon Kim. 1994. "Default Probabilities for Mortgages." *Journal of Urban Economics*, 35(3) (May): 278–296.

Kau, James B., Donald C. Keenan, Walter J. Muller III, and James F, Epperson. 1995. "The Valuation at Origination of Fixed Rate Mortgages with Default and Prepayment." *Journal of Real Estate Finance and Economics*, 11(1) (July): 5–36.

Kim, Sunwoong, and Gregory D. Squires. 1998. "The Color of Money and the People Who Lend It." *Journal of Housing Research*, 9(2): 271–284.

King, A. Thomas. 1980. "Discrimination in Mortgage Lending: A Study of Three Cities." Research working paper no. 91, Office of Policy and Economic Research, Federal Home Loan Bank Board, February. Washington, DC.

Kissinger, Terry, and Christopher A. Richardson. 2001. "An Evaluation of Automobile Loan Pricing Practices." Unpublished manuscript. Washington, DC, Federal Deposit Insurance Corporation, March.

Kushner, James A. 1995. *Fair Housing: Discrimination in Real Estate, Community Development, and Revitalization*, 2nd ed. New York: McGraw-Hill.

LaCour-Little, Michael. 1996a. "Race Differences in Demand and Supply of Mortgage Credit." Unpublished manuscript. University of Texas at Arlington, Arlington, TX.

LaCour-Little, Michael. 1996b. "Application of Reverse Regression to Boston Federal Reserve Data Refutes Claims of Discrimination." *Journal of Real Estate Research*, 11(1): 1–12.

LaCour-Little, Michael. 2000. "The Evolving Role of Technology in Mortgage Finance." *Journal of Housing Research* 11(2): 173–205.

Ladd, Helen F. 1998. "Evidence on Discrimination in Mortgage Lending." *Journal of Economic Perspectives*, 12(2) (Spring): 41–62.

Laitila, Thomas. 1993. "A Pseudo-R^2 Measure for Limited and Qualitative Dependent Variable Models." *Journal of Econometrics*, 56(3) (April): 341–356.

Lang, William W., and Leonard I. Nakamura. 1993. "A Model of Redlining." *Journal of Urban Economics*, 33(2) (March): 223–234.

Larson, Lex K. 1999. "The Civil Rights Act of 1991." In *Employment Discrimination*. 10 looseleaf volumes. New York: Matthew Bender & Co., pp. 1–34 to 1–54.1.

Lawton, Rachel. 1996. "Preapplication Mortgage Lending Testing Program: Lender Testing by a Local Agency." In John Goering and Ron Wienk, eds., *Mortgage Lending, Racial Discrimination, and Federal Policy*. Washington, DC: Urban Institute Press, pp. 611–622.

Lea, Michael J. 1996. "Innovation and the Cost of Mortgage Credit: A Historical Perspective." *Housing Policy Debate*, 7(1): 147–174.

Lederman, Jess. 1995. *Handbook of Mortgage Lending*, MBA edition. Washington, DC: Real Estate Finance Press, Mortgage Bankers Association of America.

Lee, Bill Lann. 2001. *Fair Lending Enforcement Program*. Washington, DC: U.S. Department of Justice. Available online at http://www.usdoj.gov/crt/housing/bll_01.htm.

Liebowitz, Stanley. 1993. "A Study That Deserves No Credit." *Wall Street Journal*, September 1, p. A14.

Lin, Emily Y. 2001. "Information, Neighborhood Characteristics, and Home Mortgage Lending." *Journal of Urban Economics*, 49(2) (March): 337–355.

Lindsey, Lawrence B. 1995. "Foreword." In Anthony M. Yezer, ed., *Fair Lending Analysis: A Compendium of Essays on the Use of Statistics*. Washington, DC: American Bankers Association, pp. ix–xiv.

Ling, David C., and Susan M. Wachter. 1998. "Information Externalities and Home Mortgage Underwriting." *Journal of Urban Economics*, 44(3) (November): 317–332.

Linneman, Peter, and Susan M. Wachter. 1989. "The Impacts of Borrowing Constraints on Homeownership." *Journal of the American Real Estate and Urban Economics Association*, 17(4) (Winter): 389–402.

Longhofer, Stanley D. 1996a. "Cultural Affinity and Mortgage Discrimination." *Federal Reserve Bank of Cleveland Economic Review*, 32(3) (3rd Quarter): 12–24.

Longhofer, Stanley D. 1996b. "Discrimination in Mortgage Lending: What Have We Learned?" *Economic Commentary* (Federal Reserve Bank of Cleveland), August 15.

Longhofer, Stanley D., and Paul S. Calem. 1999. "Mortgage Brokers and Fair Lending." *Economic Commentary* (Federal Reserve Bank of Cleveland), May 15.

Longhofer, Stanley D., and Stephen R. Peters. 1998. "Self Selection and Discrimination in Credit Markets." Unpublished manuscript, Research Department, Federal Reserve Bank of Cleveland.

Lundberg, Shelly J. 1991. "The Enforcement of Equal Opportunity Laws under Imperfect Information: Affirmative Action and Alternatives." *Quarterly Journal of Economics*, 106(1) (February): 309–326.

Lundberg, Shelly J, and Richard Startz. 1983. "Private Discrimination and Social Intervention in Competitive Labor Markets." *American Economic Review*, 73(3) (June): 340–347.

Lye, Linda Cheng Yee. 1998. "Title VII's Tangled Tale: The Erosion and Confusion of Disparate Impact and the Business Necessity Defense." *Berkeley Journal of Employment and Labor Law*, 19(2) (Winter): 315–361.

Maddala, G. S., and R. P. Trost. 1982. "On Measuring Discrimination in Loan Markets." *Housing Finance Review*, 1 (July): 245–268.

Mahoney, Peter E. 1998. "The End(s) of Disparate Impact: Doctrinal Reconstruction, Fair Housing and Lending Law, and the Antidiscrimination Principle." *Emory Law Journal*, 47(2) (Spring): 409–525.

Mahoney, Peter E., and Peter Zorn. 1999. "Automated Underwriting." Paper presented at FannieMae Foundation Roundtable, Washington, DC, June 30.

Mansfield, Cathy Lesser. 2000. "The Road to Subprime 'HEL' Was Paved with Good Congressional Intentions: Usury Deregulation and the Subprime Home Equity Market." *South Carolina Law Review*, 51(3) (Spring): 473.

Mansfield, Cathy Lesser. 2000. Statement before the Housing Banking and Financial Services Committee. Available online at http://www.house.gov/banking/52400man.htm.

Massey, Douglas S., and Nancy A. Denton. 1993. *American Apartheid: Segregation and the Making of the Underclass*. Cambridge: Harvard University Press.

Mayer, Christopher J., and Gary V. Engelhardt. 1996. "Gifts, Down Payments, and Housing Affordability." *Journal of Housing Research*, 7(1): 59–77.

Medine, David. 2000. "Predatory Lending Practices in the Subprime Industry: Prepared Statement of the Federal Trade Commission before the House Committee on Banking and Financial Services," May 24. Available online at http://financialservices.house.gov/banking/52400wit.htm.

Mester, Loretta. 1997. "What Is the Point of Credit Scoring?" *Federal Reserve Bank of Philadelphia Business Review* (September/October): 3–16.

Munnell, Alicia H., Lynn E. Browne, James McEneaney, and Geoffrey M. B. Tootell. 1992. "Mortgage Lending in Boston: Interpreting HMDA Data." Working paper no. 92-7, Federal Reserve Bank of Boston.

Munnell, Alicia H., Geoffrey M. B. Tootell, Lynn E. Browne, and James McEneaney. 1993. "Is Discrimination Racial or Geographic?" Unpublished manuscript. Federal Reserve Bank of Boston.

Munnell, Alicia H., Lynn E. Browne, James McEneaney, and Geoffrey M. B. Tootell. 1996. "Mortgage Lending in Boston: Interpreting HMDA Data." *American Economic Review*, 86(1) (March): 25–53.

Myers, Samuel L., Jr., and Tsze Chan. 1995. "Racial Discrimination in Housing Markets: Accounting for Credit Risk." *Social Science Quarterly*, 76(3) (September): 543–561.

Newburger, Harriet. 1995. "Sources of Difference in Information Used by Black and White Housing Seekers: An Explanatory Analysis." *Urban Studies*, 32(3) (April): 445–470.

Office of Thrift Supervision. 2000. "What about Subprime Mortgages?" *Mortgage Trends*, 4(1) (June): 1–21.

Oliver, Melvin L., and Thomas M. Shapiro. 1995. *Black Wealth, White Wealth: A New Perspective on Racial Inequality*. New York: Routledge.

Ondrich, Jan, Stephen Ross, and John Yinger. 2001. "Geography of Housing Discrimination." *Journal of Housing Research*, 12(2): 217–238.

Ondrich, Jan, Stephen Ross, and John Yinger. 2001. "Now You See It, Now You Don't: Why Do Real Estate Agents Withhold Houses from Black Customers?" Unpublished manuscript, Syracuse University, Syracuse, NY. Available online at http://webdev.maxwell.syr.edu/jyinger/nysi.pdf.

Passmore, Wayne, and Roger Sparks. 1996. "Putting the Squeeze on a Market for Lemons: Government-Sponsored Mortgage Securitization." *Journal of Real Estate Economics and Finance*, 13(1) (July): 27–43.

Patterson, Orlando. 1997. *The Ordeal of Integration: Progress and Resentment in America's "Racial" Crisis*. Washington, DC: Civitas/Counterpoint.

Pennington-Cross, Anthony, Anthony Yezer, and Joseph Nichols. 2000. "Credit Risk and Mortgage Lending: Who Uses Subprime and Why?" Working paper no. 00-03, Research Institute for Housing America, Arlington, VA.

Peterson, Richard L. 1981. "An Investigation of Sex Discrimination in Commercial Banks' Direct Consumer Lending." *Bell Journal of Economics*, 12(2) (Autumn): 547–561.

Phelps, Edmund S. 1972. "The Statistical Theory of Racism and Sexism." *American Economic Review*, 62(4) (September): 659–661.

Phillips, Robert F., and Anthony M. Yezer. 1996. "Self Selection and Tests for Bias and Risk in Mortgage Lending: Can You Price the Mortgage If You Don't Know the Process?" *Journal of Real Estate Research*, 11(1): 87–102.

Phillips-Patrick, Fred J., and Clifford V. Rossi. 1996. "Statistical Evidence of Mortgage Redlining? A Cautionary Tale." *Journal of Real Estate Research*, 11(1): 13–23.

Posey, Lisa L., and Abdullah Yavas. 2001. "Adjustable and Fixed Rate Mortgages as a Screening Mechanism for Default Risk." *Journal of Urban Economics*, 49(1) (January): 54–79.

Quercia, Roberto G., and Michael A. Stegman. 1992. "Residential Mortgage Default: A Review of the Literature." *Journal of Housing Research*, 3(2): 341–370.

Quigley, John M. 1996. "Mortgage Performance and Housing Market Discrimination." *Cityscape*, 2(1): 59–62.

Quint, Michael. 1991. "Racial Gap Found on Mortgages." *New York Times*, October 22, p. D1.

Rachlis, Mitchell B., and Anthony M. Yezer. 1993. "Serious Flaws in Statistical Tests for Discrimination in Mortgage Markets." *Journal of Housing Research*, 4(2): 315–336.

Raines, Franklin D. 2000. Statement at hearings before the Subcommittee on Capital Markets, Securities, and Government Sponsored Enterprises, Committee on Banking and Financial Services, U.S. House of Representatives, May 16. Available online at http://financialservices.house.gov/banking/51600wit.htm.

Ranney, S. I. 1981. "The Future Price of Houses, Mortgage and Market Conditions and the Returns to Homeownership." *American Economic Review*, 71(3) (June): 323–333.

Riddiough, Timothy J., and Steve B. Wyatt. 1994a. "Strategic Default, Workout, and Commercial Mortgage Valuation." *Journal of Real Estate Finance and Economics*, 9(1) (July): 5–22.

Riddiough, Timothy J., and Steve B. Wyatt. 1994b. "Wimp or Tough Guy: Sequential Default Risk and Signaling with Mortgages." *Journal of Real Estate Finance and Economics*, 9(3) (November): 299–321.

Ritter, Richard. 1996. "The Decatur Federal Case: A Summary Report." In John Goering and Ron Wienk, eds., *Mortgage Lending, Racial Discrimination, and Federal Policy*. Washington, DC: Urban Institute Press, pp. 445–450.

Roberts, Paul Craig. 1993. "Banks on the Line of Fire." *Washington Times*, March 12, p. F1.

Robinson, Carla J. 1992. "Racial Disparity in the Atlanta Housing Market." In W. A. Leigh and J. B. Stewart, eds, *The Housing Status of Black Americans*. New Brunswick, NJ: Transaction Publishers, pp. 85–110.

Rodda, David, and James E. Wallace. 1996. "Fair Lending Management: Using Influence Statistics to Identify Critical Mortgage Loan Applications." In John Goering and Ron Wienk, eds., *Mortgage Lending, Racial Discrimination, and Federal Policy*. Washington, DC: Urban Institute Press, pp. 531–560.

Rosen, Harvey S. 1985. "Housing Subsidies: Effects on Decisions, Efficiency, and Equity." In Alan J. Auerbach and Martin S. Feldstein, eds., *Handbook of Public Economics*, vol. 1. Amsterdam: North-Holland, pp. 375–420.

Rosenblatt, Eric. 1997. "A Reconsideration of Discrimination in Mortgage Underwriting with Data from a National Mortgage Bank." *Journal of Financial Services*, 11(1–2) (April): 109–131.

Rosenthal, Stuart S., and Peter Zorn. 1993. "Household Mobility, Asymmetric Information, and the Pricing of Mortgage Contract Rates." *Journal of Urban Economics*, 33(2) (March): 235–253.

Ross, Stephen L. 1996a. "Flaws in the Use of Loan Defaults to Test for Mortgage Lending Discrimination." *Cityscape: A Journal of Policy Development and Research*, 2(1) (February): 41–48.

Ross, Stephen L. 1996b. "Mortgage Lending Discrimination and Racial Differences in Loan Default." *Journal of Housing Research*, 7(1): 117–126.

Ross, Stephen L. 1997. "Mortgage Lending Discrimination and Racial Differences in Loan Default: A Simulation Approach." *Journal of Housing Research*, 8(2): 277–297.

Ross, Stephen L. 2000. "Mortgage Lending, Sample Selection, and Default." *Real Estate Economics*, 28(4) (Winter): 581–621.

Ross, Stephen L., and Geoffrey M. B. Tootell. 1998. "Redlining, the Community Reinvestment Act, and Private Mortgage Insurance." Unpublished manuscript, University of Connecticut, Storrs.

Ross, Stephen L., and John Yinger. 1999a. "The Default Approach to Studying Mortgage Discrimination: A Rebuttal." In Margery Austin Turner and Felicity Skidmore, eds., *Mortgage Lending Discrimination: A Review of Existing Evidence*. Washington, DC: Urban Institute, pp. 107–127.

Ross, Stephen L., and John Yinger. 1999b. "Does Discrimination in Mortgage Lending Exist? The Boston Fed Study and Its Critics." In Margery Austin Turner and Felicity Skidmore, eds., *Mortgage Lending Discrimination: A Review of Existing Evidence*. Washington, DC: Urban Institute, pp. 43–83.

Ross, Stephen, L., and John Yinger. 1999c. "Other Evidence of Discrimination: Recent Studies of Redlining and of Discrimination in Loan Approval and Loan Terms." In Margery Austin Turner and Felicity Skidmore, eds., *Mortgage Lending Discrimination: A Review of Existing Evidence*. Washington, DC: Urban Institute, pp. 85–106.

Ross, Stephen, and John Yinger. 1999d. "Sorting and Voting: A Review of the Literature on Urban Public Finance." In Edwin S. Mills and Paul Cheshire, eds., *Handbook of Urban and Regional Economics*, vol. 3. Amsterdam: North-Holland, pp. 2001–2060.

Royer, Stanislas, and John J. Kriz. 1999. "The New Age of Mortgage Banking." *Mortgage Banking* (January): 76–83.

Sandmo, Agnar. 1985. "The Effects of Taxation on Savings and Risk Taking." In Alan J. Auerbach and Martin S. Feldstein, eds., *Handbook of Public Economics*, vol. 1. Amsterdam: North-Holland, pp. 265–311.

Schafer, Robert, and Helen F. Ladd. 1981. *Discrimination in Mortgage Lending*. Cambridge: MIT Press.

Scheessele, Randall M. 1998. "HMDA Coverage of the Mortgage Market." Housing Finance working papers no. HF-007, Office of Policy Development and Research, U.S. Department of Housing and Urban Development, Washington, DC.

Scheessele, Randall M. 1999. "The 1998 HMDA Highlights." Housing Finance working paper no. HF-009, Office of Policy Development and Research, U.S. Department of Housing and Urban Development, Washington, DC.

Schill, Michael H., and Susan M. Wachter. 1993. "A Tale of Two Cities: Racial and Ethnic Geographic Disparities in Home Mortgage Lending in Boston and Philadelphia." *Journal of Housing Research*, 4(2): 245–275.

Schwemm, Robert G. 1994. *Housing Discrimination: Law and Litigation*. Deerfield, IL: Clark, Boardman, Callaghan.

Shear, William B., and Anthony M. J. Yezer. 1985. "Discrimination in Urban Housing Finance: An Empirical Study across Cities." *Land Economics*, 61(3) (August): 292–302.

Sheiner, Louise. 1995. "Housing Prices and the Savings of Renters." *Journal of Urban Economics*, 38(1) (July): 94–125.

Sickles, Robin C., and Peter Schmidt. 1978. "Simultaneous Equation Models with Truncated Dependent Variables: A Simultaneous Tobit Model." *Journal of Economics and Business*, 31(1) (Fall): 11–21.

Siskin, Bernard R., and Leonard A. Cupingood. 1996. "Use of Statistical Models to Provide Statistical Evidence of Discrimination in the Treatment of Mortgage Loan Applicants: A Study of One Lending Institution." In John Goering and Ron Wienk, eds., *Mortgage Lending, Racial Discrimination, and Federal Policy*. Washington, DC: Urban Institute Press, pp. 451–468.

Smith, Robin, and Michelle DeLair. 1999. "New Evidence from Lender Testing: Discrimination at the Pre-Application Stage." In Margery Austin Turner and Felicity

Skidmore, eds., *Mortgage Lending Discrimination: A Review of Existing Evidence*. Washington, DC: Urban Institute, pp. 23–41.

Smith, Shanna, and Cathy Cloud. 1996. "The Role of Private, Nonprofit Fair Housing Enforcement Organizations in Lending Testing." In John Goering and Ron Wienk, eds., *Mortgage Lending, Racial Discrimination, and Federal Policy*. Washington, DC: Urban Institute Press, pp. 589–610.

Stanton, Richard, and Nancy Wallace. 1998. "Mortgage Choice: What's the Point?" *Real Estate Economics*, 26(2) (Summer): 173–205.

Stengel, Mitchell, and Dennis Glennon. 1999. "Evaluating Statistical Models of Mortgage Lending Discrimination: A Bank-Specific Analysis." *Real Estate Economics*, 27(2) (Summer): 299–334.

Stiglitz, Joseph E., and A. Weiss. 1981. "Credit Rationing in Markets with Imperfect Information." *American Economic Review*, 71(3) (June): 393–410.

Straka, John W. 2000. "A Shift in the Mortgage Landscape: The 1990s Move to Automated Credit Evaluations." *Journal of Housing Research*, 11(2): 207–232.

Swire, Peter P. 1995. "The Persistent Problem of Lending Discrimination: A Law and Economics Analysis." *Texas Law Review*, 73 (March): 787–869.

Taylor, John E. 2000. "Prepared Testimony of John E. Taylor, President and CEO, National Community Reinvestment Coalition" before the Committee on Banking and Financial Services, U.S. House of Representatives, May 24. Available at http://financialservices.house.gov/banking/52400wit.htm.

Thomas, Lyn C. 2000. "A Survey of Credit and Behavioral Scoring: Forecasting Financial Risk of Lending to Consumers." *International Journal of Forecasting*, 16(2) (April–June): 149–172.

Thomas, Paulette. 1991. "Mortgage Rejection Rate for Minorities Is Quadruple That of Whites, Study Finds." *Wall Street Journal*, October 21, p. A2.

Thomas, Paulette. 1992a. "Blacks Can Face a Host of Trying Conditions in Getting Mortgages." *Wall Street Journal*, November 30, p. A1.

Thomas, Paulette. 1992b. "Federal Data Detail Pervasive Racial Gap in Mortgage Lending." *Wall Street Journal*, March 21, p. A1.

Tootell, Geoffrey M. B. 1996a. "Redlining in Boston: Do Mortgage Lenders Discriminate against Neighborhoods?" *Quarterly Journal of Economics*, 111(4) (November): 1049–1079.

Tootell, Geoffrey M. B. 1996b. "Turning a Critical Eye on the Critics." In John Goering and Ron Wienk, eds., *Mortgage Lending, Racial Discrimination, and Federal Policy*. Washington, DC: Urban Institute Press, pp. 143–182.

Turner, Margery Austin. 1992. "Discrimination in Urban Housing Markets: Lessons from Fair Housing Audits." *Housing Policy Debate*, 3(2): 185–215.

Turner, Margery Austin, and Maris Mickelsons. 1992. "Patterns of Racial Steering in Four Metropolitan Areas." *Journal of Housing Economics*, 2(3) (September): 199–234.

Turner, Margery Austin, and Felicity Skidmore. 1999. *Mortgage Lending Discrimination: A Review of Existing Evidence*. Washington, DC: Urban Institute Press.

U.S. Census Bureau. 2002. "Housing Vacancies and Homeownership Annual Statistics: 2001." Available online at http://www.census.gov/hhes/www/housing/hvs/annual01/ann01ind.html.

U.S. Department of Housing and Urban Development–U.S. Treasury National Predatory Lending Task Force. 2000. *Curbing Predatory Lending*. Washington, DC: Author.

U.S. Department of Housing and Urban Development. 1997. "The 1996 HMDA Data: A Closer Look." *U.S. Housing Market Conditions: 3th Quarter 1997*, November.

U.S. Department of Housing and Urban Development. 2000. "Unequal Burden: Income and Racial Disparities in Subprime Lending in America." Available online at http://www.huduser.org/publications/fairhsg/unequal.html.

U.S. Department of Housing and Urban Development. 2002. *U.S. Housing Market Conditions: 4th Quarter 2001*, February.

U.S. House of Representatives. 2000. "Witness List for Full Committee Hearing on Predatory Lending Practices," May 24. Available online at http://financialservices.house.gov/banking/52400wit.htm.

Vandell, Kerry D. 1995. "How Ruthless Is Mortgage Default? A Review and Synthesis of the Evidence." *Journal of Housing Research*, 6(2): 245–264.

Van Order, Robert. 1996. "Discrimination and the Secondary Mortgage Market." In John Goering and Ron Weink, eds., *Mortgage Lending, Racial Discrimination, and Federal Policy*. Washington, DC: Urban Institute Press, pp. 335–364.

Van Order, Robert. 2000. "The U.S. Mortgage Market: A Model of Dueling Charters." *Journal of Housing Research*, 11(2): 233–256.

Van Order, Robert, and Peter Zorn. 1995. "Testing for Discrimination: Combining Default and Rejection Data." In Anthony M. Yezer, ed., *Fair Lending Analysis: A Compendium of Essays on the Use of Statistics*. Washington, DC: American Bankers Association, pp. 105–112.

Van Order, Robert, and Peter Zorn. 2001. "Performance of Low-Income and Minority Mortgages: A Tale of Two Options." Unpublished manuscript. Freddie Mac, Washington, DC, January.

Wachter, Susan M. 1987. "Residential Real Estate Brokerage: Rate Uniformity and Moral Hazard." In Austin J. Jaffe, ed., *The Economics of Urban Property Rights*. Greenwich, CT, and London: JAI Press, pp. 189–210.

Wolff, Edward N. 1995. "How the Pie Is Sliced: America's Growing Concentration of Wealth." *American Prospect*, 22 (Summer): 58–64.

Wolff, Edward N. 2001. "Racial Wealth Disparities: Is the Gap Closing?" Public Policy Brief No. 66A, The Levy Economics Institute, Annandale-on-Hudson, NY.

Wyly, Elvin K., and Steven R. Holloway. 1999. "'The Color of Money' Revisited: Racial Lending Patterns in Atlanta's Neighborhoods." *Housing Policy Debate*, 10(3): 555–600.

Yavas, Abdullah. 1994. "Economics of Brokerage: An Overview." *Journal of Real Estate Literature*, 2(2) (July): 169–195.

Yavas, Abdullah. 1995. "Can Brokerage Have an Equilibrium Selection Role?" *Journal of Urban Economics*, 37(1) (January): 17–37.

Yezer, Anthony M. 1995. "Editor's Notes." In Anthony M. Yezer, ed., *Fair Lending Analysis: A Compendium of Essays on the Use of Statistics.* Washington, DC: American Bankers Association, pp. iii–vi.

Yezer, Anthony M., Robert F. Phillips, and Robert P. Trost. 1994. "Bias in Estimates of Discrimination and Default in Mortgage Lending: The Effects of Simultaneity and Self-Selection." *Journal of Real Estate Finance and Economics,* 9(3) (November): 197–215.

Yinger, J. Milton. 1994. *Ethnicity: Source of Conflict? Source of Strength?* Albany: State University of New York Press.

Yinger, John. 1981. "A Search Model of Real Estate Broker Behavior." *American Economic Review,* 71(4) (September): 591–605.

Yinger, John. 1986. "Measuring Racial Discrimination with Fair Housing Audits: Caught in the Act." *American Economic Review,* 76(5) (December): 881–893.

Yinger, John. 1995. *Closed Doors, Opportunities Lost: The Continuing Costs of Housing Discrimination.* New York: Russell Sage Foundation.

Yinger, John. 1996. "Discrimination in Mortgage Lending: A Literature Review." In John Goering and Ron Wienk, eds., *Mortgage Lending, Racial Discrimination, and Federal Policy.* Washington, DC: Urban Institute Press, pp. 29–74.

Yinger, John. 1997. "Cash in Your Face: The Cost of Racial and Ethnic Discrimination in Housing." *Journal of Urban Economics,* 42(3) (November): 339–365.

Zandi, M. 1993. "Boston Fed's Study Was Deeply Flawed." *American Banker,* August 19, p. 13.

Zorn, Peter. 1989. "Mobility-Tenure Decisions and Financial Credit: Do Mortgage Qualification Requirements Constrain Homeownership?" *American Real Estate and Urban Economics Association Journal,* 17(1) (Spring): 1–16.

Zorn, Peter, Susan Gates, and Vanessa Gail Perry. Forthcoming. "Automated Underwriting in Mortgage Lending: Good News for the Underserved?" *Housing Policy Debate.*

Zycher, Benjamin, and Timothy A. Wolfe. 1994. "Mortgage Lending, Discrimination, and Taxation by Regulation." *Regulation,* 17(2) (Spring): 61–73.

Name Index

Subject Index

.